# Understanding Children Through Astrology

### Revised and Expanded
### Third Edition

## by
## Samantha Marshall

**ACS Publications**
New Hampshire

Understanding Children Through Astrology
Revised and Expanded Third Edition

First Edition copyright 1992 and Second Editon copyright 1993
by Samantha A. Davis

Copyright © 2013 by Samantha Marshall

by Samantha Marshall

1st Edition 1992 and 2nd Edition (Revised) 1993
published by Top of the Mountain Publishing, Largo, Florida

Cover and book design by Maria Kay Simms

International Standard Book Number: 978-1-934976-41-8

Library of Congress Control Number: 2013935603

Published by ACS Publications
An imprint of Starcrafts LLC
334-A Calef Highway
Epping, New Hampshire 03042

Printed in the United States of America

# DEDICATION

To those who have opened their minds and are looking
for new ways to create an expanded awareness of our
future potential. To the molders of our future—
the parents, caregivers
and teachers everywhere.
May you gain better understanding, perception and
sensitivity toward the children of Mother Earth,
no matter what their age...

To the *psychotherapists* who are using astrological
charts to gain accurate information about their
patients' personalities...

And to the Inner Child within us all.

# Acknowledgments

To my daughter Gina Berney

My friend Barbara Friedman who did my first editing
(without both of their help, this book would
have never materialized).

To my good friends Judi and Tag Powell.

To ACS and Maria Simms who agreed to do
this expanded new edition for me.

To all my teachers along the way.

# CONTENTS

## Chapter 6

## Chapter 7

## Chapter 8

## Chapter 9

## Chapter 10

## Chapter 11

## Chapter 12

## Chapter 13

## Appendix

# FOREWORD

There's something remarkable about gaining that extra-special insight into personalities—whether it is your own, your loved ones' or your friends.' We all benefit when we better understand how each person functions -and when we know their likes and dislikes.

Although most of us may think that astrology and raising children do not necessarily go hand-in-hand, there's something unique and essential in recognizing that astrology does play a role in how we all develop.

This book is written for everyone—people who don't have an in-depth knowledge of what makes up an astrological personality profile, yet are concerned about the welfare of children and their interests. This book is easy-to-read and the tables are simple-to-follow for the parent, caretaker or therapist in understanding the psyche. This work is not difficult to understand, and provides a practical reference for people who want access to how they, their friends and family members tick!

With *Understanding Children Through Astrology*, Samantha takes the guess-work out of raising children. She realizes you may not have all the time in the world to sit and read a lengthy, all-engrossing guide to personality. Because of her experience as a mother of four and grandmother of ten, Samantha takes into account your time, your knowledge, your experience and your children. She completes a book that is instrumental in educating both yourself and your children.

Building communication is crucial in the early years of childhood development. It is the first step towards fulfilling and successful relationships. With this book, you can start early with your newborn... or renew already established intimacy with your children...or initiate positive relationships for improvement. Don't wait until it's too late; it's never too early—no matter what age your children are.

This book allowed me a profound look into myself and my loved ones. (I now even use astrology to better understand my employees and my sisters and brothers.) I found that Tag's "Astrological Personality Profile," described in Samantha's book, fits him like a glove! A great work for all parents, teachers and therapists!

Dr. Judith Powell
Author of *Silva Mind Mastery for the '90s*

# PREFACE

Parenthood and Caregiving are the most important and creative experiences we encounter in life. Unfortunately, most of us have little knowledge and less experience with which to handle this challenge. Where does one go to learn to be a good parent, guardian or caregiver? That's a good question! In previous decades, parenting was not as difficult to handle because children were expected to follow in their parents' footsteps and not as much emphasis was placed on the individual or their possible future potential. Now, with much less restriction in our society and more recognition of individuality, the problems of parenting, teaching, and counseling have grown tremendously. Our children are now exposed to more, are more aware...and have more potential than ever before (to rise or fall!). No wonder it has become even more challenging to be a parent, caregiver and/or therapist in this new era!

As a mother of four, astrology has helped me to understand and guide my children on an individual basis. With a better understanding of how they think, what their emotional makeup is, what they will or won't respond to, and where their talents lie, we have developed more compatible and closer, loving relationships. I have the advantage of knowing their strengths and weaknesses, giving me the ability to guide and direct them from childhood to adulthood with greater understanding. This eliminated frustrations for all of us.

I realize astrology is a complicated subject and not all parents have the time or the energy to devote to studying it as I have. This reason is what prompted me to write this book-to give an uncomplicated overview written in a way to best serve the understanding of children. It is my intention to share this small part of astrological wisdom in an easy, intelligible way...as it specifically applies to raising and guiding children.

Since each being (child or otherwise) is a complete and unique individual, it becomes very clear that each should be treated and handled on an individual basis. We are not sheep, to be herded together and driven down the same path and neither are our children. It has been said that children are merely small adults in the process of becoming, only with less experience or wisdom upon which to draw. That's where we come in as parents and teachers. We set the stage and show them the way through example; through love and understanding.

What works and is best for one child may not at all apply to the next. Astrology stresses individuality. Let's imagine a picture of the Universe (as much as we know of it) was taken at the exact moment of a

child's birth, at that specific location - and that this picture of the heavens becomes their own personal road map to their destiny. This image sounds fatalistic, as if there is no freedom of will, but that's not true ... as you will learn in this book. In fact, that is the purpose of this book -for you to guide, influence and liberate your child's free will!

Let me compare life to a trip across the country. If you started on your trip without a map, you would sooner or later (mostly later), arrive at your destination. However, along the way you may hit bad roads, detours, take the long way, take the wrong way and even get lost. Life can be the same. Each individual's astrological chart is their own personal road map to their own life's trip. We can choose to use a map for guidance or we can wander along full of only hopes and wishes.

I believe astrology is only one of several maps or tools which are here for us to use as we journey through the experience of life. The study of our palms is another, our numerological significance is still another and there are many more. They all collaborate with one another and are merely different approaches to gaining the directions and reading the road signs. Invariably, these routes all follow one basic blueprint —each person is an individual with a specific purpose and path.

The challenges arise only when we lack knowledge or comprehension of how to read these maps and use these tools. This is one time when a little bit of knowledge is not dangerous because every little bit of information will add to a better understanding.

In one's personal astrological chart, what may be considered a negative characteristic (I prefer to call them obstacles to be overcome or non-beneficial expressions) can be changed into a beneficial expression, by understanding and working with that characteristic. Remember, the planets are just energy -how each of us chooses to express these energies makes the difference. Once the obstacle is seen and understood, it can then be removed or changed. The lines on our hands can even be seen to change as we change. In astrology, we say that the non-beneficial effects will no longer be felt, that we transcend them. It's up to us to raise our level of consciousness and to help others do the same. As parents, caregivers, therapists and teachers, this education is our primary responsibility to our children and those under our care. The astrological chart is the map, how we individually follow it depends on us.

I hope you find this information enlightening. I know it will give you insight plus some very useful tools. To be covered are the two luminaries—the Sun, which is the spirit and vital force and the Moon, the emotional makeup. Also explained are the three personal planets which

are: Mercury, representing the thought processes and mental attitudes; Venus, showing the way love is experienced, as well as the appreciation of beauty, what we value and how one relates to other people; and Mars, symbolizing the type of energy, aggressiveness, and drive plus what motivates us. Also included are the two connecting planets: Jupiter, representing our abundance and good fortune and point of expansion; and Saturn, representing our discipline, limitations and lessons to be learned in this life.

There are easy-to-use tables in the back pages of the book where you can find out in what sign Sun, Moon and each of the planets fall for your children. Parents or grandparents born 1945 or later can also find their own Sun, Moon and planet signs. If you are older, check page 165 to see how to get an accurately calculated chart for yourself free, and others ar low cost. When you have your own chart you'll find, when reading this book, that you can think back about how many roadblocks or obstacles you may or may not have already overcome, and how much of your own potential you have developed. Discover too, how your chart relates to your child's chart and how you can improve your relationships with him or her. This process gets a little complicated, so I suggest that for fuller understanding, you see a professional astrologer and ask for comparison charts.

On page 165 of this book you'll find an offer for one FREE CHART offer. Order it for your child's birth date, time and place. You'll then also know his or her Ascendant sign. Read the Sun Sign description in this book for the sign of your child's Ascendant, and you will have even one more piece of your little angel's intricate personality puzzle.

It is advisable to read the brief description at the beginning of each chapter in order to understand how the energy of the planet functions. As for that extremely important (and usually baffling) subject on how to most effectively discipline the individual child, I will give practical methods of discipline which will work well for the different signs. It is important to help children develop positively and not throw roadblocks in their way! The results of using these astrological applications are a wonderful addition to your toolbox...and there is no damage to the individual child's potential!

The information in this book will help to make your daily life with your children a little more understandable, pleasant, and productive.

Thank you for having the interest and taking the time to help our children to be happier, more secure adults. The future of our world is dependent on it!

—Samantha Marshall

# INTRODUCTION

## Programming
## How it All Begins

To better understand how our programming begins, we need to know how our brain/mind works. To do that, let's start thinking of the brain as a computer (yes, we are all much more than a computer) and yet the brain is the part that works very much like a computer. So let's visualize or imagine that inside your head you have computer because the brain is the machine part of our being, the command center. Once we understand it, we can function much more effectively. As it is, most people are operating the brain-computer without instructions or guidelines, thereby not obtaining maximum benefit while allowing the computer to run without direction!

Let's pretend that you just purchased a brand new computer. You have to put programs into the computer in order to have it produce anything. What you get out is a product of what is put in. GIGO, the computer term meaning garbage in-garbage out, explains this concept well. If we put garbage into the computer, that is what we will get back —garbage. So it is the same with the brain. If we put negative or non-beneficial thoughts into our brain for programs, our lives will reflect the results of these programs. Once we realize this relationship, it simply becomes a process of clearing out or canceling out the garbage, then replacing it with beneficial thoughts or programs.

Programming, to carry on the analogy, is the learned personality developed to fit in and become accepted in the environment and by society (what Freud called the Superego). It is easy now to see the importance of early or initial programming! With beneficial programming from the beginning, limitations are lessened and potentials enhanced and accelerated. An important point to remember is this: your life up until now is a result of the programming you received, whether it was beneficial or not. And yes, our entire being is more than your programs. We all need to realize this aspect so we can tap into our own innate special selves, some of which is shown in our own special and individual horoscopes!

Consider for a moment that when we are a fetus in the womb we have oneness in physical form with another human in physical form, our mother. There is total sharing and unity. As we separate at birth from this oneness to take responsibility for our own functioning, scientific research shows we are operating at a very slow brainwave frequency. This slow frequency relates to the feeling level of our being. Whatever happens while in this frequency is impressed very strongly on our brain cells; our memory. If these feelings are beneficial impressions such as a harmonious, loving environment, we feel safe, secure and confident. If a baby lives in a hostile environment with anger, sadness or even anxiety, then the baby will develop fear and detachment. This factor is the basis of our beginning human development and cannot be stressed strongly enough! These early experiences make the difference between feeling accepted and supported...or not. Is the environment one which stimulates the survival instincts and the need to protect oneself? Or is it one which stimulates unity and is a safe place to develop one's sense of SELF!

Parents and caregivers are the first influences on their babies' biological computers.. They continue to have the strongest influence because they are the children's first authority figures. Children are dependent on adult guidance, protection and love for their very survival.

In the beginning, since babies have not developed language skills, they are functioning exclusively from the feeling and thought levels. There is actually a communication that takes place through thought on an inner level we don't yet fully understand, but we all appear to respond to it. We have found that when we attach feelings, emotions, and pictures to the thought forms, the message transmission very strong.

For example: you are tired. You start thinking, the baby might not sleep through the night. The more you think about it and remember

the last time you were up all night, or visualize your baby crying, the better chance there is of making that happen. Where our attention goes, our energy flows! This means that if we put energy into a fear—we will produce it as a reality, as easily as when we put our energy into a desire to create it as a reality. Thus, we project our fears to our children and the children under our care. They receive these feelings as programs and experience their lives accordingly. For instance, if a parent fears illness, they could have a child who often produces illness, or even a chronic problem.

We can resolve this negative projection to our children by clearing out our own fears and garbage, so that we are better able to give our children programs which bring them beneficial results. Remember that the programs we received from our parents were the best ones they had with their level of understanding at that time. Now, with this new awareness you can give your children a head start!

The best way I know to eliminate our personal fear-and-anger-based programs is to understand the true meaning of emotions. Emotions are the messengers between the inner-self or who we are at birth and the programming we have received after we arrived on earth. Since fears are learned, any fear-based emotion is the innerself saying that something in the programming is not serving our best interests. These negative emotions show us where we need to make changes and reprogram.

Since these programs either came from others or were created from early childhood experiences, it is logical that they could be inappropriate now. So work on digging out these old reactions and thoughts –and cancel, cancel, cancel, (say this to yourself 3 times). Now add and continually repeat a new beneficial/positive program to change your attitude. It is well known that 21 times is confirmed as a way to change anything. The next time the same program is activated (or someone "pulls your chain") you are better able to "respond" with conscious control... instead of with unconscious blind fear/anger reaction. As we continue this process of reinforcing the new program, the old one weakens. As we release the old program, we eliminate the negative. When there is no longer any energy put into a fear or anger, it isn't created—it is uncreated!

Unproductive emotions are based on lack of security, lack of control, or even a lack of comfort. When we experience good emotions, it is because we are receiving what we want from the environment, or something or someone is reflecting and sending something which makes us feel good.

Understanding how the brain is programmed and combining it with the new awareness that astrology gives us, we can reprogram ourselves, and we can start viewing everyone, including our children, in a new way. If others are negative, they are experiencing a lacking in some aspect of their lives. If they are positive and loving, their needs are being satisfied. They feel secure. We can project this security onto our environment, and onto our children.

I believe that by *Understanding Children Through Astrology*, and the natural inclinations of our very individualistic children, we can begin to reprogram the negative and destructive programs to be positive attitudes and unifying experiences. After reading this book, you will gain a better knowledge of how to develop each child's own creative, productive, contributing purpose and all the loving qualities they have to offer... to make this a better, safer, happier world for us all.

No one should attempt
the practice of healing
without first having a
thorough knowledge
of astrology.
—Hippocrates,
Father of Medicine

## Chapter I

# Three Master Keys in the Art of Parenting

Aside from love, good communication and the ability to motivate are the two most important considerations for mastering the art of parenting. Actually, they are important for establishing any relationship, and are especially crucial in guiding children. The word guiding is the clue here. The role of parenting or caregiving is to be a proficient facilitator. A facilitator acts as a catalyst to bring out a person's best, to help them develop and utilize their greatest potential.

As Kahlil Gibran in his infinite wisdom stated, *Your children are not your children—they are the sons and daughters of life longing for itself. They come through you but not from you, and though they are with you they belong not to you—you may give them your love but not your thoughts for they have their own thoughts.*[1]

It is not intended for us to own our children or to mold or shape them into what we think they should be. Once this is understood, we can begin to take a more objective approach to parenting and apply our unlimited creativity into handling and guiding our children's development more effectively. In this very sense, astrology is the perfect tool as it enables one to look at a child's makeup objectively, as well as it describes the various individual personality characteristics. Also we are

able to see their strengthens and weaknesses as well as their talents, inclinations and natural skills.

# I. The Communication Key

Verbal communication is one of our primary modes of interacting with one another. It is also one of our areas of most difficulty. In verbal communication, words are the tools we use to share concepts. Yet, each of us responds and reacts differently to the same words.

We have different meanings for the same words and place different importance and value on them. Some people resonate with words which create feeling and others are activated with words which stimulate thought and objectivity.

We need to understand that we all process very differently, bringing us to the question: "Who is responsible for the communication to be understood?"

The answer? "Responsibility for a mutual understanding is always placed with the person who is presenting the communication!" As parents, it is extremely important that you present your information in a manner in which your child is able to easily receive and understand it. This suggestion means you must understand how your child processes his or her information.

For example, the planet Mercury and its placement by each astrological sign will provide you insight into the frequency which each child is attuned. Think of it as a radio station. In order to have clear reception you must be tuned into the right frequency. When Mercury is placed in different signs, our mental processes function differently. Each sign has its own frequency or mode for transmission and reception. By knowing how your child's Mercury or thought process operates, you can adjust your own mode and tune into their frequency. This interaction is called establishing rapport—a valuable skill to learn for effective communication in every relationship.

For further comprehension of how this works, let's briefly examine some different placements. When Mercury is placed in the sign of Gemini it expresses itself in its purist form. This child is logical, rational, and is able to think, reason and understand easily. Their thought process is like a computer because it takes information in and processes it rapidly. These children thrive on information. They have no interference from emotions or feelings about what they take in—they simply assimilate it objectively. On the other hand, when Mercury is placed in the sign of Cancer, it is dif-

ficult for the child to have a thought without a feeling, or a feeling without a thought. This level of communication is because the sign of Cancer is emotional and sensitive, often lacking in logic. When communicating with the Mercury in Gemini, using the word think (ie. "I think this," or "what do you think about") is most effective. When communicating with the Mercury in Cancer, using the word feel (i.e. "I feel this," or how do you feel about") will provide best results. Some signs respond to a practical approach and others need pictures painted with words because they are so visual. As you can see, understanding a child's Mercury placement is a valuable asset for establishing rapport. Refer to the Mercury section in this book for complete descriptions.

## Seven Communication Skills

*1. Be aware of your tone.* Sometimes we say one thing with our words and quite another with our tone. Since children function at a more sensitive brainwave frequency, this discrepancy is very obvious to them and will cause confusion.

*2. Listen first.* Most people want to talk first. They want you to know their thoughts and feelings, and to be understood first. If you do speak first, most people will not really be listening; they either will be speaking or preparing to speak. The best approach to gaining rapport is to say, "Let me listen to you first." Next start thinking "win-win" to find the best solution for everyone involved.

*3. Always validate the other person first before presenting different or opposing information.* Since everyone has a built-in survival mechanism that automatically begins to prepare a defense when their rightness is threatened, it is necessary to validate their viewpoint (even if you disagree) to eliminate this automatic process. Simply say, "I understand how you might think that way, or, I can see how you might feel this way." By doing this you, as a parent, stop any defensiveness and can establish rapport with your children. The next step is to ask, "May I share my thoughts, feelings, or ideas with you?" The word share is important here and asking permission will open them to being receptive. This process is what I call productive disagreement.

*4. Get feedback for clarity or understanding to be sure you are being understood.* Ask questions like, "What did you hear me say?," or "What do you think I mean?" For your own clarification you can ask, "I

thought I heard you say—is that what you meant?" Remember that everyone is processing differently. The information is always entering and projecting through a person's own filters. Since no two people can stand in the same exact place, everyone's perceptions are a little different.

**5. *Become aware of body language.*** It is helpful to watch body postures and facial expressions when communicating with others, especially your child. An awareness of your own body language is also important. For instance, if you tell a child "I love you" in a cool, detached tone of voice with your arms crossed across your chest, you will not convey what you mean because of your body language. The words become insignificant; they are disregarded and the message is lost. Distance is created rather than making a loving connection. Keep in mind, the research shows that in communication about 55% is body language, 38% is tone of voice and only 7% the words. I discovered that touching your child while speaking with him or her is another very effective way of making a good connection. Hold your children's hands when explaining things to them. Finally, start talking "with" them instead of to them!

**6. *Listen...Listen...Listen.*** Most of us are not very good at doing this. As parents, we may think we listen, yet I find there is always room for improvement. This listening ability is a learned and developed skill. It is not instinctual and most of us never refine it. When I say "listen," I mean not only to hear WHAT is being said, I also mean to pay attention to HOW it is said. What kind of words are used? Learn to respond most effectively by using the same types of words, such as feel, think, see, hear, etc. This response also aids in establishing rapport. Next, start listening to yourself as well. How do you say things? This way you can tune into any negativity within yourself and become aware of what you are telling yourself and ultimately, your child. How many of us ever really listen to ourselves?

7. Honesty is mandatory! Lying to children creates insecurity, lack of trust, fear, and leads to lack of faith. Since children function primarily on the Alpha brainwave frequency, and have a very high degree of intuitive awareness, it is next to impossible to fool them. It is better not to try. It is always best to be honest. There is always a way to handle any situation honestly, even if it is something your children don't need to or shouldn't know. You can still be honest by saying, "I don't want to discuss it right now." Finally, I would like to share an idea with you. What if we were all telepathic and everyone knew what everyone else was

truly thinking all the time!? How differently do you think life would be? I suggest it would be a good exercise for us all to start living our lives as if this idea were true (on some level I think it is!).

# 2. The Motivation Key

Knowing how to motivate another person, especially a child, is half the battle of becoming a successful facilitator-parent. The trick is to create the desire within the child to want to take an initiative. Most of us will take action when we can see a benefit for ourselves; we will do or act on something for self-gratification and self-gain. Some people are more motivated to do for others, yet the result is still the same—their actions make them feel good about themselves.

Astrologically, Mars is considered the motivating factor since it describes the drive plus where and how we use our energy. Refer to the Mars section in this book for your clues on how to motivate your child to produce beneficial results.

In addition, we always need to consider the Sun's placement since it is the inner-force and primary essence within us all. The Venus placement describes what makes us feel good, comfortable, loved, how we relate to others and what we value. The Moon explains the emotional make¬up, our fears, compassions and security issues.

With all of this information available, we owe it to our future world to use it so that we will help our children to become more self-actualized and fulfilled individuals. Our children are our most valuable assets and our world's future caretakers.

## Seven Motivation Skills

*1. Create a comfort level or pleasant atmosphere for your child in order to establish rapport.* Talk first about a pleasant experience which your child has had in the past-or a pleasant experience which you shared together. This will create more comfort and open receptivity.

*2. Be aware of and keep in mind what turns your child on—what sparks his or her interests.* Awareness will enable you to present your information in a manner most appealing to the youth. Associate what you are presenting to something the subject likes or would like. Relate both of your interests to find a common meeting ground. Connect your presentation to things which will bring joy to the youth.

*3. Stimulate interest and create desire.* Find the benefit for each child. Show children you are giving them something they want, and that will make them receive pleasure. Point out the beneficial outcomes. Show them enthusiasm and excitement in your communication. Make them want what you are presenting by showing them the positive results.

*4. Ask motivating questions.* Statements such as "Wouldn't you like to..." or "Wouldn't you feel good about..." Such questions will stimulate their thought processes in a positive manner. Give them time to think about your questions, and time to respond. Ask for their ideas on how to solve problems, and give them choices. I have found that by asking for their ideas on solving problems, some very creative and beneficial solutions are discovered. You can also ask your youth what they would do if they were the parent. This position causes them to view the situation very differently than they would have before. Next, letting children make choices stimulates growth and promotes maturity. It also contributes to becoming responsible for their own actions and life. You can present the choices such as, "If you do that, then this will happen," and, "If you do this, then this will happen; the choice is yours." Not many of us are happy being dictated to. At least your children do have a choice this way. Our process of learning is through our mistakes, so sometimes it is best to let them make a few.

*5. Point out your child's other accomplishments—those that corroborate with or validate your presentation.* Praise the qualities he or she possesses that will contribute to the ability to accomplish what you are presenting. For example, recognize good listening skills in your child, and he or she will continue to listen intently and avidly. Thus, you are emphasizing a quality which will result in the development of positive behavior and trust. Make your children feel good about themselves. Build up and strengthen their confidence, and they will look to you for support, strength and guidance.

*6. Eliminate pressure tactics and maintain a level of objectivity.* Present your information in a clear and objective manner, without emotions or expectations involved. Simply present the facts, the pros and cons. You also can give your thoughts and ideas on the subject, and what you would do in a similar situation without expectation. It is vitally important to always see the circumstances from your youth's point-of-view.

*7. Back off and give your child the opportunity to process your idea.*
This final and closing comunication process is most important because
it will provide space and room for individual decision-making. Your
child will have the opportunity to make his or her own choices. Tell
the child, "It is your choice because, ultimately, everyone has to take
responsibility for his or her own beliefs, actions and selections." Help
if your child asks for it, and always support his or her decision. Even if
you don't agree with your children's choices, it is important to try to understand their point-of-view. Then let them pay their own consequences
or reap their own rewards.

# 3. The Discipline Key

The basis of all discipline is right thinking and beneficial action. How
does a person know when he or she is off-track? It is by way of our
mistakes—we all make them at one time or another. This process is
constant and applies to all areas ofl life. We make mistakes in our relationships, our emotions, our social life, our finances—even in how
we maintain our physical health. From an internal point-of-view, when
we are off-track, we begin to feel uncomfortable, unfulfilled, restricted,
resentful, angry, depressed, less energetic and even ill.

Since all we think is manifested in our physical world, it is the
thinking which will put us back on track. Any person who has ever overcome any difficulty has taken control of their thinking. Every one of us
has the ability to command our thoughts. This capability is the KEY to
good discipline.

As parent-facilitators, it is our purpose to assist our young to develop their own ability for self-discipline. It is up to us to teach them the
skill of disciplined thinking. We must all learn it—we do not arrive on
this planet having it. The sooner we learn how to govern our thoughts,
the quicker our lives are enhanced by happiness, productivity and love.
How well a person is disciplined is directly related to how much responsibility he or she has been given or has voluntarily assumed.

As you can see, it is important to give our youth as much responsibility as early in life as possible. They can then practice developing
self-discipline. Helping your child with this skill is one of the most pre-
cious gifts you could ever give to them. Inner-control over thoughts,
feelings and actions will affect how our youth learn, work, play and deal
with the many situations they must, inevitably, confront.

Somehow, most of us have equated discipline with drudgery. It would be to our advantage to associate it with joy! Some parents try to make life as easy as possible for their children—some even think they are supposed to. In many cases, these parents take total responsibility for their children, leaving them obligation free and without a set basis for striving toward achievement. Believe me, if you think non-responsibility protects our youth, you are not doing them any favors! This type of behavior only leaves them unprepared for real-life experiences, and impairs their ability to have joyful lives. Good discipline is a habit which produces beneficial results, and is formed from repetition. As parent-facilitators, our job is to help our children develop these beneficial habits. The following skills will aid you with this education process.

# Seven Discipline Skills

*1. Ask for the behavior you want* rather than telling children what you don't want. Make it a positive statement, not a negative.
    Example:
    (a) "Close the door quietly," rather than "Don't slam the door."
    (b) "Drive carefully," rather than "Don't have an accident."
    (c) "Please stop doing ..." rather than "Don't do..."
Always ask for the positive. In this manner you will be creating the most beneficial results.

*2. Think first before speaking.* When your child presents a situation to you or asks a question, answer, "Let me think about it for a minute." Two things happen: you get time to work out any feelings you have about the subject, and you get time to think through what you want to say. Then you can respond with an objective, logical, unemotional answer or solution.

*3. Modify your reactions.* Use the old saying, "Take a deep breath and count to ten." If you react to anything your children do or say with anger, disgust, shock or horror, you will be threatening their survival (and futher openness) from an inner-level of consciousness. Any time you invalidate or make anyone wrong in any way, you have threatened their survival on an unconscious level, and they will immediately prepare a defense. This response is an automatic internal process. It applies even

more so to your relationships with your children. If you attack their survival they will develop a defense. Lying becomes an easy way to avoid these unpleasant reactions from you, and you can be sure that your child won't be sharing everything with you. If your child can tell you the truth and come to you with anything, and you respond in a calm, solution-oriented manner, you will have a closer and better relationship. You also can teach them, through your behavior, that it is best to deal with life in a truthful, logical, calm manner.

*4. Start becoming solution-oriented.* Too often we tend to look at new situations concerning our children as problems. Change problems to challenges and focus on finding solutions. By doing this, you will change the energy around any given situation.

*5. Use distraction whenever possible,* with young children in particular. Divert their attention away from whatever you don't want them to do, and lead them on to something else. When dealing with or counteracting negativity, it is best to distract attention rather than fight head-on. By reading the placements of their planets, you can learn what they will respond to best.

*6. Tell them what you are going to do when they misbehave.* Example: "I will not drive the car while there is fighting." Then simply pull to the side of the road, and stop the car whenever there is fighting. Sit there until they stop misbehaving. They will soon get tired of this behavior. And moreover, they will know what to expect by your consistency of word and action.

7. Finally and most importantly is to avoid guilt. *Guilt has absolutely no beneficial result.* Not only is it unproductive, it also is a detriment to one's health. Stop using guilt to manipulate. Avoid instilling guilt in your child to gain results or effect change. Instead, find a way to create a desire within them to take action. This method is the highest form of manipulation—and a healthy one!

### Endnote:

[1]
"On Children," from *The Prophet*, Kahil Gibra

**Astrology**
does not offer
an explanation of the
Universe, nor why the
Universe exists. What it does,
to put it in simplest terms, is to
show us that there is a corre-
spondence between macrocosm
and microcosm. In short, that
there is rhythm to the Universe,
and that our own lives partake
of the rhythm...

— Henry Miller

# Chapter 2

# The ABCs of Astrology

This science of the stars was first" discovered" and recorded by the original astrologers, the Chaldeans. So renown was their wisdom of the skies, that they are mentioned as "wise men" in the *Bible's Old Testament.*

Astrology is a tool which enables us to realize the natural inclinations of each **individual** personality—his or her personal road map. The **astrological chart** provides specific information as to a person's strengths and weaknesses. Each planet symbolically represents a characteristic of the personality, and the sign that the planet is in determines the way in which a characteristic is **expressed**. The number of **degrees** between the planets forms the angle that shows us how the planet's characteristics interact with one another, whether with harmony and ease, or with conflict and tension.

Astrology gives us this knowledge so we can choose to take responsibility and **respond** rather than **react** to these influences. It also prevents us from wasting time, energy, and emotion with unnecessary resistance to another person's planetary configurations. The astrological chart shows us where to put our and our children's energy to accelerate talents and abilities, and where to modify any less desirable characteristics.

Another use of the astrological tool is as a timing device. Carl Jung called timing *synchronicity*, meaning coincidence. Since everything in

the Universe is energy, including human beings, and all energy is interrelated, astrology shows how our personal clock or timing interacts with the universal clock or timing. (Visualize gears within gears within gears, the same as when looking at the inside of a watch, with each gear interacting with the others.)

Knowing when to move forward and when to wait is invaluable information. Having this information ahead of time gives us the ability to direct events in our lives more beneficially and more productively. We can also modify or soften the effects of any undesirable events.

There has been much written about your child's Sun sign and I am sure that this alone has given you much insight. This book will go further and define additional personal components of your child's make-up. We will cover the two luminaries—the Sun and the Moon—and the three personal planets—Mercury, Venus, and Mars. Jupiter and Saturn are important connecting planets in themselves, and are also covered in this book to a lesser degree. This is because I believe that Mercury, Venus, and Mars are more pertinent in dealing with the communication and the interaction between parent, caregiver and child.

The outer planets (Uranus, Neptune, and Pluto) are further away from Earth, causing their cycles to be longer; thus, they stay in one sign for longer periods of time. It has been said that these three planets have influence over generational consciousness and possibly transformations. They can however have an important influence on the personality when they are in close contact with the Sun, Moon or faster moving planets already mentioned. This is why I strongly advise having the entire astrological chart created so you will have the complete picture.

One other important facet in the astrological chart is called the Ascendant or Rising sign. This must be calculated by an astrologer, or an astrology computer software program, according to the exact time, place, and date of birth. The Ascendant is the sign that was coming up on the horizon at the **place** of birth when a child is born. The Ascendant sign offers information about the physical body, such as its bone structure, its shape, and size, and it also represents the outward personality which we develop and learn to use as a safe or acceptable way to communicate with and interact with the outer world.

Other considerations in reading the astrological map are what we call the aspects. Aspects are formed when one planet is a specific number of degrees from another within a 360 circle, or chart wheel, that is divided into 12 thirty-degree sections that we call houses. Each house

represents part of life, such as partnerships, money, health, friends, children, love, sex. The house that a planet occupies informs us about the area of life associated with that house. Think of the planets as energy. The sign that a planet is in describes the way that the energy associated with that planet is most likely to be expressed. The house that a planet is in describes the area of life in which a planet in that house most strongly expresses itself. Following is a simple keyword list for matters associated with each house, phrased more as would apply to children.

House 1: the "I", oneself, personal appearance, behavior
House 2: what is "mine", my possessions, money, what makes me
          feel comfortable
House 3: communication, siblings, neighbors, classmates, short trips
House 4: home, roots, grandparents, the more nurturing parent
House 5: creative expression, things that are fun to do, hobbies
House 6: daily work, chores, habits, health, pets
House 7: "signficant others," partners or competitors
House 8: things that are shared with others, secrets, mysteries, endings
House 9: beliefs, ideals, teachers, places that are far away
House 10: the outside world, the more authorative parent, rules
House 11: friends, clubs or groups, hopes and wishes
House 12: one's inner private world, secrets that are kept inside

The above information is more complex than what is intended for this book. Not everyone wants to become an astrologer. It is not my purpose to give you a complete analysis of your child, but to help you relate better, to try and be a more effective 'parent-facilitator,' through an understanding of the luminaries and the three personal planets, and how they respond in the different signs. If you desire, the complete analysis of your child's chart—or your own—should be done by a fully-integrated computer program, or by a competent, helpful, positive-thinking and solution-oriented astrologer.

We are born at
a given moment,
in a given place and,
like vintage years of wind,
we have the qualities
of the year and
of the season
in which we are born.

—Carl G. Jung

# Chapter 3

# Retrogrades

Retrogrades is a term that we use to describe a planet's apparent backward motion. The fact is all the planets are always moving forward and it is only an illusion that they sometimes seem. to be going backwards. We can explain this by using the example of picturing two cars traveling down the street at the same speed. When one increases its speed, the other appears to be going backward when being viewed from the faster car. From the Earth, this is how the planets look to us.

Any planet in a retrograde motion will have its energies flowing in a different direction. Retrogrades give us the opportunity to go back over things, make changes, and eliminate any non-beneficial thoughts and situations in our lives. Retrogrades tend to stimulate internalization—we may focus more on our own growth, our needs, and desires. If planets are retrograde in the birth chart, their energies will be of a more internalized nature. We are often quick to make the word "different" mean wrong, because it is unfamiliar, and as long as a retrograde is understood it can be worked with.

A child with a retrograde planet may have to work harder to achieve the full purpose and potential of that planet's energy and it may be a longer time coming, but the strength upon which it is built can be drawn on forever. A retrograde gives the power to go back and redo or undo, and then go on again. It may take a little more discipline to develop the retrograde potential, but it is always well worth the effort.

The retrograde planet usually works on the subjective or inner-conscious level. Retrograde planets are extremely important because their significance is not as easily recognized. Since they are of an in-

ternal nature, they are keys to our personal complexities. It is an area where the potential may be delayed, or assets and liabilities may have been overlooked. Examine them closely and gain valuable tips.

The retrogrades will be described separately at the beginning of each planet section for a clearer understanding of how each planet might be acting in an internalized manner. These planets will present to you some interesting challenges.

You will be able to tell when a planet is retrograde by an R in the tables, on the day that it turns in the retrograde direction. It will stay that way until a D appears next to the sign in the tables, indicating that it has turned in direct motion (the Sun and Moon will always be going forward).

You might want to check how many days after your child's birth date a planet changes direction. Take each day to equal one year. You may see a change in your child the year it changes. For example, ten days after the child's birthday, Mercury might turn from retrograde to direct motion. So when the child is ten years old, he might start to express his thinking more openly and directly...or be more eager or able to learn. If you were to see that eight days after the birthday, the planet Mars changed from direct to retrograde, at age eight the child might internalize his anger instead of expressing it in a healthy, open manner.

The chapters on Mercury, Venus, and Mars will each have a more complete explanation of how these energies change.

Other considerations that might alter the planets' placements in the signs are important enough to bear repeating.

Aspects or angles in degrees that one planet is from another indicate a certain potential in each case. Not every aspect has the same intepretation. Some work with more harmony and ease than others, while others are more difficult or challenging. (See the Glossary for more on aspects.) The house position of the planet in the chart, or the particular area of life in which each planet works, makes a difference too. Aside from these considerations, you will find a high degree of accuracy in the following descriptions.

We and the cosmos are one.
The cosmos is a vast living body, on which we are
still parts. The Sun is a great heart whose tremors
run through our smallest veins. The Moon is a
great gleaming nerve-center from which we quiver
forever. Who knows the power that Venus has
over us, or Mars? But it is a vital power, rippling
exquisitely through us all the time.
—D.H. Lawrence, Apocalypse

# Chapter 4

# The Sun
# The Vital Force

The Sun, giver of life, is the vital force, core, or inner drive within us.
It is the energizing force of the being! No matter what else the chart
says, it will only be an extension, an addition, or modification of what
the vital force is. Some of us show this inner self and some of us don't.
We are more inclined to be true to ourselves, (our Sun sign) in early
childhood and then again in old age. The stronger of us may overcome
conditioning, programming, and expectation and remain ourselves always, but not many. No matter how obvious it is or isn't, the core of our
being will still be the same. By understanding this inner drive, we will
be better equipped to help our children develop themselves and express
their inner-selves in a more positive, productive manner.

It is important to understand this inner drive—to not damage,
destroy, or inhibit its functions. By knowing the beneficial and non-
beneficial sides of this drive, we can encourage discipline over the non-
beneficial and stimulate strength in the beneficial. Environment has an

important influence over the expression of the being, and as parents and caregivers we have the first opportunity to nurture the potential. This is a great responsibility, and a great challenge and now, with the use of Astrology, you will have some help.

First, start by thinking of your child not as a girl or a boy or even a child, but as a small person needing your assistance while growing and learning to mature. Someone once said, children are small adults in the process of becoming. All beings are equipped with their own individual set of functions and their own purpose in life. We are all happier when we are expressing ourselves as we really are and fulfilling our own purpose. If more people would or could do this, it would eliminate most frustrations and negativity. Try not to put conditions and expectations on your children, but love them for themselves; love them as they are. The only trick is to help them understand...to help them accept, discipline, and develop themselves. Stop trying to make of these little beings what you want them to be, or think they should be—or what you had wanted to be—and start helping them be the best of whom they really are!

The Sun is the energizing force of the character and should be allowed to flow freely, not blocked with restriction or filtered through limitations.

As you read the different life forces or Sun signs, you will begin to see why each being might act the way they do. It is interesting to note that Jeane Dixon in her book, *Yesterday, Today and Tommorow*, has shown us how each one of Jesus' twelve disciples may have belonged to one of the twelve astrological signs. Coincidence? Or maybe it was just to show us that each of us belonging to a specific Sun sign is needed to fulfill his or her purpose in the master plan.

# Your Child's Sun Sign—and Your Sun Sign, too!

The very simple table on the next page shows the **usual days** the Sun is in each sign of the zodiac, and also the symbol (glyph) for each sign. This table offers a quick lookup for Sun sign, which will work fine in most cases. **But, since TIME of day is also a factor, the EXACT change day can be slightly variable from one year to another.**

In the back pages of this book you'll find **Sun Tables** that show the exact days that Sun (and Moon and the planets) change signs for 1945-2025. This will allow you to look up the birth date during these years and

know the the correct signs for Sun, Moon and planets in most cases, But realize that the only absolutely sure way is to have the chart calculated for date, time and location. The data in the tables was taken from *The American Ephemeris*. Times given are for midnight UT (Universal Time, the newer term for GMT, Greenwhich Mean Time). You will need to first adjust for the time zone of the location of birth to be sure you're looking at the right day.

## Table of Sun Signs

| | | |
|---|---|---|
| January 21 — February 19 | Aquarius | ♒ |
| February 20 — March 20 | Pisces | ♓ |
| March 21— April 20 | Aries | ♈ |
| April 21 — May 20 | Taurus | ♉ |
| May 21 — June 21 | Gemini | ♊ |
| June 22 — July 22 | Cancer | ♋ |
| July 23 — August 23 | Leo | ♌ |
| August 24 — September 23 | Virgo | ♍ |
| September 24 — October 23 | Libra | ♎ |
| October 24 —November 23 | Scorpio | ♏ |
| November 23 — December 22 | Sagittarius | ♐ |
| December 22 —January 20 | Capricorn | ♑ |

Remember, for a quick look-up of Sun Sign, the table above will be correct for most people born 1945 or later, so long as the birth time was not within the hour before or after midnight. The more detailed tables in the back of this book will also be reliable in most cases. But to know for sure of the correct signs, especially for the quickly changeable Moon, a chart must be calculated for date of birth, time of birth and location of birth (longitude and latitude). On 165 of this book, there is a **"one free chart"** offer through which you can be absolutely sure of the right signs of Sun, Moon and planets for your child

## Children with Sun in Aries

Peter was the Aries apostle in Jeane Dixon's book *Yesterday, Today and Tomorrow*. He was the one whom Christ chose first, and Aries is the first sign of the zodiac. Because of being the first, and representing the early part of life, we call Aries the Child of the Zodiac. Symbolized by the Ram, it rules the head of the body. Words like headlong and headstrong are used to describe this sign.

Your Aries child may have many head injuries, headaches, or be born with a birthmark on the head or face. Most older Aries have acquired a scar in those areas. Aries hair is usually curly and their teeth may be slightly elongated. Eyes are piercingly direct. The ruler of Aries is Mars, the warrior.

The Aries nature is impatient, courageous, and aggressive. Aries children will be direct, outspoken, and blunt. Teaching them to be considerate of other people's feelings will help your Aries children in a positive way. Aries will have a tendency to charge into things impulsively, and should be taught to look before leaping; to use a small amount of caution to assure more success. Their enthusiasm is great, which stimulates others who are less initiating or courageous. They are very inventive, have a quick mind, and are wonderful at pioneering and initiating new projects and concepts.

One problem is that they are easily distracted and may turn that enthusiasm to something new before they have followed through or finished the previous undertakings. Discipline in the area of "persistence" would be a valuable attribute.

Give Aries children the opportunity for many new challenges and they will be happy. They need more freedom than most to explore untrodden areas and conquer these new vistas for themselves. If this freedom is curtailed, they will start butting their heads in some way against the restriction—or the restrictor!

Stimulate this curious Aries with a challenge when presenting anything. For instance, say to them, "See if you can pour the milk without spilling a drop," and you've immediately sparked a challenge! Don't say or order, "You must pour the milk without spilling it," or negatively say, "You can't pour the milk because you will probably spill it." Wrong! When the challenge is conquered it strengthens the natural flow of the Aries ability and directs them toward positive actions. Success with these challenges is important, so be sure to help them select realistic objectives.

Fire is their element, giving them much energy and a bit of an explosive temper. This fire may rage fiercely but it starts and stops quickly...and when it's out, it is out and forgotten. The words are not remembered and certainly not meant—it is fire being released like steam through a safety valve. If this child has plenty of physical activity, much of this energy can be expended for positive benefit. There must be some outlet for them, the more physical and active the better.

# An Aries Birthday Message

Aries, my child,
Learn that patience is power.
Temper courage with love
And as leader you'll tower!
Feel the power of Sun, but also know
That with humility, you will grow!
You'll nurture and bless all you desire.
Valient and strong, with cleansing fire!
Come, Aries warrior—protect the weak!
With valor and strength, peace you must seek!
With brightness and energy, seek highest good.
Lead with initiative, as you know you should.
Keep your sights lofty and skyward flowing,
Then temper your fires, warm energy glowing.

## Happy Birthday, my Aries!

Aries children can be quite rambunctious when they have energy which is stored up inside. To help them release this energy constructively, put a march on and let them march around the house, or take them out and run them around the block. They enjoy lively music and are quick to respond when they are encouraged to dance. Moving their bodies to music is a wonderful way for them to release any frustrations. Anything you can think of to constructively put them into physical ac-

tion will be good for them.

These children are naturally attracted to the color red since it is the color assigned to Aries, not to mention the red planet—Mars which is its ruler. You should take note that they seem to have even more energy when they wear red or when it is prominent in their environment. Since they have an abundance of energy anyway, you may want to consider calming them down by dressing them in blue, green, yellow, or white. Also choose the colors for their bedrooms with thought and care. These children are often inclined to run high fevers so be sure to dress them in these cooler, calmer colors when this occurs.

Since an Aries will dislike routine or any kind of monotony, discovering new ways of doing things will have to be developed continually. The best disciplinary methods for Aries are restriction or confinement. For an Aries child, sitting still in a chair for ten whole minutes is a dreadful chore. Be careful that the length of time is thoughtfully considered because they still need to have ample physical activity to function properly. Start with five minutes and then tell them that the next time you will have to add five more, and so on. This warning will make them think twice. The Aries child does need to think more and act less!

For young Aries children, distraction works particularly well when you wish to change their mood or behavior. The Aries is one of the signs whose attention can be diverted with almost anything, especially if action is involved. Start a new project or take a walk—their whole mood will change and you will have transformed unproductive into productive. As parent or caregiver, help them to control their impatience and to apply persistence in order to finish tasks they have started. Teach them that finishing is as important as starting. They should be allowed to develop their natural initiative; and be encouraged to be logical and think before acting with blind courage. Your Aries is strong and vital. Do not push your Aries child, or you'll have much resistance, even a young rebel. Aries children are energetic, courageous, inventive, and bright. Help them to know it, and to use it for good. Refer to Mercury in Aries for key words to use in your communications with your Aries child.

## Children with Sun in Taurus

The apostle in Jeane Dixon's book whose Sun was in Taurus was Simon. As a young man he was uncompromising, determined, and stubborn, much like the bull which is the symbol for Taurus. Simon was slow to accept the concept of unity, slow to change his attitude from

preaching war to preaching peace and bringing all people together. It is the same with most Taureans: they are slow to make changes, because they are stubborn.

The part of the body governed by Taurus is the throat, and the planet that rules it is Venus. It is no wonder that we have so many famous singers born with the Sun in Taurus. Keep in mind that the part of the body which a sign rules or governs may have weakness as well as strength. It may be wise to protect these children's necks, and by all means keep them warm in cold weather...they may have a predisposition toward sore throats. Sometimes these are caused because these children have an inclination to hold feelings in and not say what they think or feel. Teach them that holding back or trying to endure something is not helpful to any situation.

These children are attracted to pastel colors and soft hues. They enjoy gentle, sensual music. When they are ill or just generally out of sorts, put them in soft plushy clothes, soften the lights, and put on Nat King Cole, or a soft rock station. They will soon be soothed.

Through the use of speech they can accomplish almost anything as they are convincing as well as persistent. Arguing with them can present quite a challenge. The best way to win with them is through indirect action -back off and give them time. They can't be pushed. If you do -watch out! They are generally peaceful, but if you try to force them or anger them they have a fierce volcanic temper, and you will be well advised to wait until they cool down. You will get nowhere until then. They also have a tendency to hold on to hurt feelings

The element for Taurus is earth and since it is a fixed sign we are dealing with "rock." Taurus can be like the Rock of Gibraltar and have the same endurance. They are strong and steady. They are not easily discouraged and will stay with things that they believe have value.

They can brave the challenge, no matter how difficult. They usually accomplish more than most, but need to learn the difference between persistence and stubbornness. Taureans hate to change, so your best approach is to show them the value of any change you are asking for and how it will serve their purpose. Gain their cooperation because they are tough competitors. Your Taurus will have great powers of persuasion, persistence, and determination. They can resist and persist with a vengeance.

The Taurean can be jealous, possessive, and greedy. They are materialistic, and they are sensual, and are attached to having their com-

forts satisfied. They will be attracted to and enjoy all of the finer things in life. They have a tendency to overindulge and need to learn discipline with their eating and drinking to avoid being overweight and unhealthy. Sauces and rich foods can be a weakness. Teach them to enjoy healthier foods that taste good. Taste is an important sense to a Taurean, as sight is to an Aries.

You will win points by lovingly touching them or doing anything that gives them pleasure. Stroking or hugging them when you are eliciting their cooperation will help.

An important lesson for Taureans to learn is detachment. They are too possessive. They are attached to everything and everyone. They will want to hold on to and own people and things. Teach them that the true values in life are not in possessions, but in one's self and in one another. Once they value themselves and value the unity of us all, they will be a strong force in motivating others. Teach them that principle and purpose are more important than all the material possessions in the world.

The best disciplinary method to use if you have been unsuccessful getting their cooperation is to deny them their comforts and pleasures. Taking away their dessert, television, back rubs, or anything else which is pleasurable to them will have an effect. By the same token, rewarding them with the same for good behavior will give Taureans incentive to cooperate. But do not, I repeat, do not use corporal punishment on a Taurean! It only makes them more stubborn and also unforgiving -for they deeply feel physical pain along with the emotional pain and they won't forget it.

Help your Taureans to know their strengths and weaknesses, develop patience yourself, and enjoy an affectionate, loving relationship. Refer to Mercury in Taurus for key words to use in your communication with your Taurus child.

# Children with Sun in Gemini

The apostle according to Jeane Dixon's book, born with the Sun in Gemini was James (The Less). He was called The Less only because of his physical structure, so don't think less in any other aspect for Gemini. Gemini is ruled by the planet Mercury and is associated with the arms, shoulders, nervous system, and lungs. Its element is air. When we think about air we realize that it is all around us and it moves as we move

# A Taurus Birthday Message

Happy Birthday, Taurus, the Bull's own sign.
Stand strong and firm, of body and mind.
You're persistent, determined,
but slow to adjust ....
So to know not to push you, for us is a must.

You're gentle and kind...unless you're provoked.
With love for comfort, you might overindulge,
so learn how too much
makes the wrong kind of bulge!

It's important to be just a little detached–
Your true sense of values cannot be matched.

We know you'll succeed, so stop fearing loss.
Know that you can and that God is the boss!

You're devoted and patient, steadfast and true,
Deliberate, thrifty—we're glad you are you!
Have faith in yourself—
move ahead with good cheer.

## Happy Birthday, my Taurus—
## Have a wonderful year!

through it. All air signs are mental and intellectual in quality, and since Gemini is mutable in its Mode of Action, their thoughts are all over the place! Mutable means flexible, changeable, adaptable, flowing, and spontaneous. Therefore, Gemini children are bright, quick, mercurial and full of action—probably too much action at times to suit most parents. They are also quite capable of doing more than one thing at a time. There is never a dull moment with them. In fact, for these children boredom is truly horrendous. They are very quick to learn anything, being the mimic of the zodiac so watch your own bad habits. Theirs is a mind that never stops. They must be fed constantly with positive material or they will find their own material, and that can be dangerous.

Geminis are fond of humor and have a natural quick wit. Their remarks at times may be considered by some as being smart alecky or flippant, but to them it is just humor and a natural loquaciousness.

Talking is one of their long suits. Speaking of long suits, sharing could be another. They are not possessive in anything. They enjoy having new things as much as anyone but once they have something, if it breaks or is lost, it won't be important. Chances are that something newer has caught their eye anyway. Their attention span is rather short but they absorb so quickly, it just means that they are ready for more material. They may have trouble doing or learning anything with which they have no interest. Help them to develop good reading habits and your biggest problem of keeping them occupied will be solved. Their thirst for knowledge can then be satisfied. They are ambidextrous and very good at doing anything with their hands. Challenge them with crafts.

The astrological symbol for Gemini is the Twins, representing a duality, and they are definitely changeable, often confusing and maddening to everyone and seeming like two very different people indeed. Because of this characteristic a Gemini can espouse an idea on one occasion and have the opposite idea on another. They can change as quickly as you can change a TV channel. It is wise for the Gemini to become aware that this extreme flexibility can often be perceived by others as inconsistent, not dependable, or fickle.

With all this quickness and manual dexterity, a lot of Geminis are quite good at sports (particularly golf and tennis). Maybe this is because they like games. At times, life may even appear to be a game to these free spirits, always moving on to the next experience. When it comes to discipline, this very mental child will respond best if you give an explanation of why an action is taken. Just be sure that you have good, sound

# A Birthday Message
## for Gemini

Hello, playful Gemini, quick-witted youth.
Learn perseverance, and find your truth!
Twins you are, not just one mind but two,
Loving surprises and anything new!
Energetic and active in so many ways—
You must learn how focus most strongly pays.
You're adaptable, versatile, with logical mind.
Don't let it be scattered—
your truth you must find!
I see you inquiring, curious, diverse,
Though sometimes too restless
to "get there" first.
So, my child, concentrate!
See things through!
With love, best wishes and
Happy Birthday, too!

## Have a wonderful birthday, my Gemini Child!

logical reasons if you expect results. For the young Gemini, distraction works very well, as they are intrigued with anything new. Because they want to learn and experience everything, their attention is easily diverted. Another effective disciplinary measure would be isolation. Com-

munication is primary to them so they are not good loners. They need to have someone to talk to and will not be comfortable when shut off by themselves. (Now that would be the proper punishment!)

Speaking of communication, Geminis are not always the best listeners -they are more interested in doing the talking themselves. In fact, sometimes they are not even aware of whether others are listening or not. At times, they don't even care! Teach them that communication is a two-way street. Let them know that it is important for others to share ideas as well.

Geminis are very adaptable and will easily adjust to change. A new residence or a new school will not be traumatic. In fact, it's stimulating— new friends! Obviously, they are not attracted to tradition or ritual. They relate and respond on a mental level rather than an emotional one. In fact, they may even have difficulty understanding people who display great emotion unless of course there are other things in the chart that say otherwise. These children are usually wondering why. Teach them to become aware of others' sensitivities whether they are understood or not.

Feed this airy mental computer with plenty of positive material and have fun with your Gemini. Refer to Mercury in Gemini for key words to use in your communications with your Gemini child.

## Children with Sun in Cancer

As referenced in Jeane Dixon's book, we find the lovable apostle, Andrew, born with his Sun in Cancer. He was a fisherman and Peter's older brother. Since Cancers have such strong natural needs for spirituality to help eliminate their fears, Andrew was already working closely with John the Baptist. He had no doubts about his purpose of serving others in self-sacrificing humility. He had no need to be the leader or to have a position of great importance; he only had to be a part of the family and to serve to the best of his ability.

The symbol for Cancer is the Crab. When we think of the crab we remember that it moves sideways to avoid anything approaching it. Cancer people are much the same—they are not direct with their approach. When threatened, they withdraw and retract like the crab, hiding and pulling into its shell. The crab actually carries its home, or shell, with it wherever it goes. This may be why home is so important to Cancerians, and why wherever they go, they set about making it homelike.

Cancer is a water sign and is ruled by the Moon. This gives them qualities of being receptive and responsive. They feel everything, and

# A Birthday Message
# for Cancer

For you, gentle Cancer, child of the Moon,
May bright birthday wishes be
granted quite soon!
Though unsure you may be,
try not to scurry—
Away to hide where you sit and worry.
Tender inside your outer shell
Where feelings are deep and hard to tell...
But blend them with reason,
for surely you see
That I'm here for you,
just as you're here for me.
Protective and nurturing,
A good kind of friend,
Dependable always—beginning to end.
You're perceptive and psychic,
with wisdom of old.
May your year bring you happiness,
all you can hold!

# Happy Birthday,
# my Moon Child!

will be especially affected by the cycle of the Moon. The new Moon and the full Moon can cause them to be more emotional and sensitive. Teach them to be aware of this monthly cycle so they can be prepared and armor themselves.

Although Cancer is a water sign, notice that the crab is comfortable on both land and in the water. A good way to calm and soothe your Cancer is with a bath or playing in water. The sea also has a great calming effect upon the Cancerian. Teach them early to swim and they will always have a way to work out any frustrations. Some of the great amateur sailors of the world are born in this sign.

The sign of Cancer has influence over the stomach, breast, and solar plexus. Cancer children might have a tendency to have a nervous stomach and should be careful about what and when they eat. In extreme cases, they could get an ulcer. They should avoid eating when emotionally upset or highly excited, and should never be forced to eat! The breast is symbolic of their need to be nurtured and to nurture others. Moon children have a strong need to feel protected in their environment. They must feel secure in the love from those close to them, secure that their environment is safe and stable and secure that they will be taken care of.

Since the solar plexus is a strong area of psychic reception, this may explain why the Cancerian is so sensitive to everyone and everything around them. They have highly developed intuitive and psychic abilities, and are operating almost totally on the feeling level. These strong feelings and psychic experiences can be frightening to them so it is important to teach your Cancer child that it is a gift and to not be afraid of it!

These children need to be taught to affirm on a daily basis that they are protected from all negative input. This will build belief and become fact. They are psychic sponges and will absorb whatever energy and feelings are in the environment. They will feel what other people are feeling. If there is sadness, they will be sad; if there is happiness, they will be happy. Obviously one of the most important things that a parent can do is to keep the environment as tranquil, peaceful, and as happy as possible. Help them select positive "up" people for friends and teach them to see a protective bubble around them that keeps all negativity out and away from them.

Cancerian children like old familiar things, and can become too attached to objects and people. They are inclined to collect things and

will enjoy any hobby that includes collecting. But, if they don't learn to let go of some possessions, their life will be filled with clutter. Teach them the very necessary art of organization. Also, teach them the value of change—of letting go of things, people, and unworthy concepts. Most importantly, teach them that placing their security in anything outside of themselves is an insecure position. Security has to come from within. Amassing great quantities of things to surround themselves with won't help. If this is not learned, Cancer can be quite selfish, quite unturned and always trying to protect themselves. On the other hand, when they are secure in their own minds they can be outgoing, affectionate, and generous.

Family is important to Cancer, so planning family activities and doing things together is a must. Let them help you plan and they will love it. When you want their cooperation with anything, tell them how you feel when they do something wrong and ask them how they would feel if they were in your place. Usually they will come around. Use a lot of feeling words in your communication. They are devastated with any harsh or brash disciplining. Sharing feelings works best.

Be sure to give these Cancer children lots of hugs and always be aware of their sensitivities. Refer to Mercury in Cancer for key words to use in your communications with your Cancer child.

## Children with Sun in Leo

In Jeane Dixon's book, she suggests that apostle John best represents Sun in Leo. He was the youngest and joined with Peter, an Aries, another fire sign, to spread the word throughout Asia Minor. He was still writing and teaching until his death which demonstrates the persistence of Leo.

Leo is the heart and spine in the physical body. The heart shows us the powerful love and warmth of which Leos are capable. All energy needs proper expression so even love needs direction. The Leo needs to understand how to balance the love of self and love given to others. Leos usually have positive self-esteem; unfortunately, when it is overdone they can be egotistical and arrogant. Learning to send the power of their love out to the world will empower others to be loving too. They are natural leaders and like to be looked up to, and they will best fulfill their role by incorporating some humility into their personalities.

The spine is what gives Leo a strong backbone. They will accept a challenge no matter how difficult, and will stand tall with their heads high. When Leos enter a room, they command attention by the way they carry themselves, as their symbol is the regal lion. They walk

erectly, with dignity, and demand respect as if they were royalty. They have been called regal and lofty yet should be advised to stay in touch with their" subjects" if they expect cooperation. Thinking that they are better than anyone else should be kept to themselves. They must learn to control their words and actions, or it will cause resentment in others. A good leader needs to focus on being of service to all.

Ruled by the Sun, Leo is a fixed fire sign. The Sun shows the power and radiance, and is the giver of life. The fixed fire can be either contained fire as in a fireplace which keeps us warm, or it can be a welder's torch which can be very dangerous and harmful. Leos need to learn that other people don't have the same high energy and that their fire might get too hot for others or prove exhausting, causing others to move away. Leos want approval and applause more than most people but they will benefit their purpose if made aware to occasionally share the spotlight. A little moderation will go a long way.

Leo the actor always wants center stage, and demands recognition. If they don't get enough loving attention in childhood, they could become the unstoppable show-off. It is best to inspire them to participate in plays or any productive way of performing. They are very dramatic and have great flair. It is always better when they use these attributes on stage or in some other beneficial way.

Respect is important to Leos and they yearn to achieve some importance in life. Being a fire sign, they are usually direct and honest. They are not likely to lie and will not treat others kindly who do. They are demanding of themselves and will also be demanding of those whom they love and are close to. Everything these children do they feel is a reflection of themselves so they will work harder than most to do their best, always reaching for perfection. They will expect the same from others and will be amazed that others can be happy with less. Because of this, they have a hard time delegating authority—when they are to be held personally responsible for the work. (Their motto is: When you want something done right, do it yourself!) Otherwise, they will be great at delegating and giving directions, because they need the detail people to plan the nitty gritty and carry out their grand schemes.

Leo's lesson to learn is that perfection is seen differently through each person's eyes. Life is too short and they may even be hurting their own health (heart) with this attitude. When they can depersonalize, allowing their thinking to become more objective, they will be able to see that others have needs too! Then they can give their great abundance of warmth and love that brings them and those around them such joy.

# Leo Birthday Poem

Leo—Lord of the jungle, king of kings,
A salute from your subjects who wish you all things.
We're loyal to you 'cause you're loyal to us.
We'll submit to your will without any fuss.
You're blessed wieth leadership, brave and direct,
Done with affection which brings right effect.
You're honest, brave and reliant, too.
You show confidence with dignity,
So determined are you!
Who cares if you're dramatic, a showman at heart.
It's part of your vitality that's seen from the start.
Besides you're magnetic—passion we can't resist,
and none are more generous of
themselves and their gifts.
With all of this talent, beware of extremes,
for things overdone can soon change the whole theme.
Your power, when dictatorial, is not pleasant to feel.
Arrogance, overbearing, is not a good deal.
So, step out of your ego, humility try,
And you'll shine like the Sun, bright at dawn in the sky.
This year should be yours, from now to the end.
Here's luck and much love—all that we have to send.

# Happy Birthday, my Leo!

In disciplining a Leo always try to do it with respect and dignity. Never threaten their integrity or you may arouse a temper with the force of Mount St. Helens. The best way to get cooperation is to praise them for their accomplishments. If you tell them that they did a great job, you will get an even better one next time. Even if it wasn't the best, it will get better. If they seem to be frustrated about something or unusually pushy and aggressive, take them for a brisk walk in nature. This will usually calm them down.

It is Leo who roars and scares the enemy. It is Leo who protects (at any sacrifice, even life) its loved ones! Leo stands tall in the face of adversity, inspires the faltering, and puts spunk into the timid.

Without Leo this would be a world with less color, less courage, less conviction. They believe supremely in themselves, and inspire others to take heart (a symbol of Leo). In short, Leo is bigger than life! And oh how a petty, frightened world does need them!

But one caution. A little Leo, with difficult, frustrating, non-beneficial aspects in their chart could be the Cowardly Lion, who cries out, and mews like a kitten, for your help. You, as did Dorothy, can give Leo children heart and courage through your love and belief in them.

Your Leo will look for the good in situations, and is creative, loyal, forgiving, even magnanimous in mind and purse, sometimes to a fault (a true Leo is always an "easy touch"). Help them to use their strengths to empower the world.

Refer to Mercury in Leo for key words to use in your communications with your Leo child.

## Children with Sun in Virgo

Phillip was the apostle who in Jeane Dixon's book *Yesterday, Today and Tomorrow* best fit the description for the sign of Virgo. He was the business manager who took care of practical things, such as where they all would stay and where they would eat. Like other Virgos, he had no need for recognition, and, in fact, isn't mentioned that often in the scriptures. Most Virgos are like that—they quietly go about their work knowing what is most important is to do the job to the best of their ability. The fame and even the money is not as important as doing the job well. Success to them is based on performance. They are methodical and meticulous. They are analytical and neat, using both their head and their hands. They are always an asset because they present the facts, and put form and organization into life. It makes sense that Virgo is an earth

# Virgo Birthday Poem

To the sign of the Virgin, a part of our wheel,
All the best wishes our poem can reveal,
And how does one share with our Virgo friends?
With logic and reason—its how this mind extends.
We'll meet on a chord that's effective, reserved.
We'll serve and be served
with the balance deserved,
And with the methods you're refined to precise.
So practical—you are skilled—in giving advice.
You are cautious, discriminate—part of your whole,
But to leave out your feelings inhibits your soul.
So don't be so skeptical, or pick at perfection.
Accept what you have—for it is your selection.
You are our worker—fastidious and clean,
And your need to be useful and neat is well seen.
Let's analyze now, and then join our forces,
For all must be pure—we came
from the same sources!
We know you are shy, so to you we extend
Our invitation to the best of all we can send.

# Happy Birthday, my Virgo!

sign and is ruled by Mercury.

Virgo symbolically represents the assimilation process in the physical body, and is symbolized by the Virgin. A virgin represents purity and perfection, two characteristics that are strong in Virgos. The statement "cleanliness is next to Godliness" comes to mind, and maybe we all need a little more Virgo in our lives. They certainly like having themselves clean and groomed, and most of them want their environment clean, organized, and neat. They will think better when their surroundings are orderly. The problem is that if they set their standards too high, they become nitpicks and nervous, the typical type "A" personality. When they set the same high standards for others (and they do), not only are they disappointed, but others will see them as too critical and impossible to please or satisfy. Since they really are happiest when they are helping someone else, learning to be non-judgemental will be the quality which will bring results. Being less critical and more loving will make their service to others more effective. Helping Virgo to accept other people as they are gives your child a better starting point to really help others.

Virgo children have wonderful mental powers. They have great concentration and a retentive memory. Their brain is like a masterful computer, always taking in information, categorizing it, detailing it, organizing it, and then using it. They are great with detail, when they're working with their hands or their brain. They like to work with projects which are practical and will develop skills in these areas. They also like to handle routine jobs. They are much more realistic than most.

Virgos are very interested in health and diet. They can be hypochondriacs always worrying about their own health, or they will study nutrition and attempt to lead healthy lives. They are not only concerned with the quality of the food, but they will also want it to look appealing. Some Virgos become vegetarians; some are just finicky eaters. They will have definite ideas about what they will and won't eat. If you keep their diet simple, plain, with no sauces, and only a few combinations, they will be happier. If you tell them the health benefits of the food you are serving them, they are more apt to eat what you present. Just be sure that you have your facts straight because they will probably check them out. Many Virgos end up in the field of nutrition. Many make wonderful surgeons because they not only are concerned about the body, but are so level-headed, unemotional and exact.

One area in which they have difficulty is being able to express their personal feelings. They are not very gregarious and can appear

distant and aloof. This is the reason why they need love, assurance, and acceptance. They appear aloof because they are shy and uncertain of themselves. Be sure to make the effort to approach them and give them plenty of affection even if you have to initiate it most of the time. One of their lessons is to learn to be more open and loving... and by your doing this, you will help them.

To discipline a Virgo you might ask them what they would do if they were you or ask what they think is the best way to handle the situation. You just might be surprised at what they come up with. Usually if you keep them busy with new things to learn, little jobs to do, and plenty of craft projects, they won't get into any trouble.

Refer to Mercury in Virgo for key words to use in your communications with your Virgo

## Children with Sun in Libra

Bartholomew fits the sign of Libra well so I agree with Jeane Dixson's assessment in her book because Libra is an air sign, meaning that it is strongly influenced by the intellect. Bartholomew appears to have been the best educated of all the apostles, having a strong love of knowledge. He was observed as handling all difficulties and hostilities with a calm, logical approach. As a Libra, he was able to see both sides of a situation and attempted to administer assistance to all with fairness. He is sometimes called Nathaniel in the scriptures, which points to the duality so characteristic of Libra. At times, Libran natives appear fickle because they seem to vacillate and can be so evasive. The main reason for this behavior is because they are always weighing both sides of everything. This sign can see, understand, and sympathize with each point of view. No wonder the symbol for Libra is the scales, always looking for and trying to balance, as well as being the symbol for justice. This sign is continually weighing and evaluating.

The children who are born under Libra are charming and diplomatic. They will want to have a very active social life and are sometimes called social butterflies. They are friendly, outgoing, generally good natured, and will work hard at being liked. It is very important to them to be liked by everyone. The problem is that they have a tendency to try to be all things to all people. This can be overwhelming and may bring out some of the non-beneficial characteristics such as appeasing, pacifying, and settling for peace at any price -since they basically dislike discord and are always striving for harmony. They can become non-committal,

seem indecisive, or be easily influenced. They also are inclined to be gullible, especially while they are young. Because popularity is so important to them, be sure to teach Libra children to avoid sacrificing their principles to obtain it, because they have all the natural abilities to be liked without doing so.

These children will want to help everyone and are strong catalysts in inspiring others. They are sometimes called the peacemakers of the zodiac. No wonder so many choose professions as lawyers and counselors. They generally enjoy and work well with most people. You will find large numbers of them on any list of *Who's Who.*

If all this sweetness doesn't sound like your little Libra, be aware that there is another side to this sign. They can be dominating and strong-willed. These children sometimes enjoy the contest of argument for argument's sake; they enjoy all one-on-one encounters as long as it is kept on a high intellectual level! Many generals and strategists were born in this sign.

Libras have been known to be great perfectionists with high personal standards, sometimes making them difficult to live with. On the plus side, they are fastidious, modest, neat, and refined. These children appreciate, even need beautiful surroundings. They will feel best and be far more cooperative when their environment is peaceful, harmonious, and beautifully arranged.

They have an eye for quality and are attracted to culture and all forms of the fine arts. These children can be very creative and artistic. They have a developed sense of color and balance, and love all beautiful things. Be sure to help them develop a practical sense too.

Since Libra is the relationship sign, it is not unusual for them to always want to do everything with someone. They dislike doing anything alone. It is as though they need the reflection of someone else to know who they are. It is important to help them learn the discipline of working alone. And most importantly, the discipline of getting started, and then completing! It is also important to give them some tests or responsibilities, or they can grow up "spoiled" and have great difficulty adjusting to the real world.

You will get their best cooperation by working with them or assigning them to work with someone else. Since they dislike any type of work that is dirty, put your efforts into selecting jobs where they will be able to use their talents of beautifying.

In the physical body, Libra rules the kidneys, the purifying system of the body.

# Libra Birthday Poem

How thankful we are for Libra,
Sign of beauty in our zodiac—
The one who speaks of justice,
Who's refined with charm and tact.
Our airy social butterfly
Brings color and grace to our world.
And touches all with gentle love
As a bud to a blossom uncurled.
You blend harmony with understanding,
And show the way to peace,
That cooperating and compromise
Make feelings of separateness cease.
You're creative and liberal,
loving all forms of art.
You've no need for evasion
In matters of the heart.
Let's join together 'round our zodiac wheel,
To be part of its beauty and oneness to feel.
We'll sing you a tribute of love and your worth,
Wishing you all the best
from the stars and our Earth.

# Happy Birthday, My Libra!

The planet of love, Venus, is the planet which rules Libra and so it is love that purifies the soul. Children of this sign are very affectionate and have a lot of love to give. They also need the love returned. They are generous and sharing and want to be appreciated for that. They are very "other-people" oriented. They will love to entertain so mothers, be prepared to have the neighborhood at your house. You may find your home the meeting place for clubs and party planning, and usually the place where the parties are held.

Since friends are so important to Librans, be sure to teach them to choose their friends with care. They need models who are positive and loving, with high principles and integrity—just as they have—so they won't later suffer the agonies of disillusionment from those who don't have high standards.

If it is necessary to discipline these children they will respond best when you go about it in a calm, logical and reasoning way. Be sure they understand. Be as tactful as you can and be sure you are fair, for the concept of fairness is a fetish with Librans. These children react poorly to harshness and dislike anything ugly, vulgar, or unjust. Ask for their cooperation, discuss the matter together, elicit their suggestions. Compromise if you can, then they will feel that together you both have created a win-win situation.

A devastating punishment for these children would be to have phone privileges removed, or being told they will be unable to attend the next party or social event. Remember, if you choose to attack or confront them you will likely get the same behavior in return. Mirror to them what you want. They will prefer pleasant interaction when cooperating with you.

Libra children are romantic by nature, and are inclined to be idealistic at times. They are liberal, broadminded, and tolerant. They are willing to fight for justice and are fair minded. Help them to choose worthwhile causes so that their energy and time can be beneficially utilized and not spent on futile causes. They can sometimes remind one of Don Quixote! They usually have good judgment on their own but can sometimes, in their zeal to please, be taken in by others who will use and misuse them. These children have high principles - when given a choice between two undesirable options they will refuse to compromise these principles and will choose neither option.

As you can see, you have a fascinating combination here. They are easy to work with once you understand them. These children will

want to live life to the fullest so I am sure it will be an exciting experience for all whom they share it with. Have fun, they will insist on it!

Refer to Mercury in Libra for key words to use in your communications with your Libra child.

## Children with Sun in Scorpio

*Dear Thomas, our doubting Thomas,* as Jeane Dixon put it! Truly our Scorpio apostle—remembering that he was the one who would not believe that Christ had risen without first seeing him and touching his wounds. This is so typical of Scorpio who says, "Prove it to me." Scorpio is always the skeptic, wanting personal experience before believing and accepting. However, once Scorpios have been convinced and decide to commit themselves they show passionate determination and great loyalty. Scorpios are real fighters and live the motto: *When the going get's tough, the tough get going.* These are the children who won't cry when they are hurt or spanked, because they don't want to show weakness. Instead they will clench their teeth or look back at the inflicter with their penetrating defiant eyes, often thinking, "Just wait. I'll get you back some day." They have a tendency to be vindictive. so it is most important for them to learn at a young age to forgive and forget. Help them realize it is unhealthy in every way to hold grudges and keep negative thoughts.

Scorpios are among the strong-minded signs of the zodiac, if not the strongest sign. How these children use their power, for benefit or not, will be determined by the type of guidance they receive in their early years. It is extremely important for them to establish strong spiritual values as young as possible. When these children use their power in a positive way their influence can help others make transformational changes. It is critical that they be directed wisely.

There is no halfway or in-between with these children. It is either black or white, devil or angel, due to their fixed watery sign. To give an example: Jonas Salk is a Scorpio using his power with positive expression; Charles Manson is a Scorpio using his power in the most negative expression.

The symbols that are given to Scorpio explain very clearly the choices they have. Scorpio is the only sign that has three different symbols! First, there's the scorpion which is the lowest expression of the sign, with strong self-preservation and survival instincts, yet will sting itself for lack of something else to sting. Second, there is the eagle that

shows the heights to which these children can soar. Third, is the Phoenix Bird rising out of the ashes, having died and then transformed. Transformation is a keyword for Scorpio, and each person in this sign must undergo this process in order to fulfill their destiny. They must surrender the ego or personality to the spirit and use their strength in service to the world. These children need to learn about the powerful leaders throughout history, both the good and the destructive. This will help to stress the importance of the choices they make through life and guide them to follow the high path. The negative side unfortunately has given us some of the most clever and brutal criminals ever known. However, examples of famous Scorpios who have soared high are Theodore Roosevelt, Charles Atlas, Picasso, John Phillip Sousa, Marie Curie, George Patton, Nehru, Martin Luther and Daniel Boone!

In the body, Scorpio rules the reproductive organs, which explains why these children have such dynamic and creative energy. They also have strong regenerative powers, both physically and psychically, and will recover from even the most devastating experiences, becoming even stronger as a result. They are filled with courage and conviction and lack understanding or patience with those who are timid or weak. These children will approach situations with single-minded enthusiasm, accepting them as stimulating challenges. Many Scorpios are destined to become famous through great accomplishments.

Often people find Scorpios hard to know because they are so secretive. On the other hand, because they have such highly developed psychic abilities and are able to see beneath the surface, it is difficult to keep a secret from them! As their parent, trying to hide a truth will be useless. They will expect and need honest answers to their questions and are usually able to handle the truth of any situation. When disciplining them, be sure to think the situation through before taking action and be sure to make the punishment fair. In projects always remember to ask for their assistance rather than telling them what to do. Don't demand their cooperation. This action only would bring out the streak of perversity in them, making them do just the opposite!

Scorpio children have strong emotions and experience life with extreme intensity. One of the greatest lessons you can teach them is to learn how to separate from their feelings by objectively observing themselves. This lesson will be a lifelong challenge but well worth the effort. The danger is that when the emotions are not controlled or used positively, the intensity involved can cause unbelievable destruction to

# Scorpio Birthday Poem

Here's an offering to Scorpio, power of the signs
With love and respect from soul, heart and mind.
Your fierce determination is a wonder to see,
A quality you use well, as you show how to be.
Like apostle Thomas, your doubting is strong,
Keeping your reserve, slow to join in the throng.
You perceive, understanding,
    things not easily seen,
You know depths of wisdom,
    and show us what they mean.
We know you have secrets,
    that you choose to keep
Silent within you, instinctively deep
But when you choose to share, we trust in you
To be sharing only what you know to be true.
We love your strength,
    hope that you'll love yourself
We wish you happiness, peace and good health.
May your new year bring beauty
With all gifts your world can give.

# Happy Birthday, my Scorpio,
# and for each year you live!

themselves ( like the scorpion stinging itself) as well as to others. These children have sharp tongues, stinging wit, and are prone to sarcasm. They must be made aware that their words can do great and lasting harm. Once they develop compassion and humility, their passions can rise to a higher level and be used to benefit others. It will be wise to teach them the law of cause and effect, meaning that what one puts out, one gets back—or what goes around comes around. This will be a good incentive to get them to act in kinder, more beneficial ways. Learning to turn the other cheek will curb their vindictiveness. The earlier they are helped to see this, to work on purifying themselves of Scorpio venom, the better for all.

Finally, these children, like the scorpion, seem to be always on the defensive, so you might as well give up trying to deceive or mislead them, or manipulate them in any way. They are the masters of manipulation. Treat them openly, and honestly. Enlist them as an ally and you will be protected by their strength, and have their loyalty for life.

Refer to Mercury in Scorpio for key words to use in your communications with your Scorpio child.

## Children with Sun in Sagittarius

Once again as referenced from Jeane Dixson's book, James the Greater, called the "son of thunder" by Christ, demonstrates the qualities of Sagittarius. The Greater was added to his name to distinguish him from the other James who was shorter. His responses were optimistic and enthusiastic, and he was always ready to gallop off to a new adventure. His comments were brutally frank like a clap of thunder, often unnerving those exposed. Expect the same from these children born in the sign of Sagittarius. One of your most important challenges as their parent or caregiver will be to teach them the art of diplomacy, and how to pause and think and then choose their words carefully. They never mean harm—there is nothing vicious in the Sag nature, only unthinking spontaneity!

Sagittarius is a mutable fire sign, causing these children to be outgoing, and impulsive. It also causes a quick fiery temper that burns furiously... and then out. To assist in extinguishing this blast, don't feed it any response and the blaze will quickly dissipate. Simply observe the outrage and then calmly redirect their attention to something else. Taking them for a walk is an excellent way to diffuse any lingering hostility (and this sign does not store up negative feelings). Walking will always be the best way

# Sagittarius Birthday Poem

What would the world be without
the truth of a Sagittarian,
But pay heed, my friend, and
let me remind you once again,
Your words  can come like flying arrows,
Shot direct and straight wth a pierce
so painful without loving tact
Now, nobody's perfect and
we need people like you,
Who are frank, optimistic, sincerely honest, too.
At dinner you charm us with philosophy and such,
It's your outgoing nature that we love so much.
No one is more jovial, brighter than you,
nor lives a life of freedom more than you do.
You spread yourself generously, as does the Sun.
Please teach what you know,
for you hold wisdom.
Thank you for daring just to be you.
Here's sending a Happy Birthday.
May your wishes come true!

# Happy Birthday,
# my Sagittarius!

for these children to release any anxieties or frustrations actually anything requiring the use of their legs so biking, hiking, etc.

There are two reasons which explain why a walk works so well at dissipating emotions. The first is because Sagittarius has influence over the hips and thighs in the physical body, therefore the freedom and movement that walking creates releases any pent-up energy. Secondly, the symbol for Sagittarius is the centaur, half horse and half man. When the children of this sign get to expend the physical energy charging through the animal part of their symbol, then they are free to utilize their human ability of logic and wisdom and can more clearly think through situations.

These children's approach to life is direct like the centaur archer's arrows. You will always know where you stand, and they don't hesitate to tell you what is on their minds. Unless you are prepared for the blunt truth, don't ask for their opinions. They are seldom shy or timid about telling you exactly what they think. They dislike beating around the bush and will let everyone know it. They are honest and will tell the truth as they see it. One caution is that they can be careless with details and may not have all the facts. Another is that they may have a tendency to be reckless or rash, so do you best to teach them to think before speaking or taking any action.

Freedom is mandatory for Sagittarius. Their theme is "Don't fence me in!" When these children feel penned in too tightly they will kick and carry on like a wild mustang held in a confined area. That's the centaur showing itself again. The best way to handle this need for freedom is to allow them to take the lead whenever feasible, and give them many opportunities to make their own choices. Explain to these children that if they make wise choices and act in a responsible manner they can continue to choose for themselves. Let them know that this is the way to the freedom they crave. If you should find your young Sagittarian child cranky or irritable, check to see if you have dressed them in something too tight. These children will even need freedom with their clothing!

You will discover that the children of this sign are very independent and they find it difficult to stay within any boundaries. They will even end a friendship or any relationship rather than be restricted by it. For young children, anyone telling them who they can or can't have as a friend is fatal. For older children who have begun to date, anyone of the opposite sex expecting to possess them should be prepared to have the relationship be of short duration.

These children are easily bored, going from one thing to another. This mental scatterdness can also move into the physical, with them being a bit messy and disorganized. They are always looking to the future, thinking up new things to do and new places to go. They like continuous activity so be prepared. The natives of this sign love sports and travel. They are good with animals, especially large ones, and will feel at home in the forest. These suggestions should give you some ideas of how to keep them busy. Keeping their days filled with activities which they enjoy will create happy children who will require little or no discipline. However, when discipline is required the worst punishment for these children is any form of restriction or confinement. It is always wise to be truthful with them to retain their respect. It is also important to be fair and just. They will respond better with discussions that are direct and to the point. These are children who will give you some interesting feedback if you ask for their suggestions and opinions—and many times they will give you the solutions!

Your Sag will be lucky and no matter how close to the wire they may come, something will save their day at the eleventh hour. It is almost as if they know this deep inside. This luck is also why they are such big gamblers, and will gallop forth where others fear to tread. They have a natural ability to see the whole picture rather than any particular part. They look at the whole of society rather than individuals. They expand their interest to all nationalities and are not prejudiced or biased. Their philosophies are far reaching and futuristic. They are comfortable with abstract ideas ... and I'm sure these children will present you with many new ways of looking at life. They like to be acknowleged for their abilities so I suggest that you compliment them, love them -and give them plenty of space to be themselves.

Refer to Mercury in Sagittarius for key words to use in your communications with your Sagittarian child.

## Children with Sun in Capricorn

In her book *Today Tomorrow and Forever*, Jeane Dixson says that the apostle who aligns with the sign of Capricorn is Matthew, the tax collector. When we realize that the natural instincts of a Capricorn are to be in a position of authority, and that they need to be respected by others, it is clear to see why Matthew had chosen his profession. Capricorns do make wonderful administrators. They are serious and responsible. They take time to assess the situation, which makes them able to respond with

practical, useful solutions.

The symbol for Capricorn is the goat who surefootedly and very carefully places each foot, always looking for solid ground before moving on. They are persistent, determined, and will climb to great heights. Professionally, Capricorns aspire to high positions no matter what arena they choose, but, usually they choose to work within the status quo in fields that are socially acceptable and well-respected. This obviously is a sign which clings to customs and is comfortable with tradition. They have a strong appreciation for money and will usually focus on obtaining financial success. They are achievement-oriented and will strive to accomplish in areas that have strong purpose.

Most of the time these children are so serious they appear old for their years. They seem to be born as adults and will act in very mature ways. You can count on them to behave well in situations where adult contact is required. Even as young children, Capricorns are easy to discipline and can be trusted with responsibility. They are almost overly conscientious. They thrive on others taking them seriously, and on receiving praise for performing well. They will want to please you, to gain your respect. They are wonderfully self-disciplined.

These children are ambitious and are hard workers. In fact, they feel that work is virtuous and that everyone should work for whatever they get. These are the children who will want to have a job at an early age or will always be thinking up ways to earn money. They may even start their own little business. They are very persistent and will still be plugging along after most would have given up.

Capricorn is an earth sign which causes the children of this sign to gravitate toward the material side of life. They are realistic and place little value in fantasy or intangibles. They are interested in accumulating material substances, both money and possessions. They are often good at using materials to build with, many even become contractors. In fact, they excel at building structures of any nature. And figuratively, they are always building their lives, and climbing like the mountain goat.

It is not surprising to discover that Capricorn rules the skeletal system and the skin in the physical body; one is the structure and the other is the form. This sign also rules teeth and the knees. Since the knee is one of the most complex joints in the body and is necessary for good mobility, it is important for these natives to take care of their knees. Teach them the value of life-long, daily-done exercise to keep them flexible and to avoid becoming rigid, mentally as well as physically. Re-

# Capricorn Birthday Poem

To our responsible Capricorn, here and out there,
A few words of tribute to show that we care.
Your sense of self-preservation is strong,
Both here and above, whether right or wrong.
But don't be fearful—or let down your guard
Do taste of love, and of sincere regard.
You're ruled by Saturn, so tests can be stiff.
Life will give lessons of patience and thrift.
Your self-discipline and perfection, we admire to see,
But while here on Earth we would not be
If compared to the One whom we call Thee.
We need your caution—dependable, enduring...
Practical, productive and most reassuring.
Just remember for you there is strength in humility.
Don't be pessimistic—you have strong ability.
We hope that this year, and all the rest, too,
Bring the happiest of birthdays, always for you!

## Happy Birthday, my Capricorn!

member, one is apt to develop a weakness in that area of the body that a sign rules. Since Capricorn rules knees and skeletal system, they often develop arthritis later—all the more reason for exercise and flexibility!

These children are collectors, and like to hold on to everything they accumulate. The caution here is that in extreme cases accumulating too much around oneself can be immobilizing, giving them no

room to move or grow! Also holding on too tightly can cause rigidity, and without movement psychic atrophy sets in. The same problem exists with patience, a characteristic of this sign, if carried to its extreme and they wait too long, an opportunity could be missed.

When these children reach school age, don't be surprised if they show little or no interest in subjects which they consider to have no practical application. They are primarily interested in learning about what can be useful to them. Since they tend to be focused on the past and are establishment-oriented, you will be able to teach them wisdom through reading and learning about the people throughout history who reached positions of great authority and respect. These children will work very hard in school and usually make excellent students. They are organized and will respect teachers who are. They are concerned about their reputation and will do everything to acquire a good one; woe to him who sullies their reputation, or embarrasses them in any way!

Two of the worst things anyone can do to a Capricorn is to imply that they are incompetent, or to treat them with disrespect. If they are commended for their accomplishments they will eagerly take on more responsibility. But be sure to watch they don't take on so much that their lives are filled only with work and duty. They need to be encouraged to play and sometimes have fun. Help them to develop a sense of humor.

These children appear to be pessimistic because they have a tendency to look first at the down side of situations. For them it is a form of self-protection. They feel that by looking for the pitfalls they can more easily avoid them. Help them to become aware of how others might react to this "downer" approach so that they won't be considered a wet blanket, or the one who rains on other people's parades! The best advice I can think of is for you to teach them to always keep one thought in mind—lighten up!

Refer to Mercury in Capricorn for key words to use in your communications with your Capricorn child.

## Children with Sun in Aquarius

Thaddaeus, nicknamed Jude, is our apostle for the sign of Aquarius. This is again referenced from the book *Today, Tomorrow and Forever.* He was one of the least known of the apostles, supposedly the brother of James the Less. It is so typical of Aquarius to work behind the scenes and to shun the spotlight. Their need seems only to be able to fight for the cause rather than to be the center of attention. Thaddaeus or Jude is known as the

apostle of the impossible and is prayed to as a last resort when all seems hopeless. It makes sense when we know that the planet Uranus, with its unpredictable nature, rules the sign of Aquarius. The key phrase for Uranus is: expect the unexpected! These natives are capable of a powerful love for all mankind and they possess a strong desire for humanitarian service. If needed, they will stand alone against the status quo to eliminate suffering, and will fight for any worthwhile cause.

The symbol for Aquarius is the water bearer. Since water is a necessity to live, it is thought that he is pouring forth in abundance the substance of life. This thought may be the mission of Aquarius, to bring new life to us all. Although he is pouring water, it should be remembered that Aquarius is an air sign. Sometimes this gets confused.

Like all air signs, Aquarius children will operate in a logical, and intellectual manner. They are objective, and experience life using a mental approach. Because of a lack of emotional display, to some they may seem impersonal and aloof. They are definitely independent and have no need for approval. This characteristic causes them to be comfortable going their own way without becoming concerned about what others may think. They are quite self-sufficient and march to their own drummer. These children are the entrepreneurs of the world. They are individuals in every sense of the word. They are often unconventional and always unique, to say the least.

Freedom is extremely important to the children born under this sign. They need the freedom to be who they are and to do their own thing. Their approach may be unorthodox, and sometimes they are defiant of established customs and tradition. This behavior may take some getting used to, but how would we ever find new ways to live life and make improvements if we never tried something different?

Aquarian children are non-conformists and totally indifferent to their environment, especially in the sense of how they dress. They are not likely to get caught up in the latest fad or even know what they should wear to a particular event. They will need your guidance in this area, but I suggest that you insist only when it is absolutely necessary. They still need their individual freedom to be themselves, plus they can be quite stubborn and can NOT be pushed. They have their own ideas about most everything so you will need to be creative and discover ways to motivate them to make necessary changes or concessions. Sometimes presenting what you want in the form of a suggestion and then backing away, will give them the needed space to make the change on their own.

Remember, they must decide for themselves so present your ideas in a calm, logical way and give them space and time to come around.

Your main challenge with these children will be to keep enough variety in their lives. They will always want to be learning new things, especially subjects pertaining to science, exploration, and new technology—especially computers—and they love science fiction!

Aquarian children are very curious about everything. Generally they like study and they have good retentive memories. You will find that they will need a minimum amount of supervision when it comes to schoolwork. They can also be very creative and innovative in the areas of art, music, and literature. They will produce very original and unusual material, and always pursue a broad range of interests, activities, and people. In reference to the latter, be prepared, because they may choose some very different, unusual types for friends. These choices may not make sense to you but please be patient with them since your Aquarian probably has a reason. Know that these children of Aquarius are their own persons, so the company they keep does not have that great an influence over them. Besides, they will have many friends who are all very different.

These children are sometimes viewed as the rebels of the zodiac, because they are often seen as fighting for reform. They look for causes as they are true humanitarians. They will join groups who work for social and political reform. After all, a key word for Uranus, their ruler, is liberation. Sometimes Aquarians seem radical in their approach; however, they are intellectually rational. Although they are progressive free thinkers and the revolutionaries of the world, appeal to that rational side if they go overboard and become fanatic—and there is that danger, within this free-thinking fixed sign! They will often want to participate in marches and protests, for they are real crusaders. Direct them to worthwhile causes so that they won't simply become a renegade and a rioter. Show them how to use their enthusiasm in peaceful, constructive, nondestructive ways.

Before Uranus was discovered, the old rulership of Aquarius was the planet Saturn. You may remember that Saturn rules Capricorn so you know it represents responsibility, order, and perseverance, so thse children do have some of those qualities, too. I see older Aquarians more inclined to demonstrate the Saturn side, and younger Aquarians demonstrating the experimental, futuristic, unconventional side. It is natural for Aquarians to have keen intuitions and good psychic powers

# A Birthday Message for
## Aquarius

It's a pleasure to know you, and
how well you add to our group
You point to the future, and
discover new ways to lead our troops.
Your intuitive intellect, unconventional as it is,
Creates originality that others might miss
Your philosophy of individual pursuit
Teaches us independence and freedom to boot
As  a spirited reformer for humanity,
for universal truth
You're resourceful, and determined,
though sometimes aloof.
Please don't detach from us, and don't rebel
We know you're self-sufficient and
non-conforming, as well.
Besides, who is more inventive and practical, too.
We need your discerning genius—
that comes only from you!
Here's hoping your days are extraordinary
all year through,
And we wish you success in whatever you do.

# Happy Birthday, my Aquarius!

—so they may see and know things that others are as yet unaware.

One problem this sign has is that they are so focused on the masses that sometimes they neglect their families. Teach them that charity begins at home. A detached attitude is not as appropriate in family matters as it is in dealing with worldly matters. They can be very warmhearted—they just need you to help them work on expressing it at home with the family!

Aquarius rules the ankles and circulation in the physical body. The ankles are part of the foundational structure, therefore they need to be strong. Encourage these children to walk, to do up-and-down ankle exercises, and to choose activities which will create strength in this area, such as dancing! And these same activities will help the circulation. Aquarians have a tendency to be more mental than physical, so do see to it that they add some physical activities to their daily routine.

I am sure that by now you have a pretty good idea of the fun in store for you with your interesting little Aquarian, so I will leave you with this: do NOT try to control or force them. Keep daily life filled with as many new experiences as possible, and you will enjoy an exciting life together. Remember, they are the Age of Aquarius!

Refer to Mercury in Aquarius for key words to use in your communications with your Aquarius child.

## Children with Sun in Pisces

Last, but definitely not least, is Pisces. Here we find individuals who have amazing abilities and are very complex. Those born under this sign are often misunderstood, just as (from Jeane Dixon's book), the apostle Judas Iscariot. He is often thought of as the traitor, but when we reexamine the events to understand his motives and intentions, the picture changes. His motive was to end the oppression and suffering which the people endured under the cruel and brutal rulership of the Romans. His intention was to bring Jesus together with this political power, believing that Jesus would confront them and bring the wrath of God upon them. Then Jesus could become emperor of Rome, thereby ending suffering and restoring decency. Judas was so desperate for social and political reform that he completely missed the point that Jesus wasn't here to rule the Earth, but that His mission was to leave a message which would change it for all time. This factor makes it seem very probable why Jesus chose Judas—because of his zeal for the people, and because Jesus knew full well what was going to happen.

In retrospect, the part Judas played was most important, since singularly his actions birthed the beginning of Christianity, which was all part of the divine plan. Judas didn't want to hurt Jesus; he wanted to empower Him. When his plan didn't work, he became despondent and committed suicide. The other apostles then chose Matthew to take his place.

The symbol for Pisces is the two fish swimming in different directions. This indicates that the children born under this sign have a choice of two directions. One of their problems is that they are too susceptible to external influences, so whatever is the greatest force in their environment, determines which way they swim. As their parent or caregiver, it is most important that you stimulate them in the best direction, and help them develop their spiritual nature. Once this becomes their main direction, they will be able to accomplish much in this too realistic world.

Without a strong spiritual background and solid foundation, they can be misled into squander and deception. These children may have a tendency to want to escape the world of reality and to spend their time daydreaming and in fantasy land. Sometimes the world is too harsh, cruel, and hurts too much for them to endure. This is because they "feel" everything so personally. Pisces children need to learn to view the world and other people more objectively. When they can do this, everything that happens around them will affect them less. Otherwise they will always feel like the victim—vulnerable, and at the mercy of their environment.

Pisces is a water sign so we find these children emotional, sensitive, and intuitive. They can be like sponges, soaking up everyone's feelings. This, of course, causes them to be not only sympathetic, but also empathetic. They literally can feel the pain and the joy of others, even while watching a play or the evening news. That is why they must be very careful not to become moody or sink into the problems of others. I hope you can see how important it is to surround them with as much positivity as possible. When you do this they can blossom and develop all of their artistic and creative abilities.

These children are very imaginative and will show great inspiration. Teach them to work at and to follow through with their ideas, and to produce the results for this the material world. They sometimes lack persistence and need lots of encouragement in this area. To start with, help them to set and complete short-term goals. As they succeed with

these, it will become easier to complete long-term goals. These children are susceptible to procrastination and are sometimes 'afraid' to take that first step. So, gently guide them in the direction that is needed. They are adaptable and flexible so this shouldn't be too hard.

Children of this sign are very visual, so when you are teaching them, paint pictures with your words and they will better remember. For example: if you are giving them directions to reach a certain destination, rather than saying, "Turn right at the third street down," say, "Turn right at the street that has the yellow house on the corner, with a marble bird-bath by the big fur tree and a red-white-and-blue mailbox by the road." They are quick to" see" mental pictures, and in this way will learn rapidly. Also, when they are school age, the more visual aids you can use the better. They will enjoy television so utilize any video aids you can. But don't let them become TV-addicted—or addicted to any escape, or fantasy world. Later in life, without early guidance into the real world, they could escape into alcohol or worse. But do allow them some time alone to imagine and dream up something wonderful for the rest of us earthbound creatures.

It is very important to be affectionate and give the children of Pisces a lot of reassurance, because they are inclined to feel unworthy or experience some feelings of inferiority (because they don't feel quite at home on Earth!). They are easily hurt and can cry readily. Be gentle about discipline and always be aware of how sensitive they are—never use corporal punishment on them!

The part of the physical body that Pisces rules is the feet. Since the feet are the support for the rest of the body, it is necessary to have strong, well-formed feet for good mobility. When the foundations of your Pisces children is built on the strength of the spiritual, their physical world can stand tall.

This sign of the fish is known for its accomplishments in the worlds of art and music, as well as in religion and medicine. They have great compassion and are capable of great sacrifice. They serve with devotion and can truly be the healers of us all, in mind and body. As they develop the perseverance of the disciple Matthew, they will become determined to excel in the world.

Because these children have such highly developed psychic sensitivity, teach them to see a bubble of white light surrounding them and protecting them at all times from any negativity. Help them to develop

# A Birthday Message for Pisces

Hail to Pisces, the last and most needed
of all our zodiac friends
For how can we have a beginning, until we have an end?
You show us that we must leave Earth
In order to ascend,
And do it by dreaming of things beyond the now and then.
Your visions will take us away with inspiration, too
If you'll utilize your genius and show us what to do.
Take us to lands of fantasy
Where dreams are strong and true,
You know the way past darkness
Please help us to get through.
We need your perception, creative as it is,
God shared with you the secrets
that once were only His.
You're sensitive, caring and filled with compassion,
Serving the masses in charitable fashion.
As masquerader or poet, your gifts of emotion
Inspire imaginaton and intuitive devotion.
Is it illusion? Confusion> Delusion...or what?
Show us the way through a door that is shut.
How can you feel unworthy, and martyr yourself,
When you have all this talent—the best kind of wealth?
To you, Happy Birthday–Success and Good health!

# Happy Birthday, my Pisces!

their natural intuitive ability and to use it to make decisions. Let them know that it is a gift and that it should be used wisely.

Pisces children need your attention and your encouragement. Reward them with doing things together —and reward them often. Be sure to give them lots of love and reassurance, and be considerate of their sensitivity. This will ensure a joyful and rewarding life together.

Refer to Mercury in Pisces for key words to use in your communications with your Pisces child.

**An estimated 32 million people, according to a recent "Gallup Poll," believe that the movement of the planets affect their lives.**

**—Sydney Omarr, national syndicated columnist**

# Chapter 5

))

# The Moon
## The Messages of Emotions

The Moon is the fastest moving celestial body in our solar system. It travels through the entire zodiac, each one of the twelve signs, every month. It stays in each sign for approximately two and a half days which is the average of 28 days, the lunar cycle. The Moon is the activator, or trigger which causes events to happen, and mood changes to occur. As it moves through the different signs each month, it makes contact with and activates each planet in everyone's individual horoscope. This is why we have highs and lows and is what causes our feelings and reactions to change from day-to-day. When we understand this, we become less apt to expect anyone, including ourselves, to feel or act consistently the same all of the time!

Symbolically the Moon represents the emotions—our feelings about and our reactions to our environment. The sign that our Moon is in describes how we experience the emotions and how they will be expressed. The Moon also represents security. It denotes how comfortable we are with our environment. It shows whether we feel like an important necessary part of our society, with a purpose in this world. It shows whether we are needed and whether the world fills our needs. By understanding what your child's needs are, we as parents and caregivers can begin to provide what is necessary.

When you read the description for each child's Moon place-ment, you will understand how his or her emotional nature functions. This will help clarify how you should develop your child's security and fulfill his or her needs.

## Your Child's Moon Sign

The Moon moves very quickly through the signs each month, staying in a sign approximately two and a half days. The Moon may change signs at almost any time of day, so look-up tables for a sign per day are not re-liable. The exact day and time of day that Moon changes signs can vary from one year to the next. The best and easiest way for you to know the correct Moon sign (as well as all other planetary placements) for your child's chart would be to send the coupon in the back of this book for the **One Free Chart Offer** to Astro Computing Services. The chart will be the Student Chart that lists under the chart wheel what each glyph or symbol means. When you look at a chart, the signs and planets will appear as glyphs. Here is a key to the glyphs:

### SIGNS

| ♈ | Aries | ♉ | Taurus | ♊ | Gemini |
|---|---|---|---|---|---|
| ♋ | Cancer | ♌ | Leo | ♍ | Virgo |
| ♎ | Libra | ♏ | Scorpio | ♐ | Sagittarius |
| ♑ | Capricorn | ♒ | Aquarius | ♓ | Pisces |

### PLANETS

| ☉ | Sun | ☽ | Moon | ☿ | Merucry |
|---|---|---|---|---|---|
| ♀ | Venus | ♂ | Mars | ♃ | Jupiter |
| ♄ | Saturn | ♅ | Uranus | ♆ | Neptune |
| ♇ | Pluto | | | | |

So that you can look up the Moon sign for your children without having to wait for the free chart, tables of the date Moon entered each sign, in Eastern Standard Time, from 1945 through 2025 are in the back of this book beginning on page **167**. Scan down the tables for your child's birth date (or your own if you were born in 1945 or after), or the closest date prior to the birth date, and the sign listed is most likely the correct one. Do understand, though, that Moon changes signs every two or three days at most. Only with a chart calculated for birth date, time and place can you be absolutely sure of the position of Moon in a chart.

# Children with Moon in Aries

The Moon in Aries gives the emotional nature an aggressive, impulsive way of expressing itself. These children will rush headlong into any relationship or project without first looking things over. They need to be taught to sit back a minute, to count to ten, and think it through. Otherwise, they will find themselves in situations of difficulty before they realize what has happened. In Aries, the emotions are fiery and strongly expressed. Their aim tends to be selfish because they unconsciously believe their feelings are more important and should come first. Teach them to understand other people have feelings that are just as important. A little understanding can help them curb this self-oriented tendency. In any case, they must be taught to think before they act or speak and not to be so impulsive. Otherwise they will have to face the consequences.

They are very courageous and will fight for what to them seems right. They will fight not only for themselves but others as well. They need to understand that their actions are triggered more from an emotional response... if they don't stop and think first they could make many mistakes.

They have a strong desire to learn the truth, and are so concerned with what should be, that they are rarely satisfied with what is. Teach them to work on improving themselves, and then all other things will improve automatically. Teach them to sometimes sit still and to study the lives and philosophies of the great people in history so they can expand their understanding of just what is truth. They will generally try anything once just because it is new and different. They are quite inventive and will come up with many original things to explore. As a toddler they are into everything, so be forewarned. And later, Aries goes where angels fear to tread!

When these children are emotionally upset, they are likely to have and be headaches! Aries carries their tension in the head. (Remember? Mars and Aries rules the head part of the body.) This is a tension which must be dealt with throughout life. Two ways to help this challenge are by releasing the tension through some vigorous activity or by talking out their feelings.

Moon in Aries has a fiery temper, and like fire, erupts quickly and goes out just as fast. They won't hold a grudge as might other signs. But they need to learn to control themselves because they say things they don't mean and can deeply hurt others. They must be taught that others may be as much or more sensitive than they.

They are idealists and will want to blaze their own trail. Teach

them that by learning from the past they will be better equipped to lead into the future.

When you challenge their actions or feelings, you arouse a will of unbelievable strength. This can be a tremendous asset when directed for a productive cause and in a positive manner. Teach them to be the keeper of and to stoke their own fire. Then they control it and spread only enough that warms, and not so much that it burns.

The Aries Moon will have trouble with a demanding or controlling mother, father, or teacher. They will be fighting them at every turn whenever they try to restrict them in any way. They have a strong need for independence and will continue to fight to maintain it, so give them the lead whenever the opportunity arises. Help them to consciously withhold their need for that independence, or they could waste their lives and energy on acting the rebel.

## Children with Moon in Taurus

The Moon is exalted in the sign of Taurus. This means that from the beginning the emotions and personality are functioning with a high degree of efficiency. These children will be fairly stable emotionally and will have a good idea of what they want. They want comfort and luxuries and all the "good things" of the material world. It will be necessary to teach them how to develop values that go beyond possessions. They will be security-oriented and inclined to place their security in not only material things but attachments to people. They must be taught to not place undue emphasis on this kind of security because all material things can be lost, and undue attachments to people cause the negative attribute of over-possessiveness which in later life can lead to heartache. Moon in the sign of the Bull can be quite stubborn with both their ideas and with any need to make changes, especially in their immediate environment. Getting them to change anything may be a challenge. If you can show them how a change (that you want them to make) can be beneficial to them, you have a chance. But they are naturally more comfortable with familiarity.

Your child will be a very determined little one with this Moon placement—which, of course, can be a tremendous asset when directed properly. If you direct them in a beneficial, productive manner they will accomplish a great deal. They have great staying power and can be formidable opponents. Teach them the correct use of these attributes. Show them that the overuse of determination is being obstinate. Point out that

the world is constantly changing and they would do well not to resist forced changes. They should be encouraged to broaden their scope and expand their values beyond just the immediate and external world. Help them achieve a good self-image, with an attitude of high self-worth ... which will bring the benefits of the external world to them.

They will be conservative and cautious with their possessions and self-indulgent about "the finer things in life." They will love good food, music, art, and anything that represents comfort. They are very affectionate and will enjoy both giving and receiving love. They have a lot of charisma and will use it charmingly.

They may not be a self-starter but once you get them in motion they'll generally see things through. They are very patient, sympathetic, and gentle when unprovoked. However, they do have a temper and, if they are prodded long enough, can be furious when angered. Indirect action works best and given time, they will come around on their own. But try always to be gentle with them, for they deeply feel emotional and physical pain. Also, logic doesn't always work, especially when they set their stubborn mind against it and tune you out—something the little Bull is especially proud of doing. If punishment is needed, deny some "goodies"—that should do it.

To these children, values will be very important and they tend to see things as either black or white, right or wrong. Teach them not to limit their knowledge with a narrow frame of reference, but to read about different cultures in order to enhance their attitudes and broaden their values. They may be a little lazy, so give them a gentle nudge.

Since security is so important, teach them inner security. Teach them to like themselves and to live life with an open heart.

## Children with Moon in Gemini

The Moon in Gemini gives the emotions a more intellectual approach, because it gives the ability to think the feelings through and the ability to discuss them, In fact, these children enjoy talking about all their feelings and reactions about people and events. They are very adept at expressing themselves. They also are very articulate and tell stories well. Short stories, that is. They have a restlessness about them that causes a short attention span. Thus, these children get bored easily, especially with routine. Keep them happy by presenting them with new things and diverse experiences. They will be content and easy to handle if you take them places with you and give them plenty of diversions in

life. They like to travel with you even if it is only to the grocery store. To them, every outing is a little adventure—and better for their active, curious minds. This insatiable curiosity must be properly fed for it is imperative they be learning constantly so that they can more positively use their emotional energy. Their emotional moods can be quite changeable. When the mood is positive and high, they can be very humorous but when the mood is negative and low, they feel persecuted and filled with self-doubt. At these times they will be nervous and scattered, or they may talk more, as well and faster. It should be fairly easy to change their mood to a more positive expression by simply presenting a new experience of some kind.

They do need to learn self-discipline in staying with things long enough to absorb the whole meaning, as they have a tendency to skim the surface. Teach them that this leads to being superficial. If they want people to listen to them, they will need to have all their statements backed up by facts. Tell them that they have plenty of time in their lives to have millions of new experiences and still have time to be thorough too.

They should also be made aware that there are a lot of people whose feelings are more sensitive than theirs, and some who are unable to think their feelings through. By understanding this they will be less inclined to hurt others with tactless words and inconsiderate actions.

They have the continual need to receive and dispense knowledge. They are always on the move both physically and mentally. They may even have a nervous stomach. Again, the best remedy is an interesting change in environment, and an occasional quiet period so they can assimilate all their incoming data!

These children are versatile and can be good conversationalists. When nervous or upset, they can be real chatterboxes. Help them to calm down and you will enjoy their company.

## Children with Moon in Cancer

The Moon is in her natural home in the sign of Cancer, since the Moon rules Cancer. Here, her influence is unaltered, her characteristics projected in full strength. Your Cancer Moon child will be sensitive, responsive, emotional, intuitive and possibly psychic. The Moon's monthly cycle will have a strong effect on them and they will be inclined toward moodiness. The relationship with mother is most important for strong emotional security. Any insecurity causes overindulgence, and modera-

tion is one of the keys to success. You would do well to give this child lots of love and affection, to help them feel wanted and accepted. The nurturing principle is very strong. These children need a lot of nurturing and also need to nurture others. They need to feel secure with their emotional energies in order to utilize and give nurturing in a healthy way. These children will do well with pets or younger children because it gives them an opportunity to care for someone or something and will allow this need to nurture develop in a positive manner. They have a lot of compassion and are sympathetic, even empathetic, so much so that you need to teach these children not to be quite so sensitive to those around them and not to respond so much to their environment. Feelings are more important to them than logic, so appeal to their feelings when you need cooperation. Because they may look for security through material possessions and therefore may be disappointed, they must be shown that true security comes from love and faith in themselves and, to a lesser degree, in others. Shower them with love and affection and they will return it in good measure.

Because of such strong emotional reactions and feelings, it will be difficult to reason with them when they are upset or disturbed. For better results, wait until their mood has quieted.

This Moon placement has a tendency for stressful emotions to affect the physical body through the stomach. They may not want to eat when upset, or if they do, they may get sick. Bland foods are best and if possible have them eat only when calm. Don't make them eat if they are upset.

When there is a full or new Moon, this child may be noticeably more high strung. It would be to their advantage to learn at a young age to become aware when these times occur each month. In this way they can be prepared and can learn to control their feelings more, to understand that this will shortly pass.

Their sensitivities are so well developed that they know things which will amaze you. It is an instinctive tuning in to people and environment. This is marvelous, but once again, teach them not to be such sponges, for the psychic energy they are absorbing could be non-beneficial (as well as beneficial) and could severely affect them emotionally. Strong positive training will help them block out and not let anything negative become a part of them. It would be good to have these children say out loud each morning, "I will block out all negativity today and resist letting it become a part of me." In the evening at bedtime ask if they "felt" any negative "vibes" coming into them that day—and teach your

child to throw them out! Cancel them! To say, "Cancel, cancel, cancel." They will adore this little game—and it gives them a protective shield against the bad, the hurtful.

## Children with Moon in Leo

These children's emotions are warm and strongly affectionate. They are loving yet need a lot of love in return. Most of all, they need reassurance that they are appreciated. If you can teach them to be proud of themselves, they will have less need to be applauded by others. Otherwise, they will become show-offs who demand attention any way they can get it. They need to feel special and important—and they should learn that this must first be developed from within.

They are generous with their time and with their belongings. If this positive trait is overdone, they may become extravagant. They need to learn discipline, to establish a realistic set of values, and learn that generosity makes a fine showing, but extravagance is showing off. Too much of anything is not good. They are sensitive, have strong feelings, and can be easily offended. This comes partly from an inner insecurity or a strong need for approval. They also like things their way! The better they feel about themselves the more difficult it will become to offend them. They should also learn that as much as they need to be themselves, others need to be themselves too.

Moon in Leo children can be egotistical, overbearing, arrogant, and stubborn when challenged. Teach these children to control their emotions and to use self-discipline over these non-productive characteristics. On the positive side, they are noble, honorable, loyal, and have strong leadership abilities. They try to be outstanding and usually are. They are outgoing and need to be with people. They will feel frustrated and unfulfilled if they are not allowed center stage to get the attention they need.

These children may have a tendency to exaggerate so this trait should be carefully watched, and minimized so that other people can believe and trust in them. If they want to be effective leaders, a certain amount of realism is necessary. But as for outright lies—never. A true Leo Moon would never stoop to that, or have so little courage.

Pride runs strongly in these personalities. Self-esteem is so important to them that it is the basis of how they experience their lives. Be sure to always keep this factor in mind. One of the quickest ways to trigger a bad, negative response in them is to insult their integrity or

humiliate them. For best results, try to present criticism in a considerate way, sandwiched between two compliments! Show them that by making necessary corrections, they will improve themselves and garner the approval they so ardently desire!

These children are often attracted to the theater. Being on stage and playing different parts is a good way for them to let their dramatic feelings flower, plus get that applause they crave. A Leo Moon loves luxury and glamour. They have a keen appreciation for artistic and creative talents and are blessed with many themselves. They love to have fun and are usually fun to be with. Give them as much praise and respect as possible and you will be contributing to their emotional security.

## Children with Moon in Virgo

Children with the Moon in Virgo will have fewer emotional highs and lows than some of the other placements. They are inclined to be both orderly and conservative. These children tend to be nitpicks and place too much importance on minor things. Since they want to be useful and are so good at analyzing (Virgo being a thinking, thoughtful sign), show them how valuable they can be if they expose themselves to new experiences. Because their instincts are inclined to be somewhat narrow and critical, they need to expand, to investigate new situations and people, to accept other points of view.

With this Moon placement, they not only set high standards for themselves but will expect others to follow the same standards, especially those they consider close to them. They need to understand that all people must do what is best for themselves and that each has different priorities and values. They should also learn to stop being so critical of themselves and of others. No one is perfect.

These children are compulsive about health and cleanliness, so you can be assured, they will take good care of themselves and their surroundings. Teach them to relax a bit, stop being so fussy, and most importantly, to let others just be. Teach them that moderation is the key to success. Just because they need to be busy, sometimes compulsively so, others don't! Teach them to set goals for themselves only. Goal-setting will make them happy because they dislike aimlessness. They will be meticulous workers and like to participate in activities in which they can use both their hands and their minds. Their intellectual abilities are excellent and they are able to learn easily. They also have good memory skills. But teach them the importance of applying feeling to their think-

ing and their knowledge. This, in the long run, will bring more happiness to themselves and others.

It is the nature of these children to want to be helpful, to serve in a meaningful way, to accomplish. Being by their nature rather detached and unemotional, they need to learn about others' feelings and emotions. Since they are concerned with health, they must learn that they will destroy their own through their nervous drive of wanting everything to be perfect. Things and people just aren't that way. Show them that we still need the imperfect in order to know what is perfect, and that perfection would be boring because then there would be nothing for them to do!

The Moon in Virgo children will be happiest when following some intellectual pursuit and are capable of great dedication. They will admire others who are also dedicated. Show them that these are wonderful attributes, and if everyone in the world were the same it would be a pretty sterile and dull place.

They may not be as loving as you would like, but you can have closeness in other ways. They will be great verbalizers and will communicate with you and love sharing ideas. Learn together and become good friends. They may be shy and reserved so you should make the first effort. They may not need your hugging as much as they need your reassurance. Show them your appreciation for their efforts. In return, they will appreciate you and give you respect and loyalty.

## Children with Moon in Libra

The Moon placement in Libra, ruled by Venus gives these personalities a gentle, peace-loving nature. If this trait is carried to extremes, we have children who give in too easily, are too agreeable, and will try to achieve peace at any price. Show them it is a valuable attribute to have understanding, but it must be used without sacrificing values and principles. Harmony at any price will not work.

It is very important for them to be liked by people and to be socially accepted. Because they have such strong needs to interact with people, you will almost never find them doing anything alone. If they are taught a little discretion in their choice of associates, they will be able to achieve balance (Libra is always trying to achieve balance) without giving up their values or abandoning their principles.

They are affectionate, warm-hearted, good-natured, and generally make friends easily. They are apt to see only the good in others and can be taken advantage of by those with selfish motives. Their successes

can be so dependent upon and influenced by those around them, that they must be helped in choosing their friends wisely. Teach them that they cannot be all things to all people, no matter how they try, and that they really don't need to be.

These Moon in Libra children have an appreciation for beauty in all forms—art, music, design, adornment, fashion, and luxury. They are refined and have good taste in all things. Music is an excellent way to soothe these children when they become too sensitive and inclined to brood. Show them that it is impossible to have harmony all the time, that one cannot always control one's environment. Teach them that they can learn to control the peace and balance within themselves with a little practice. Once they learn to be less affected by outside stimuli, they will be able to stabilize and control their reactions, and their emotions.

Family ties are important to these children and they need those close to them to have faith in them.

Moon in Libra has more than an ample amount of charm, and they need to learn the proper use of this talent. Natural charm gives a tremendous advantage for advancement in life and should not be misused by sweet-talking one's way out of chores or any difficult situation. Speaking of chores, work or any task, they will not be too eager in this department, especially if they have to do it alone. They work better when others are involved, cooperation is one of their long suits. Just be careful that they don't sweet-talk someone else into doing their share. Teach them that although work can sometimes be unrefined (even getting one's hands dirty!), it is nevertheless a constructive and positive endeavor. Afterwards, they'll feel good about accomplishing something, especially the glow of group effort.

One of the more important lessons caregivers must bring to their Moon Libra children, for their very survival in the cold harsh world, is to self-start! Too often they seem to need prodding, sometimes even a fire lit under them! So emphasize the value of their initiating a task, and carrying it through, whether it's homework or cleaning their room. Reward them with something beautiful, such as one perfect flower, a lovely tune, or just cuddling and reading them a poem or story!

## Children with Moon in Scorpio

The Moon in Scorpio indicates a nature very intense and emotional. These children are often hypersensitive, yet they rarely show it to others. This trait is a challenging placement for the Moon as it causes them to

have great difficulty in freely expressing their feelings. Emotions are so internalized that they are sometimes buried too deeply to surface. These children need to learn to recognize and appreciate their emotions, to look at them objectively, and then to verbally express what they feel. Teach them that by holding in and bottling everything up, they only hurt themselves—and those they love, when finally the dam bursts. Many times these internalized feelings may even manifest in real physical illness.

Nothing is lukewarm with these children. When they are happy it is total; when they are sad it is extreme. Everything is intense, everything is all or nothing. They have strong convictions and can be obstinate about changing them. It will be extremely difficult to sway them once they have made up their minds. If you should attempt to, you will have a better chance at succeeding if you re-examine your facts, and then have a very open mind when you converse with them. Because they have the ability to see beyond the surface in stuations, and people, you may end by admitting that they are correct.

Since Moon in Scorpio children have keenly developed intuitive abilities, they will make wonderful detectives, researchers, and scientists. They will enjoy investigating the secrets of people, nature, and the universe. They want to know all there is to know about the world around them—and the world within them. They often become psychiatrists.

Although it may be hard for a parent to sit by and watch, these children learn best from experience. They are quite energetic, very self-reliant, and in all probability will have to experience and want to experience more than most people throughout their lives. It is important that they learn to understand their own complicated feelings, and to stop getting so involved with their own emotions. Teach them to lighten up and not to be quite so serious all the time. Show them through your example how to laugh at what life brings, that they can laugh at themselves when something unfortunate happens. Laughing is a better way in which to release their intense emotions.

These Moon in Scorpio children have a tendency to go to extremes in all things, so teach them to discipline themselves and to avoid any excessive indulgence—whether in emotion or food or later, drink. They have strong wills and accomplish whatever they set out to do. With loved ones, they are inclined to be jealous and possessive. Since their mother is a primary love, she may find that these children put many demands on her. They will want her for themselves, entirely.

They are quick to attach and again, want to control. Help them

learn that it is selfish to put demands and expectations on others. Show them that if the same demands were put on them, they would NOT tolerate it. Because they have an astonishing ability to be perceptive and see the truth, it is most important for you to avoid any manipulation or deception. But they have a tendency to manipulate, to control, so it is very important that you teach them to deal openly and fairly with others. Teach them to respect the integral being of another as they wish to be respected. Help them become aware of this need to control so that they can work at "canceling" that out—or they could lose friends and loved ones!

## Children with Moon in Sagittarius

Children with their Moon in Sagittarius will have a great love of outdoors, sports, and travel; going places and doing things! They will learn a great deal from. traveling, and are fun to travel with. They are naturally interested in foreign places, foreign cultures—and foreign people, often later marrying one. They are immensely curious about everything, and want to learn as much as they can about the world. They love any place that is new to them because it satisfies their need for mental stimulation, which is such an important part of their personality. They also have a great attraction to animals and nature.

Sagittarian Moon children are very frank about their ideas which others sometimes take as being too blunt. They easily speak their minds and will tell you exactly what they feel. This is an admirable charteristic, however too often they are not very diplomatic. Help them to develop tact and understand how other people might react to this direct approach—and also how easily others might misunderstand their well-intentioned words and get their feelings hurt!

These idealistic, and in many ways, naive children want the world to be honest, honorable, and pleasant. They try always to act this way themselves and just naturally expect others to do the same. They must be taught to accept people and life as it is or they will continually find disappointments. Because they are constantly adding new information and new thoughts, they often may change their attitudes. They have boundless energy and are very active, both physically and mentally, but they have a tendency, if not properly guided, to be disorganized—both physically and mentally!

Since Sagittarius is a fire sign, these children may be quick to anger, but their sudden blaze is just as quickly doused. They are not

inclined to hold a grudge and are generally very good natured. Their values are lofty and most honest in origin. They hate hypocrisy. An important lesson for them to learn is to set their goals more realistically, and to forgive others for falling short.

One of their most desirable traits is their great sense of humor. These children seem to be able to laugh at themselves and laugh at whatever happens to them—and even to make others laugh. In the most serious, desperate situations, they somehow come up with the flip side of it. The only caution here is that they need to realize that others with serious natures may not appreciate making light of sober and serious situations. In the long run, their inborn wise judgment and a little self-discipline in touchy situations will make their lives much easier.

In disciplining them, you should be direct and honest. If you can give them the reasons for your actions, you will more likely gain their cooperation. These children are unable to stay sad or unhappy for any length of time. They are the bouncy optimists of the zodiac. They are very curious and may ask many questions about all the facets of life, God, and the Universe. They will expect direct and thoughtful answers, so be prepared. If you don't know, tell them so and you will gain their respect. It can be fun to discover the answers together—an intellectual adventure!

They are natural students and will enjoy studying the lives of men and women who have changed the world. Life will be exciting with these fun-loving children—but be sure to love them with an open hand, and an open honest heart, and especially an open mind. In fact, open can be a key word for these little extroverts. Restricted they are miserable, and eventually will rebel—or when older just won't be there!

## Children with Moon in Capricorn

The Moon in Capricorn is one of the more challenging placements. These children need more love, more nurturing, and more attention in the early part of their lives than any other sign. Their need for security is so consuming that you will need to satisfy it in their primary years. If not, security needs may create emotional problems throughout their lives. On the emotional level, they are filled with fears of inadequacy which must be addressed. In whatever they do, they want to succeed and be given respect, and be recognized. Because they need to feel in control of any situation, they will do well in positions of authority, and often they are the controlling force behind the front man or woman. In

other words, they can be a king or queen maker.

These children are very strong-minded, determined, and will work hard at acquiring their needs. In fact, work too often can become an obsession with them—the typical workaholic. Their sense of self-worth is directly related to how important they feel. For these children, the amount of affection, reassurance, nurturing, and time that a parent or caregiver gives will determine how positively their self-worth will develop. They have powerful needs to feel accepted, and to belong as a significant part of the world.

The person who is providing the care for these children in their primary years will have a very important role in creating their very much needed sense of emotional security. Many times you find children with a Capricorn Moon will have parents that don't mean to neglect the children and in fact don't. However, if the parents themselves are detached or are emotionally not gregarious, or just too busy, the effect is the same—these children would feel neglected. Sometimes a child with this Moon placement has parents who are actually physically absent, living elsewhere or even deceased, in which case some family member must provide them with a strong sense of security. Optimally, their parents should be people whom these children can look up to and respect, and who give to these children much love and commitment.

Always remember to praise your little Capricorn Moon child because he or she needs a lot of positive reinforcement. Make these children feel secure and wanted, that they are a necessary part of your life. Help them realize that they have an important purpose, that they are worthy. Teach them to like themselves, to release the fear, and to stop building a fence around themselves. This is very important because if they don't learn to like themselves, they will constantly demand affection from others. More than attention, it's a true nurturing love and acceptance which is so needed.

Help them to understand their demands often are greater than what other people can understand, greater than what most people are able to give. Therefore, they must learn to first love themselves and then to give this love to others unselfishly. Help them to openly express their feelings. Once they feel secure with this love principle, they have a tremendous amount to give to others. Teach them to be happy, accepting the type and amount of love that other people are able to give. They must try to stop strangling everyone close to them with their demands and expectations. To feel accepted and to feel loved–these are the two

prime psychological needs for the Capricorn Moon child's emotional security and development. You as parents and guardians have, from your child's birth to approximately age six (the crucial years), the opportunity to fulfill these basic needs.

## Children with Moon in Aquarius

The Moon placed in the sign of Aquarius is one of the least emotional placements. Feeling is primarily expressed through the intellect. Children with this Moon sign think rather than spontaneously react, and are not influenced through feelings and emotions. In fact, they can be quite uncomfortable with the emotional displays of others. These children need to understand that other people may be different and have less control over their feelings. They need to develop tolerance and patience for those with a different emotional makeup.

These children are often considered unconventional. They are stimulated by new ideas, unorthodox methods, and original or unusual approaches. They like to have the freedom in which to experiment with any new findings. They want to do what they want to do when they want to do it! They can be quite stubborn when these freedoms are taken away or restricted. Because of their unorthodox approach to life, they often become categorized as eccentrics.

They are generous and care about groups and society at large. They are humanitarians and have good intentions but don't always have practical applications to support their ideas. They like applause and they like to be patted on the back. Praising them will go a long way. Because they want to be a friend to all the world, approach them intellectually by pointing out how they can benefit the world through their serving it... but in a realistic practical way, so as to make the world a better place.

Friends are especially important to children with this Moon placement and they will get pleasure from all sorts of group activities. They will want to join clubs or organizations where they can share ideas, pleasures, and thoughts with others. Since changing the world for the better is one of their great drives, they need to learn to be less rigid, to be willing to work with others of possibly less "vision," and how to accept criticism thoughtfully.

Moon in Aquarius children will be fascinated with all facets of space and space travel. They enjoy science fiction as well as dream interpretation, astrology, and hypnotism, and any New Age subject-for they are the New Age! They are often eager to try anything that is new.

Stimulate their natural mental acuity by exposing them to these kinds of experiences. They will love visiting natural history museums, space exhibitions, science fairs, and computer trade shows!

When correcting this child you will receive favorable responses by administering discipline without emotions—with logic, not anger. They almost always block out emotional outbursts and impulsive actions by their parents, so the whole point of the lesson will be lost.

Think through any discipline before presenting it. If you should happen to react emotionally or get a bit out of control, the best recovery is to explain that sometimes powerful emotions are difficult for some people to control.

These Aquarian Moon children truly want to help, so teach them to first learn how to help themselves, and then they will be able to help others. They can become a great force for social good; making the world a better place to live will fulfill many of their deepest desires. But be sure to teach them that while they are busy changing the world for the better, they should not neglect their own family! They are unconventional but loving when understood.

## Children with Moon in Pisces

Having one's Moon in Pisces is one of the more, if not the most, sensitive placement of this luminary. For these children, emotions can rule and ruin their lives.

Because they are very receptive and easily influenced by everyone and everything around them, they take almost everything personally. They cry easily and must be allowed this outlet (boys too!). Perhaps the most important lesson with this Moon placement is to teach them to be realistic, and much more objective. This is necessary because they have a tendency to feel misunderstood, feel sorry for themselves, and over-dramatize life's experiences, whether their own or someone else's. Help them to be less vulnerable and develop thicker skins. This process will surely stand them in good stead as they mature.

Moon in Pisces children also have a tendency to live in a dream world. Their fantasies are, for them, easier to live with than reality. They need to learn to not only stand up for their own rights, but they also must stop taking the line of least resistance. This lesson will aid in eliminating some of their moodiness and changeability, guiding them to bend with the breezes.

Because emotion is such a major factor with these children,

nothing being experienced without feelings, they have tremendous creative potential and a vivid imagination. This is one of the reasons why they are so attuned to music, to poetry of love, and particularly to acting, or any other activity that requires creative expression.

Another area in which Piscean Moon children excel is one in which they care for people, especially the injured or ill—but they must be careful not to take in their vibrations, particularly those mentally or physically ill. They are quite gifted with animals. These children are so acutely attuned to other creatures that they empathetically "feel" them.

Feeling for others is a marvelous gift but because they are so sensitive, they need to learn more stability in their ideas, feelings, and attitudes. Too often they "go with the flow" of others because it is the path of least resistance. They must be taught confidence in their own beliefs and to stand by them! If not learned, doubt and depression can be their enemy. Worse, they can lose their own sense of identity, their feelings of self. Teach them not to be self-indulgent, to not wallow in their sensitivities.

Moon in Pisces children will be most happy and will function best when their environment is kept positive, peaceful, and pleasant. Any negativity, depression, arguing, or fighting from those close to them may be extremely traumatic and deeply felt. Soothing, soft music and a calm environment help these children feel most content.

Have some fun with these children by asking them to tell you their dreams. Quite often they will be prophetic as well as psychic. Most importantly, teach them to recite this statement every morning: "I will let all negativity pass me by today. I will push it out and away from me!"

"...astrology is not to discover what is going to 'happen' to us, it is not to forestall the blows of fate, that we should look to our horoscopes. A chart, when properly used should enable one to understand the overall patterns of one's life."
—Henry Miller

# Chapter 6

# Mercury
## The Messenger of the Gods & the Key to Communication Modes

Mercury influences our thinking reaction to our physical environment. Mercury is thought itself. It is our mental reaction to our five senses ... our thoughts about odors, tastes, sounds, sights and tactile feelings. It is the logical and rational part of the mind that deals with reason. It is by itself void of emotions or feelings. Its purpose is to think, analyze, and understand. Mercury is communication both given and received. It is how our thoughts are expressed, and how the communication from others is received and interpreted. Needless to say, when Mercury is placed in the different signs, it takes on different expressions. Again, *the planet is the energy, the sign that it is in is the way that the energy is expressed.* In some signs, Mercury is able to express itself easily because there is compatibility other signs are more challenging. Some signs color the logic with emotion and feeling, some are more coolly intellectual; while some will be practical, and others abstract, even mystical. Some think quickly, others slowly. Some probe the depths (and get caught there), others scan a broader surface. Different expression is necessary and important to give us an expanded perspective of all possibilities of the thought process, adding variety to life.

Mercury will also show how your child's learning ability is affected, and since you are their primary teacher, this test is of inestimable importance. We are all teachers and students simultaneously, therefore we need to communicate well. The Mercury connection is one of our most effective tools at the present time.

How can you communicate well with your children if their thinking is on another channel unless you know what channel it is on... and then switch yours to the same one for a direct connection? We are all naturally drawn to people who think the same as we so there is no strain in communicating. Many times you will even know what the other person means before the thought is completely expressed. This idea is great but with some people it works just the opposite. Most of the problems in any relationship can be traced to lack of or misunderstood communication.

Everyone wants to express themselves in the way that most easily satisfies their own needs, and everyone wants at the same time to be understood. Too often, this desire is impossible. It is possible, however, to change your channel or wavelength in order to understand others. All you need is the necessary knowledge and the desire to apply it. In the case of your child, or others with whom you communicate often, it is well worth the effort. The following interpretations of Mercury in the signs will help you "change your channels" at will.

This brings me to the question, who is responsible for the understanding in the communication the one giving or the one receiving? The answer is that it is always the one who is doing the communicating. It is the responsibility of the one sending the message to get their meaning across, and be understood... that is, if they want to have unified communication and sharing. If they don't, of course it won't matter, and they might as well talk to a door, then no one else will have to experience the separateness either. Of course, with your children you will still be the one making the effort.

Think of the importance of what we project and say to our children! In the beginning they learn everything from us, including the meanings and attitudes we have about different words and thoughts. They even learn how to develop the parent and adult parts of their personality from us. We teach them. how to interact socially, professionally, and ethically. They develop attitudes about family, one-on-one relationships, the world —and most importantly, they learn how to think and feel about themselves! What kind of a picture has the on-

going programming created on their mental computer screen? Is it one of assurance and acceptance, or one of fear and doubt? With this in mind, it is important to start "listening" to what we say, how we say it, and whether it is beneficial or not.

Some things to keep in mind when working with children is that their computer brains are storing new information rapidly, more so than at any other time in their lives. They focus generally on what is happening at the moment. When we get their attention with, "Don't open the door!" their attention will go to the door; the "don't" is heard as a general restriction, if it is even heard at all. What can we expect other than them focusing on the door? Statements like, "Will you help me keep the door closed?" are heard more clearly...or better yet, to get the desired focus on "close" and to get attention away from the "open" we could say, "We need to keep the door closed, will you help me? Thank you." The child's main drive is to learn, and to get approval and acceptance. Help them to satisfy these drives through better communication with them. After all, learning is a process of taking in information, and of making mistakes and adjustments. Learning from error is an important concept for us all to remember, and particularly for children to understand.

It is always good to validate first. By that I mean, give accepting compliments like, "I can understand why you want to...," or "It is okay for you to feel..." (Then add, "and" (not "but" because "but" takes away from, while "and" adds to it, as in "and we are going to do..." Everyone's computer is built for survival. It will automatically resist when invalidated and will create separation for self-preservation. Obviously the closer we are with our children the better we communicate, and the more effective parents or caregivers we will be.

# Mercury Retrograde

Before we start with some of the possible expressions of Mercury retrograde I would like to make it very clear that the descriptions of this placement will not apply in all cases because how it is placed in the chart by sign, the area of the chart it falls into and the connections to other planets at the time of birth. All of these factors will all have an effect on how it is experienced. Some people with Mercury retrograde will only experience the benefits of it, and will have no challenge with it at all. The reason that I am pointing out some of the possible difficulties with the placement is strictly to bring an awareness to you and to signal your attention in case your child does show signs of the challenge side.

With awareness, you will not add to the challenge, but will understand it and with my suggested solutions, treat it in the best possible way. Most important is to help the child understand that his/her brain works differently from the majority, and has special abilities. This helps the child to avoid frustration if he/she thinks somewhat differently from others. Mercury travels in a retrograde direction three times a year for approximately 21 days each time. This adds up to approximately 63 days out of the entire year, a relatively short amount of time so those born during these periods will be in the minority. Since Mercury symbolically represents the thought processes and communications, any children born at a time when Mercury retrograde occurs will require more understanding with how they express their mental abilities.

When a planet is in a direct motion its energy is flowing in an open, normal, forward way. Because retrograde means going back over and back into, any retrograde planet has its energy restricted and turned inward. Since we are talking about mental abilities here, children with this situation at birth will often repeat what they say, and will also ask others to repeat. At times, it may seem like they are trying to be antagonistic or 'sassy.' Have patience with them because it seems to take at least two repetitions for anything to mentally register.

Keep a full supply of erasers on hand because these are the children who will need them! Buy them erasable ink pens. They are the original, "Play it again Sam" types. Somehow, they do most everything over again.

Help these children to understand that the way they think and the way their brains work is different otherwise, they can become quite frustrated, and feel they are out-of-step with the rest of the world. Teach them that different does not equal wrong. It is more important for them to accept their differences than it is for them to try to change themselves to fit the way other people think and act. Explain that there are other people who think the same way they do, just not as many.

These children often have difficulty expressing their thoughts and feelings, especially if they feel the slightest rejection to their ideas. This will cause them to withdraw, turn inward, and ultimately give up. It is most important for them to learn to understand and accept their differences, so that they can feel secure and not just "different".

School can be a challenge for these children because they don't learn easily from the conventional methods of teaching. They are apt to feel that they are not smart since their thought processes are marching

to a different drummer. They have their own unique methods of solving problems, and when given the opportunity to use their own methods, they can solve problems faster than most. I sometimes wonder if they're not using more of their 'psychic brain' than the so-called normal Mercury direct people. And I feel very strongly that if a study were to be done, the results would show that most dyslexic children were born when Mercury was retrograde.

Comprehension of the written word may be difficult for some, while others will be unusually good writers as well as avid readers. It seems that Mercury retrograde people are capable of reading entire sentences at a glance—but are afraid of missing something important! Because of this, they go back and repeat each word one by one to make sure that nothing is missed. After they develop their own inner-confidence they can become excellent speed readers. They have superb memories because of this special ability to think back and to retrieve information from their "internal computers."

These children may be inclined to be nervous types and may worry or fuss over everything. This is because they are trying so hard to do everything perfectly. Help them learn that although striving for perfection is acceptable, the attaining of it is in another dimension. Accepting each outcome for what it is—this is realistic and less stressful.

Most importantly, teach these children that just because it sometimes takes them longer to learn through the usual conventional methods, it does not mean they are less intelligent. In most cases they will end up with a better understanding and better retention of what they have learned.

Each year during the times that Mercury is retrograde, these children will think and speak very clearly...because it is their time! So, it is a good time for them to clear up any prior misunderstandings. They will want to organize and take action with anything left undone. Check the tables to discover when these times occur. Encourage them to make their plans and prepare to take action—but not until after Mercury goes direct!

Many believe that it is important to wait until transiting Mercury is in direct motion to take action on anything, but this does not always hold true. Just as some of those born with Mercury retrograde have excelled in Mercury type occupations, some activities or businesses begun during Mercury retrograde do quite well. Avoid making Mercury retrograde a superstition. Watch its forward and backward motion and

see what happens in your personal life. Keep notes on it to make your own references.

## How To Find Your Child's Mercury Sign!

Find the year and month of birth in the Mercury Tables beginning on page **208**. The sign of Mercury is given for each day that it changes signs, and the **time** of the change is in Eastern Standard Time. If the birth took place in a different time zone or it was daylight time then, you will need to interpolate accordingly. Be sure to "Spring forward" to add an hour for daylight time births. If you aren't sure how to do time changes, try an online converter. This one does any year, any location:

*http://www.timeanddate.com/worldclock/converter.html*

Again, you can be absolutely sure of exact signs and of retrograde or direct motion if you send for that free chart! In an accurately calculated chart, Mercury retrograde will be shown with a symbol next to the Mercury glyph. It will look like this: ☿R. If you see just the Mercury glyph **without** the little R after it, you'll know that Mercury is direct.

## Children with Mercury in Aries

Mercury in Aries is an interesting placement. These children will be quick thinking and witty, with inventive minds. They want to be first with their ideas, so they have a tendency to jump to conclusions too quickly. Teach them that making rash, impulsive decisions can cause them many problems, and they need to learn to count to ten before opening their mouths. Help them learn that it's not enough to just come up with original ideas -they have to follow through to get any results!

They will be quick on the switch and will love arguments. They will be very good at this and should be encouraged to join the debate team to learn the skill of constructive argument. But when they become contentious, it would be wise for you as a parent to say, "Oh it's debate time!" or something similar, and then accept the challenge with a smile. They will often take the opposite viewpoint just for the challenge of the contest. It doesn't mean they always believe what they are saying, they just enjoy the battle of wits!

They are able to express themselves with a fluent, direct approach. But show them the difference between directness and brashness! Teach them to be sensitive to other people's feelings. Being abrasive will not create positive experiences.

These children may become quickly angered at something that is said, and may spout off and say things they don't mean. Fortunately their anger is over as quickly as it started and the experience is forgotten. They will be very attuned to sound (Aries rules the ears as well as eyes) and should be encouraged in developing this ability and understanding music. Pleasant, comfortable sounds in their environment will calm some of their impulsive energy.

They should be excellent students as long as they are allowed enough independence to explore and express their own originality. They must be stimulated with plenty of new material. Teach them it is good to pursue and pioneer the new, but that it is important to complete one thing before moving on to the next! Teach them to discipline themselves with this follow through. They are anxious to explore any and all new methods of communication and should have no trouble utilizing them. Be sure to put lots of positive action and energy into what you tell them, and you will be able to direct them beneficially.

Key words to use in your communications with Mercury in Aries children are: courage, pursue, drive, energy, lead, compete, brave, active, initiate, assert, sound, hear, listen and experience.

Make your communications to the point—stimulating, full of action, and short—they get bored easily and are often way ahead of you! The more dynamic you are, the more Aries will pay attention. Threaten them and they are off to war. Talking things out with them while you both are doing something physical... while walking, biking, playing tennis ... works well. Eliminate any form of boredom or confinement Aries is not interested in the practicality of things, only in the excitement and adventure of them. Remember! These children born with Mercury in Aries love mental challenge, so prepare yourself!

## Children with Mercury in Taurus

Those of you who have children with Mercury in Taurus will need quite a bit of patience. Their thinking will be slow and methodical. They are cautious and will have difficulty in changing their ideas or opinions quickly. They are very practical and determined. They will appear stubborn and obstinate, and you cannot force or push them to change -they will resist and not cooperate. There are several ways to handle this. One is to put out the new information and then back off—give them time to think about it, assimilate it, and change at their own pace. Two, present things to them in some way so that they can see things

visually through pictures or diagrams ... so they can feel or experience them. For example, these children will not respond well or understand if you just verbalize it when you tell them not to touch the fire. Take them to it, hold their hand (safely) close to it so they can feel the heat. They will get the message. They respond best to visual and sensual stimuli rather than audible. Paint them a picture with your words, and tell them about all the feelings involved, both emotional and tactile. They learn readily from travel, movies, and television.

It may appear that they are slow and not too bright, but they are certainly not stupid (Freud, Edison, Brahms and General Grant, to name a few!). Once they have learned something, it sticks. They think about any new information thoroughly and carefully to be sure that it is solid and usable before they accept it. They also are inclined to feel most comfortable holding onto ideas they have, because it is in their nature to feel safer and more secure with holding!

Mathematics can be a problem for them as can any abstract subject. To stimulate interest here, show them the usefulness of these subjects and they will respond. For example, explain that they might be taken advantage of in money situations if they can't add and subtract well. This was a turning point with one of my children who had been stumbling with Math and he jumped two grades ahead with this simple comment.

They also respond well to common sense. They are persistent and follow through. You will find yourself delegating responsibility to these children because they will be very dependable. Just be sure to be patient with their inflexibility and slowness in all forms of communication.

Key words to use in your communications with Mercury in Taurus children are: worth, comfort, quality, ease, increase, stable; value, see, look, visualize, feel, and sense.

Because physical comfort is so important to these children, the best way to put them in a cooperative mood is to make sure they are comfy. For example, give them a plushy chair, put them in their pajamas and make sure the room temperature is just right. If you can physically touch them or stroke them in some way while you are talking, you will tame the natural resistance within them. Reassure them that their comforts and pleasures will still be secure with any changes that you want them to make. Most importantly, show these children the value, benefits, practicality, and usefulness of what you are presenting ... and how it will work for them!

# Children with Mercury in Gemini

Mercury in Gemini creates very active thought processes. They are extremely quick to assimilate information and are always looking for more. These children are even capable of absorbing more than one thing at a time. It is important for children with Mercury in Gemini to receive a lot of intellectual stimulation early in their lives. As their parent or caregiver you can show them how to learn by reading. Provide them with the time and the materials to read each day. This is most important. They should also be encouraged to write. Since their need to communicate is so strong, writing out some of their thoughts will cut down on the amount of verbalizing—otherwise, they will chatter incessantly and talk your ear off.

Guide them to discern when they are really saying something or are just babbling. They have the ability to be extremely articulate and express themselves clearly. They will amaze you with a continuous flow of new information. Communicating with these children can be fascinating. When you communicate with them, using words that concern feelings, what you say will likely fall on deaf ears. It is very important that you refrain from using any emotion when conversing with these quick, logical thinkers. Preface your statements with "I think" and ask them what they think. Because they love games, you can get them to cooperate by saying, "Let's play a game and see if we can do..." or, "Let's see how fast we can do it"

One problem with this energetic curious mind is that it gets bored too quickly, and too easily. Their mind changes from one thing to another so fast that it often never finishes anything or follows through far enough to completely learn something. Teach them the discipline of steadiness and of staying with it long enough to get the whole picture.

These children are versatile, have high energy, and love change. They can be very nervous. They can scatter themselves in too many directions and burn themselves out. It is important for you to teach them the importance of taking time each day to be quiet, to relax. They also need to keep an orderly environment to have thoughts operate clearly and calmly, so they should learn early to be organized.

Key words to use in your communications with Mercury in Gemini children are: intelligent, smart, clever, rational, think, look, listen, logical, quick, mental, change, and exciting.

Your little Mercury in Gemini "computer" will have no problem learning and communicating as long as they are programmed properly

and positively. Present information to them with as much variety as possible, making the same point in different ways and citing many different examples. Be sure you approach everything from a logical point of view. Keep the conversation lively and exciting. Add as much humor as you can as they are witty creatures and will love the stimulation. Since these children are most comfortable when they have several different activities going on at the same time, it is advisable to approach them with subjects you need to discuss when you are both engaged in some type of activity. Otherwise, if you plan to just sit and talk, be sure to make your discussion very dynamic. And remember, most important of all, always be sure to give them the opportunity to express their own ideas as much as possible!

## Children with Mercury in Cancer

Mercury in Cancer creates an emotionally-based thought process. That is, they let their emotions rule how they think. They will always have a feeling connected to every thought and will personalize every communication they experience. They are so receptive that they are influenced too much by what is happening around them. They can take on the opinions of whomever is close at the moment. They need to learn to step back and see things more objectively. They have a very retentive mind and will find it difficult to change habits and attitudes.

It is important for them to establish beliefs that are workable for them. They have a tendency to accept what other people think and feel without thinking things through. They will be especially vulnerable to their parents and to the family's projections because family is so important to them. It is important for them while they are still very young to learn how to step outside of themselves and look things over. A little objectivity will be very helpful.

These children will be very emotionally responsive and often won't know why they think the way they do. When they are upset, their thoughts about the world will be distorted. Teach them to throw away these thoughts and to become aware of the difference in how they think when they are calm!

It is not advisable to argue with these children or ever make a direct attack. This will arouse resistance and stubbornness. You will get better results by appealing to their sympathy. They have such sensitive feelings that they always relate to things in a feeling way. Logical, cold, or harsh communication will be very ineffective with Mercury

in Cancer children. Rather than giving them a direct order or making a frontal attack, tell them how you feel about it and they will respond. Always remember to ask them how they feel about doing whatever it is you want. Avoid using the word "think"—it will not appeal to their emotions.

These children will be very psychic and will know things without knowing how. They should be encouraged to rely on their instincts and intuitions. They may have some trouble in school because they learn best by listening. It is difficult for them to study, especially factual subject matter. They will learn faster through movies, television, or exposure to travel and people than through reading. Once they have grasped something, they won't forget it. Approach them through their feelings and you will experience much closeness and will grow together. Key words to use in your communications with Mercury in Cancer children are: sensitive, support, emotion, intuitive, protect, care, feel, respond, listen, need, sympathetic, and safe.

Communicate with them from your heart, and preferably choose a very safe, cozy place in which to do it. Tell them how you feel about your subject and that you care how they feel about it. Help them to feel secure about changes that are to be made, and let them know that their cooperation is needed. Feeling needed is an important part of what makes them feel good inside, so be sure that this is satisfied.

## Children with Mercury in Leo

These are the children who will crave center stage, and will have very decisive ideas. The problem is that Mercury in Leo children will identify personally with whatever they think. A challenge to their beliefs or thinking is a direct challenge to them. It is important to teach them that a difference of opinion doesn't make one right and the other wrong... it is simply a different point of view. Show them that contrary ideas shouldn't be taken as a personal insult.

These children try very hard to be sure that they have the truth of anything, and then they are cocksure they do! However, they need to be shown that truth is in a constant state of change and they may not have the only valid point of view. They need to learn to be a little more flexible and open to new ideas. It will do no good to try and force the new on them, so try to present the information in a way that is non-threatening and then they will change by themselves. Do teach them to present their ideas with a little humility. They have a tendency to

be arrogant which causes others to feel inferior or just annoyed. This of course, will cause an unfavorable response to their ideas and an unwillingness in others to communicate with them.

They will put great energy into organizing and solving problems. They have the ability to see things on a large scale and as a whole. The bigger the project the better. They need to apply a little discipline so that they pay attention to all the little details to be sure that they do have the complete picture. Their communications are presented with great flair and sometimes with extreme dramatics. They take great pride in what they think, so always treat them with dignity. They will do well in life as long as the flair and dramatics are kept under control.

The comment, "Flattery will get you everywhere," was coined for Leos. The more you compliment them, the better they want to and will do. Sharp criticism can be devastating -to them and to your communicating! They are very warm and loving, and the more you approach them in a loving way the more cooperation you will get. They have strong needs to be accepted and validated, so give them applause and praise often. Since they are good planners and can organize and direct others well, make them the chief and they will get the Indians to perform!

Key words to use in your communications with Mercury in Leo children are: creative, entertain, exciting, respect, appreciate, care, talent, noble, dignified, generous, and loving.

An interesting approach to disciplining these children is to ask them to play your role as the parent, and ask them how they would handle the situation. Do role playing-they'll love it! You might be surprised with the creative solution they suggest. When you communicate with them allow them to feel dignified and to leave their pride intact. Acknowledge their ideas by saying, "I can appreciate how you might think that way," and then say, "I have a different view point -may I share it with you?" By using this approach, you will eliminate hurt feelings and defensiveness. Most importantly, continue to compliment them on their good ideas and your conversations will always be open and loving.

## Children with Mercury in Virgo

Mercury is right at home in the sign of Virgo. These children will have a very analytical and logical way of receiving and transmitting their communications. Their minds are quick and alert. They will assimilate and categorize facts with ease. They can be very intolerant of stupidity. They can be quite critical of themselves, not to mention the world in

general. You must show them that the world does not run on logic and reason alone. And they need to recognize that their thought processes allow them to function with a high degree of common sense but not everyone has this ability. They should learn to be a little more flexible, tolerant... and have more acceptance of life as it is.

They will analyze everything and could do with a little more spontaneity. Teach them to let their heads rest sometimes, to let their feelings develop, and their hearts blossom. Show them that some people think only with their feelings and emotions. A balance of both heart and mind is best. Also, show them that by being overly critical of themselves and others they not only damage their own confidence, but their relationship with everyone else. Teach them to see that the world is perfect just as it is and that everything has its own beauty.

They can be neat, and clean, to the point of persnickety, and picky about their food. They will be interested in learning about nutrition and what is good for the body. Health is very important to them. These children are good with their hands and will work well with detail and with great precision. They will especially like to work on things that are practical. They are good in school and will approach their studies meticulously and methodically. The biggest problem here is that if they can't see the usefulness of a subject they may not apply themselves. Show them what might have no value at the present could be important later. They also may have trouble retaining information that they think is superfluous. Teach them that most facts can be used at one time or other.

Teach them to use their discriminating, analytical skills in a helpful way, by learning to understand the difference between beneficial and non-beneficial. Show them it is more beneficial, when interacting with people, to balance thought with feeling. Help them to look for the good in others and to add warmth to their communications.

Key words to use in your communications with Mercury in Virgo children: organize, analyze, order, discriminate, think, look, specific, proficient, facts , detail, skill, and practical.

Be sure that your conversations with these children are organized and realistic. Leave emotions out. Think of how to get practical responses to your well thought-out and coolly-administered disciplinary procedures. Give them the ABC's of why you are taking specific actions. Write these actions down or ask the child to write them down. It helps these children when they can see what they are dealing with. Post your rules. These children are list makers so let them help you

organize. Tell them how capable they are and they will help you with everything.

## Children with Mercury in Libra

When Mercury is in Libra we find children who are born diplomats. They will not like harsh or abrasive situations. Being natural peacemakers, they will try to smooth troubled waters for both themselves and others. But because they want both sides to be completely considered before a decision is made, they may appear to be argumentative...this is their way of bringing attention to alternative views. It usually is done in good taste and with carefully chosen words! This is because they always want to have harmonious experiences and never to offend anyone. It may even appear that they are vacillating and cannot make up their minds, or that they are unwilling to take a stand, because they want to be fair and keep peace with everyone at the same time. The fact is, they would rather settle for a compromise than to actually take one side or the other. They do have the ability to see validity on both sides of things. Teach them to tune into their hearts, conscience, and souls for answers. When "tuned in," making decisions throughout their lives will become easier. Also, help these children learn that life can't always be peaceful and harmonious or friendly. They can get really "bent" when people are rude, unfriendly, or - heaven forbid - ill-mannered! Tell them that life is not all sweetness and light, that we need some negative to appreciate the positive. Their rational intellectualizing mind should love that! Also, do help them get over a very serious problem with procrastinating - probably because they can't bear to face unpleasant situations. All of this of course, fits together - they must learn early to "bite the bullet" and do what's necessary, when and with whomever. The operative word here is "DO"—Libras would rather not.

These children are sensitive, pliable, and have good judgment. They have a natural proclivity towards all the arts. They are very creative -music and writing and painting may be good ways for them to express themselves. They will like order and beauty, and have excellent taste. They will prefer quality to quantity. They also will be very social. They are good speakers and express themselves well. In fact, they will be very convincing when they want you to do something!

Mercury in Libra children love parties and are very good at planning them. Their creative ideas will make any occasion beautiful, elegant, and in good taste. At the party they will become a social

butterfly, flitting from one person to another and making sure that they have given each guest a bit of their time.

Key words to use in your communications with Mercury in Libra are: cooperate, charm, balance, sociable, tactful, appreciate, diplomatic, look, feel, value, beauty, peace, and harmony.

Present your conversations to these children diplomatically and tactfully with never any harsh, abrasive, or vulgar expressions. Ask them to cooperate with you. Tell them that you will help and work with them... they want to do everything with another person rather than alone. If you offer to work with these children you will eliminate a large portion of their resistance. On the other hand, a stern discipline for them is just having to do a job, having to do it alone, having to do a dirty job! Have patience with them while they are weighing and evaluating all sides of things before making their decisions - at least you will know that they have given most decisions much thought!

## Children with Mercury in Scorpio

Because children with their Mercury in Scorpio have very penetrating minds, there is a powerful depth to their thinking. These children will want to investigate and delve into the reasons for everything. They are born asking the question "why?" and discover the whys of nature, people, life, and death. These great little investigators actually find the solving part of a problem more exciting than the answer itself. Anything that is mysterious or hidden will attract their minds. They have a very keen sense of perception. Listen to them carefully because they will present insights that you might not have even previously considered. They are able to see beyond the obvious. Because their sixth sense is highly developed, they are able to go beneath the surface and get to the real meaning of people and things, cabbages and Kings.

They can be very secretive and hard to pin down. It will be difficult to find out what they are thinking unless they want you to know. Sometimes they think so deeply that they won't even have the thoughts sorted out themselves! Be patient, they might let you know what they were thinking when they have it all in order.

They may be critical of themselves and others, and they tend to be suspicious...always looking for ulterior motives. Teach them to be nonjudgmental. Also, they can be very sarcastic at times. Show them that most people's feelings are too sensitive to endure their bite. If they want friends, they must learn to control these characteristics. Reassure

them that they have a sharp, strong, perceptive mind and that they have no need to belittle or destroy other people's confidence. Some may already feel intimidated by their awareness and penetrating questions.

Always answer their questions directly and honestly. They will see right through lies and manipulation anyway. These children will need to see a good example of truth from you so that they will learn to be truthful themselves. They may ask many questions about sexuality so be prepared. They need to understand the hows and whys, and to learn healthy, even spiritual values about their purpose and usefulness.

Key words to use in your communications with Mercury in Scorpio children are: purpose, focus, investigate, discover, transform, delve, meaning, feel, sense, power, and empower.

In your communications with them present any situation objectively. Then ask the Scorpio to help you find a solution and they will turn their thinking to finding the answer. Also, let them help you to determine the conditions of their own discipline. They may be sterner than what you would have suggested. When an action is decided upon, these children will keep their word and follow through once they have made the commitment. If they think you have lied to them, betrayed them, or been unjust to them - they will remember and have great difficulty ever forgiving you. Teach these children the transforming power of forgiveness. You must!

## Children with Mercury in Sagittarius

Your child with a Mercury in "Sag" will love communicating on all levels. They are perpetually in search of the great truth. By that, I mean that they will want to know all about nature, why humankind thinks and acts as it does, what makes the Universe as it is, and how everything fits together! To them it seems important to develop a solid philosophy of life and afterlife. They will be constantly seeking out new information to enhance this philosophy. They tend to see things as a whole, in a broad perspective, and will often skim over or leave out pertinent facts. They need to be taught to slow down and get all the details before they speak so they can be sure they have the whole picture.

Because of their lofty thinking and idealism, they can easily be taken advantage of. Therefore, they should learn to be more reflective, and look at situations and people with a bit of skepticism. They seem not to realize that the whole world is not as truthful as they. These children are very direct in their thinking and in their communications, sometimes

to the point of being blunt. They need to know that other people may be offended by this. Teach them to be honest and "tactful" at the same time; to think a minute and choose their words carefully before speaking.

Mercury in Sagittarius children should be pleasures to be with because they are generally enthusiastic, upbeat, and love anything that is new. They will adjust easily and actually welcome change. They love to travel, and learn a great deal this way. They will be concerned with people in general rather than those who are close. Remind them to not overlook the importance of those closest and dearest to them. Also - they cannot tolerate deception, so don't lose their respect by telling them untruths.

Their thinking is expansive, and they are basically optimistic. Since they are direct and up front with everything, you can always count on what you see and hear as being what you get. This will eliminate any doubts about whether you are being appeased, or that they might be pretending in any way.

In dealing with school and academics, teach these children to go back over all tests and assignments. They do them so quickly that they may easily make mistakes. They have a tendency to be careless -and they don't like it either!

Key words to use in your communications with Mercury in Sagittarius children are: wise, benefit, truth, understand, honest, expand, abundance, optimistic, faith , knowledge, perception, and opportunity. When you converse with these children their responses are fiery and quick. Have patience with this because they don't mean to be abrasive. Present your ideas to them with enthusiasm and with plenty of excite-ment. Once again, always communicate with these children directly and honestly. Speak from your heart.

## Children with Mercury in Capricorn

Here we find the children who seem old before their time. They are serious in their thinking and cautious in their actions. They don't think quickly because they are practical and deliberate. It is challenging for them to change and to accept new ideas—unless they can see the usefulness of what is being presented. These children relate best to things that pertain to the physical, material world. Because they are very serious in their thinking, they can take being responsible to an extreme—even sacrificing themselves to their duty, for the job or for others. This can cause them to become dull, and miss out on the joys and

excitement in life. Let them know that it is healthy to have fun and to do lighthearted things from time to time. They should learn to develop a sense of humor. Because they take life so seriously, they need to learn to laugh more. They can be quite moody and at times may seem to be negative and depressing to others. Understand and help them pull out of their moods, or it could affect their health—in mind and body.

These children need to be encouraged to develop faith and to be less attached to the physical and material. They are very earth-oriented and you need to help them create a balance in their lives between earth and heaven—between always being practical and of trusting in spirit. This can be very important in their lives. They have the tendency to get caught in the "never enough" syndrome, meaning that they are looking for security by accumulating more and more possessions, and it is never enough. Until they learn to place their security in their own abilities, and to have the belief that everything is always in right order, they will always feel insecure.

They are good organizers and have an instinctive urge to organize everything and everyone they come in contact with. "Messy" thinking, messy anything upsets them - they can be overly fastidious. They will communicate with diplomacy, carefully choosing the way they express themselves. They have great ability to concentrate and will be disciplined in their thinking. They can be taskmasters both for themselves and others - and will demand precision in themselves, and others. Teach them to "lighten up" some and learn to be more tolerant of others. These are the children to whom you can delegate responsibility. Let them help you organize and plan—they love it and you will be surprised at how well they do.

Mercury in Capricorn children love to learn and do things that are useful. They think in a very practical way so when you present ideas to them, be sure to show them just how the ideas are useful. Superfluous information or abstract concepts have no value to them.
Because they are so competent at business and organization, give them books on successful people to establish good role models.

They have the potential to get stuck in a rut so show them how life can be a joy and a pleasure, and that they can still be responsible at the same time. Give them as much authority as possible and let them enjoy feeling responsible. These children need very little discipline because they have so much self-discipline. On the other hand, should they know they really need a bit of punishment - if you don't administer

it (justly and fairly and coolly, of course) they'll lose respect for you! One of the dangers of disciplining them is their biggest mental challenges - a feeling they have "muffed it," failed in some way. This sign has a great intolerance for failure - in others, but most of all, in themselves. Help them early to judge themselves less harshly! Give them many sincere compliments, and much recognition. This may help them be less judgmental on everything and everyone.

Key words to use in your communications with Mercury in Capricorn children are: mature, responsible, practical, useful, plan, organize, efficient, achievement, recognition, authority, respect, success, manage, solid, and structure.

They have a tendency to see the down side of every new proposal and will tell you why it won't work or can't be done. Acknowledge their comments as being helpful in avoiding pitfalls, rather than taking them as negative. Encourage them to look for the potential, to see the possibilities. Teach them to add humor to what they are saying so that their ideas will be more easily accepted by others. And remember, when you communicate with these children, always treat them with respect.

## Children with Mercury in Aquarius

These are children with quick minds and original thoughts. In fact, there will be very little which is traditional in their thinking. They are attracted to unusual and unconventional ideas and concepts. Mercury in Aquarius children are futuristic, non-conforming, and love the unorthodox - in all things and people too. They have logical minds and can be stubborn about their ideas, however they have highly developed intuition, so they usually know when something is correct. Get them to slow down a little so they have a chance to use these intuitive abilities beneficially. They are quickly attracted to anything new and different. They are very idealistic about how they think the world and everyone in it should function. Show them that some traditional ideas have merit and that sometimes adding the new to the old brings steadier results. In other words, don't throw out the baby with the bath water!

Mercury in Aquarius is not emotional. The thinking is clear, clean, and logical. These children will probably do well with mathematics and science and be very good with computers. Their minds enjoy stimulation and excitement-and they could become the inventors who create wonderful new things. They will communicate well with others, and are always willing to listen to new information. Everything

is fodder for their creative, inventive minds.

They will choose unusual friends and will usually like anyone who is exciting and different, or has any NEW ideas to offer them. They can become so involved in humanity in general and saving the world that they forget themselves and those who are close to them. Since they naturally are such space cadets, they need to plant their feet firmly on the ground and become more practical. Since Aquarians are so adept, they would be well advised to have patience with those who are less able to separate out their feelings so as to be left with the pure essence of their thoughts.

They may be rebellious and quick to organize protests. They will want to protect and help the abused, to help minorities and to make sure the downtrodden gain their rights. They will fight against injustice, especially political injustice. They make very good lawyers. They will join the fight for almost any cause, so teach them to carefully choose only those which have real value.

These children will love airplanes and flying and will be curious about subjects such as astronomy, astrology, and anything else dealing with space, science and modern technology.

Key words to use in your communications with Mercury in Aquarius children are: unique, unusual, create, invent, discover, rational, individual, independent, original, experiment, humanitarian, innovative, different, change and futuristic.

Try not to be shocked with their progressive ideas, nor try to discourage them from thinking that way. Instead, teach them how to add practicality to their thoughts. If these children develop strong reading habits early, they will always have new information available to them. Also, fill their lives with opportunities to have new experiences...and the need to discipline them will be minimal. Your biggest challenge might be the cost for all these new endeavors, and the fact that their interest in them might be short-lived! Have fun stimulating these interesting minds.

## Children with Mercury in Pisces

The position of Mercury in Pisces causes the persons thought process to be emotionally-based. These children will think with their feelings. They are very sensitive and greatly influenced by their environment and the people in it. Other people's beliefs will become their beliefs whether they are beneficial to them or not until they are made aware of this tendency. They need to learn to think things out for themselves

and to decide what is good for them personally. Their moods are also influenced by what and whom they are exposed to. Negative people and negative environments can cause these children to be depressed or even psychically ill. It is absolutely imperative for them to learn how to insulate themselves from negativity so they will be less affected. Without this awareness their moods will be up and down without knowing why, and possibly out of their control. You would do well to encourage them to incorporate some cool-thinking and reason into their character. If they learn to relate to the world that we are living in with a more objective approach, they will benefit greatly. Teaching them to make it a daily habit of protecting themselves with a bubble/shield from negative influences or anything not good for them would time well spent.

These children are so imaginative, poetic, and sensitive, that they are capable of bringing great beauty into this world. Show them how to create their ideas and visions and bring them into some material form. They are dreamers and visionaries with highly developed psychic abilities. They will love fantasy and romance and may be found daydreaming much of the time. Gently, positively help them NOT to dream their way through school and instead do it at some more appropriate times! Reading poetry and other literature will aid them in learning how to put their ideas into writing for the world to enjoy.

They need to get in touch with the inner part of themselves so they can establish their own values, ideas, and philosophies. When they are able to do this, they will experience more stability in their lives. They are so aware and tuned into other people that they are entirely too receptive. They are much like a sponge, absorbing everything. Music is a good way to lift and calm them, even to inspire them.

Subjects that deal with hard cold facts usually have little interest to them—yet, they might benefit by learning the value of facts, reason, and logic. This could present an interesting challenge for you as a parent or caregiver. Remember, these children have a gentle nature and can be reached through their feelings...so present information or correction to them in a sensitive way. When communicating with them about anything you will get better results if you express it with feeling and sensitivity and use the word "feel" as much as possible. They also think in pictures more than most, so learn to tell stories and paint pictures with your words. They will then more clearly understand.

Keywords to use in your communications with Mercury in

Pisces children are: imagine, create, visualize, feel, sensitive, sympathy, intuition, inspire, empathize, service, help, and unify.

When disciplining them let them know how you "feel" when they do something you don't approve of and you will get a favorable reaction. Also, you can ask them how they would feel if they were in your position. And always remember to be gentle; firm but gentle. If you are the hot-tempered type—don't take it out on them.

If these children are given many opportunities to use their rich imaginations and bountiful creativity, they will always be a pleasure to be around—as well as having great gifts to give to the world.

> "Astrology is assured of recognition from psychology without further restrictions because astrology represents the summation of all psychological knowledge of antiquity."
> — Carl G. Jung

## Chapter 7

♀

# Venus
# The Goddess of Love

Venus represents the capacity to give and receive love and affection. She represents the appreciation of and the need for beauty, harmony, and unity. She relates to relationships, the ability to cooperate, and how one experiences social interaction. These are certainly loaded statements and rightfully so. Venus is an all important consideration for us humans on Earth. Love is what makes the difference between merely existing and truly living. It is one of the most positive and powerful energies we know. This has been demonstrated throughout history and literature, and even more importantly, through the lives of all of our great spiritual leaders who understood love in its total sense. How well and in what manner each one of us expresses this important facet of our being must be understood, nurtured, and developed. Venus is at her best when she is radiating love, and contributing to the happiness and pleasures of others. She is the what, when, where...and how we love. Venus also shows us how the personal value system operates. Her placement in the sign describes not only what is valued but also how it is expressed. Venus describes how each individual feels about possessions, and their attitude toward money and prosperity. She relates to the need for pleasure and

creature comforts. The sign in which Venus is placed describes how a person experiences pleasure and also how the tactile senses respond... to velvet, to skin, to clay. She shows artistic abilities and creative talents. And she depicts the appreciation, awareness, and understanding of all forms of beauty ... both natural and those which are created. Venus represents the harmony, balance and joy with which we experience our daily life.

Furthermore, the Venus placement shows how an individual will get along with others...how one makes friends, how many, and what types they are attracted to (Venus attracts, pulls, magnetizes). This is the planet which represents relationships and sociability, so important because no one is an island. In fact, relationship may be the single most important process which we experience as human beings. Since other people reflect and ignite our own inner selves, both the strengths and the weaknesses, sociability then becomes our strongest area of growth. Those people who are closest to us—such as parents and other family members, teachers, friends and enemies, partners and mates—are the most intense relationships. These give us the best lessons of both where we are lovingly unifying and where we are disapproving and causing separation. Venus shows us where love is within each of us and where it is lacking. Understanding this placement will bring information of how you and your children will express yourselves in all relationships, and how you can help to create growth for all.

When the Venus energies are restricted or excessive, or out of balance in any way, the expression can manifest itself in vanity, greed & self-indulgence, unhealthy love relationships, dependencies and lack of self worth.

## Venus Retrograde

When Venus is retrograde, her energies may be restricted, internalized, or undemonstrative. These children may have a difficult time believing that they are lovable. They could be filled with self-doubt and may lack a true sense of self-worth. Instead of acting in life, they seem to react to life. They need a lot of reassurance and, although what you give may be rejected, keep giving it. Venus retrograde children often fear intimacy. Learning to accept love as it is, how and when it is given is an important challenge for these children. They are naturally suspicious and critical of love...wanting it to be as they idealize it which is often unrealistic or too demanding. This can cause disappointments and reinforce their

problem. Teach them not to expect what they think should be, but to feel good about whatever is given and to receive it joyfully. Teach them to trust love. Experience builds trust so it is very important to give children with retrograde Venus as much love, acceptance, and approval as possible. This positive programming will help them develop their own self-esteem. and self-worth. Eventually they will learn to stop evaluating their worth by what others project and will establish self-esteem on their own. Explain to them that self-love is just as important as, and must come before, love from outside. Teach your child that when we love ourselves we automatically have love...help them learn to allow their Venus energies to flow.

These children are often uncomfortable in social situations and will attempt to avoid them as often as possible. They have their own value system and refuse to play the usual social games. You will find them wearing whatever suits them rather than dressing for the occasion. They will not be found wasting their time in polite conversations - in fact, they can lack refinement and may even appear crude. Sometimes they become a behind-the-scene troublemaker. Venus retrograde children are non-materialistic, and are not interested in climbing the social ladder, or winning any popularity contests. The most important lesson for these children will be to learn how to open their hearts to others and to let the love of others come in, so that they avoid becoming hard, cold, unloving adults.

## How To Find Your Child's Venus Sign

Find the year and month of birth in the tables beginning on page 215. The sign of Venus is given for each day that it changes signs, and the **time** of the change in Eastern Standard Time. If the birth took place in a different time zone or it was daylight time then, you will need to interpolate accordingly. "Spring forward" to add an hour for daylight time births. If you were born on the West Coast, add three hours to your birth time to get the EST equivalent. If you were born in the Mountain time zone, add two hours. If you were born in the Central time zone, add one hour. "Spring forward" to add an hour for daylight time births.

If you see that on a particular day the sign listed has gone back to the sign before, this indicates that Venus is in a retrograde period. When you see that Venus has moved ahead again in the signs, you'll know it is now in direct motion. It is beyond the scope of this book to list all exact times of retrograde and direct stations for Venus. The more important information is the Venus sign.

**Example:** under the year 2025 above, note that Venus enters Aries on February 4 and then enters Pisces on March 27. But on April 30, Venus enters Aries again. By this we know that at some point while Venus was in Pisces, it must have retrograded and then turned direct again some days later. Again, you can be absolutely sure whether Venus might be retrograde if you send for that free chart! In an accurately calculated chart, Venus retrograde will be shown with a symbol next to the Venus glyph. It will look like this: ♀ℝ

## Children with Venus in Aries

Aries represents the sign of self—it is number one, so when Venus is placed here the individual tends to think more about their own satisfaction. They are inclined to be more into receiving than giving in almost everything, including love and affection. Lessons for these natives to learn are cooperation, compromise, and how to put themselves in the other person's place! They tend to want things their own way. If you teach them early to share more, they will become less abrasive to others.

The nature of Aries is fiery and aggressive, not blending well with the gentle, passive, and receptive nature of Venus. This is easy to understand when you remember that Mars is the natural ruler of Aries as Venus is of Libra—and that these two signs oppose each other in the zodiac just as Mars and Venus naturally oppose each other in what they represent. Therefore, this placement creates an interesting challenge - to learn to balance these conflicting forces!

These children sometimes put too little effort into making friends, and those they do make may be hard to keep. They can be quite touchy, easily offended, and often inconsiderate. Help them to think of other people's feelings and what others might need or want. Socially they may have the same problem as they make little effort to be popular and can sometimes be even rude.

They value their independence and will dislike being tied down by any person or situation. If they feel uncomfortable they simply leave. Some people will consider them unstable because they are so impulsive and changeable in their relationships—unless there is something else in their chart to compensate, or they learn to understand this tendency and choose to change it.

Like all fire signs, Aries has lots of energy and can be passionate when motivated. These children are dynamic and experimental. They like the color red and music which has high energy, like marches, or classical

Rachmaninoff—who had an Aries Sun! In art they like anything with action, such as mobiles. They won't value money for security reasons, but only for how it can serve them to get what they want. Also, the value of any possession is short-lived as they will move quickly on to something else they will want. As you can see, this is not an easy placement to contend with and these natives will need much guidance. Consider these children as a crude stone...and you are going to help them smooth their rough edges and polish themselves to a warm and loving glow.

## Children with Venus in Taurus

Since Venus rules Taurus, she is now at home. Her energy is expressed here in a very earthly manner. These natives' have a natural love of Mother Earth. These are the children who will stop and smell the flowers. Although they are passive and somewhat shy, they generally won't seek out others to love. When it does come to them as it usually does, they give their love easily. Actually they crave all forms of touching, caressing, hugging, and kissing. They are extremely affectionate, sensual, and require physical contact. Don't be surprised if when young, they will toddle over to anyone.

These children are fond of comfort and enjoy luxury. An excessive focus on the same can create overindulgence or even laziness. They have an innate sense of what makes "value." They seem to be magnets for prosperity and good fortune. Possessions are important to them, especially those which contribute to their comfort and pleasure. They like money and the luxury that it can provide. They are usually socially adept and will want to participate in functions which provide entertainment and which gratify their pleasure principle. They are loyal in both love relationships and in friendships. They may have a tendency to hold onto or become overly attached to people which could cause problems. Help them to become aware and to overcome this tendency by teaching them to love with an open heart.

These Venus in Taurus natives are creative in the fields of finance and real estate and also in any area which has to do with luxury, such as jewelry, furs, fine restaurants, or entertainment. Their appreciation for beauty and art is usually with items which are useful or have value. They have a need for and a great love of music, usually romantic. They are stubbornly steadfast in their pursuit of their needs and usually acquire more than most. This is a good placement for Venus, as she is able to express all of her benefits in a physical earthly manner.

# Children with Venus in Gemini

Children who have Venus placed in Gemini will express their love verbally and in a light, airy manner. They are able to share with a large number of people as long as they can keep the exchange on a surface level. They find it difficult to become involved with deep emotional intensity or to form strong attachments. The responsibility and also the restriction which go along with getting close to others is not comfortable for them. These children do not display a great deal of emotion and will not appreciate it when others do. They are common-sense oriented and logical, and will respect actions that are based on the same. As their parent or caregiver or teacher, you will accomplish most by staying cool and logical, in control of yourself. When you use this approach, you will create a cooperative admirer.

Venus in Gemini is the bright, witty social butterfly. These children flit from flower to flower blessing each one with their charm... and the more the better. The motto here is "Variety is the spice of life." These natives make friends easily and are attracted to a multitude of types. They seem to understand and tolerate the differences in people because they enjoy diversity. The mundane is boring to them and won't be tolerated long. Since these children have such a strong need for people and social interaction, they are happiest and at their best when in contact with others.

You will find Venus in mercurial Gemini delightfully humorous and very entertaining. All mental stimulation gives them great pleasure and they will know a little bit about a lot of things. They love to communicate because their interests are unlimited. They value words and the way they are used, respecting and appreciating articulate expression in all forms. They are lively, entertaining, and make great companions as long as the other person doesn't want or need attachment. These children will enjoy traveling from place to place, and from thing to thing, both literally and figuratively. A change of surroundings is always refreshing to them. Their lessons are to learn steadfastness, as well as to develop loyalty and dependability. Their simple creative abilities could be well utilized as writers, teachers, actors, and public speakers. Make sure that they avoid long periods of isolation as this may cause some form of repression, even depression. Finally, have fun exposing your Venus in Gemini child to new types of social activities, new ways of learning, and all forms of artistic pursuit.

# Children with Venus in Cancer

As with all water signs, there is great sensitivity when Venus is placed in Cancer. The need for love and affection is strong. These children need parental affection more than most, especially from their mother. They are very demonstrative and will need to have affection returned. They are good at giving emotional support to others and will require great amounts for themselves. These natives require large doses of reassurance because if they feel unloved or insecure they can become timid and withdrawn. Sometimes this may result from and lead to sibling rivalry. These children are too dependent on others for their security, especially their parents, and later their mate. Be sure to show your love for them often, and teach them to learn to be less needy and more emotionally self-reliant.

Individuals with this placement are naturals at mothering others, sometimes even to the extent that they may be smothering. (If immature at any age, they could have a selfish need for the flip side of that—to be always babied.) They have a tendency to hold on to relationships long after it would have been better to let go. These children do not need a large number of friends; they will be happy with a few good ones. Generally Venus in Cancer people are good friends to have because they are sensitive to other's needs and will not hurt anyone, unless they are hurt first.

Socially these children are apt to be a little shy and retiring. In fact, they may not want to participate in social activities at all. They are more comfortable in their own home. They feel more secure when surrounded by their own belongings. Don't be surprised if these children resist leaving home to go to school. For the young ones, be sure to familiarize them with the school they will be attending before the first day.

Venus in Cancer children are inclined to use their creative abilities in domestic areas such as home decorating and gourmet cooking. They are attracted to art work which activates sentiment within themselves. They will want their environments to be cozy and safe like the shell of the crab. Sometimes these natives become excellent business people (often preferring to operate a business out of their homes), because they value money for the security it can bring. This security is important to them. If they don't receive enough love as a child, they could later hold on too tightly to money. Teach them that security lies in the heart, not in the pocket.

Nurture well the children with this Venus in Cancer placement... to encourage them to shed their protective shell and to love more open-heartedly...to become as they develop, more adventuresome about life.

## Children with Venus in Leo

Venus expresses her love and affections with great gusto and flair in the fiery sign of Leo. These natives are truly the lovers of life. These children are gregarious, demonstrative types, having no difficulty expressing how they feel or in lavishing others with affection. They are dramatic and are born romantics. They are warmhearted and loyal in close relationships and also in friendships. They will have many friends as they are the actors who need a large audience. They want to be, and usually are, very popular wherever they go. They also have a tendency to choose people for associates who will make them look good. They prefer to give and attend social events which are glamorous and theatrical, expensive and lavish...befitting any king of the jungle! They often become the entertainment at these gatherings as they are always ready to be on stage and in the spotlight. It will be obvious that they take great pride in all that they do, both personally and socially.

Children with Venus placed in Leo value money for the luxury and glamour it can provide. Their choice of possessions runs to the expensive, often extravagant, and they will want to have them in abundance. They will appreciate all of your grand gestures to them with money. They will be willing to work for anything they might want, and are usually quite capable of doing whatever is necessary to acquire it.

These children are blessed with many creative talents expressed in numerous areas and in a royal fashion! One of their finest attributes is the ability to inspire others. They are masters at stimulating enthusiasm, and are gifted at helping others to become their very best. They enjoy being around children and can become great motivators when working with them. These children are outgoing, warm, entertaining personalities who will undoubtedly bring great sparkle to your days.

## Children with Venus in Virgo

This is a challenging place for Venus because her energies have difficulty integrating with the mental, analytical characteristics of Virgo. Since Virgo, ruled by Mercury, thinks everything and the energy of Venus is feeling, there is difficulty in expressing her Venusian characteristics well. This combination interferes with and hinders spontaneous loving

and giving. These natives may not even understand love, or at the very least will have trouble expressing it. To learn how to give and receive, plus eventually feel love, is the most important lesson for this placement. They are inclined to show their love and friendship by doing things for others because they have a strong desire to serve. These children also need to learn to love themselves as they often feel undeserving, and they underestimate their own worth. Help them with this as early as possible. This is the placement of the perfectionist. These children can be quite critical. Occasionally we find one that is not neat, clean, and orderly—but not often. These natives have such high standards, they are apt to face many disappointments. They need to learn that by having impossible expectations they put themselves and others through unnecessary frustration. Teach them that imperfection is part of being human, and is all in the way one looks at it—that everything has its own beauty just the way it is. Have them learn the saying, "Don't try to change the world—change the way you look at it"

These children are shy and retiring personalities and have difficulty making friends easily. They lack confidence and are uneasy in social situations. You will help them immensely if you will teach them the social graces and prepare them adequately for any social occasion they may be required to experience. This will strengthen their confidence and help them to find more pleasure at any gathering. If they don't learn to lovingly relate to people early in their lives, they may repress their affections completely, expending these affections on animals, or using this energy in their work. These children do like to work as they can avoid personal contact with other people this way. (They can develop into touch-me-nots!) In fact they can become all work and no play. Help them to have fun and enjoy the pleasures of life and the stimulation of other people.

Venus in Virgo children may have difficulty in seeing art and beauty as a whole because they will take each part individually and analyze it. They are born critics. They have a natural ability to express themselves in words. Some of our most famous literary and social critics have had this placement. Any craft or artistic project they undertake will be done to perfection as they are good with their hands. They may become good seamstresses or fashion designers, woodworkers, or food planners because of their interest in health and the body.

Basically most of their lessons can be learned by developing humbleness, tolerance, and forgiveness of others for their human

failings—and by accepting themselves for being just slightly less than perfect. Remember to praise them for whatever they do!

## Children with Venus in Libra

Since Libra is one of the two signs that Venus rules, her energy is expressed most naturally and comfortably when placed here. These children possess all of the refinement and charm for which Venus is noted, and they are easily offended by any coarseness and uncouth behavior.

Since Libra is an air sign, they are stimulated through mental activity as are all air signs. They are especially adept at communicating in one-to-one situations. They make wonderful counselors because they see both sides of situations and will present ways to resolve differences and create harmony. They also have the ability to say things in a way that is pleasing and comfortable for others; never offensive or intimidating, which makes what they say easier to accept. This sign placement represents the masters of cooperation, for they are definitely people-oriented. For these children, sharing love is second nature, wishing to please others and to be pleasing themselves. They are usually very attractive and present themselves with classic style.

Relationship is a primary goal for all Libra placements, and with Venus here it is accentuated. These natives do not like to be alone. They must have others around them most of the time. They thrive on the feedback from others, needing to reflect off of others in order to know themselves. This is an area to watch carefully because this need is so strong they have a tendency to become too dependent on other people. They also may attract people who will use, to their own advantage, Venus in Libras' willingness to openly share.

There is an eternal naivete and trust about them which can lead to heartache. It is important these overly-pleasing children learn to be themselves in all friendships as well as in all close relationships. They need to be sure that they are receiving as much as they are giving in all of their personal exchanges. Too often they want to avoid conflict at all costs because discord can sometimes affect their health, and they have a horror of being rude or offensive to anyone. Remind them that the extreme people-pleaser can become a sick door mat. Venus Librans, when they have reached their breaking point with someone, never say a word—they just close the door and disappear.

As well as harmonious relationships, these children value a pleasant active social life, and a beautiful peaceful environment. They

will choose friends who are intellectually stimulating and who have good social manners. They place high priority on social know-how, which therefore, makes them excellent hosts and hostesses. They have a good aesthetical sense with a natural instinct for color and design, and are talented in many areas which include: art, literature (poetry!), music, fashion, entertainment, and counseling. They make good caterers, restaurant owners, home decorators, social directors, and ambassadors. Encourage these adaptable, loving children to eliminate the tendency for indecision and settle on a direction that will benefit themselves as well as others.

## Children with Venus in Scorpio

The love of Venus placed in the sign of Scorpio is expressed with extreme intensity. These children have powerful and deep feelings, penetrating to the core of their beings. There is nothing lukewarm or moderate about these natives; it is always all or nothing. In the few close relationships which they form, they will be warmly affectionate, and must feel trust and loyalty for that other person, and visa versa. They are not good at speaking their feelings, which may cause them to appear as if they are secretive and calculating. This is not always true. Sometimes the feelings are too deep for words, and sometimes they haven't yet figured out what they feel—they just know they have these strong feelings. There may be some challenges in their relationships because they have a need to control. Some natives with this placement are very possessive. Any relationships that these children have, including friendships, will always be intense...never superficial. They either like someone very much or not at all.

In social situations they like to stay in the background so they can observe everyone, quietly studying the behavior of others like a master sleuth looking for clues. They also have a tendency to ignore and dismiss people with whom they are not involved, or who seem too bland or uninteresting. They can be quite abrupt and rude about this—and do not suffer as fools if they can help it!

These Venus in Scorpio children value the honor and power which comes with financial success, and this in turn motivates them to accomplish and achieve a great deal. They have strong personal pride and conduct themselves with dignity. They are shrewd and reserved and make excellent business people.

These natives have a dramatic taste in art, loving black and whites,

red and blacks, and artwork with sharp design. In their environment they prefer decor with clean, angular lines. They may have a flair for modern art if they choose to use these creative abilities. Some of these natives have been powerful writers, others great composers. Whatever they do, it's done intensely—but be careful it doesn't become obsessive! You can help these children by becoming aware of their deep sensitivity and by teaching them to be less suspicious, to not always look for a dark motive. Also watch for a cruel side and teach them to treat others as they would like to be treated. They are intensely magnetic, and can draw both good and bad into their lives. Teach them to discriminate —to not just plunge into a relationship with something or someone who intrigues them. If properly guided, these children can bring much benefit to the world.

## Children with Venus in Sagittarius

Since Sagittarius is a fire sign, Venus placed here is outgoing and friendly. There is always a certain amount of gusto with all of the fire signs and Sagittarius is no exception. These children have no difficulty expressing their affections and will love spontaneous giving and receiving. They are very outspoken about telling you how they feel, being direct and honest...and will appreciate others who also are to the point. In fact they value honesty so much that they will end any friendship or relationship in which there is deceit. They also will have difficulty with people who try to restrict them in any way, as they have no tolerance for possessive types. They place a high value on their freedom and cannot be forced or pressured into commitments of any kind. The result of any attempt is that they will bolt. They need a wide berth to decide for themselves.

The friends that Venus in Sagittarius children choose most likely will have similar religious or philosophical beliefs...or will need to have an open mind about these beliefs. There is a strong need for associates with whom they can have lively discussions and share their hypotheses, since they are very sociable and enjoy the interaction with others.

In matters of art and creativity, these natives appreciate natural art forms and in bigger-than-life sizes. They love anything which is done in grand style or with flamboyant colors. Their tastes may be extravagant, and they are sometimes called gamblers. They are often attracted to art which relates to religion or pieces from Greek or Roman history. These children take pleasure participating in almost all sports and particularly those which are individualistic such as horseback riding, tennis, skiing, mountain climbing, and hiking. They handle their

money and their possessions with an easy-come-easy-go manner, being generous and impulsive with regards to giving and spending. You could teach them a little discipline in both these areas. Basically you should have great fun with Venus in Sagittarius children—especially if you remember to give them their freedom.

## Children with Venus in Capricorn

This is another challenging sign placement for Venus. In the cautious, conservative sign of Capricorn, the love and affection expressions of Venus are restricted and withheld for Capricorns are very reserved when it comes to expressing their feelings. They are not demonstrative and are not fond of gregarious, excessive type personalities. They keep their feelings under control because they have a fear of being hurt. Since Capricorn is an earth sign, these natives need tangible assurance from others to trust or believe that it is safe for them to open their hearts and minds. They exercise great control over their desires, and simply won't allow themselves to become self-indulgent. However, when they do feel safe they will enjoy the pleasure of tactile exchanges.

These children value prestige and status. Socially they will do whatever is required to obtain positions of authority and recognition. They may even use their friends to get ahead, and will usually choose those individuals who will be helpful. You will not find them associating with frivolous or irresponsible people, or attending a gathering just for the fun of a party; they have a secondary agenda in mind. They are often attracted to older, more mature people because they not only want to draw on their experience and wisdom, they also seem to feel more comfortable with them. When they do establish a close friendship it will last, as they are loyal and willing to take on personal responsibility. These Venus in Capricorn children value money because they want the control that it brings to them. They may not appreciate art for its own sake because they value only that which is useful...unless, of course, the object brings them recognition and prestige! They respect and have creative abilities which produce beauty in practical, useful results such as carpentry, furniture making, or metal-working. They enjoy the world of business and are greatly attracted to politics, with many becoming very successful in these arenas.

The most needed lesson for these natives is to learn how to extend themselves to others more readily and to allow themselves to experience the joys and pleasures of life just for its own sake.

# Children with Venus in Aquarius

This is not one of the most comfortable placements for Venus because the Aquarian instincts are to be impersonal and aloof. This causes these children to have trouble with loving and forming close ties. Their loving is usually expressed in the form of detached friendships and for humanity in general. This, of course, does not mean that they are incapable of loving—just that the intensity of a one-to-one involvement is not their natural mode.

These natives value freedom and independence to the point that when any relationship becomes restrictive or confining they will drop it. Also, when an association loses its excitement they will look elsewhere, making them rather unpredictable in relationships. In social situations they tend to be themselves, the nonconformist of the group. Their mottoes are: "Take me as I am or not at all," and "What you see is what you get." The good side to this is that they are unique, interesting, and exciting...plus you always know where you stand!

Venus in Aquarius children are not emotional, sentimental, or interested in tactile touching. They are not the romantics of the zodiac, so don't take it personally if they appear detached. Their stimulation is usually mental and comes from the excitement of learning or experiencing something new and different. Originality is one of their strong points and they will demonstrate plenty of it. This placement can be drawn to modern art, and they are entrepreneurs who pursue originality to create new means and methods. Their minds are quick, inventive, and unconventional in style. They are apt to find their pleasures in the act of discovery, so be prepared. Help them direct their search in areas that will be useful to humanity, and do be patient with their idiosyncrasies.

# Children with Venus in Pisces

Venus in Pisces children are filled with love and empathy which they are quite willing to share with the world. They have no difficulty expressing how they feel or giving what they have. They feel so much tenderness and compassion for all, that one lesson which they need to learn is to be more discerning about whom they choose to love. Sometimes they are too interested in "saving" someone, regardless of that person's desire to change. And they are so willing to serve others that they could find themselves the victim of abusive types - whether mental, emotional, or worse. Help them to guard against any of this by becoming selective - to

feel a little less and think a little more before "falling" in love.

These children are truly the romantics and poets. They are inspired by all artistic creativity. They are very talented in this area as they have vision and a very creative imagination. They visualize easily and need to be motivated to put their ideas into concrete form, so encourage them to take action—to write the poem or book, to paint the picture!

These natives are supersensitive, both for others and for themselves. They can be easily hurt emotionally and can have difficulty coping with that pain, so they need much reassurance and a sensitive ear. They appreciate touching and caressing in all forms, and they are big huggers and kissers! They usually make friends easily even though they may be a little shy at first, and they are pleasant and amiable. They are not likely to rock the boat or take control in any situation, including their relationships. Children with this Venus in Pisces placement have values and ideals not geared to this Earth—and sometimes they may feel that they don't even belong here! They have very little use for money, rich people, or material possessions, being more interested in the "real" person and in feelings. These children have a beautiful spiritual nature which will be a pleasure to experience. Help them learn how to protect themselves from less sensitive types so they can safely and freely express the very beautiful side of themselves.

# Chapter 8

# Mars
## The Double Edged Sword of Energy

Mars is energy! It is masculine, physical energy... it is assertive energy ... it is creative energy. His energy is the fuel supply for the Sun. It might be said that Mars is the Sun's right-hand man. Mars stimulates "action" which causes reaction, which stimulates growth. He represents the ability to express individuality, telling us about an individual's get-up-and-go. Mars also represents deepest conflicts and greatest challenges—what turns us on, and what motivates us. He assists in expressing where the greatest drive and ambition will be focused in the self, where each one of us will take initiative and lead—or may not. The sign that Mars is in tells "how" our energy is expressed.

Like everything else in this world there is a beneficial and a non-beneficial expression. Mars is a two-edged sword. He is the warrior able to attack and/or to defend. His energy is like fire—it can either warm or burn., and it needs to be used constructively or it can cause much destruction. Some words used to describe Mars are aggressive, protective, restless, initiative, combative, courageous and, of course, impatience, spontaneous action, and energy. Patience is the biggest lesson of Mars. If your child has a strong Mars placement, one of your

greatest challenges will be to help them learn the lesson of patience, and also, one of your greatest accomplishments.

An important factor which will be helpful for you to know, since Mars rules anger, is to avoid being too upset when your child expresses this anger. Just be happy that he or she is able to get it out.

Do teach children with strong Mars placements not to be destructive or abusive with it to themselves, the environment or any other thing or person. Mars also rules sex and sports, and its placement shows how that energy will be expended or controlled. Children with high energy levels need to be encouraged to participate in competitive sports. Contact sports are especially good because they seem to satisfy the need for physical contact which might otherwise lead to early sexual activities. A serious interest in a sport can often satisfy these early strong sexual drives. And for all the sign placements for Mars, to encourage sport participation, or, some form of physical movement of the body will be helpful for the health of the mind and body, to learn to focus and to have some control over their physical body, or to learn fair play and to understand the value of teamwork.

Mars is the planet which tells us about our physical world, and the placement tells the what and why, as well as how action will be taken. Mars is the need to express oneself unconditionally, without restriction. Only the harmful or uncontrolled expressions of Mars should have to be moderated or redirected, for there is always a positive outlet for this energy. Guide your child into using their Mars energy constructively.

## Mars Retrograde
When Mars is retrograde at birth, its energy is restricted and turned inward, causing a lack of spontaneous expression. The energy of Mars may be just as strong but it is short-circuited in its output. Since Mars deals with anger, if it can't be expressed outwardly, it will be turned inwardly. We all know that pent-up anger is dangerous and unpredictable. It can cause not only frustration, but an inability to defend oneself (necessary for survival!) can cause depression, physical illness, even accidents. There is also a fear of letting go that can build to a point where there is no control—the energy is stuffed and then explodes. It will be very important as a parent or caregiver to teach retrograde Mars children how to express this energy in a positive way and as soon as it is felt, so that it doesn't internalize or build. This can be done by providing these children with creative projects, or healthy physical activities.

The biggest problem you could have with retrograde Mars children is that they often won't have the necessary motivation, and you will have to supply the stimulation using your creative imagination. This lack of motivation can stem from a physical source. The adrenalin production may be slow, or the oxidation and metabolic process sluggish, or there could be a psychological cause. Mars retrogrades are lacking in initiative and are not inclined to be competitive, since they can be filled with self-doubt and fear taking risks. They will need to hear statements such as: "It's not the **winning** that is so important, it's the **doing** that counts," and that, "Winners are just those who are willing to take risks because they are not afraid of failure."

Most of their battles take place on an internal level—constantly competing with themselves, and becoming angry, to boot! They need to know that anger is a normal human function that can be acknowledged and handled. It is not healthy to self-inflict or repress these feelings, so get these children to write about what they are thinking and feeling inside, so as to help them to alleviate a build-up of negative energy.

Teach these children that they will have to put a little more extra effort into using their Mars than most people, and to not feel defeated before they start. They need to know that every living person has his or her own personal difficulties to deal with. Once they are able to handle and express energy constructively, it will no longer be a point of concern.

## How to Find Your Child's Mars Sign

Turn to Mars Tables on page 221 and scan to find the year of birth. Next locate the month under that year. The dates listed indicate the day Mars moves into a sign. It stays in that sign until the next date listed.

**Example:** In the year 1900 Mars was in Capricorn on January 1 and stayed in Capricorn through January 20. On January 21, it entered Aquarius and stayed in Aquarius through February 28. March 1, it entered Pisces—and so on.

The D and R after the sign indicates whether Mars was Direct or Retrograde. When the R appears it means Mars turned Retrograde on that day and will remain Retrograde until the next date a D appears after the Sign.

**Example:** In the year 1901 Mars turned Retrograde on January 13, and stayed Retrograde through March 1. On March 2, Mars turned Direct again.

## Children with Mars in Aries

This is the most comfortable placement for Mars, since it rules Aries; it is at home, so to speak. It enables Mars to express its energy in the most natural and direct way. Mars in Aries is highly energetic, powerful and has spontaneous physical energy—sometimes leaping into action before looking or thinking. This placement makes good starters and poor finishers, so they will need to learn perseverance. Inclined to have hot tempers, these children should be taught to take a deep breath and count to ten before reacting and saying anything that might be harmful. Their anger, although quickly ignited, is usually short in duration.

These natives can be easily directed when motivated by challenge. As parents, caregivers, or therapists choose wisely and carefully in which direction you send them. They are courageous and forceful, and they like to be first in anything, whether in the classroom, in business, in driving a car! Mars in Aries is a strong and very personalized placement, so they can be consumed with self-importance. For these children, self-preservation levels are extremely high. It seems obvious that they will excel in sports especially individual sports.

In relationships, these children will want to dominate, although they usually will choose those who are also strong, as well as interesting as friends and associates. But sometimes they come on too strong, causing others to back away. They will tend to be direct, so teach them how to do it with less force and more diplomacy. A little modification in their desire to dominate is also a good idea...they need to learn cooperation. If others refuse to do what they want, they should go do it themselves! Teach them about balance, to give and take, and about equality.

These children make very good leaders. They like to be in charge and they make good executives. In school, career, or anything else the important factor is "challenge." They are very assertive, love competition, and dislike repetition or anything and anyone boring! Use this information as your tool for motivating them wisely.

## Children with Mars in Taurus

Mars is uncomfortable in Taurus because it is restricted in this Venusian earth sign—the physical energy being low and slow to move. These natives are motivated on a sensual level by things which bring them comfort, and on a practical level by accumulating material possessions. These children need to express their assertiveness through solid achievements and in endeavors that require patience, persistence, and

efficiency. One of the most positive assets of this position is persever-ance. Once they are motivated, they will work very hard and follow through to get what they want. They also will do a better-than-average job with what-ever they undertake.

These natives are stubborn and cannot be pushed, resisting any efforts to change them or to make them move more quickly. Since their drive is to accumulate material possessions and to receive physical comfort, as parent or caregiver, you will do best by stimulating these children with rewards that bring them comfort and pleasure. They love affection so lots of hugs and kisses can be a wonderful way to motivate and reward them.

Children with this placement find it difficult to express anger naturally because they hold it in, causing it to build up and then explode! - usually out of proportion and at inappropriate times. Sometimes they will even get a sore throat as a result of holding back or of having too much anxiety. (Taurus rules the throat, and having Mars in a sign shows where to expect physical problems.) Their patience is enduring - in fact, so enduring that they are sometimes taken advantage of by others. On the surface they are controlled, and inside they may be steaming. Teach these children to verbalize the way they feel to avoid any emotional or physical repercussions.

Any problems that may occur in relationships stem from jealou-sy and possessiveness. These natives tend to treat people the way they do their possessions, preferring to own them! The old adage that states, "If you set something free and it comes back, then it belongs with you," is a good thought for these children to learn and keep in mind. If they hear it often enough from you it will become a part of them.

## Children with Mars in Gemini
Children with Mars placed in Gemini are motivated by intellectual stimulation. They will use a great deal of their energy in mental pur-suits; having very active minds they thrive on learning. All information, especially anything new, will be attractive and exciting to them. They excel in areas that require mental activity, from school to quiz games. Their major downfalls in school will be their lack of follow-through, and diminished concentration when they are bored. If you find that they are slacking off in a particular study, check for monotony and help them to find a way to make it more mentally challenging. They are very re-sourceful so most times, once you direct them along this line, they will

find their own solution. As for the follow-through, they simply need to learn the importance and the discipline of perseverance. They will start many things (sometimes simultaneously!), and will need to learn the significance of finishing them.

These children are gifted with manual dexterity and will be able to work very quickly. They need to use this Mars energy both mentally and physically by using their hands; otherwise, it will manifest as nervousness. Computers are a great way to use both. Often these children have a talent for writing and make good reporters and critics. They are quick-witted, and when misdirected their wit can be taken as sarcastic and abrupt. Help them to use their quickness in beneficial ways. For optimum results, keep them active with fresh, stimulating information and many challenging discussions. Silence is not golden, and will be next to impossible with these children! Teach them to "edit" what they want to say, beforehand—so it doesn't come out as a garrulous stream!

## Children with Mars in Cancer

This is not one of the more comfortable places for Mars. The fiery Martian's aggressive physical nature gets water-logged in Cancer. Mars represents assertion but Cancer, like the crab, withdraws and goes within their own protective shell, when they feel in the least threatened. Since these children have difficulty being assertive, and rarely use a direct approach to gaining what they desire, they can be very devious. Sometimes they will use guilt as a method of manipulation to get their results. It is very important to help them see this manipulative nature, and to help them be more direct!

These children are super-sensitive and can become very hurt and angry inside when they feel offended, bitter, or put-upon—and, of course, they usually will not express this anger openly. Repressed hostility can make them seem moody and worrisome, and can be the cause of many physical illnesses, even ulcers. Teach them to express and discuss their angry feelings, bringing these feelings out in the open to avoid much of the emotional frustration so typical of this placement. Have a little session every night and ask them if anything is bothering them, help them express the resentment and rage.

The key motivation for these children is to gain security. Cancer is a sign that has strong protective drives, both for themselves and toward others. In fact, sometimes they are so protective of those they care about they can be smothering. They are very good at nurturing others

and will want to take care of those in need. This characteristic, when overdone or indiscriminative, can make them slaves to those who may take advantage. Teach them to serve only those people who will appreciate them, and to nourish in ways that will bring benefits to each. They have good instincts and strong intuition, which they should learn to use more.

These natives will put huge amounts of energy into domestic issues, building safety for home and family. At the same time they can make excellent business people—often doing best operating their own business and preferably from home! Many are very good at home repairs too. These children are conservative, so they usually stay out of troubles caused by the usual Mars impulsive actions. Help them to release all fears about security and especially their pent-up feelings about people...thereby eliminating most of their problems.

## Children with Mars in Leo

Leo is a fire sign so this is a powerful position for Mars as it provides tremendous vitality. Children with this placement will be forceful, impulsive, dynamic, dramatic, restless, enthusiastic, creative, and very ambitious.

These natives are best motivated with applause and by the recognition they will gain. They are driven to develop their own talents, which are numerous, because they want to achieve something of great importance in the world. These natives are loaded with personal magnetism and passion—passion for people, passion for the deed. Their enthusiasm and self-confidence which inspire others are characteristics which make this personality so attractive. Teach them that nothing is exciting or glamorous all the time, and that they will be stronger and happier and accomplish more if they don't let their enthusiasm dwindle too much when things slow down or become routine.

Pride is another strong characteristic inherent in Mars in Leo children. This is a fine trait which is necessary for accomplishment, however excessive pride can lead to arrogance. Teach them the advantage of this trait and the disadvantage of its misuse. Point out that humility is also necessary for advancement and for getting along with people...this is a very important quality for these children to develop. Sometimes they feel that they are better than others, so help them to see the difference between liking themselves and feeling confident...and looking down on others from their lofty heights.

These natives have a great deal of courage, and will often become leaders. Show them that the great leaders were not dictators. They earned their positions through respect and admiration, and for their deeds done. These children will not take kindly to being dictated to, so this example presents a useful way to show them how others feel!

They are not afraid of work, and will want to show you that you can rely on them. They want you to think of them as being physically and emotionally strong at all times. With all this high energy they are usually good at sports, and are naturally drawn to physical activities of all kinds. They have a quick temper, though usually not dangerous. They have strong will power and can be defiant or authoritative. Teach them to modify these forces within themselves. They like center stage and will cooperate best when you appeal to their sense of the dramatic, as well as to their sense of fairness. Help these children to channel their powerful energy into constructive directions, and you will be amazed at all they can accomplish.

## Children with Mars in Virgo

Mars in Virgo children are motivated to put their energy into achieving perfection in all aspects of their lives. It is their main drive. These are the children who plan their activities before taking action, as they want to do everything as perfectly as possible. Since Virgo is an earth sign, they are inclined to only take action in areas which will bring practical results, producing material value and gain. They will not want to use their energy on anything unproductive. These natives focus on details and are good not just with their heads but with their hands. This makes them excellent crafts people. They put their efforts into keeping organization in their lives, and in their environment as well. The force and energy of Mars is carefully directed with this placement. They systematically become skilled in any area they choose. These children will do well in all areas of the medical field especially as surgeons, or computer programming is another good option.

The challenging side of this placement is that these natives may also expect other people to adhere to the same perfectionistic standards which they set for themselves. They can be very critical and picky, finding fault in others and in their work, which will cause much dissension in their lives. People won't like it! Teach them to lighten up a little, especially on others. If they look to the larger plan they will become aware that all might already be in the right order.

# Children with Mars in Libra

Children with Mars placed in Libra may have some challenges as to how they express their energy. (Mars rules the sign Aries—opposite Libra!) Since Mars is self-oriented and Libra is other-oriented, you can see the conflict. One part of them wants to be partners focusing on cooperation, and another part of them is very competitive. The competitive side wants to take action, and the other side is afraid to because they need approval so desperately. Oh, what a see-saw they're on!

With this placement we see the fire of Mars expressed through the mental mode of Libra, the air sign. These children can be motivated and will take physical action only through mental stimulation. They do not like hard or dirty physical work; menial tasks have little appeal. They also don't take orders very well, so you will need to ask for their cooperation. For best results, work along with them.

These are the natives who like to use their energy working very hard creating social events and initiating parties. They also are very skilled at inspiring others to cooperate and contribute to their projects. (They're great at fund-raising!) Socializing and relationships are their prime motivators. Keep this in mind with your disciplines and rewards. These children will be the ones who will want to have a girlfriend or boyfriend at an early age. Teach them how to be discriminating with those they choose. Sometimes they can be taken advantage of because of their strong need for a partner, their willingness to do whatever is necessary to make it work, and their trusting naivete. Often they jeopardize their own needs and priorities. If the relationship doesn't work out, they can feel like a failure. This dependency on others may cause them many problems.

Children with Mars placed in Libra can become real warriors, and will fight vigorously when justice is violated. When "fairness" is the question, they will exhibit anger and display courage to make corrections, whether they are involved personally or not. Again, discrimination is the key to assure that their efforts are not wasted or misplaced. Sometimes they seem to have a tendency to tilt at windmills! Help these children to use their energy so that they will not become the eternal people-pleasers, and will become decisive individuals who can stand on their own feet ... as they go about in life, creating social benefit.

# Children with Mars in Scorpio

Mars placed in the sign of Scorpio creates a powerful, combustible combination. The fiery forceful nature of Mars is coupled with the intensity, endurance, and power of Scorpio! These natives are motivated by the desire for power and control. These children are very determined, persistent types who must be motivated and guided to use their strong power in beneficial ways. Otherwise, it can cause great destruction, as these natives are quite capable of accomplishing whatever they decide —for or against.

These children have very strong physical and emotional desires, and their intensity can be overwhelming. (They are also inclined to be very sensual.) They have deep feelings and are unable to experience anything in a moderate manner. When they are angry it is usually internalized and the pressure continues to build. Holding on to their anger in this fashion causes them to hold grudges and to think about revenge. You can tell when they are angry because they will become sarcastic and make biting remarks. Teach them to release all hostility, so they can channel their energy into productive causes. This negativity serves no beneficial purpose, and can be detrimental to any relationship, whether personal or business.

The physical energy of these children is high and enduring. They are active and forceful, and you may find them challenging to keep up with. Their energy is applied in a steady, persistent manner... they are not likely to give up when the going gets tough. In fact, this will activate their courage, and oblige them to apply all of their energy. They are quite willing to fight for what they want. These children, more than others, will need to learn about the win-win concept. Teach them to use their power to benefit others just as they benefit themselves in their own endeavors. The main lesson to teach them is to always choose the high road. Since they have such great power, this will cause them to become the catalyst for many great accomplishments. They are motivated to succeed and do well in the world, and they make excellent business people.

# Children with Mars in Sagittarius

Natives with this placement will expend large amounts of their Mars energy rebelling against any form of restriction. You can motivate these natives by showing them how they can gain more freedom. As their parent, caregiver or teacher, I would advise loosening the reins and giving

these children some elbow room. This will eliminate wasting a lot of time and energy for both of you. They have strong needs for freedom and spontaneity. If you use your creativity to guide them into using their own judgment wisely, restricting them won't be as necessary.

These children love being outdoors and participating in sports, especially those which are played outside and require lots of physical energy, are most appealing. They also love travel and adventure. Motivate them with rewards along these lines. They are open and direct people (sometimes too much so!), and you will obtain your best results by being the same way with them.

The lessons Mars in Sagittarius children need to learn are endurance and discrimination. They can spread themselves too thin, and scatter their energy, resulting in sloppy work and unfinished projects. Also, they seem to be careless with material objects, because their minds are racing ahead. They tend to act without thinking and need to slow down. Teach them to count to ten. Their lack of follow-through can create problems with deadlines, so you will need to redirect their energy into matters which need completing.

These children are the crusaders who have lofty goals. They will fight for the good of the country, the world, humankind, and God. Teach them to discriminate, so they will use their energy appropriately to best serve these ideals. Your challenge is great, but the rewards can be greater.

## Children with Mars in Capricorn

Mars is well placed in the sign of Capricorn because the caution of Capricorn slows, modifies, and brings practicality and discrimination to the impulsiveness of Mars. These natives are motivated by ways to gain positions of authority and respect from others. These children are not reckless. When they take action it is well planned. They use their physical energy carefully in disciplined ways. They will want to put their energy into work which brings them concrete results.

They are not afraid of hard work and will demonstrate great perseverance. Be careful they don't become work-alcoholics. They are so ambitious that they are often planning their career at a very early age. They are strongly motivated by professional ambitions, and want to achieve positions that have prestige or bring recognition. They have a compelling drive to get ahead materially, as they take seriously their duty to take care of and fulfill their responsibilities. Sometimes they can

become too calculating or seem cold with this strong drive for success. They will take active leadership roles, but may be inclined to step on others on their way up. Be sure to teach them the value of caring about people so they won't lose sight of the humanistic side of life. These natives make good executives, politicians, and military personnel.

When these children become angry, they exhibit control over their actions. However, you will know when they are angry because they will act aloof and become as cold as ice. Sometimes their hostility comes from the fact that they have no tolerance for, and in fact, will vehemently disrespect laziness. They will not associate with people who have no ambition. Whenever they are exposed to these types, it becomes very distressing for them because they simply cannot understand it! Help them to learn to apply their standards to themselves only, and to tolerate people who have other priorities. Oddly enough this placement can be thin-skinned (Capricorn rules the skin). It might be that their sense of dignity has been breached, and their feeling of self-worth sullied. So help them build another top layer!

## Children with Mars in Aquarius

With this placement we find the raw physical energy which Mars represents frustrated, because it is expected to express itself through the mental channel of the air sign Aquarius. This may not be one of the better placements for Mars as it can cause low physical energy. When blocked, this Mars energy may build up and cause nervous tension. However, these children will gladly use their physical energy when motivated by any "cause" or some exciting mental pursuit.

Their natural instinct is to use their energy to obtain freedom and avoid restriction. They require the room to be independent and to find their own way, using their own originality. As a parent or teacher, you need to know that these are the children who the more you try to control them, the more they fight to get free. They remind one of a song entitled "I Did It My Way." For best results, keep their need for independence in mind. You will also see a practical side to these children, so direct them toward productive causes where they can expend their Mars energy for the benefit of many. The Aquarians are naturally inclined to have goals which will benefit others as well as themselves, so this should be easy.

In relationships, these gregarious and friendly children are not comfortable with and have no need for displays of emotion. The Aquar-

ians do not usually form deep attachments to others, and do not understand nor tolerate well the possessiveness of some signs. They like and enjoy many friends. The best approach to Mars in Aquarian children is through logical, intelligent, and practical means.

Since these children have an inability to follow orders very well, you will get better results by suggesting, rather than telling. Then, as a parent, caregiver or teacher, try to stay open to experiencing a new way of doing things since they have so many different ideas!

Too often these children are inclined to resist any kind of authority, or form of restriction. If they grow up with lightly held reins, and are made aware of this anti-authority tendency in a friendly and logical way, it could cause much fewer problems when they are adults! In fact, these children, who can be so rebellious and impatient, can always be reached by your cool-headed logic. Since basically they are inspired by intelligence, they shouldn't go too far for too long, unless, of course, those reins were held too tightly. The key to working with them is to lighten the control, and motivate them through their intellect.

These children are naturally very enterprising and original. Appeal to that side of them. Some of the world's great inventors and thinkers have had this placement. They love to do and think new things and have new experiences. So be willing to also, and your life with them can be an adventurous joy!

## Children with Mars in Pisces

This is not one of the more advantageous places for fiery aggressive Mars to reside. Motivate these natives to use their creativity and fertile imaginations to benefit others. In the sensitive watery sign of Pisces, its expression is dampened and somewhat stifled. This is what might be considered an uncomfortable placement. They tend to not make waves and will look for ways to avoid pressure since they are not forceful, assertive types. They are more reactive as opposed to initiating. These children live in a world of feelings and imagination rather than in the world of action. They are not likely to set goals as they prefer to wander through life based on how they feel. They are always motivated by feelings rather than thoughts—a very important point for you to remember. These children are apt to have low physical energy and will not expend what they do have on strenuous activities. A thoughtless parent or teacher might call them "lazy" a harmful label that they will remember forever. If you ask them, they'll say they're waiting to be "inspired." Be

clever and think of a way to do just that! It is very difficult for them to come up from their imaginings and become self-starters, even harder to follow through. See if you can turn their task into a story of some kind. Train them to do this, and they can play this little game on all their work—and they might eventually use their fertile imaginations to create something important!

Too often their energy is used on their emotional sensitivity and over-responsiveness to just about everything. Sometimes these natives have low levels of self-confidence. This, plus their low levels of physical energy, may be what inhibits their ability to take decisive action. They tend to be shy, timid, and apologetic. However, they do make good listeners and would make excellent psychologists.

These children need help in releasing their anger. They tend to suppress it, many times feeling they are to blame. Help them to develop strong self-esteem and to eliminate all tendencies to internalized guilt, which can cause many illnesses. These feelings of guilt can actually be a wallowing in emotion instead of coldly looking at something and taking responsibility for it! Again, less guilt, more action.

Sometimes individuals with this Mars in Pisces placement put much energy into their own weaknesses, and project that out on others, whom they then dominate with their helplessness and their dependency! Help them to learn self-responsibility by praising what they do...and in the beginning, every little effort! Don't criticize if it isn't done just the way you want it. Appreciate their efforts, and help them appreciate themselves. Get their focus away from their inner-imaginings and out to where it can serve others. Service and sacrifice {within healthy limits!} are two of the noblest traits of this placement.

> Divine being has permitted me to learn
> from the revolution of the stars.
> —Nostradamus

# Chapter 9

# ♃

# Jupiter
# The Point of
# Expansion, Opportunity and Luck

Jupiter is considered one of the good guys in the zodiac; that is, if there were truly good and bad guys. Obviously, each planet has its own best use and highest manifestation, as well as its excessiveness and misuse. Although Jupiter is called the great benefactor, he also has his extremes and inappropriate expressions.

Jupiter's placement in the chart is considered the lucky spot. He represents the area of ease, where one receives the little benefits of life. He is our optimism., our expansion point, where we feel unlimited. Jupiter symbolizes our abundance. He is the planet which puts us in search of higher knowledge and broader horizons. With Jupiter, we seek our own truths and philosophies. This planet always sees the "big picture" ¬the overall plan.

We all have a Jupiter in our chart. However, where he is placed and how he aspects the other planets depicts how his influence is felt. **For example**, he is restrained when in contact with Saturn and energized when contacted by Mars. Jupiter's energies, like Saturn's, are most strongly felt on a personal level when he is making a close connection to the Sun, Moon, Mercury, Venus, Mars or the angle's of the chart. He is in each sign for approximately one year. Therefore, all who are born during that particular year have Jupiter in the same sign. We will not describe Jupiter through the twelve signs. It is really necessary to have a chart cast to discover how he affects individual personality traits. Please do consider having a chart consultaton with a competent astrologer, so you can get a clear picture and accurate information. Also be sure to take advantage of the "One Free Chart" offer from Astro Computing Services in the back of this book. You can then be absolutely sure you're reading the correct interpretations for your child. The tables, alone, may be off for some planets if they are very close to changing signs. A true chart must be calculated for exact birth time.

**Key words that describe Jupiter are:** expansion, opportunity, luck, optimism, abundance, enhancement, idealism, benevolence, humor, honesty, truth, education, knowledge, understanding, wisdom, philosophy, exploration, adventure, travel, freedom, exuberance, carefree, happy and positive. Negative expressions are: overconfident, careless, gullible, flippant, cocky, tactless, procrastination, reckless, undisciplined, presumptuous, wasteful and foolhardy.

## How to Find Your Child's Jupiter Sign
Turn to the tables beginning on page 224, and scan down the list to your child's date range that includes your child's birthdate.

## Children with Jupiter in Aries
There is no shortage of personality here. Strong charisma, strong self-esteem, and definitely not lacking - well - in most anything. Hates to wait, loves to be first, takes risks and usually wins. It is definitely a go for the gusto placement with a positive pulse. Knowing that you are good is handy but bragging on yourself too soon deprives you of compliments you surely would get if you gave them a few seconds to show up. Selling yourself is a natural so put it to good use. Perfect combo for leadership, is independent and rings the bell for freedom.

## Children with Jupiter in Taurus

To say that money and comfort play big in your world is like saying that there will be snow in Alaska! Of course you like the pleasures of life! They make you happy and so does sharing them with others. The good news is that you usually are good at creating a lot of money. Here we find a very sensual being with a love of food and a great appetite. Watch the waist line. Luxury is a word Jupiter in Taurus loves, and piling up the gold coin is always fun, too. With Jupiter here, the little bull not easily pushed, but is at heart, loving and giving at heart.

## Children with Jupiter in Gemini

Talk talk talk – questions questions questions - well just a bit! Learning never stops and is a must. Just let them travel off into another place whether it is a journey of the mind or a foreign country. Good placement for selling, teaching or communicating in any fashion. These personalities are very diverse in fact maybe too much so at times so focus would be a good skill to learn. Be sure to keep the information coming so boredom is avoided and restlessness takes over. Generally this is a happy person with a carefree attitude who enjoys the nuances of everyday life.

## Children with Jupiter in Cancer

This is a very caring person with a good antenna for understanding other people's feelings and needs, always looking to protect the needy and feed the hungry. Nurturer of the world would be an appropriate description. They will probably want to learn to cook at a young age and will always make others feel at home and comfortable where ever they are. Home and family are important as is the security that comes with having both. These natives attract benefits just because of their nature in that they work well with people and the public.

## Children with Jupiter in Leo

We might expect to see a bit of drama in the personality of this placement. Leo the sign is big and bold on its own and when you combine that with the bigger than any planet Jupiter you have some pretty huge expression. This is one of the more optimistic placements and one who needs to shine. They love the Sun, yellow, gold and glamor. Look for a desire to have showy possessions. Jupiter in Leo has a flair for style

or for the right costume, can dynamic on the stage. Overall, he or she will be the life of the party —the lead performer. This child is generous, maybe to a fault, and has a tendency to overspend.

## Children with Jupiter in Virgo

Here the expansiveness of Jupiter is drawn in somewhat since Virgo is interested in methodical, useful and practical uses of time and energy. These are the kids who love to have a job so let them help you with as much as you can. Help them to develop as many skills as you can and praise them for their precision and cleanliness. They like to work and are willing to earn what they get. You might just have to help them to learn to have some fun along way with their projects. Health, diet and medicine might be topics they are interested in.

## Children with Jupiter in Libra

This placement can mean a social butterfly—maybe—the one who always wants a party and is probably good at planning them too. There also is a potential for artistic interests, so give it a try. Bring out the paints with lots of colors and big papers or canvases, then see what happens. At any rate, beauty is important to these children. Also, they have a strong sense of fairness and will be the peacemaker wherever they see conflict. This is a soul who needs an active social life and will want to have lots of friends, so prepare for company in your home.

## Children with Jupiter in Scorpio

This is an interesting combination. Jupiter is the magnifier and Scorpio is the intensifier. Wow, what is your guess on that one? Well Scorpios also love mystery and anything that needs to be figured out, so here is the detective. Maybe a chemistry set or a magic kit? These children are the ones who will see beneath the surface and into your psyche, but you probably won't be able to probe too far into theirs because they are good at creating an aura of secrecy about themselves. They like to be the ones asking the questions. Tell them about astrology and other occult subjects—they most likely will be interested.

## Children with Jupiter in Sagittarius

Here we have double the influence of similarity since Jupiter is the ruling planet of Sagittarius. Optimism, honor, nobility and justice personified

are some of the characteristics we find here. Those are some pretty high concepts for a child but they will grow into them. These are the kids who need to have lots of freedom to discover their own world their own way, and on a path of discovery they are. The higher truths and the wisdoms of the ages will catch their attention. So will foreign cultures and distant lands plus any kind of travel where they are exploring new information to help them figure out the world and beyond. Adventure and expansion are the key words here. This is a trusting soul and generous as well. So keep an eye on their friends to be sure they are not being taken advantage of. They will amaze you with what they have learned.

## Children with Jupiter in Capricorn

These children trust and respect that which is stable, reliable, practical and pretty much the status quo. They look to authority and will work to get themselves in those positions as well. Work is a positive and accomplishment is the reward. These are the ones who will strategize and plan their future so they are sure they will succeed. Reaching the top of the pile in whatever pursuit they take on is the goal. They are motivated by achievement, results and status. Going for President would not be outrageous. They will want to rub elbows with people of influence and will start young. This placement may have coined the phrase "it isn't what you know, it is who you know that is important".

## Children with Jupiter in Aquarius

This is generally a youth with high intellectual abilities who is capable of original innovated and unconventional thinking. The ideas will keep you thinking because they are so creative and unusual. Watch out you may have an inventor extraordinaire on your hands. Building robots and computer games are high on the list for keeping the attention of this keen busy mind. Freedom is priceless to them so don't fence them in, they probably will escape anyway. These kids will start new clubs or lead groups that fight for the rights of others and humanitarian causes that bring equality for all. Friends are important and will always come first so it's nothing personal when they choose to be with the friend rather than the family. Honesty is golden so never lie to them.

## Children with Jupiter in Pisces

Sympathetic, sensitive, caring and understanding are characteristics that go way over the top for these loving souls. These are the idealistic imaginative children who are able to create special worlds where fairies and fantasy live. You may have to help them deal with the harsher realities that may present themselves as they go out into the real world. They feel sorry for all who are in need and tend to take on more than would be in their own best interest. Help them to discriminate in choosing friends because of their strong natural empathetic abilities being around less compassionate people can be emotionally disturbing. Many with this placement become the helpers of the world, taking care of the sick and weak. Strong spiritual beliefs will be helpful for the challenges here.

# Chapter 10

$$\hbar$$

# Saturn
# The Taskmaster

Saturn is the guy with the bad reputation. He has been called the task-master of the zodiac, and probably was the originator of the "bread and water" treatment for punishment. One thing for sure - Saturn is the plan-et of discipline! Even more true is that he will teach us discipline until we learn to discipline ourselves. It is true he does catch a lot of flack, yet ultimately, he can become our greatest strength. Saturn represents how we build our structures, and how we utilize self-discipline. Sat-urn's placement in the chart depicts each person's life lessons. Saturn's placement by sign and house, along with his relationship to the other planets in a birth chart, show the areas of life which (once mastered) will become the foundations and strengths. These same areas also can be the source of difficulty, denial and challenge in life. It is going to be the challenge until it is mastered.

With this planet in the signs, there is a forced opportunity to develop discipline through the particular sign in which Saturn is placed. We are forced to blend and utilize Saturn's qualities with the qualities of the sign. The contacts it makes to the other planets show the dynamics and how Saturn affects personality traits, and the house or area of the chart it falls in show the areas of life involved. Saturn and discipline are synonymous. He challenges us with the weaknesses inherent in the sign

in which he is placed, and forces us to develop the strengths of that sign. The quicker we do it the better.

In broad terms, Saturn symbolizes the structure of the world. All the laws apply, both naturally such as gravity and time, and manmade laws such as beaucracy and culture. He symbolizes the father and authority; he is truly a serious consideration in life. He always demands we earn what we receive. When we apply the necessary discipline, we become the master, and then the lesson brings joy. Resisting or avoiding the lesson brings unpleasant experiences which cause feelings of being restrained, limited, resentful, angry, depressed, having a lack of energy or even an illness. These are manifestations of Saturn's misuse, or our failure to take responsibility for using his energy properly. Knowing what the lessons are and how to develop them is paramount.

It takes Saturn twenty-nine years to complete his cycle through the zodiac, which means he is in each sign approximately 2 1/2 years. All people born within this time frame will have Saturn placed in the same sign. This occurrence means the sign placement tends to be generational and describes the characteristics of entire groups of people. Unless Saturn makes a strong aspect to the luminaries, the personal planets, or the chart angles, you will not (personally) experience his influence.

For a complete understanding of how Saturn operates in any person's life, a comprehensive astrological chart must be cast.

**Key words that describe Saturn are:** caution, practicality, seriousness, reservation, dependability, reliability, responsibility, discipline, maturity, self-control, restraint, integrity, authority, status, recognition, stability, tradition, perseverance, persistence, diligence, endurance and structure. Negative expressions are: fearfulness, limitation, restriction, deprivation, denial, inhibition, selfishness, solitary, cruelness, rigidity, coldness and pessimism.

## How to Find Your Child's Saturn Sign
Turn to the tables beginning on page 225, and scan down the list to your child's date range that includes your child's birthdate.

## Children with Saturn in Aries
**Fear**—of being inhibited or restrained by others, of outside control, of identity loss.

**Challenge**—with patience, other people's priorities.
**Lessons**— to learn responsible action and consideration.
**Needs to Eliminate**—selfishness, hastiness.
**Beneficially Applied**—an enduring competitor, disciplined leader.

## Children with Saturn in Taurus

**Fear**—not having enough, of deprivation and denial, loss of comfort and possessions.
**Challenge**—with stubbornness and possessiveness.
**Lessons**—to learn moderate indulgence and non-attachment.
**Needs to Eliminate**—greed, indulgence, inflexibility.
**Beneficially Applied**—displays responsible values, financial benefactor.

## Children with Saturn in Gemini

**Fear**—of boredom and inactivity, loss of mental stimulation.
**Challenge**—with consistency, endurance, dedication.
**Lessons**—to learn disciplined intellectual pursuit and application, perseverance and practical learning.
**Needs to Eliminate** — scattering self, becoming the know-it-all.
**Beneficially Applied**—provides solid authoritative information, production of material resources, persevering useful study.

## Children with Saturn in Cancer

**Fear**—of not being cared for, loss of security, safety and protection.
**Challenge**—with moodiness, ability to feel secure within self.
**Lessons**—to develop self-confidence and mature emotional responses.
**Needs to Eliminate**—insecurity, hiding feelings, hoarding belongings.
**Beneficially Applied**—provides protection for others, disciplined feelings.

## Children with Saturn in Leo

**Fear**—of not being or having love, loss of praise and admiration, dignity and approval.

**Challenge**—with humility and being of service to others.

**Lessons**—to learn to applaud self inwardly.

**Needs to Eliminate** —arrogance and the need to dominate others.

**Beneficially Applied**—inspires responsibility in others, organized
    leader, respectable status

## Children with Saturn in Virgo

**Fear**—of being criticized, loss of appreciation.

**Challenge**—with imperfection and lack of order.

**Lessons**—to learn productive discrimination and acceptance of current reality.

**Needs to Eliminate**—judgment and intolerance.

**Beneficially Applied**—brings skillful creation of form, mastery in
    health areas.

## Children with Saturn in Libra

**Fear**— of rejection and loneliness, loss of unity.

**Challenge**—with relationships, indecisiveness, vacillation.

**Lessons** —to learn responsible cooperation, confidence
                and independence.

**Needs to Eliminate**—inconsistency and being a people-pleaser.

**Beneficially Applied**—provides an enduring peacemaker, justice
    based on integrity.

## Children with Saturn in Scorpio

**Fear**—of becoming vulnerable, loss of control.

**Challenge**—with exposing self, being secretive.

**Lessons**—to learn to trust, to place importance on control of the self.

**Needs to Eliminate**— harmful manipulation, need for revenge.

**Beneficially Applied**—learns how to empower others,
                responsible perceptions, teaching others self-control.

## Children with Saturn in Sagittarius

**Fear**—of being limited or restricted, loss of movement and space.

Challenge—with confinement and commitment.

Lessons— to develop practical philosophies, master wisdom.

Needs to Eliminate—tactlessness and bluntness, dissipating
   resources and energies.

Beneficially Applied—provides organized adventures,
   reliable enduring truths.

## Children with Saturn in Capricorn

Fear—of being in a subservient position, loss of respect, and authority.

Challenge—with experiencing warmth, learning to lighten-up.

Lessons— to develop humor and compassionate administration.

Needs to Eliminate— being overly structured, rigid and isolated.

Beneficially Applied—displays administrative responsibility,
   diplomatic ambassador

## Children with Saturn in Aquarius

Fear—of having to conform or of becoming attached, loss of freedom.

Challenge—with authority and tradition, making commitments.

Lessons–to learn reasonable limitations, stable changes
   and reconstruction.

Needs to Eliminate—detachment, irresponsible rebellion.

Beneficially Applied—shows practical innovation,
   reform with integrity.

## Children with Saturn in Pisces

Fear—of having a routine mundane existence, loss of
   imagination and fantasy.

Challenge—with physical reality, depression.

Lessons—to learn stability, bring spirituality to earth.

Needs to Eliminate—over sensitivity, escapisms.

Beneficially Applied—provides practical spiritual application,
   creative artistic structures.

# Chapter II

# The "Transpersonal" Outer Planets

Uranus    Neptune    Pluto

## Important reasons of why you need to have the whole chart done

This book just wouldn't be complete without talking about the outer planets or sometimes referred to as the transpersonal or outer planets. Even though they are further away they still have important influences. They are called the outer planets because they are beyond personal. The fact that they stay in a sign for a long time causes their influence to be generational and will affect a large group of people in a similar way. However, if they are closely connected to one of the personal planets such as Mercury, Venus, Mars, the luminaries (Sun and Moon), or Jupiter and Saturn or the ascendant in a person's chart, they definitely will change the expression of whatever they are contact.

For example my oldest son has a Virgo Moon, but he has Pluto at the same degree as his Moon in Virgo. Since Pluto is ruler of Scorpio, it changes the normal way a Virgo moon would be expressed to be now expressing as a Virgo/Scorpio combination. This "ups the ante" a bit, making his emotional make-up far more intense and complex.

My younger son has Neptune on his Scorpio moon making it a Scorpio/Pisces expression, and Uranus on his Libra Ascendant changing

the people pleasing Libra and combining it with the detached Aquarius energy. It does make a difference. I have a Leo Sun with Pluto—Scorpio in contact with it and I can assure you that it definitely changes the normal outgoing Leo to a more reserved observing Scorpio.

These are just a few examples to show you how important it is to know the whole chart. I strongly recommend that you take one step further and pursue having the charts done for your children and yourself to gain a clearer understanding then I am able to cover in this book.

# URANUS

Following are the individual characteristics of each of the outer planets. Let's start with Uranus, which stays in one sign for about seven years, 84 years for a full circle, and it rules Aquarius. I will be calling the planet "he "although I believe it is androgynous. (That's just me by the way.) The effects of Uranus in each sign are expressed differently, and as I have already mentioned, since he is in a sign for about seven years, his sign theme will influence all those born during that seven year period in a similar way. However, the specific placement of Uranus in each specific chart will create the individual expressions of what the meaning of Uranus will be for that person.

A birth chart with a strong influence of Uranus will bring many unusual and individualistic characteristics to the personality. This child will not be the conformist or the one to go along with the crowd. He/she will usually rebel at any form of restriction so beware. You have a unique character in your life. This child needs his/her freedom! These children as they get older and begin to journey out into the world may feel like they don't fit in but most of the time they don't really care. The truth is they are different. Different is good. Just look back through history and most of the people who made an impact on the world were unique and non-conformist. They were the trend setters blazing new trails and changing the status quo for the better. Your mission is to encourage them and help them develop high self-esteem. Also, most definitely show them how to use their uniqueness in a way that is grounded with a balance of a practical approach, rather then just causing changes for the sake of change itself. These children are tuned into the Universal Mind. They are the ones who show us the way, so be sure to encourage their special genius.

Although Uranus might be considered the most disruptive type of energy especially to people who like the status quo, normally the

fixed signs—Taurus, Leo, Scorpio and sometimes Aquarius—he is the one who moves us out of our ruts changing the things that make us boring, ho hum and keep us from being all we really can become. Uranus is known as the liberator so he brings us the freedom and the independence to be our unique selves. One astrologer said that Uranus is "Freedom from the Known." To me that means moving beyond what is to what can be—new possibilities. When we don't resist and we simply let go and go with the flow, Uranus can be very exciting and open the doors to many new opportunities.

You may be able to tell that even though I have fixed signs I have learned to like Uranus' energy. This is because in my birth chart he is closely sextile my Mercury, semi-sextile Venus and Moon, trine Neptune and squares the MC—all the things that may not make sense to you, and you don't need to or want to know. Simply put, Uranus is connected to many parts of my personality and is strongly placed in my chart. This is why you go to an astrologer or even have a computer chart done, so you can understand in plain English what all that means! You need to know how Uranus is placed and what and where and how strong his influence is in the chart.

The other reason I like Uranus is because I have many interesting experiences with his transits, such as when he contacts planets in my chart. Some were great right away, meaning I chose to initiate or not resist them. Some were not so great at first, when I did not choose them or I resisted them, but then turned out to be great when I let go and experienced them with an open heart and trust. Sometimes it is only when you are on the other side of of a time period when Uranus made a direct contact to a chart that you really can see the benefits.

The points about Uranus that are of most interest to you are to know whether any of your child's planets (or yours) are in close aspect (relationship). This helps you understand why a person is the way he or she is. Also, we all have times when Uranus is in a position in the zodiac or sky (called transiting) that has a strong relationship to a your chart or your child's. Keep in mind that Uranus is the planet of change, revolution, rebellion, and freedom from oppression. When it is in contact with our charts we should expect the unexpected at any moment.

Wouldn't it be good to know when this is going to happen or if it is happening now, and that's why things are the way they are—plus to know the timing of how long it will last??? It was important for me! When I knew that one of my kids would be, or was having, a Uranus

transit, I knew it would be pointless to try to restrict their need for freedom. Instead I needed to have clear communication with them and let them know that I understood what they were about to feel or were feeling first. I let them know of any possible pit falls that could occur, and then I gave them their heads with a guiding hand, love and trust.

We need to keep in mind that our children's journey is their journey. It is what they came here to experience for their own soul growth, and we have been blessed with the opportunity to share that experience with them. We are not supposed to control them or mold them into what we think they should be. We are only supposed to facilitate their process and do our best to keep them safe. The more you understand about them and that process, the easier it can be—and astrology can help you a lot. As Carl Jung (who studied astrology) said, you can quickly see the personality profile of a person by looking at their astrology chart, and then you can begin to understand and eliminate much frustration right away. To me it is our "Astro DNA"—much can be learned from looking at it.

**Key Words For Uranus:** change, individuation, liberation, freedom, detachment, reform, rare, eccentric, different, strange, intuitive, can be erratic, radical and unpredictable, cause upheaval, loves exploration, spontaneous solutions, original, loves technology, is electrifying and revelations abound. Have fun with him, resisting is futile. One astrologer said, "Uranus helps to synchronize individual effort into a collective whole. He is about equality and freedom from oppression" The Aquarian ideal is unity in diversity. There is a revolutionary tone here. However he is Universal Brotherhood and a higher level awareness.

## Representatives of Uranus
futurists, inventors, astrologers, technicians, space travelers, computer experts, artists, revolutionaries, pilots, researchers, visionaries, eccentrics, philosophers, astronomers.

## The Lesson of Uranus
To bring about reform in a peaceful way that is good for all of humanity.

# NEPTUNE
Neptune, also one of the outer planets so again, it effects generations and will bring its characteristics to an even larger number of people at the same time in similar ways. Personally its influence will depend on

where it is in the individual chart, what other planets it is in contact with and how. It takes 156 years to go through the entire zodiac which is an average of 14 years in each sign. For example when it passed through the sign of Libra 1942 to 1956 the "Flower Children" were born. Since one of the characteristics of Neptune is what we hold near and dear and even worship, these children were all about peace and love—both expressions of Libra—and they even held them as sacred.

Illusion falls into the Neptunian realm and while illusion is fun with magic shows and very important in the filming industry if it is prominent in your little ones chart it might be wise to make sure it is channeled into a productive creative expression such as filming, art or music. Neptune is very creative and imaginative. Sometimes the challenge for the person with strong Neptune is in balancing that imagination with a dose of earthliness and practicality. They are the dreamers and the day dreamers from which come the visions of the future. Based on Walt Disney's huge and continued success, there can be a lot of lot of pleasure associated with the use of Neptune.

On the other hand, sometimes with a Neptune transit, (when it makes a contact in a person's chart), one might feel like being in and passing through a thick fog. You can't really see clearly and don't know what is ahead until you are on top of it. For some this can be exciting, especially if Neptune is strong in the birth chart. For others it can be a disaster. It has a lot to do with the faith which is associated with Neptune.

I have also heard that to be in a state of uncertainty or confusion is to be in high state of consciousness. This must be where the concepts of mysticism, spirituality, enlightenment, divine compassion and uUniversal love parts of Neptune come into play.

Dreams (the kind we have at night or lucid dreams and visions )are all under Neptune's domain. Your child's imaginary playmate is another possible expression of Neptune, and by the way, this should not be discouraged because it could shut down the child's powerful quality of imagination that simply needs to be encouraged in a positive direction so that it is in balance with the physical world. The point here is that there is a time and a place for everything, and an appropriate use for this planet's energy. Neptune is the psychic, the unexplained, the world of no time or space, and in some way it is a part of each of us. It has produced our fantastic artistic creations which only needed a little Saturn or the material world so they could be put into physical form.

Neptune is definitely creative and romantic, but it could be

termed as unstable or at least unpredictable. It also can be deceptive and that creates the illusions that may cause problems. Also, the last area I want address concerning Neptune is that when it is strong in a chart, there can be a tendency and sometimes even an out-of-control desire to want to escape! There are lots of ways to do this and you probably are aware of some, such as alcohol and drugs. But also, about phobias, eating disorders, smoking, and yes even excessive meditation. For young children it coudl staying in the world of make believe early ALL the time. You may know of even more ways to escape.

The bottom line is when a person has a Neptune transit, their behavior can change. They may become spacey, forgetful and may even experience some physical sensations of being dizzy or disorientated. Before running off for a brain MRI or accusing them of doing drugs, it might behoove you to have the chart looked at to see if good old Neptune is making an appearance.

I had that experience with my younger daughter, who is the most responsible, organized, practical and disciplined person you could ever meet. If I hadn't known to look at her chart, I would have sworn she had gotten in with the wrong crowd and was doing drugs. She was in college at the time, and fortunately I was able to understand what was happening and let her know that I understood. I also was able to tell her some things she could do that would be helpful and ease the challenges, so she could be prepared for the things that were happening in her life.

This can be a big heads up for you if you go through a period like this with your child at any point in their growth. Have the chart done. Since children are for the most part naturally tuned into the Neptune part of themselves when they are young, mostly because they have not yet been conditioned to squelch it, and have not yet fully developed the rational part of themselves, I feel that we would do best by them by helping them to keep it active, understand it, value it and help them learn to use it appropriately and in balanced healthy way with the physical world reality. They are just different realities, both needed and both real.

**Key words for Neptune:** fantasy, dreams, mysticism, intuitive. Intangible, spirituality, enlightenment, illusion, delusion, escapism, deception, uncertainty, confusion, dissolution, idealization, compassion, sensitivity, martyrdom, imagination, intangible, melancholy, self-deception

## People of Neptune prediposition

Artists, musicians, actors and actresses, poets, mystics, priests, psychologist, doctors, nurses, chemists. occultist , astrologers, as well as swindlers, addicts and criminals.

## The Lesson of Neptune

To serve for the highest good of all

# Pluto

Pluto – the last but by no means the least! Discovered by Percival Lowell on February 18 1930, Pluto orbits the entire zodiac in about 248 years, an average of 21 years in each sign. Its orb is elliptic, so the time varies from 11 to 30 years. Pluto is the planet of transformation and my two descriptions of him are the cosmic colonic and the roto-rooter of the zodiac. That might not sound like a lot of fun and for most people it usually isn't, but boy do you feel good when it is all over. He has a way of bringing anything to the surface and to the awareness—anything that has collected or is buried deep in your consciousness and your life, but is not currently doing you any good – it could be anything emotionally, mentally, physically, materially and maybe even spiritually. Get ready for the clean sweep and the big cleanse. This is, of course, when you (or your child, your friend, your spouse or your parent experiences a contact of Pluto to any part of the natal chart. Pluto is also about death and rebirth, so this type of life experiences are apt to show up. Pluto is all about transformation and regeneration, the process of letting go of old in order to give birth to something new. He is the stimulus for drastic change, and can bring upheaval that turns life inside out and upside down. He can mean awareness that has been buried or suppressed is brought to the surface and must be dealt with. He makes us deal with the demons within us, and all the fears that so often keep us paralyzed. He is about bringing light to the darkness to set us free. Pluto's process is intense, extreme and often uncomfortable, to say the least, but as I described at the beginning, you will feel lighter, brighter and so much better when the process is completed.

So far I have been talking about Pluto transits, when he makes a connection with something in the personal chart as he moves through the heavens and through the signs. Now I have to ask: wouldn't you like to know about this before it happens—when it will happen—for how

long—and maybe even what you can do to minimize the effects of it??? Don't you think consulting a professional astrologer would be helpful and a good idea?

Now let's talk about people who have Pluto prominent in their natal chart. They will have lives where upheaval happens often and may be filled with traumatic events. The good news is, they have the strength, the power of regeneration and the internal fortitude to deal with such things and overcome them. Power is a key word here, and children with Pluto strong in the birth chart must be taught to use their power to assist and empower others, because by doing so, they will always be protected. It is only the misuse of power that causes them problems. For you as the parent, understanding this and teaching your child about it will save you and the child a lot of unpleasant moments. Many may still have near death experiences, but with this awareness it won't be because of an experience with the corrupt or the underworld.

An example of higher use of Plutonian energy is Mahatma Gandi. An example of the misuse is James Manson. Teach your children to take the high road to avoid destructiveness and harm to themselves and others. Help them to be the Supermen and the Wonder Women of the world.

With strong Pluto placements, personalities are intense. Nothing is half way—it is all or nothing, black or white. They could exhibit compulsive behavior, or they could be extremists. I don't think you can easily change this because if you try to force a child with strong Pluto to do what he/she does not want to do, you will have a battle on your hands. The child will fight for control. Realize that people with strong Pluto are as they are, because they are supposed to be the way in order to fulfill their purpose in this life. Your best option is to melt them with love and gently guide them with reason. Figure out a way for them to see benefit from what you want them to do—or better yet, if you can figure out how to make it seem like it's their idea, you will do far better. The bottom line is that you need to have the chart erected, because you need to to understand your child, and to know how to help him or her develop in the best way possible.

## Key words for Pluto:

transformation, regeneration, transmutation, evolution, rebirth, empowerment, purification, intensity, extremism, purpose, focus, concentration, power, control, catharsis, obsession, compulsiveness, crisis, upheaval, manipulation, purging.

## Pluto People:

researchers, doctors, scientist, speculators, dictators, charismatics, leaders, demagogues, hypnotist, occultists, analysts, phycologists, detectives, healers, masters of manipulation for good —or for harm.

## The Lesson of Pluto

To use power to empower others.

# The Outer Planets in Aspect to Other Planets

The signs that your child's outer planets are in are generational—all children in the same age group will have Uranus, Neptune and Pluto in the same sign. For this reason, knowing the sign alone, does not give you personal information about this one special child that is yours. But when a child has an inner planet in a close relationship to one of the three outer planets, that can be a quite important key to understanding the child's personality, talents, needs and potential. Following are a few key words for what it might mean for each of the inner planets to be in close relationship (aspect) to each of the three outer planets. For more detailed information on how this works, a personal consultation with an experienced astrologer is recommended. Or, if this book sparks your interest in learnng more about astrology, you will find among the few ads in the back pages of this book,infomation about books that cover the astrological aspects more thoroughly.

## Key Words for Uranus

unique, creative, impulsive, tense, needs freedom, unconventional.
**With Sun**—the child may be all of the above and "shine" through them.
**With Moon**—emotional tension is heightened. Feelings are very strong.
**With Mercury**—the child is an original, creative thinker, who may be
    especially adept at modern technology
**With Venus**—expect sudden passions or beng in love with love.
    Artistic or musical talents are likely.
**With Mars**—the child is assertive, impulsive and unconventional,
    with freedom needs. His/her dexterity in making things may
    be quite good
**With Jupiter**—upbeat, optimistic, original, and inclined to overdo
**With Saturn**—tension, challenges in handling freedom vs. restriction,
    or in balancing control with freedom, strong willed

## Key Words for Neptune

imaginative, creative, space-cadet, a dreamer, who may be deceptive and/or unrealistic

**With Sun**—the child may be all of the above and "shine" through them

**With Moon**—the child is emotionally sensitive. He or she may be very intuitive and ends to absorbs others' feelings

**With Mercury**—the child likes to makes up stories, enjoys make-believe play, may be deceptive, may have talent for creative writing

**With Venus**—he or she is in love with love, a natural romantic, with special feelings and/or talents for art, music and beauty.

**With Mars**—there may be challenges in assertiveness or physical energy, Channel this child's positive energy toward helping healing activities or physical activities that express beauty

**With Jupiter**—expect expanded emphasis on any or all of the above.

**With Saturn**—anticipate grounded, practical expression of any or all of the above

## Key Words for Pluto

intensity, power, focus, obsessive, compulsive, transformative

**With Sun**—strong, powerful, internalizes, manipulative, strong body, very focused and intense

**With Moon**—ntense emotions kept inside, broods, deep feelings, picks up on other's feelings, intuitive

**With Mercury**—deep thinker, sees beneath the surface, good researcher

**With Venus**—deep love, compulsive, manipulative in relationships, intense feelings and/or artistic expression

**With Mars**—explosive, dynamic, transformative energy, able to move mountains

**With Jupiter**—strong success potential, tendency to overdo, obsessive

**With Saturn**—workaholic, self-disciplined, strong desire to achieve

# Chapter 12

# Gift Giving
# Through the Signs

Here are some ideas for those birthdays and other gift-giving occasions when you are shopping for something special to please a child. I'll give you suggestions for each of the Sun signs.

## Aries

Aries children love being first, so are likey to like anything that they are the first on the block to have, the newest thing on the market. They love the color red and things that are action orientated. Just make sure it isn't something that they will get bored with by having to figure it out or it takes to long to finish. They like excitement and completion. Just about any kind of sports gear particularly for the head. Give them anything that is noisy or fast such as racing cars or video games, bikes, kites and scooters. How about martial arts lessons? Now that would be a great way to channel all that energy wouldn't it? Even the girls like action and sports so maybe finding something that they can do or go to that has excitement and is the new rage.

## Taurus

Taurus children love things that are soft, luxurious and feel good to the touch like a plush robe or a cuddly furry stuffed animal—or maybe an angora scarf, since Taurus rules the throat. Things that smell good, taste

good and make them feel indulged will work well—think of perfume, aroma therapy and chocolate. Music is big hit with Taurus, so Cd's, music boxes or even a calming waterfall appeals to their senses. I'd bet that a microphone or a sing along toy will work too. They also appreciate money, (monopoly and banks), practical gifts and things of value like jewelry. The young ones will like it even if it is just pretty. Pastels and green would be their color choices.

## Gemini

Gemini children should be simple to choose for, since since they have varied interests. It probably would be hard to miss, but let's try some suggestions. They are intellectual, so for sure they'd like books. Since they are also good with their hands, any kind of craft or building toys are good—pottery, weaving, wood working etc, They like to be on the move, so consider baby walkers to bikes, rollerblades, razor scooters, skis, snowboards etc. I guess you get the point. They are also great with puzzles, board games, computer games, electronics , science or magic. Communication is important to them, so phones, walkie talkies, morse code and recorders are possible choices. Or, how about a gift certificate to a video store? It really is hard to go wrong, but they do like things that reflect who they are, so if they are into art then get the latest thing going in that department because they are also up on the trends. Keep that in mind. Mostly, though, they like your company.

## Cancer

Cancerian children, our domestic nurturerers, will love pets of all kinds, live pets or and even pretend pets, and also doctor sets, dolls, doll houses, cooking and baking sets, dishes, pots and pans, or kitchen sets like toy stoves ovens and sinks. They are attracted to cameras and photography probably because they are sentimental, and this lets them capture the moments of family and friend gatherings. Photo albums and collages would work too. They also like collectables, limited editions, antiques heirlooms memorabilia and things that increase in value. Cancerians are quite traditional, so they love homemade items and anything relating to family. Food and cooking catches their attention, as do water sounds and things from the ocean. Make sure the family is close by and they will be happy.

# Leo

Oh my gosh—anything glamorous, elegant, sparkly, shiny or gold will attract Leo! Consider huge stuffed toys, fancy doll houses, glamorous dolls, castles, crowns and rhinestone tiaras ,or better yet, since they love to dress up and put on costumes, get them a big chest of dress up stuff. They love to be on stage and play theater, so let your imagination go, selecting party clothes, hair items and anything they can show off. They also love stories and movies about the Prince and Princes. The most important thing to remember with Leo is that they prefer first class things as in name brands and designers, or at the very least, something that seems expensive. So, avoid the knock-offs and anything that is tacky. Just think deluxe and you can't go wrong. Oh well—you can always wrap it in gold paper with fancy sparkly bows.

# Virgo

This sign is much like Gemini only a little more discriminating. Virgo children like to work with their hands and are experts at crafts and hobbies. Since Virgo is an earth sign, they are remarkable with wood. A wood burning kit or any type of wood working kit will appeal. You might choose a work bench for the boys, a pottery wheel for the girls. Mosaic kits, stained glass kits, paint by number, painting figurines or anything requiring detailed work will make them happy. Mental and manual dexterity which are areas that make them tick, and this covers a wide variety of things you can come up with. I think another area is hygiene and items to be used in the bath or shower, a rubber ducky or bubble bath. I know you can be more creative than that, but you get the idea—toys and accessories.

# Libra

There are several things to consider for Libra and the most important would be to give them something you can enjoy or do together or at least something they can do with someone else. A perfect gift would be taking them to a social event or an art museum or maybe to the art store to buy a kit to paint tee shirts or to tie dye. Maybe your Libra is into music so a trip to the music store will be fun. They might like a musical instrument. A rainbow in their room would work, too, or a sound machine, a bright light, or coloring books, or books that have beautiful illustrations. These children like things to be peaceful, calm and bal-

anced. They also value friendship, so maybe something that they can make and give to their friends would please...as it goes without saying, all games that take two to play.

## Scorpio
While some might think this is a hard one, I think it is easy! Anything involving mystery, magic, intrigue or suspense will do. Spy kits, challenging puzzles, archeological dig kits, chemistry sets, crystal growing kits, or the famous Labyrinth game are possible choices. Or, how about microscopes, I Spy books, or any books that are about mysteries, unexplained phenomena or that explain the "why" of anything. What about IQ puzzles and games, maybe the board game Clue (that one has got to be a favorite!) or any other kind of mind game. For the little ones, the toys that you match the shapes and insert the correct one, or mechanical toys and dolls that move—the easy stuff—would be good choices.

## Sagittarius
These children are the outdoor types, so bikes are big along with bow and arrows, tree houses, swings, dart games—or of course, you could always get them a horse. They love to hike and camp and mountain climb. The little ones like to climb on the jungle gyms, or jump with trampolines and pogo sticks. They love puppies better than anything, except ponie, so if at all possible get them a pet, since they are among the biggest animal lovers if not the biggest. My next thought might be a cowboy or cowgirl suit with holster and pistol, even if it is a water pistol. These kids love to travel and also love books that take them to other places in thier imagination. Music to dance, jog, or ski to, and clothes that are casual and comfortable. are also good choices. So, there you have it—easy.

## Capricorn
Wow—how about a gift certificate so they can get what they want! I guess for the little ones, they might enjoy military games, a set of army soldiers, a captian's cap, or maybe some building blocks or an erector set. These are the children who are old for their age and are practical from the start. How about things made of wood, or a fleet of trucks or ships, something that is useful? Or consider books about great leaders

and masters, or classical and traditional items. They like leather and appreciate things that are made well. Good luck—I think you should ask them what they want.

## Aquarius

This one should be easy because they like a lot of things. I think their favorite, even as a little tyke, would be computer games and computer learning, probably for both girls and boys. They have natural inclinations towards technical, electronic and futuristic areas. They are attracted to telescopes, and newfangled gadgets. You can be safe with anything to do with space, like a planetarium on their ceiling. How about a portable miniature arcade game, a radio kit, a chemistry set or high tech strobe lights? They like all the new stuff, especially if it is exciting colorful and fun, so its hard to go wrong here.

## Pisces

These children are fun because they are all about fantasy and imagination—just what kids are supposed to be like, whimsical, mystical and filled with wonder. They will like all of the toys and films and books that are made for children. Some other ideas are music that they can sing along with, goldfish or aquariums, slippers, videos they can dance with, cameras, paints, crafts ----do I need to go on? Have fun, take them shopping and enjoy the fact that they will love all things magical that are made for kids.

The ancient popularity of astrology is not
a threat to religion but an opportunity, a
chance to show searching minds how they
can combine all the world's wisdom into
one cohesive

# Chapter II

# Conclusion

In the great dance of life and relationship, the material in this book is but a first step toward understanding the complexities of human behavior as they relate to the role of parenting, caregiving, teaching, and counseling. Also, keep in mind there may be other factors in a chart which can modify the descriptions given here. Sometimes there is so much strength in another area it may weaken a placement so that it is almost unnoticed. A complete chart drawn up by a professional astrologer will present a clearer picture with specific information of one's characteristics, life purpose, and direction. It will present a more complete personality profile plus the timing of developments throughout the individual's life! I feel that one would be missing a great opportunity if they do not take the time to have the entire chart drawn up and described in detail by a competent astrologer. One who can explain it in a positive manner and with constructive suggestions.

Please realize that each description presented here, of a planet in a sign, will also apply to any adult with that placement. After all, we all had to be children some time, didn't we? From a broader perspective, we are all still children in the process of becoming! So apply this understanding and use these guidelines for all of your relationships, as well as for understanding yourself. The astrological approach provides us with the opportunity to look at ourselves from a detached viewpoint, and in an objective manner. I believe that all people are capable of changing their reactions and behavior...and this becomes possible

once they understand what to change, and when they will have a strong enough desire. The desire is the motivation, it then becomes a matter of persistence. The more times we repeat a behavior, the more it becomes automatic - an ingrained habit.

Start thinking of each of us here on the planet as a sprinkling of diamonds. As we touch one another through our contact in our relationships, we reflect our different facets. We are all made of the same substance, each with the potential to shine. It is our gift to help one another —love is the way!

# Astrology's Birthday Wishes for Each Sun Sign

**Happy Birthday to Aries**—here's to a life charged with new things that bring you excitement and that you are always the first to experience whatever you wish.

**Happy Birthday to Taurus**— may your life be filled with pleasure, comfort and a peaceful environment with plenty of fine dining in beautiful places.

**Happy Birthday to Gemini**—here's to inviting the universe to bring you fun filled days and see you playing with new information in many different ways.

**Happy Birthday to Cancer**—sending a big wish for you to have the security of family, sound foundations and that your home is as you'd love it to be.

**Happy Birthday to Leo**—seeing you filled with plenty of gusto and center stage of your bigger than life and glamorous experiences.

**Happy Birthday to Virgo**—thanks for bringing order and discrimination to our world—may you always be appreciated for your contributions.

**Happy Birthday to Libra**—let the world be your party grounds as the best social butterfly on earth you deserve to always have plenty of people around.

**Happy Birthday to Scorpio**—let it be known that you are intense but not a threat unless threatened, so may we send you understanding and the love you deserve.

**Happy Birthday Sagittarius**—Wow—what you need is all the adventure, travel, nature and fun that the world has to offer—may you always have as much as you can handle.

**Happy Birthday Capricorn**—lucky you—you start out old/mature and get younger with each year that passes—may you enjoy your newest childhood year.

**Happy Birthday Aquarius**—our humanitarians who will fight for our causes – may your friends be many and new cause abound.

**Happy Birthday Pisces**—may all of your fantacies fill your heart with joy and your creative ideas materialize into successful people toys.

## Recommended books for parents or teachers
### who would like to learn more about astrology and how it works

*The Only Way to Learn Astrology, Volume 1*
Marion D. March and Joan McEvers
(Book #1 of a six volume series, each book with more advanced material)

*Your Magical Child*
*Astrology for Nurturing Your Child or Inner Child, Expanded 3rd Edition*
Maria Kay Simms
(interprets planets in signs, houses and in aspect to other planets, plus synastry—how to evaluate parent-child relationships.)

*Easy Astrology Guide*
*How to Read Your Horoscope*
Maritha Pottenger
(easy lookup interperetations for planets in signs, houses, and aspects)

## See ONE FREE CHART offer on page 166!

# Samantha – isms
## Everything is always in Right Order – WHAT IS, IS!

The only time we experience negative emotions is when we are trying to control the outside world and it isn't working. In other words we are resisting and trying to change what is.

What anyone else thinks about me is none of my business— they are all just doing what they need to do for their own growth.

There is no such thing as failure—only delay

People treat you the way you teach them to treat you

You are not your programs—you are so much more—your life may be the results of your programs and can be changed when you take control of your thinking.

Control your thinking and you control your experience of the world— open your heart and you connect with the world.

Our relationships with others are like looking in the mirror because they reflect to us where we are loving and accepting ourselves— and—where we are not.

## WORK ON YOUR OWN HEAD!

# Tables to look up
# Sun, Moon and the Planets
## HOW TO USE THE SUN SIGN TABLES

These Sun Sign tables show the day of the month for each year that the Sun moved into a new sign, as taken from *The American Ephemeris* in which time are calculated for midnight, Universal Time (Greenwich Mean Time). Obviously, most people were not born at midnight GMT, so for an accurate birth chart, you must correct for the time zone of birth. In most cases, you will find that the tables for your birth date show your correct Sun sign. However, if your birthdate is on the day that Sun changes signs (in astrological terms, meaning you were "born on the cusp") the accurate time for your zone is important. You may need to have an accurately calculated chart to know for sure what Sun sign you have.

The tables in this book begin with 1945, so in addition to looking up the Sun, Moon and planet signs for your children, you'll also be able to look them up for your own birthdate—in some cases even if you are the grandparent! Hint: It's easier and will help avoid mistakes, if you use a ruler to help you scan across the pages.

**Example:** Just below, at left, is is a key to abbreviations given in the tables to indicate the signs, and in the box to the right is the first three years of the Sun Signs (1945-1947). For example, to look up the Sun sign for the birthdate August 28, 1946, scan down to AUG, and then scan across to the 1946 column. The number 24 is the date that Sun entered VIR (Virgo). Sun will be in Virgo until September 24 when it enters Libra. So, the Sun sign on August 28 is definitely Virgo. Births **on** August 24 and September 24 are cusp days, so uncertain. For cusp days a chart calculation based on birth date, birth time and birth location are necessary to be absolutely certain what the correct Sun sign is. **Note that there is an offer for one free chart calculation on page 165 of this book.**

## Sign Abbreviations

| ARI | Aries | LIB | Libra |
|-----|-------|-----|-------|
| TAU | Taurus | SCO | Scorpio |
| GEM | Gemini | SAG | Sagittarius |
| CAN | Cancer | CAP | Capricorn |
| LEO | Leo | AQU | Aquarius |
| VIR | Virgo | PISC | Pisces |

|  | 1945 | | 1946 | | 1947 | |
|-----|-----|------|-----|------|-----|------|
| JAN | 21 | AQU | 21 | AQU | 21 | AQU |
| FEB | 19 | PIS | 20 | PIS | 20 | PIS |
| MAR | 21 | ARI | 22 | ARI | 22 | ARI |
| APR | 21 | TAU | 21 | TAU | 21 | TAU |
| MAY | 22 | GEM | 22 | GEM | 22 | GEM |
| JUN | 22 | CAN | 22 | CAN | 23 | CAN |
| JUL | 24 | LEO | 24 | LEO | 24 | LEO |
| AUG | 24 | VIR | 24 | VIR | 24 | VIR |
| SEP | 24 | LIB | 24 | LIB | 24 | LIB |
| OCT | 24 | SCO | 24 | SCO | 25 | SCO |
| NOV | 23 | SAG | 23 | SAG | 23 | SAG |
| DEC | 22 | CAP | 23 | CAP | 23 | CAP |

# Sun Signs 1945-2025

| | 1948 | 1949 | 1950 | 1951 | 1952 | 1953 |
|-----|---------|---------|---------|---------|---------|---------|
| JAN | 21 AQU | 21 AQU | 21 AQU | 21 AQU | 21 AQU | 21 AQU |
| FEB | 20 PIS | 19 PIS | 20 PIS | 20 PIS | 20 PIS | 19 PIS |
| MAR | 21 ARI | 21 ARI | 21 ARI | 22 ARI | 21 ARI | 21 ARI |
| APR | 20 TAU | 21 TAU | 21 TAU | 21 TAU | 20 TAU | 21 TAU |
| MAY | 21 GEM | 22 GEM | 22 GEM | 22 GEM | 21 GEM | 22 GEM |
| JUN | 22 CAN | 22 CAN | 22 CAN | 23 CAN | 22 CAN | 22 CAN |
| JUL | 23 LEO | 23 LEO | 24 LEO | 24 LEO | 23 LEO | 23 LEO |
| AUG | 24 VIR | 24 VIR | 24 VIR | 24 VIR | 23 VIR | 24 VIR |
| SEP | 23 LIB | 24 LIB | 24 LIB | 24 LIB | 23 LIB | 24 LIB |
| OCT | 24 SCO | 24 SCO | 24 SCO | 25 SCO | 24 SCO | 24 SCO |
| NOV | 23 SAG | 23 SAG | 23 SAG | 23 SAG | 23 SAG | 23 SAG |
| DEC | 22 CAP | 22 CAP | 23 CAP | 23 CAP | 22 CAP | 22 CAP |

| | 1954 | 1955 | 1956 | 1957 | 1958 | 1959 |
|-----|---------|---------|---------|---------|---------|---------|
| JAN | 21 AQU | 21 AQU | 21 AQU | 21 AQU | 21 AQU | 21 AQU |
| FEB | 19 PIS | 20 PIS | 20 PIS | 19 PIS | 19 PIS | 20 PIS |
| MAR | 21 ARI | 22 ARI | 21 ARI | 21 ARI | 21 ARI | 22 ARI |
| APR | 21 TAU | 21 TAU | 20 TAU | 21 TAU | 21 TAU | 21 TAU |
| MAY | 22 GEM | 22 GEM | 21 GEM | 22 GEM | 22 GEM | 22 GEM |
| JUN | 22 CAN | 22 CAN | 22 CAN | 22 CAN | 22 CAN | 22 CAN |
| JUL | 24 LEO | 24 LEO | 23 LEO | 23 LEO | 24 LEO | 24 LEO |
| AUG | 24 VIR | 24 VIR | 23 VIR | 24 VIR | 24 VIR | 24 VIR |
| SEP | 24 LIB | 24 LIB | 23 LIB | 24 LIB | 24 LIB | 24 LIB |
| OCT | 24 SCO | 24 SCO | 24 SCO | 24 SCO | 23 SCO | 24 SCO |
| NOV | 23 SAG | 23 SAG | 23 SAG | 23 SAG | 23 SAG | 23 SAG |
| DEC | 23 CAP | 23 CAP | 22 CAP | 22 CAP | 23 CAP | 23 CAP |

| | 1960 | 1961 | 1962 | 1963 | 1964 | 1965 |
|-----|---------|---------|---------|---------|---------|---------|
| JAN | 21 AQU | 21 AQU | 21 AQU | 21 AQU | 21 AQU | 21 AQU |
| FEB | 20 PIS | 19 PIS | 19 PIS | 20 PIS | 20 PIS | 19 PIS |
| MAR | 21 ARI | 21 ARI | 21 ARI | 22 ARI | 21 ARI | 21 ARI |
| APR | 20 TAU | 21 TAU | 21 TAU | 21 TAU | 20 TAU | 21 TAU |
| MAY | 21 GEM | 22 GEM | 22 GEM | 22 GEM | 21 GEM | 22 GEM |
| JUN | 22 CAN | 22 CAN | 22 CAN | 22 CAN | 22 CAN | 22 CAN |
| JUL | 23 LEO | 23 LEO | 24 LEO | 24 LEO | 23 LEO | 23 LEO |
| AUG | 23 VIR | 24 VIR | 24 VIR | 24 VIR | 23 VIR | 24 VIR |
| SEP | 23 LIB | 24 LIB | 24 LIB | 24 LIB | 23 LIB | 24 LIB |
| OCT | 24 SCO | 24 SCO | 24 SCO | 24 SCO | 24 SCO | 24 SCO |
| NOV | 23 SAG | 23 SAG | 23 SAG | 23 SAG | 23 SAG | 23 SAG |
| DEC | 22 CAP | 22 CAP | 23 CAP | 23 CAP | 22 CAP | 22 CAP |

| | 1966 | 1967 | 1968 | 1969 | 1970 | 1971 |
|-----|---------|---------|---------|---------|---------|---------|
| JAN | 21 AQU | 21 AQU | 21 AQU | 21 AQU | 21 AQU | 21 AQU |
| FEB | 19 PIS | 20 PIS | 20 PIS | 19 PIS | 19 PIS | 20 PIS |
| MAR | 21 ARI | 22 ARI | 21 ARI | 21 ARI | 21 ARI | 22 ARI |
| APR | 21 TAU | 21 TAU | 20 TAU | 21 TAU | 21 TAU | 22 TAU |
| MAY | 22 GEM | 22 GEM | 21 GEM | 22 GEM | 22 GEM | 22 GEM |
| JUN | 22 CAN | 22 CAN | 22 CAN | 22 CAN | 22 CAN | 22 CAN |
| JUL | 24 LEO | 24 LEO | 23 LEO | 23 LEO | 24 LEO | 24 LEO |
| AUG | 24 VIR | 24 VIR | 23 VIR | 24 VIR | 24 VIR | 24 VIR |
| SEP | 24 LIB | 24 LIB | 23 LIB | 24 LIB | 24 LIB | 24 LIB |
| OCT | 24 SCO | 24 SCO | 24 SCO | 24 SCO | 24 SCO | 24 SCO |
| NOV | 23 SAG | 23 SAG | 23 SAG | 23 SAG | 23 SAG | 23 SAG |
| DEC | 23 CAP | 23 CAP | 22 CAP | 22 CAP | 23 CAP | 23 CAP |

# Sun Signs 1945-2025

| | 1972 | | 1973 | | 1974 | | 1975 | | 1976 | | 1977 | |
|-----|----|-----|----|-----|----|-----|----|-----|----|-----|----|-----|
| JAN | 21 | AQU | 20 | AQU | 21 | AQU | 21 | AQU | 21 | AQU | 20 | AQU |
| FEB | 20 | PIS | 19 | PIS | 19 | PIS | 20 | PIS | 20 | PIS | 19 | PIS |
| MAR | 21 | ARI | 21 | ARI | 21 | ARI | 22 | ARI | 21 | ARI | 21 | ARI |
| APR | 21 | TAU | 21 | TAU | 21 | TAU | 22 | TAU | 21 | TAU | 20 | TAU |
| MAY | 21 | GEM | 21 | GEM | 22 | GEM | 22 | GEM | 21 | GEM | 21 | GEM |
| JUN | 22 | CAN | 22 | CAN | 22 | CAN | 22 | CAN | 22 | CAN | 22 | CAN |
| JUL | 23 | LEO | 23 | LEO | 24 | LEO | 24 | LEO | 23 | LEO | 23 | LEO |
| AUG | 23 | VIR | 24 | VIR | 24 | VIR | 24 | VIR | 23 | VIR | 24 | VIR |
| SEP | 23 | LIB | 23 | LIB | 24 | LIB | 24 | LIB | 23 | LIB | 23 | LIB |
| OCT | 24 | SCO | 24 | SCO | 24 | SCO | 24 | SCO | 24 | SCO | 24 | SCO |
| NOV | 22 | SAG | 23 | SAG | 23 | SAG | 23 | SAG | 22 | SAG | 23 | SAG |
| DEC | 22 | CAP | 22 | CAP | 23 | CAP | 23 | CAP | 22 | CAP | 22 | CAP |

| | 1978 | | 1979 | | 1980 | | 1981 | | 1982 | | 1983 | |
|-----|----|-----|----|-----|----|-----|----|-----|----|-----|----|-----|
| JAN | 21 | AQU | 21 | AQU | 21 | AQU | 20 | AQU | 21 | AQU | 21 | AQU |
| FEB | 19 | PIS | 20 | PIS | 20 | PIS | 19 | PIS | 19 | PIS | 20 | PIS |
| MAR | 21 | ARI | 22 | ARI | 21 | ARI | 21 | ARI | 21 | ARI | 21 | ARI |
| APR | 21 | TAU | 21 | TAU | 20 | TAU | 20 | TAU | 21 | TAU | 21 | TAU |
| MAY | 22 | GEM | 22 | GEM | 21 | GEM | 21 | GEM | 22 | GEM | 22 | GEM |
| JUN | 22 | CAN | 22 | CAN | 22 | CAN | 22 | CAN | 22 | CAN | 22 | CAN |
| JUL | 23 | LEO | 24 | LEO | 23 | LEO | 23 | LEO | 23 | LEO | 24 | LEO |
| AUG | 24 | VIR | 24 | VIR | 23 | VIR | 24 | VIR | 24 | VIR | 24 | VIR |
| SEP | 24 | LIB | 24 | LIB | 23 | LIB | 23 | LIB | 24 | LIB | 24 | LIB |
| OCT | 24 | SCO | 24 | SCO | 24 | SCO | 24 | SCO | 24 | SCO | 24 | SCO |
| NOV | 23 | SAG | 23 | SAG | 22 | SAG | 23 | SAG | 23 | SAG | 23 | SAG |
| DEC | 23 | CAP | 23 | CAP | 22 | CAP | 22 | CAP | 22 | CAP | 23 | CAP |

| | 1984 | | 1985 | | 1986 | | 1987 | | 1988 | | 1989 | |
|-----|----|-----|----|-----|----|-----|----|-----|----|-----|----|-----|
| JAN | 21 | AQU | 20 | AQU | 21 | AQU | 21 | AQU | 21 | AQU | 20 | AQU |
| FEB | 20 | PIS | 19 | PIS | 19 | PIS | 19 | PIS | 20 | PIS | 19 | PIS |
| MAR | 21 | ARI | 21 | ARI | 21 | ARI | 21 | ARI | 21 | ARI | 21 | ARI |
| APR | 20 | TAU | 20 | TAU | 21 | TAU | 21 | TAU | 20 | TAU | 20 | TAU |
| MAY | 21 | GEM | 21 | GEM | 22 | GEM | 22 | GEM | 21 | GEM | 21 | GEM |
| JUN | 21 | CAN | 22 | CAN | 22 | CAN | 22 | CAN | 21 | CAN | 22 | CAN |
| JUL | 23 | LEO | 23 | LEO | 23 | LEO | 24 | LEO | 23 | LEO | 23 | LEO |
| AUG | 23 | VIR | 23 | VIR | 24 | VIR | 24 | VIR | 23 | VIR | 23 | VIR |
| SEP | 23 | LIB | 23 | LIB | 24 | LIB | 24 | LIB | 23 | LIB | 23 | LIB |
| OCT | 24 | SCO | 24 | SCO | 24 | SCO | 24 | SCO | 23 | SCO | 24 | SCO |
| NOV | 22 | SAG | 23 | SAG | 23 | SAG | 23 | SAG | 22 | SAG | 23 | SAG |
| DEC | 22 | CAP | 22 | CAP | 22 | CAP | 23 | CAP | 22 | CAP | 22 | CAP |

| | 1990 | | 1991 | | 1992 | | 1993 | | 1994 | | 1995 | |
|-----|----|-----|----|-----|----|-----|----|-----|----|-----|----|-----|
| JAN | 21 | AQU | 21 | AQU | 21 | AQU | 20 | AQU | 21 | AQU | 21 | AQU |
| FEB | 19 | PIS | 19 | PIS | 20 | PIS | 19 | PIS | 19 | PIS | 19 | PIS |
| MAR | 21 | ARI | 21 | ARI | 21 | ARI | 21 | ARI | 21 | ARI | 21 | ARI |
| APR | 21 | TAU | 21 | TAU | 20 | TAU | 20 | TAU | 21 | TAU | 21 | TAU |
| MAY | 22 | GEM | 22 | GEM | 21 | GEM | 21 | GEM | 22 | GEM | 22 | GEM |
| JUN | 22 | CAN | 22 | CAN | 21 | CAN | 22 | CAN | 22 | CAN | 22 | CAN |
| JUL | 23 | LEO | 24 | LEO | 23 | LEO | 23 | LEO | 23 | LEO | 24 | LEO |
| AUG | 24 | VIR | 24 | VIR | 23 | VIR | 23 | VIR | 24 | VIR | 24 | VIR |
| SEP | 24 | LIB | 24 | LIB | 23 | LIB | 23 | LIB | 24 | LIB | 24 | LIB |
| OCT | 24 | SCO | 24 | SCO | 23 | SCO | 24 | SCO | 24 | SCO | 24 | SCO |
| NOV | 23 | SAG | 23 | SAG | 22 | SAG | 23 | SAG | 23 | SAG | 23 | SAG |
| DEC | 22 | CAP | 23 | CAP | 22 | CAP | 22 | CAP | 22 | CAP | 23 | CAP |

# Sun Signs 1945-2025

| | 1996 | 1997 | 1998 | 1999 | 2000 | 2001 |
|-----|--------|--------|--------|--------|--------|--------|
| JAN | 21 AQU | 20 AQU | 21 AQU | 21 AQU | 21 AQU | 20 AQU |
| FEB | 20 PIS | 19 PIS | 19 PIS | 19 PIS | 20 PIS | 19 PIS |
| MAR | 21 ARI | 21 ARI | 21 ARI | 21 ARI | 21 ARI | 21 ARI |
| APR | 20 TAU | 20 TAU | 21 TAU | 21 TAU | 20 TAU | 20 TAU |
| MAY | 21 GEM | 21 GEM | 22 GEM | 22 GEM | 21 GEM | 21 GEM |
| JUN | 21 CAN | 22 CAN | 22 CAN | 22 CAN | 21 CAN | 22 CAN |
| JUL | 23 LEO | 23 LEO | 23 LEO | 24 LEO | 23 LEO | 23 LEO |
| AUG | 23 VIR | 23 VIR | 24 VIR | 24 VIR | 23 VIR | 23 VIR |
| SEP | 23 LIB | 23 LIB | 24 LIB | 24 LIB | 23 LIB | 23 LIB |
| OCT | 23 SCO | 24 SCO | 24 SCO | 24 SCO | 23 SCO | 24 SCO |
| NOV | 22 SAG | 23 SAG | 23 SAG | 23 SAG | 22 SAG | 23 SAG |
| DEC | 22 CAP | 22 CAP | 22 CAP | 23 CAP | 22 CAP | 22 CAP |

| | 2002 | 2003 | 2004 | 2005 | 2006 | 2007 |
|-----|--------|--------|--------|--------|--------|--------|
| JAN | 21 AQU | 21 AQU | 21 AQU | 20 AQU | 20 AQU | 21 AQU |
| FEB | 19 PIS | 19 PIS | 20 PIS | 19 PIS | 19 PIS | 19 PIS |
| MAR | 21 ARI | 21 ARI | 21 ARI | 21 ARI | 21 ARI | 21 ARI |
| APR | 21 TAU | 21 TAU | 20 TAU | 20 TAU | 21 TAU | 21 TAU |
| MAY | 22 GEM | 22 GEM | 21 GEM | 21 GEM | 21 GEM | 22 GEM |
| JUN | 22 CAN | 22 CAN | 21 CAN | 22 CAN | 22 CAN | 22 CAN |
| JUL | 23 LEO | 24 LEO | 23 LEO | 23 LEO | 23 LEO | 23 LEO |
| AUG | 24 VIR | 24 VIR | 23 VIR | 23 VIR | 24 VIR | 24 VIR |
| SEP | 23 LIB | 24 LIB | 23 LIB | 23 LIB | 23 LIB | 24 LIB |
| OCT | 24 SCO | 24 SCO | 23 SCO | 24 SCO | 24 SCO | 24 SCO |
| NOV | 23 SAG | 23 SAG | 22 SAG | 23 SAG | 23 SAG | 23 SAG |
| DEC | 22 CAP | 23 CAP | 22 CAP | 22 CAP | 22 CAP | 23 CAP |

| | 2008 | 2009 | 2010 | 2011 | 2012 | 2013 |
|-----|--------|--------|--------|--------|--------|--------|
| JAN | 21 AQU | 20 AQU | 20 AQU | 21 AQU | 21 AQU | 20 AQU |
| FEB | 20 PIS | 19 PIS | 19 PIS | 19 PIS | 20 PIS | 19 PIS |
| MAR | 21 ARI | 21 ARI | 21 ARI | 21 ARI | 20 ARI | 21 ARI |
| APR | 20 TAU | 20 TAU | 20 TAU | 21 TAU | 20 TAU | 20 TAU |
| MAY | 21 GEM | 21 GEM | 21 GEM | 22 GEM | 21 GEM | 21 GEM |
| JUN | 21 CAN | 22 CAN | 22 CAN | 22 CAN | 21 CAN | 21 CAN |
| JUL | 23 LEO | 23 LEO | 23 LEO | 23 LEO | 23 LEO | 23 LEO |
| AUG | 23 VIR | 23 VIR | 24 VIR | 24 VIR | 23 VIR | 23 VIR |
| SEP | 23 LIB | 23 LIB | 23 LIB | 24 LIB | 23 LIB | 23 LIB |
| OCT | 23 SCO | 24 SCO | 24 SCO | 24 SCO | 23 SCO | 24 SCO |
| NOV | 22 SAG | 22 SAG | 23 SAG | 23 SAG | 22 SAG | 22 SAG |
| DEC | 22 CAP | 22 CAP | 22 CAP | 23 CAP | 22 CAP | 22 CAP |

| | 2014 | 2015 | 2016 | 2017 | 2018 | 2019 |
|-----|--------|--------|--------|--------|--------|--------|
| JAN | 20 AQU | 21 AQU | 21 AQU | 20 AQU | 20 AQU | 21 AQU |
| FEB | 19 PIS | 19 PIS | 20 PIS | 19 PIS | 19 PIS | 19 PIS |
| MAR | 21 ARI | 21 ARI | 20 ARI | 21 ARI | 21 ARI | 21 ARI |
| APR | 20 TAU | 21 TAU | 20 TAU | 20 TAU | 20 TAU | 21 TAU |
| MAY | 21 GEM | 22 GEM | 21 GEM | 21 GEM | 21 GEM | 22 GEM |
| JUN | 22 CAN | 22 CAN | 21 CAN | 21 CAN | 22 CAN | 22 CAN |
| JUL | 23 LEO | 23 LEO | 23 LEO | 23 LEO | 23 LEO | 23 LEO |
| AUG | 23 VIR | 24 VIR | 23 VIR | 23 VIR | 23 VIR | 24 VIR |
| SEP | 23 LIB | 24 LIB | 23 LIB | 23 LIB | 23 LIB | 24 LIB |
| OCT | 24 SCO | 24 SCO | 23 SCO | 24 SCO | 24 SCO | 24 SCO |
| NOV | 23 SAG | 23 SAG | 22 SAG | 22 SAG | 23 SAG | 23 SAG |
| DEC | 22 CAP | 22 CAP | 22 CAP | 22 CAP | 22 CAP | 22 CAP |

# Sun Signs 1945-2025

| | 2020 | | 2021 | | 2022 | | 2023 | | 2024 | | 2025 | |
|-----|----|-----|----|-----|----|-----|----|-----|----|-----|----|-----|
| JAN | 21 | AQU | 20 | AQU | 20 | AQU | 21 | AQU | 21 | AQU | 20 | AQU |
| FEB | 19 | PIS | 19 | PIS | 19 | PIS | 19 | PIS | 19 | PIS | 19 | PIS |
| MAR | 20 | ARI | 21 | ARI | 21 | ARI | 21 | ARI | 20 | ARI | 21 | ARI |
| APR | 20 | TAU | 20 | TAU | 20 | TAU | 21 | TAU | 20 | TAU | 20 | TAU |
| MAY | 21 | GEM | 21 | GEM | 21 | GEM | 22 | GEM | 21 | GEM | 21 | GEM |
| JUN | 21 | CAN | 21 | CAN | 22 | CAN | 22 | CAN | 21 | CAN | 21 | CAN |
| JUL | 23 | LEO | 23 | LEO | 23 | LEO | 23 | LEO | 23 | LEO | 23 | LEO |
| AUG | 23 | VIR | 23 | VIR | 23 | VIR | 24 | VIR | 23 | VIR | 23 | VIR |
| SEP | 23 | LIB | 23 | LIB | 23 | LIB | 24 | LIB | 23 | LIB | 23 | LIB |
| OCT | 23 | SCO | 23 | SCO | 24 | SCO | 24 | SCO | 23 | SCO | 23 | SCO |
| NOV | 22 | SAG | 22 | SAG | 23 | SAG | 23 | SAG | 22 | SAG | 22 | SAG |
| DEC | 22 | CAP | 22 | CAP | 22 | CAP | 22 | CAP | 22 | CAP | 22 | CAP |

## Sign Abbreviations

| | | | |
|-----|--------|-----|-------------|
| ARI | Aries  | LIB | Libra       |
| TAU | Taurus | SCO | Scorpio     |
| GEM | Gemini | SAG | Sagittarius |
| CAN | Cancer | CAP | Capricorn   |
| LEO | Leo    | AQU | Aquarius    |
| VIR | Virgo  | PIS | Pisces      |

## ONE FREE CHART CALCULATION OFFER!

In most cases, the tables in this book will give you the correct sign—but in some cases, if the time of birth was hours away from the GMT time listed, the sign may have changed. If you want to be sure, it is best to have an accurately calculated chart for the exact birth date, time and location.

### ASTRO COMPUTING SERVICES

will send you ONE FREE CHART, if you bought the book from us or can send us proof of purchase of the book elsewhere. Be sure to include birth date, time of birth and location of birth, and your mailing address (or email address if you'd prefer to receive the chart as a PDF file). The chart will be our Student Chart, a clear graphic chart wheel with a list beneath it that identifies each glyph, plus the aspects between the planets, in English.

**Astro Computing Services, operated by Starcrafts LLC**
**ACS Publications and Starcrafts Publishing**
**334-A Calef Highway, Epping, NH 03042**
*www.astrocom.com*

# HOW TO USE THE MOON SIGN TABLES

The Moon moves very quickly through the signs each month, staying in a sign approximately two and a half days. These Moon Sign tables show the date that the Moon moved into a new sign for each month.

If you are checking a birthdate that was on a day when the Moon is listed as having been in a different sign on the day prior to the birthday, or will be in a different sign on the day after the birthday, then **it is not possible to know for sure which is the correct sign unless you obtain a calculation for the birth chart based on date, time and location of birth.**

It is likely that you might intuitively know which of the signs on, and just before or after cusp days, is the correct one, if you read the interpretive text in this book for Moon in each of the signs. Adjacent signs have quite different traits, so if you read both profiles, you should sense and know which sign best fits the person in question.

Find the year and month of the birth, then use a ruler across the page to help you move down the page to the right day.

## Moon Signs 1945-2025

**1945**

| JAN | | FEB | | MAR | | APR | | MAY | | JUN | |
|---|---|---|---|---|---|---|---|---|---|---|---|
| 2 | VIR | 1 | LIB | 3 | SCO | 1 | SAG | 1 | CAP | 2 | PIS |
| 4 | LIB | 3 | SCO | 5 | SAG | 4 | CAP | 3 | AQU | 4 | ARI |
| 7 | SCO | 6 | SAG | 8 | CAP | 6 | AQU | 6 | PIS | 6 | TAU |
| 9 | SAG | 8 | CAP | 10 | AQU | 8 | PIS | 8 | ARI | 8 | GEM |
| 12 | CAP | 10 | AQU | 12 | PIS | 10 | ARI | 10 | TAU | 10 | CAN |
| 14 | AQU | 12 | PIS | 14 | ARI | 12 | TAU | 12 | GEM | 12 | LEO |
| 16 | PIS | 14 | ARI | 16 | TAU | 14 | GEM | 14 | CAN | 15 | VIR |
| 18 | ARI | 17 | TAU | 18 | GEM | 16 | CAN | 16 | LEO | 17 | LIB |
| 20 | TAU | 19 | GEM | 20 | CAN | 19 | LEO | 18 | VIR | 20 | SCO |
| 22 | GEM | 21 | CAN | 22 | LEO | 21 | VIR | 21 | LIB | 22 | SAG |
| 25 | CAN | 23 | LEO | 25 | VIR | 24 | LIB | 23 | SCO | 25 | CAP |
| 27 | LEO | 26 | VIR | 27 | LIB | 26 | SCO | 26 | SAG | 27 | AQU |
| 29 | VIR | 28 | LIB | 30 | SCO | 29 | SAG | 28 | CAP | 29 | PIS |
| | | | | | | | | 31 | AQU | | |

| JUL | | AUG | | SEP | | OCT | | NOV | | DEC | |
|---|---|---|---|---|---|---|---|---|---|---|---|
| 1 | ARI | 2 | GEM | 2 | LEO | 2 | VIR | 1 | LIB | 3 | SAG |
| 3 | TAU | 4 | CAN | 5 | VIR | 4 | LIB | 3 | SCO | 6 | CAP |
| 6 | GEM | 6 | LEO | 7 | LIB | 7 | SCO | 6 | SAG | 8 | AQU |
| 8 | CAN | 8 | VIR | 10 | SCO | 10 | SAG | 8 | CAP | 10 | PIS |
| 10 | LEO | 11 | LIB | 12 | SAG | 12 | CAP | 11 | AQU | 12 | ARI |
| 12 | VIR | 13 | SCO | 15 | CAP | 14 | AQU | 13 | PIS | 15 | TAU |
| 15 | LIB | 16 | SAG | 17 | AQU | 17 | PIS | 15 | ARI | 17 | GEM |
| 17 | SCO | 18 | CAP | 19 | PIS | 19 | ARI | 17 | TAU | 19 | CAN |
| 20 | SAG | 21 | AQU | 21 | ARI | 21 | TAU | 19 | GEM | 21 | LEO |
| 22 | CAP | 23 | PIS | 23 | TAU | 23 | GEM | 21 | CAN | 23 | VIR |
| 24 | AQU | 25 | ARI | 25 | GEM | 25 | CAN | 23 | LEO | 25 | LIB |
| 26 | PIS | 27 | TAU | 27 | CAN | 27 | LEO | 26 | VIR | 28 | SCO |
| 29 | ARI | 29 | GEM | 30 | LEO | 29 | VIR | 28 | LIB | 30 | SAG |
| 31 | TAU | 31 | CAN | | | | | 30 | SCO | | |

# Moon Signs 1945-2025

## 1946

| | JAN | | FEB | | MAR | | APR | | MAY | | JUN |
|---|---|---|---|---|---|---|---|---|---|---|---|
| 2 | CAP | 1 | AQU | 2 | PIS | 1 | ARI | 2 | GEM | 1 | CAN |
| 4 | AQU | 3 | PIS | 4 | ARI | 3 | TAU | 4 | CAN | 3 | LEO |
| 6 | PIS | 5 | ARI | 6 | TAU | 5 | GEM | 6 | LEO | 5 | VIR |
| 9 | ARI | 7 | TAU | 8 | GEM | 7 | CAN | 8 | VIR | 7 | LIB |
| 11 | TAU | 9 | GEM | 11 | CAN | 9 | LEO | 11 | LIB | 10 | SCO |
| 13 | GEM | 11 | CAN | 13 | LEO | 11 | VIR | 13 | SCO | 12 | SAG |
| 15 | CAN | 13 | LEO | 15 | VIR | 14 | LIB | 16 | SAG | 15 | CAP |
| 17 | LEO | 16 | VIR | 17 | LIB | 16 | SCO | 18 | CAP | 17 | AQU |
| 19 | VIR | 18 | LIB | 20 | SCO | 19 | SAG | 21 | AQU | 20 | PIS |
| 22 | LIB | 20 | SCO | 22 | SAG | 21 | CAP | 23 | PIS | 22 | ARI |
| 24 | SCO | 23 | SAG | 25 | CAP | 24 | AQU | 26 | ARI | 24 | TAU |
| 27 | SAG | 26 | CAP | 27 | AQU | 26 | PIS | 28 | TAU | 26 | GEM |
| 29 | CAP | 28 | AQU | 30 | PIS | 28 | ARI | 30 | GEM | 28 | CAN |
| | | | | | | 30 | TAU | | | 30 | LEO |

| | JUL | | AUG | | SEP | | OCT | | NOV | | DEC |
|---|---|---|---|---|---|---|---|---|---|---|---|
| 2 | VIR | 1 | LIB | 2 | SAG | 2 | CAP | 1 | AQU | 3 | ARI |
| 4 | LIB | 3 | SCO | 5 | CAP | 4 | AQU | 3 | PIS | 5 | TAU |
| 7 | SCO | 6 | SAG | 7 | AQU | 7 | PIS | 5 | ARI | 7 | GEM |
| 9 | SAG | 8 | CAP | 9 | PIS | 9 | ARI | 7 | TAU | 9 | CAN |
| 12 | CAP | 11 | AQU | 12 | ARI | 11 | TAU | 10 | GEM | 11 | LEO |
| 14 | AQU | 13 | PIS | 14 | TAU | 13 | GEM | 12 | CAN | 13 | VIR |
| 17 | PIS | 15 | ARI | 16 | GEM | 15 | CAN | 14 | LEO | 15 | LIB |
| 19 | ARI | 17 | TAU | 18 | CAN | 17 | LEO | 16 | VIR | 18 | SCO |
| 21 | TAU | 20 | GEM | 20 | LEO | 20 | VIR | 18 | LIB | 20 | SAG |
| 23 | GEM | 22 | CAN | 22 | VIR | 22 | LIB | 20 | SCO | 23 | CAP |
| 25 | CAN | 24 | LEO | 25 | LIB | 24 | SCO | 23 | SAG | 25 | AQU |
| 27 | LEO | 26 | VIR | 27 | SCO | 27 | SAG | 25 | CAP | 28 | PIS |
| 30 | VIR | 28 | LIB | 29 | SAG | 29 | CAP | 28 | AQU | 30 | ARI |
| | | 31 | SCO | | | | | 30 | PIS | | |

## 1947

| | JAN | | FEB | | MAR | | APR | | MAY | | JUN |
|---|---|---|---|---|---|---|---|---|---|---|---|
| 1 | TAU | 2 | CAN | 1 | CAN | 2 | VIR | 1 | LIB | 2 | SAG |
| 3 | GEM | 4 | LEO | 3 | LEO | 4 | LIB | 3 | SCO | 5 | CAP |
| 5 | CAN | 6 | VIR | 5 | VIR | 6 | SCO | 6 | SAG | 7 | AQU |
| 7 | LEO | 8 | LIB | 7 | LIB | 8 | SAG | 8 | CAP | 10 | PIS |
| 9 | VIR | 10 | SCO | 10 | SCO | 11 | CAP | 11 | AQU | 12 | ARI |
| 12 | LIB | 13 | SAG | 12 | SAG | 13 | AQU | 13 | PIS | 14 | TAU |
| 14 | SCO | 15 | CAP | 15 | CAP | 16 | PIS | 16 | ARI | 16 | GEM |
| 16 | SAG | 18 | AQU | 17 | AQU | 18 | ARI | 18 | TAU | 18 | CAN |
| 19 | CAP | 20 | PIS | 20 | PIS | 20 | TAU | 20 | GEM | 20 | LEO |
| 22 | AQU | 23 | ARI | 22 | ARI | 23 | GEM | 22 | CAN | 22 | VIR |
| 24 | PIS | 25 | TAU | 24 | TAU | 25 | CAN | 24 | LEO | 25 | LIB |
| 26 | ARI | 27 | GEM | 26 | GEM | 27 | LEO | 26 | VIR | 27 | SCO |
| 29 | TAU | | | 28 | CAN | 29 | VIR | 28 | LIB | 29 | SAG |
| 31 | GEM | | | 31 | LEO | | | 31 | SCO | | |

| | JUL | | AUG | | SEP | | OCT | | NOV | | DEC |
|---|---|---|---|---|---|---|---|---|---|---|---|
| 2 | CAP | 1 | AQU | 2 | ARI | 1 | TAU | 2 | CAN | 1 | LEO |
| 4 | AQU | 3 | PIS | 4 | TAU | 4 | GEM | 4 | LEO | 3 | VIR |
| 7 | PIS | 6 | ARI | 6 | GEM | 6 | CAN | 6 | VIR | 6 | LIB |
| 9 | ARI | 8 | TAU | 9 | CAN | 8 | LEO | 8 | LIB | 8 | SCO |
| 12 | TAU | 10 | GEM | 11 | LEO | 10 | VIR | 11 | SCO | 10 | SAG |
| 14 | GEM | 12 | CAN | 13 | VIR | 12 | LIB | 13 | SAG | 13 | CAP |
| 16 | CAN | 14 | LEO | 15 | LIB | 14 | SCO | 15 | CAP | 15 | AQU |
| 18 | LEO | 16 | VIR | 17 | SCO | 17 | SAG | 18 | AQU | 18 | PIS |
| 20 | VIR | 18 | LIB | 19 | SAG | 19 | CAP | 20 | PIS | 20 | ARI |
| 22 | LIB | 20 | SCO | 22 | CAP | 22 | AQU | 23 | ARI | 23 | TAU |
| 24 | SCO | 23 | SAG | 24 | AQU | 24 | PIS | 25 | TAU | 25 | GEM |
| 27 | SAG | 25 | CAP | 27 | PIS | 26 | ARI | 27 | GEM | 27 | CAN |
| 29 | CAP | 28 | AQU | 29 | ARI | 29 | TAU | 29 | CAN | 29 | LEO |
| | | 30 | PIS | | | 31 | GEM | | | 31 | VIR |

# Moon Signs 1945-2025

## 1948

| | JAN | | FEB | | MAR | | APR | | MAY | | JUN |
|---|---|---|---|---|---|---|---|---|---|---|---|
| 2 | LIB | 3 | SAG | 1 | SAG | 2 | AQU | 2 | PIS | 1 | ARI |
| 4 | SCO | 5 | CAP | 3 | CAP | 5 | PIS | 5 | ARI | 3 | TAU |
| 6 | SAG | 8 | AQU | 6 | AQU | 7 | ARI | 7 | TAU | 6 | GEM |
| 9 | CAP | 10 | PIS | 8 | PIS | 10 | TAU | 9 | GEM | 9 | CAN |
| 11 | AQU | 13 | ARI | 11 | ARI | 12 | GEM | 11 | CAN | 10 | LEO |
| 14 | PIS | 15 | TAU | 13 | TAU | 14 | CAn | 14 | LEO | 12 | VIR |
| 16 | ARI | 17 | GEM | 16 | GEM | 16 | LEO | 16 | VIR | 14 | LIB |
| 19 | TAU | 20 | CAN | 18 | CAN | 18 | VIR | 18 | LIB | 16 | SCO |
| 21 | GEM | 22 | LEO | 20 | LEO | 21 | LIB | 20 | SCO | 18 | SAG |
| 23 | CAN | 24 | VIR | 22 | VIR | 23 | SCO | 22 | SAG | 21 | CAP |
| 25 | LEO | 26 | LIB | 24 | LIB | 25 | SAG | 25 | CAP | 23 | AQU |
| 27 | VIR | 28 | SCO | 26 | SCO | 27 | CAP | 27 | AQU | 26 | PIS |
| 29 | LIB | | | 28 | SAG | 30 | AQU | 29 | PIS | 28 | ARI |
| 31 | SCO | | | 31 | CAP | | | | | | |

| | JUL | | AUG | | SEP | | OCT | | NOV | | DEC |
|---|---|---|---|---|---|---|---|---|---|---|---|
| 1 | TAU | 2 | CAN | 2 | VIR | 1 | LIB | 2 | SAG | 2 | CAP |
| 3 | GEM | 4 | LEO | 4 | LIB | 3 | SCO | 4 | CAP | 4 | AQU |
| 5 | CAN | 6 | VIR | 6 | SCO | 6 | SAG | 7 | AQU | 6 | PIS |
| 7 | LEO | 8 | LIB | 8 | SAG | 8 | CAP | 9 | PIS | 9 | ARI |
| 9 | VIR | 10 | SCO | 11 | CAP | 10 | AQU | 12 | ARI | 12 | TAU |
| 11 | LIB | 12 | SAG | 13 | AQU | 13 | PIS | 14 | TAU | 14 | GEM |
| 13 | SCO | 14 | CAP | 16 | PIS | 15 | ARI | 17 | GEM | 16 | CAN |
| 16 | SAG | 17 | AQU | 18 | ARI | 18 | TAU | 19 | CAN | 18 | LEO |
| 18 | CAP | 19 | PIS | 21 | TAU | 20 | GEM | 21 | LEO | 20 | VIR |
| 21 | AQU | 22 | ARI | 23 | GEM | 23 | CAN | 23 | VIR | 22 | LIB |
| 23 | PIS | 24 | TAU | 25 | CAN | 25 | LEO | 25 | LIB | 25 | SCO |
| 26 | ARI | 27 | GEM | 27 | LEO | 27 | VIR | 27 | SCO | 27 | SAG |
| 28 | TAU | 29 | CAN | 29 | VIR | 29 | LIB | 29 | SAG | 29 | CAP |
| 30 | GEM | 31 | LEO | | | 31 | SCO | | | 31 | AQU |

## 1949

| | JAN | | FEB | | MAR | | APR | | MAY | | JUN |
|---|---|---|---|---|---|---|---|---|---|---|---|
| 3 | PIS | 2 | ARI | 1 | ARI | 2 | GEM | 2 | CAN | 2 | VIR |
| 5 | ARI | 4 | TAU | 3 | TAU | 5 | CAN | 4 | LEO | 5 | LIB |
| 8 | TAU | 7 | GEM | 6 | GEM | 7 | LEO | 6 | VIR | 7 | SCO |
| 10 | GEM | 9 | CAN | 8 | CAN | 9 | VIR | 8 | LIB | 9 | SAG |
| 12 | CAN | 11 | LEO | 10 | LEO | 11 | LIB | 10 | SCO | 11 | CAP |
| 15 | LEO | 13 | VIR | 13 | VIR | 13 | SCO | 12 | SAG | 13 | AQU |
| 17 | VIR | 15 | LIB | 15 | LIB | 15 | SAG | 15 | CAP | 16 | PIS |
| 19 | LIB | 17 | SCO | 17 | SCO | 17 | CAP | 17 | AQU | 18 | ARI |
| 21 | SCO | 19 | SAG | 19 | SAG | 19 | AQU | 19 | PIS | 21 | TAU |
| 23 | SAG | 22 | CAP | 21 | CAP | 22 | PIS | 22 | ARI | 23 | GEM |
| 25 | CAP | 24 | AQU | 23 | AQU | 24 | ARI | 24 | TAU | 25 | CAN |
| 28 | AQU | 26 | PIS | 26 | PIS | 27 | TAU | 27 | GEM | 28 | LEO |
| 30 | PIS | | | 28 | ARI | 29 | GEM | 29 | CAN | 30 | VIR |
| | | | | 31 | TAU | | | 31 | LEO | | |

| | JUL | | AUG | | SEP | | OCT | | NOV | | DEC |
|---|---|---|---|---|---|---|---|---|---|---|---|
| 2 | LIB | 2 | SAG | 1 | CAP | 3 | PIS | 2 | ARI | 1 | TAU |
| 4 | SCO | 5 | CAP | 3 | AQU | 5 | ARI | 4 | TAU | 4 | GEM |
| 6 | SAG | 7 | AQU | 6 | PIS | 8 | TAU | 6 | GEM | 6 | CAN |
| 8 | CAP | 9 | PIS | 8 | ARI | 10 | GEM | 9 | CAN | 9 | LEO |
| 11 | AQU | 12 | ARI | 11 | TAU | 13 | CAN | 11 | LEO | 11 | VIR |
| 13 | PIS | 14 | TAU | 13 | GEM | 15 | LEO | 14 | VIR | 13 | LIB |
| 15 | ARI | 17 | GEM | 15 | CAN | 17 | VIR | 16 | LIB | 15 | SCO |
| 18 | TAU | 19 | CAN | 18 | LEO | 19 | LIB | 18 | SCO | 17 | SAG |
| 20 | GEM | 21 | LEO | 20 | VIR | 21 | SCO | 20 | SAG | 19 | CAP |
| 23 | CAN | 23 | VIR | 22 | LIB | 23 | SAG | 22 | CAP | 21 | AQU |
| 25 | LEO | 25 | LIB | 24 | SCO | 25 | CAP | 24 | AQU | 24 | PIS |
| 27 | VIR | 27 | SCO | 26 | SAG | 28 | AQU | 26 | PIS | 26 | ARI |
| 29 | LIB | 30 | SAG | 28 | CAP | 30 | PIS | 29 | ARI | 29 | TAU |
| 31 | SCO | | | 30 | AQU | | | | | 31 | GEM |

# Moon Signs 1945-2025

## 1950

| | JAN | | FEB | | MAR | | APR | | MAY | | JUN |
|---|---|---|---|---|---|---|---|---|---|---|---|
| 3 | CAN | 1 | LEO | 1 | LEO | 1 | LIB | 1 | SCO | 1 | CAP |
| 5 | LEO | 3 | VIR | 3 | VIR | 3 | SCO | 3 | SAG | 3 | AQU |
| 7 | VIR | 6 | LIB | 5 | LIB | 5 | SAG | 5 | CAP | 5 | PIS |
| 9 | LIB | 8 | SCO | 7 | SCO | 7 | CAP | 7 | AQU | 8 | ARI |
| 11 | SCO | 10 | SAG | 9 | SAG | 10 | AQU | 9 | PIS | 10 | TAU |
| 14 | SAG | 12 | CAP | 11 | CAP | 12 | PIS | 12 | ARI | 13 | GEM |
| 16 | CAP | 14 | AQU | 13 | AQU | 14 | ARI | 14 | TAU | 15 | CAN |
| 18 | AQU | 16 | PIS | 16 | PIS | 17 | TAU | 17 | GEM | 18 | LEO |
| 20 | PIS | 19 | ARI | 18 | ARI | 19 | GEM | 19 | CAN | 20 | VIR |
| 22 | ARI | 21 | TAU | 21 | TAU | 22 | CAN | 22 | LEO | 22 | LIB |
| 25 | TAU | 24 | GEM | 23 | GEM | 24 | LEO | 24 | VIR | 25 | SCO |
| 28 | GEM | 26 | CAN | 25 | CAN | 27 | VIR | 26 | LIB | 27 | SAG |
| 30 | CAN | | | 28 | LEO | 29 | LIB | 28 | SCO | 29 | CAP |
| | | | | 30 | VIR | | | 30 | SAG | | |

| | JUL | | AUG | | SEP | | OCT | | NOV | | DEC |
|---|---|---|---|---|---|---|---|---|---|---|---|
| 1 | AQU | 2 | ARI | 2 | GEM | 3 | CAN | 2 | LEO | 1 | VIR |
| 3 | PIS | 4 | TAU | 5 | CAN | 5 | LEO | 4 | VIR | 3 | LIB |
| 5 | ARI | 7 | GEM | 8 | LEO | 7 | VIR | 6 | LIB | 6 | SCO |
| 8 | TAU | 9 | CAN | 10 | VIR | 10 | LIB | 8 | SCO | 8 | SAG |
| 10 | GEM | 11 | LEO | 12 | LIB | 12 | SCO | 10 | SAG | 10 | CAP |
| 13 | CAN | 14 | VIR | 14 | SCO | 14 | SAG | 12 | CAP | 12 | AQU |
| 15 | LEO | 16 | LIB | 16 | SAG | 16 | CAP | 14 | AQU | 14 | PIS |
| 17 | VIR | 18 | SCO | 18 | CAP | 18 | AQU | 16 | PIS | 16 | ARI |
| 20 | LIB | 20 | SAG | 21 | AQU | 20 | PIS | 19 | ARI | 19 | TAU |
| 22 | SCO | 22 | CAP | 23 | PIS | 23 | ARI | 21 | TAU | 21 | GEM |
| 24 | SAG | 24 | AQU | 25 | ARI | 25 | TAU | 24 | GEM | 24 | CAN |
| 26 | CAP | 27 | PIS | 28 | TAU | 28 | GEM | 26 | CAN | 26 | LEO |
| 28 | AQU | 29 | ARI | 30 | GEM | 30 | CAN | 29 | LEO | 28 | VIR |
| 30 | PIS | 31 | TAU | | | | | | | 31 | LIB |

## 1951

| | JAN | | FEB | | MAR | | APR | | MAY | | JUN |
|---|---|---|---|---|---|---|---|---|---|---|---|
| 2 | SCO | 2 | CAP | 2 | CAP | 2 | PIS | 2 | ARI | 3 | GEM |
| 4 | SAG | 4 | AQU | 4 | AQU | 5 | ARI | 4 | TAU | 5 | CAN |
| 6 | CAP | 7 | PIS | 6 | PIS | 7 | TAU | 7 | GEM | 8 | LEO |
| 8 | AQU | 9 | ARI | 8 | ARI | 9 | GEM | 9 | CAN | 10 | VIR |
| 10 | PIS | 11 | TAU | 11 | TAU | 12 | CAN | 12 | LEO | 13 | LIB |
| 12 | ARI | 14 | GEM | 13 | GEM | 14 | LEO | 14 | VIR | 15 | SCO |
| 15 | TAU | 16 | CAN | 16 | CAN | 17 | VIR | 16 | LIB | 17 | SAG |
| 17 | GEM | 19 | LEO | 18 | LEO | 19 | LIB | 19 | SCO | 19 | CAP |
| 20 | CAN | 21 | VIR | 20 | VIR | 21 | SCO | 21 | SAG | 21 | AQU |
| 22 | LEO | 23 | LIB | 23 | LIB | 23 | SAG | 23 | CAP | 23 | PIS |
| 25 | VIR | 25 | SCO | 25 | SCO | 25 | CAP | 25 | AQU | 25 | ARI |
| 27 | LIB | 28 | SAG | 27 | SAG | 27 | AQU | 27 | PIS | 28 | TAU |
| 29 | SCO | | | 29 | CAP | 29 | PIS | 29 | ARI | 30 | GEM |
| 31 | SAG | | | 31 | AQU | | | 31 | TAU | | |

| | JUL | | AUG | | SEP | | OCT | | NOV | | DEC |
|---|---|---|---|---|---|---|---|---|---|---|---|
| 3 | CAN | 1 | LEO | 3 | LIB | 2 | SCO | 1 | SAG | 2 | AQU |
| 5 | LEO | 4 | VIR | 5 | SCO | 4 | SAG | 3 | CAP | 4 | PIS |
| 8 | VIR | 6 | LIB | 7 | SAG | 6 | CAP | 5 | AQU | 6 | ARI |
| 10 | LIB | 9 | SCO | 9 | CAP | 8 | AQU | 7 | PIS | 9 | TAU |
| 12 | SCO | 11 | SAG | 11 | AQU | 11 | PIS | 9 | ARI | 11 | GEM |
| 14 | SAG | 13 | CAP | 13 | PIS | 13 | ARI | 11 | TAU | 13 | CAN |
| 16 | CAP | 15 | AQU | 15 | ARI | 15 | TAU | 14 | GEM | 16 | LEO |
| 18 | AQU | 17 | PIS | 18 | TAU | 17 | GEM | 16 | CAN | 19 | VIR |
| 20 | PIS | 19 | ARI | 20 | GEM | 20 | CAN | 19 | LEO | 21 | LIB |
| 23 | ARI | 21 | TAU | 23 | CAN | 22 | LEO | 21 | VIR | 23 | SCO |
| 25 | TAU | 24 | GEM | 25 | LEO | 25 | VIR | 24 | LIB | 25 | SAG |
| 27 | GEM | 26 | CAN | 28 | VIR | 27 | LIB | 26 | SCO | 27 | CAP |
| 30 | CAN | 29 | LEO | 30 | LIB | 29 | SCO | 28 | SAG | 29 | AQU |
| | | 31 | VIR | | | | | 30 | CAP | 31 | PIS |

# Moon Signs 1945-2025

## 1952

| JAN | | FEB | | MAR | | APR | | MAY | | JUN | |
|---|---|---|---|---|---|---|---|---|---|---|---|
| 3 | ARI | 1 | TAU | 2 | GEM | 1 | CAN | 3 | VIR | 2 | LIB |
| 5 | TAU | 3 | GEM | 4 | CAN | 3 | LEO | 5 | LIB | 4 | SCO |
| 7 | GEM | 6 | CAN | 7 | LEO | 6 | VIR | 8 | SCO | 6 | SAG |
| 10 | CAN | 9 | LEO | 9 | VIR | 8 | LIB | 10 | SAG | 8 | CAP |
| 12 | LEO | 11 | VIR | 12 | LIB | 10 | SCO | 12 | CAP | 10 | AQU |
| 15 | VIR | 14 | LIB | 14 | SCO | 13 | SAG | 14 | AQU | 12 | PIS |
| 17 | LIB | 16 | SCO | 16 | SAG | 15 | CAP | 16 | PIS | 15 | ARI |
| 20 | SCO | 18 | SAG | 19 | CAP | 17 | AQU | 18 | ARI | 17 | TAU |
| 22 | SAG | 20 | CAP | 21 | AQU | 19 | PIS | 21 | TAU | 19 | GEM |
| 24 | CAP | 22 | AQU | 23 | PIS | 21 | ARI | 23 | GEM | 22 | CAN |
| 26 | AQU | 24 | PIS | 25 | ARI | 23 | TAU | 25 | CAN | 24 | LEO |
| 28 | PIS | 26 | ARI | 27 | TAU | 26 | GEM | 28 | LEO | 27 | VIR |
| 30 | ARI | 29 | TAU | 29 | GEM | 28 | CAN | 30 | VIR | 29 | LIB |
| | | | | | | 30 | LEO | | | | |

| JUL | | AUG | | SEP | | OCT | | NOV | | DEC | |
|---|---|---|---|---|---|---|---|---|---|---|---|
| 2 | SCO | 2 | CAP | 1 | AQU | 2 | ARI | 1 | TAU | 2 | CAN |
| 4 | SAG | 4 | AQU | 3 | PIS | 4 | TAU | 3 | GEM | 5 | LEO |
| 6 | CAP | 6 | PIS | 5 | ARI | 6 | GEM | 5 | CAN | 7 | VIR |
| 8 | AQU | 8 | ARI | 7 | TAU | 9 | CAN | 7 | LEO | 10 | LIB |
| 10 | PIS | 10 | TAU | 9 | GEM | 11 | LEO | 10 | VIR | 12 | SCO |
| 12 | ARI | 13 | GEM | 11 | CAN | 14 | VIR | 13 | LIB | 15 | SAG |
| 14 | TAU | 15 | CAN | 14 | LEO | 16 | LIB | 15 | SCO | 17 | CAP |
| 16 | GEM | 18 | LEO | 16 | VIR | 19 | SCO | 17 | SAG | 19 | AQU |
| 19 | CAN | 20 | VIR | 19 | LIB | 21 | SAG | 19 | CAP | 21 | PIS |
| 21 | LEO | 23 | LIB | 21 | SCO | 23 | CAP | 21 | AQU | 23 | ARI |
| 24 | VIR | 25 | SCO | 24 | SAG | 25 | AQU | 24 | PIS | 25 | TAU |
| 26 | LIB | 27 | SAG | 26 | CAP | 27 | PIS | 26 | ARI | 27 | GEM |
| 29 | SCO | 30 | CAP | 28 | AQU | 29 | ARI | 28 | TAU | 30 | CAN |
| 31 | SAG | | | 30 | PIS | | | 30 | GEM | | |

## 1953

| JAN | | FEB | | MAR | | APR | | MAY | | JUN | |
|---|---|---|---|---|---|---|---|---|---|---|---|
| 1 | LEO | 3 | LIB | 2 | LIB | 1 | SCO | 2 | CAP | 1 | AQU |
| 4 | VIR | 5 | SCO | 4 | SCO | 3 | SAG | 5 | AQU | 3 | PIS |
| 6 | LIB | 7 | SAG | 7 | SAG | 5 | CAP | 7 | PIS | 5 | ARI |
| 9 | SCO | 10 | CAP | 9 | CAP | 7 | AQU | 9 | ARI | 7 | TAU |
| 11 | SAG | 12 | AQU | 11 | AQU | 10 | PIS | 11 | TAU | 9 | GEM |
| 13 | CAP | 14 | PIS | 13 | PIS | 12 | ARI | 13 | GEM | 12 | CAN |
| 15 | AQU | 16 | ARI | 15 | ARI | 14 | TAU | 15 | CAN | 14 | LEO |
| 17 | PIS | 18 | TAU | 17 | TAU | 16 | GEM | 18 | LEO | 16 | VIR |
| 19 | ARI | 20 | GEM | 19 | GEM | 18 | CAN | 20 | VIR | 19 | LIB |
| 21 | TAU | 22 | CAN | 22 | CAN | 20 | LEO | 23 | LIB | 21 | SCO |
| 24 | GEM | 25 | LEO | 24 | LEO | 23 | VIR | 25 | SCO | 24 | SAG |
| 26 | CAN | 27 | VIR | 27 | VIR | 25 | LIB | 27 | SAG | 26 | CAP |
| 28 | LEO | | | 29 | LIB | 28 | SCO | 30 | CAP | 28 | AQU |
| 31 | VIR | | | | | 30 | SAG | | | 30 | PIS |

| JUL | | AUG | | SEP | | OCT | | NOV | | DEC | |
|---|---|---|---|---|---|---|---|---|---|---|---|
| 2 | ARI | 1 | TAU | 1 | CAN | 1 | LEO | 2 | LIB | 2 | SCO |
| 5 | TAU | 3 | GEM | 4 | LEO | 4 | VIR | 5 | SCO | 5 | SAG |
| 7 | GEM | 5 | CAN | 6 | VIR | 6 | LIB | 7 | SAG | 7 | CAP |
| 9 | CAN | 8 | LEO | 9 | LIB | 9 | SCO | 10 | CAP | 9 | AQU |
| 11 | LEO | 10 | VIR | 11 | SCO | 11 | SAG | 12 | AQU | 11 | PIS |
| 14 | VIR | 13 | LIB | 14 | SAG | 13 | CAP | 14 | PIS | 14 | ARI |
| 16 | LIB | 15 | SCO | 16 | CAP | 16 | AQU | 16 | ARI | 16 | TAU |
| 19 | SCO | 18 | SAG | 18 | AQU | 18 | PIS | 18 | TAU | 18 | GEM |
| 21 | SAG | 20 | CAP | 21 | PIS | 20 | ARI | 20 | GEM | 20 | CAN |
| 23 | CAP | 22 | AQU | 23 | ARI | 22 | TAU | 22 | CAN | 22 | LEO |
| 26 | AQU | 24 | PIS | 25 | TAU | 24 | GEM | 25 | LEO | 25 | VIR |
| 28 | PIS | 26 | ARI | 27 | GEM | 26 | CAN | 27 | VIR | 27 | LIB |
| 30 | ARI | 28 | TAU | 29 | CAN | 28 | LEO | 30 | LIB | 30 | SCO |
| | | 30 | GEM | | | 31 | VIR | | | | |

# Moon Signs 1945-2025

## 1954

| | JAN | | FEB | | MAR | | APR | | MAY | | JUN |
|---|---|---|---|---|---|---|---|---|---|---|---|
| 1 | SAG | 2 | AQU | 1 | AQU | 2 | ARI | 1 | TAU | 2 | CAN |
| 3 | CAP | 4 | PIS | 3 | PIS | 4 | TAU | 3 | GEM | 4 | LEO |
| 6 | AQU | 6 | ARI | 5 | ARI | 6 | GEM | 5 | CAN | 6 | VIR |
| 8 | PIS | 8 | TAU | 7 | TAU | 8 | CAN | 8 | LEO | 9 | LIB |
| 10 | ARI | 10 | GEM | 10 | GEM | 10 | LEO | 10 | VIR | 11 | SCO |
| 12 | TAU | 13 | CAN | 12 | CAN | 13 | VIR | 12 | LIB | 14 | SAG |
| 14 | GEM | 15 | LEO | 14 | LEO | 15 | LIB | 15 | SCO | 16 | CAP |
| 16 | CAN | 17 | VIR | 16 | VIR | 18 | SCO | 17 | SAG | 19 | AQU |
| 19 | LEO | 20 | LIB | 19 | LIB | 20 | SAG | 20 | CAP | 21 | PIS |
| 21 | VIR | 22 | SCO | 21 | SCO | 23 | CAP | 22 | AQU | 23 | ARI |
| 23 | LIB | 25 | SAG | 24 | SAG | 25 | AQU | 25 | PIS | 25 | TAU |
| 26 | SCO | 27 | CAP | 26 | CAP | 27 | PIS | 27 | ARI | 27 | GEM |
| 28 | SAG | | | 29 | AQU | 29 | ARI | 29 | TAU | 29 | CAN |
| 31 | CAP | | | 31 | PIS | | | 31 | GEM | | |

| | JUL | | AUG | | SEP | | OCT | | NOV | | DEC |
|---|---|---|---|---|---|---|---|---|---|---|---|
| 1 | LEO | 2 | LIB | 1 | SCO | 1 | SAG | 2 | AQU | 2 | PIS |
| 4 | VIR | 5 | SCO | 4 | SAG | 4 | CAP | 5 | PIS | 4 | ARI |
| 6 | LIB | 7 | SAG | 6 | CAP | 6 | AQU | 7 | ARI | 6 | TAU |
| 9 | SCO | 10 | CAP | 9 | AQU | 8 | PIS | 9 | TAU | 8 | GEM |
| 11 | SAG | 12 | AQU | 11 | PIS | 10 | ARI | 11 | GEM | 10 | CAN |
| 14 | CAP | 14 | PIS | 13 | ARI | 12 | TAU | 13 | CAN | 12 | LEO |
| 16 | AQU | 16 | ARI | 15 | TAU | 14 | GEM | 15 | LEO | 14 | VIR |
| 18 | PIS | 19 | TAU | 17 | GEM | 16 | CAN | 17 | VIR | 17 | LIB |
| 20 | ARI | 21 | GEM | 19 | CAN | 19 | LEO | 20 | LIB | 19 | SCO |
| 22 | TAU | 23 | CAN | 21 | LEO | 21 | VIR | 22 | SCO | 22 | SAG |
| 24 | GEM | 25 | LEO | 24 | VIR | 23 | LIB | 25 | SAG | 24 | CAP |
| 27 | CAN | 27 | VIR | 26 | LIB | 26 | SCO | 27 | CAP | 27 | AQU |
| 29 | LEO | 30 | LIB | 29 | SCO | 28 | SAG | 30 | AQU | 29 | PIS |
| 31 | VIR | | | | | 31 | CAP | | | 31 | ARI |

## 1955

| | JAN | | FEB | | MAR | | APR | | MAY | | JUN |
|---|---|---|---|---|---|---|---|---|---|---|---|
| 3 | TAU | 1 | GEM | 2 | CAN | 1 | LEO | 2 | LIB | 1 | SCO |
| 5 | GEM | 3 | CAN | 4 | LEO | 3 | VIR | 5 | SCO | 4 | SAG |
| 7 | CAN | 5 | LEO | 7 | VIR | 5 | LIB | 7 | SAG | 6 | CAP |
| 9 | LEO | 7 | VIR | 9 | LIB | 8 | SCO | 10 | CAP | 9 | AQU |
| 11 | VIR | 10 | LIB | 11 | SCO | 10 | SAG | 12 | AQU | 11 | PIS |
| 13 | LIB | 12 | SCO | 14 | SAG | 13 | CAP | 15 | PIS | 13 | ARI |
| 16 | SCO | 15 | SAG | 16 | CAP | 15 | AQU | 17 | ARI | 16 | TAU |
| 18 | SAG | 17 | CAP | 19 | AQU | 18 | PIS | 19 | TAU | 18 | GEM |
| 21 | CAP | 19 | AQU | 21 | PIS | 20 | ARI | 21 | GEM | 20 | CAN |
| 23 | AQU | 22 | PIS | 23 | ARI | 22 | TAU | 23 | CAN | 22 | LEO |
| 25 | PIS | 24 | ARI | 25 | TAU | 24 | GEM | 25 | LEO | 24 | VIR |
| 28 | ARI | 26 | TAU | 27 | GEM | 26 | CAN | 27 | VIR | 26 | LIB |
| 30 | TAU | 28 | GEM | 29 | CAN | 28 | LEO | 30 | LIB | 28 | SCO |
| | | | | | | 30 | VIR | | | | |

| | JUL | | AUG | | SEP | | OCT | | NOV | | DEC |
|---|---|---|---|---|---|---|---|---|---|---|---|
| 1 | SAG | 2 | AQU | 1 | PIS | 1 | ARI | 1 | GEM | 1 | CAN |
| 3 | CAP | 5 | PIS | 3 | ARI | 3 | TAU | 3 | CAN | 3 | LEO |
| 6 | AQU | 7 | ARI | 5 | TAU | 5 | GEM | 5 | LEO | 5 | VIR |
| 8 | PIS | 9 | TAU | 8 | GEM | 7 | CAN | 7 | VIR | 7 | LIB |
| 11 | ARI | 11 | GEM | 10 | CAN | 9 | LEO | 10 | LIB | 9 | SCO |
| 13 | TAU | 13 | CAN | 12 | LEO | 11 | VIR | 12 | SCO | 12 | SAG |
| 15 | GEM | 15 | LEO | 14 | VIR | 13 | LIB | 15 | SAG | 14 | CAP |
| 17 | CAN | 18 | VIR | 16 | LIB | 16 | SCO | 17 | CAP | 17 | AQU |
| 19 | LEO | 20 | LIB | 18 | SCO | 18 | SAG | 20 | AQU | 19 | PIS |
| 21 | VIR | 22 | SCO | 21 | SAG | 21 | CAP | 22 | PIS | 22 | ARI |
| 23 | LIB | 25 | SAG | 23 | CAP | 23 | AQU | 24 | ARI | 24 | TAU |
| 26 | SCO | 27 | CAP | 26 | AQU | 26 | PIS | 27 | TAU | 26 | GEM |
| 28 | SAG | 30 | AQU | 28 | PIS | 28 | ARI | 29 | GEM | 28 | CAN |
| 31 | CAP | | | | | 30 | TAU | | | 30 | LEO |

# Moon Signs 1945-2025

## 1956

| | JAN | | FEB | | MAR | | APR | | MAY | | JUN |
|---|---|---|---|---|---|---|---|---|---|---|---|
| 1 | VIR | 2 | SCO | 3 | SAG | 1 | CAP | 1 | AQU | 3 | ARI |
| 3 | LIB | 4 | SAG | 5 | CAP | 4 | AQU | 4 | PIS | 5 | TAU |
| 6 | SCO | 7 | CAP | 8 | AQU | 6 | PIS | 6 | ARI | 7 | GEM |
| 8 | SAG | 9 | AQU | 10 | PIS | 9 | ARI | 8 | TAU | 9 | CAN |
| 11 | CAP | 12 | PIS | 12 | ARI | 11 | TAU | 11 | GEM | 11 | LEO |
| 13 | AQU | 14 | ARI | 15 | TAU | 13 | GEM | 13 | CAN | 13 | VIR |
| 16 | PIS | 16 | TAU | 17 | GEM | 15 | CAN | 15 | LEO | 15 | LIB |
| 18 | ARI | 19 | GEM | 19 | CAN | 17 | LEO | 17 | VIR | 18 | SCO |
| 20 | TAU | 21 | CAN | 21 | LEO | 20 | VIR | 19 | LIB | 20 | SAG |
| 22 | GEM | 23 | LEO | 23 | VIR | 22 | LIB | 21 | SCO | 22 | CAP |
| 24 | CAN | 25 | VIR | 25 | LIB | 24 | SCO | 24 | SAG | 25 | AQU |
| 26 | LEO | 27 | LIB | 28 | SCO | 26 | SAG | 26 | CAP | 27 | PIS |
| 28 | VIR | 29 | SCO | 30 | SAG | 29 | CAP | 29 | AQU | 30 | ARI |
| 31 | LIB | | | | | | | 31 | PIS | | |

| | JUL | | AUG | | SEP | | OCT | | NOV | | DEC |
|---|---|---|---|---|---|---|---|---|---|---|---|
| 2 | TAU | 1 | GEM | 1 | LEO | 1 | VIR | 1 | SCO | 1 | SAG |
| 4 | GEM | 3 | CAN | 3 | VIR | 3 | LIB | 3 | SAG | 3 | CAP |
| 6 | CAN | 5 | LEO | 5 | LIB | 5 | SCO | 6 | CAP | 6 | AQU |
| 8 | LEO | 7 | VIR | 7 | SCO | 7 | SAG | 8 | AQU | 8 | PIS |
| 10 | VIR | 9 | LIB | 10 | SAG | 10 | CAP | 11 | PIS | 11 | ARI |
| 12 | LIB | 11 | SCO | 12 | CAP | 12 | AQU | 13 | ARI | 13 | TAU |
| 15 | SCO | 13 | SAG | 15 | AQU | 15 | PIS | 16 | TAU | 15 | GEM |
| 17 | SAG | 16 | CAP | 17 | PIS | 17 | ARI | 18 | GEM | 17 | CAN |
| 20 | CAP | 18 | AQU | 20 | ARI | 19 | TAU | 20 | CAN | 19 | LEO |
| 22 | AQU | 21 | PIS | 22 | TAU | 22 | GEM | 22 | LEO | 21 | VIR |
| 25 | PIS | 23 | ARI | 24 | GEM | 24 | CAN | 24 | VIR | 24 | LIB |
| 27 | ARI | 26 | TAU | 26 | CAN | 26 | LEO | 26 | LIB | 26 | SCO |
| 30 | TAU | 28 | GEM | 29 | LEO | 28 | VIR | 29 | SCO | 28 | SAG |
| | | 30 | CAN | | | 30 | LIB | | | 31 | CAP |

## 1957

| | JAN | | FEB | | MAR | | APR | | MAY | | JUN |
|---|---|---|---|---|---|---|---|---|---|---|---|
| 2 | AQU | 1 | PIS | 3 | ARI | 1 | TAU | 1 | GEM | 1 | LEO |
| 5 | PIS | 3 | ARI | 5 | TAU | 4 | GEM | 3 | CAN | 4 | VIR |
| 7 | ARI | 6 | TAU | 7 | GEM | 6 | CAN | 5 | LEO | 6 | LIB |
| 9 | TAU | 8 | GEM | 10 | CAN | 8 | LEO | 7 | VIR | 8 | SCO |
| 12 | GEM | 10 | CAN | 12 | LEO | 10 | VIR | 9 | LIB | 10 | SAG |
| 14 | CAN | 12 | LEO | 14 | VIR | 12 | LIB | 12 | SCO | 12 | CAP |
| 16 | LEO | 14 | VIR | 16 | LIB | 14 | SCO | 14 | SAG | 15 | AQU |
| 18 | VIR | 16 | LIB | 18 | SCO | 16 | SAG | 16 | CAP | 17 | PIS |
| 20 | LIB | 18 | SCO | 20 | SAG | 19 | CAP | 18 | AQU | 20 | ARI |
| 22 | SCO | 21 | SAG | 22 | CAP | 21 | AQU | 21 | PIS | 22 | TAU |
| 24 | SAG | 23 | CAP | 25 | AQU | 24 | PIS | 23 | ARI | 25 | GEM |
| 27 | CAP | 26 | AQU | 27 | PIS | 26 | ARI | 25 | TAU | 27 | CAN |
| 29 | AQU | 28 | PIS | 30 | ARI | 29 | TAU | 28 | GEM | 29 | LEO |
| | | | | | | | | 30 | CAN | | |

| | JUL | | AUG | | SEP | | OCT | | NOV | | DEC |
|---|---|---|---|---|---|---|---|---|---|---|---|
| 1 | VIR | 1 | SCO | 2 | CAP | 2 | AQU | 1 | PIS | 1 | ARI |
| 3 | LIB | 4 | SAG | 5 | AQU | 4 | PIS | 3 | ARI | 3 | TAU |
| 5 | SCO | 6 | CAP | 7 | PIS | 7 | ARI | 5 | TAU | 5 | GEM |
| 7 | SAG | 8 | AQU | 10 | ARI | 9 | TAU | 8 | GEM | 8 | CAN |
| 10 | CAP | 11 | PIS | 12 | TAU | 12 | GEM | 10 | CAN | 10 | LEO |
| 12 | AQU | 13 | ARI | 15 | GEM | 14 | CAN | 13 | LEO | 12 | VIR |
| 15 | PIS | 16 | TAU | 17 | CAN | 16 | LEO | 15 | VIR | 14 | LIB |
| 17 | ARI | 18 | GEM | 19 | LEO | 18 | VIR | 17 | LIB | 16 | SCO |
| 20 | TAU | 21 | CAN | 21 | VIR | 21 | LIB | 19 | SCO | 18 | SAG |
| 22 | GEM | 23 | LEO | 23 | LIB | 23 | SCO | 21 | SAG | 21 | CAP |
| 24 | CAN | 25 | VIR | 25 | SCO | 25 | SAG | 23 | CAP | 23 | AQU |
| 25 | LEO | 27 | LIB | 27 | SAG | 27 | CAP | 26 | AQU | 25 | PIS |
| 28 | VIR | 29 | SCO | 29 | CAP | 29 | AQU | 28 | PIS | 28 | ARI |
| 30 | LIB | 31 | SAG | | | | | | | 30 | TAU |

# Moon Signs 1945-2025

## 1958

| JAN | | FEB | | MAR | | APR | | MAY | | JUN | |
|---|---|---|---|---|---|---|---|---|---|---|---|
| 2 | GEM | 3 | LEO | 2 | LEO | 1 | VIR | 2 | SCO | 3 | CAP |
| 4 | CAN | 5 | VIR | 4 | VIR | 3 | LIB | 4 | SAG | 5 | AQU |
| 6 | LEO | 7 | LIB | 6 | LIB | 5 | SCO | 6 | CAP | 7 | PIS |
| 8 | VIR | 9 | SCO | 8 | SCO | 7 | SAG | 8 | AQU | 10 | ARI |
| 10 | LIB | 11 | SAG | 10 | SAG | 9 | CAP | 11 | PIS | 12 | TAU |
| 12 | SCO | 13 | CAP | 12 | CAP | 11 | AQU | 13 | ARI | 15 | GEM |
| 15 | SAG | 16 | AQU | 15 | AQU | 13 | PIS | 16 | TAU | 17 | CAN |
| 17 | CAP | 18 | PIS | 17 | PIS | 16 | ARI | 18 | GEM | 19 | LEO |
| 19 | AQU | 21 | ARI | 20 | ARI | 19 | RAU | 21 | CAN | 21 | VIR |
| 22 | PIS | 23 | TAU | 22 | TAU | 21 | GEM | 23 | LEO | 24 | LIB |
| 24 | ARI | 26 | GEM | 25 | GEM | 23 | CAN | 25 | VIR | 26 | SCO |
| 27 | TAU | 28 | CAN | 27 | CAN | 26 | LEO | 27 | LIB | 28 | SAG |
| 29 | GEM | | | 29 | LEO | 28 | VIR | 29 | SCO | 30 | CAP |
| 31 | CAN | | | | | 30 | LIB | 31 | SAG | | |

| JUL | | AUG | | SEP | | OCT | | NOV | | DEC | |
|---|---|---|---|---|---|---|---|---|---|---|---|
| 2 | AQU | 1 | PIS | 2 | TAU | 2 | GEM | 1 | CAN | 3 | VIR |
| 4 | PIS | 3 | ARI | 5 | GEM | 4 | CAN | 3 | LEO | 5 | LIB |
| 7 | ARI | 6 | TAU | 7 | CAN | 7 | LEO | 5 | VIR | 7 | SCO |
| 9 | TAU | 8 | GEM | 9 | LEO | 9 | VIR | 7 | LIB | 9 | SAG |
| 12 | GEM | 11 | CAN | 11 | VIR | 11 | LIB | 9 | SCO | 11 | CAP |
| 14 | CAN | 13 | LEO | 13 | LIB | 13 | SCO | 11 | SAG | 13 | AQU |
| 17 | LEO | 15 | VIR | 15 | SCO | 15 | SAG | 13 | CAP | 15 | PIS |
| 19 | VIR | 17 | LIB | 18 | SAG | 17 | CAP | 16 | AQU | 18 | ARI |
| 21 | LIB | 19 | SCO | 20 | CAP | 19 | AQU | 18 | PIS | 20 | TAU |
| 23 | SCO | 21 | SAG | 22 | AQU | 22 | PIS | 20 | ARI | 23 | GEM |
| 25 | SAG | 23 | CAP | 24 | PIS | 24 | ARI | 23 | TAU | 25 | CAN |
| 27 | CAP | 26 | AQU | 27 | ARI | 27 | TAU | 25 | GEM | 27 | LEO |
| 29 | AQU | 28 | PIS | 29 | TAU | 29 | GEM | 28 | CAN | 30 | VIR |
| | | 31 | ARI | | | | | 30 | LEO | | |

## 1959

| JAN | | FEB | | MAR | | APR | | MAY | | JUN | |
|---|---|---|---|---|---|---|---|---|---|---|---|
| 1 | LIB | 1 | SAG | 1 | SAG | 1 | AQU | 1 | PIS | 2 | TAU |
| 3 | SCO | 4 | CAP | 3 | CAP | 4 | PIS | 3 | ARI | 5 | GEM |
| 5 | SAG | 6 | AQU | 5 | AQU | 6 | ARI | 6 | TAU | 7 | CAN |
| 7 | CAP | 8 | PIS | 7 | PIS | 8 | TAU | 8 | GEM | 9 | LEO |
| 9 | AQU | 10 | ARI | 10 | ARI | 11 | GEM | 11 | CAN | 12 | VIR |
| 12 | PIS | 13 | TAU | 12 | TAU | 14 | CAN | 13 | LEO | 14 | LIB |
| 14 | ARI | 15 | GEM | 15 | GEM | 16 | LEO | 16 | VIR | 16 | SCO |
| 17 | TAU | 18 | CAN | 17 | CAN | 18 | VIR | 18 | LIB | 18 | SAG |
| 19 | GEM | 20 | LEO | 20 | LEO | 20 | LIB | 20 | SCO | 20 | CAP |
| 21 | CAN | 22 | VIR | 22 | VIR | 22 | SCO | 22 | SAG | 22 | AQU |
| 24 | LEO | 24 | LIB | 24 | LIB | 24 | SAG | 24 | CAP | 24 | PIS |
| 26 | VIR | 27 | SCO | 26 | SCO | 26 | CAP | 26 | AQU | 27 | ARI |
| 28 | LIB | | | 28 | SAG | 28 | AQU | 28 | PIS | 29 | TAU |
| 30 | SCO | | | 30 | CAP | | | 30 | ARI | | |

| JUL | | AUG | | SEP | | OCT | | NOV | | DEC | |
|---|---|---|---|---|---|---|---|---|---|---|---|
| 2 | GEM | 1 | CAN | 2 | VIR | 1 | LIB | 2 | SAG | 1 | CAP |
| 4 | CAN | 3 | LEO | 4 | LIB | 3 | SCO | 4 | CAP | 3 | AQU |
| 7 | LEO | 5 | VIR | 6 | SCO | 5 | SAG | 6 | AQU | 5 | PIS |
| 9 | VIR | 8 | LIB | 8 | SAG | 7 | CAP | 8 | PIS | 8 | ARI |
| 11 | LIB | 10 | SCO | 10 | CAP | 10 | AQU | 10 | ARI | 10 | TAU |
| 13 | SCO | 12 | SAG | 12 | AQU | 12 | PIS | 13 | TAU | 13 | GEM |
| 16 | SAG | 14 | CAP | 15 | PIS | 14 | ARI | 15 | GEM | 15 | CAN |
| 18 | CAP | 16 | AQU | 17 | ARI | 17 | TAU | 18 | CAN | 18 | LEO |
| 20 | AQU | 18 | PIS | 19 | TAU | 19 | GEM | 20 | LEO | 20 | VIR |
| 22 | PIS | 20 | ARI | 22 | GEM | 22 | CAN | 23 | VIR | 22 | LIB |
| 24 | ARI | 23 | TAU | 24 | CAN | 24 | LEO | 25 | LIB | 25 | SCO |
| 27 | TAU | 25 | GEM | 27 | LEO | 26 | VIR | 27 | SCO | 27 | SAG |
| 29 | GEM | 28 | CAN | 29 | VIR | 29 | LIB | 29 | SAG | 29 | CAP |
| | | 30 | LEO | | | 31 | SCO | | | 31 | AQU |

# Moon Signs 1945-2025

## 1960

| | JAN | | FEB | | MAR | | APR | | MAY | | JUN |
|---|---|---|---|---|---|---|---|---|---|---|---|
| 2 | PIS | 3 | TAU | 1 | TAU | 2 | CAN | 2 | LEO | 1 | VIR |
| 4 | ARI | 5 | GEM | 4 | GEM | 5 | LEO | 5 | VIR | 3 | LIB |
| 6 | TAU | 8 | CAN | 6 | CAN | 7 | VIR | 6 | LIB | 6 | SCO |
| 9 | GEM | 10 | LEO | 9 | LEO | 10 | LIB | 9 | SCO | 8 | SAG |
| 11 | CAN | 13 | VIR | 11 | VIR | 12 | SCO | 11 | SAG | 10 | CAP |
| 14 | LEO | 15 | LIB | 13 | LIB | 14 | SAG | 13 | CAP | 12 | AQU |
| 16 | VIR | 17 | SCO | 15 | SCO | 16 | CAP | 15 | AQU | 14 | PIS |
| 19 | LIB | 19 | SAG | 17 | SAG | 18 | AQU | 17 | PIS | 16 | ARI |
| 21 | SCO | 21 | CAP | 20 | CAP | 20 | PIS | 20 | ARI | 18 | TAU |
| 23 | SAG | 23 | AQU | 22 | AQU | 22 | ARI | 22 | TAU | 21 | GEM |
| 25 | CAP | 26 | PIS | 24 | PIS | 25 | TAU | 24 | GEM | 23 | CAN |
| 27 | AQU | 28 | ARI | 26 | ARI | 27 | GEM | 27 | CAN | 26 | LEO |
| 29 | PIS | | | 28 | TAU | 30 | CAN | 29 | LEO | 28 | VIR |
| 31 | ARI | | | 31 | GEM | | | | | | |

| | JUL | | AUG | | SEP | | OCT | | NOV | | DEC |
|---|---|---|---|---|---|---|---|---|---|---|---|
| 1 | LIB | 1 | SAG | 2 | AQU | 1 | PIS | 2 | TAU | 2 | GEM |
| 3 | SCO | 3 | CAP | 4 | PIS | 3 | ARI | 4 | GEM | 4 | CAN |
| 5 | SAG | 5 | AQU | 6 | ARI | 6 | TAU | 7 | CAN | 7 | LEO |
| 7 | CAP | 7 | PIS | 8 | TAU | 8 | GEM | 9 | LEO | 9 | VIR |
| 9 | AQU | 10 | ARI | 11 | GEM | 10 | CAN | 12 | VIR | 12 | LIB |
| 11 | PIS | 12 | TAU | 13 | CAN | 13 | LEO | 14 | LIB | 14 | SCO |
| 13 | ARI | 14 | GEM | 16 | LEO | 15 | VIR | 16 | SCO | 16 | SAG |
| 15 | TAU | 17 | CAN | 18 | VIR | 18 | LIB | 19 | SAG | 18 | CAP |
| 18 | GEM | 19 | LEO | 20 | LIB | 20 | SCO | 21 | CAP | 20 | AQU |
| 20 | CAN | 22 | VIR | 23 | SCO | 22 | SAG | 23 | AQU | 22 | PIS |
| 23 | LEO | 24 | LIB | 25 | SAG | 24 | CAP | 25 | PIS | 24 | ARI |
| 25 | VIR | 26 | SCO | 27 | CAP | 26 | AQU | 27 | ARI | 26 | TAU |
| 28 | LIB | 29 | SAG | 29 | AQU | 28 | PIS | 29 | TAU | 29 | GEM |
| 30 | SCO | 31 | CAP | | | 31 | ARI | | | 31 | CAN |

## 1961

| | JAN | | FEB | | MAR | | APR | | MAY | | JUN |
|---|---|---|---|---|---|---|---|---|---|---|---|
| 3 | LEO | 2 | VIR | 1 | VIR | 2 | SCO | 2 | SAG | 2 | AQU |
| 5 | VIR | 4 | LIB | 3 | LIB | 4 | SAG | 4 | CAP | 4 | PIS |
| 8 | LIB | 6 | SCO | 6 | SCO | 6 | CAP | 6 | AQU | 6 | ARI |
| 10 | SCO | 9 | SAG | 8 | SAG | 9 | AQU | 8 | PIS | 8 | TAU |
| 12 | SAG | 11 | CAP | 10 | CAP | 11 | PIS | 10 | ARI | 11 | GEM |
| 14 | CAP | 13 | AQU | 12 | AQU | 13 | ARI | 12 | TAU | 13 | CAN |
| 16 | AQU | 15 | PIS | 14 | PIS | 15 | TAU | 14 | GEM | 16 | LEO |
| 18 | PIS | 17 | ARI | 16 | ARI | 17 | GEM | 17 | CAN | 18 | VIR |
| 20 | ARI | 19 | TAU | 18 | TAU | 19 | CAN | 19 | LEO | 21 | LIB |
| 23 | TAU | 21 | GEM | 21 | GEM | 22 | LEO | 22 | VIR | 23 | SCO |
| 25 | GEM | 24 | CAN | 23 | CAN | 25 | VIR | 24 | LIB | 25 | SAG |
| 28 | CAN | 26 | LEO | 26 | LEO | 27 | LIB | 27 | SCO | 27 | CAP |
| 30 | LEO | | | 28 | VIR | 29 | SCO | 29 | SAG | 29 | AQU |
| | | | | 31 | LIB | | | 31 | CAP | | |

| | JUL | | AUG | | SEP | | OCT | | NOV | | DEC |
|---|---|---|---|---|---|---|---|---|---|---|---|
| 1 | PIS | 2 | TAU | 1 | GEM | 3 | LEO | 2 | VIR | 1 | LIB |
| 4 | ARI | 4 | GEM | 3 | CAN | 5 | VIR | 4 | LIB | 4 | SCO |
| 6 | TAU | 7 | CAN | 5 | LEO | 8 | LIB | 6 | SCO | 6 | SAG |
| 8 | GEM | 9 | LEO | 8 | VIR | 10 | SCO | 9 | SAG | 8 | CAP |
| 10 | CAN | 12 | VIR | 10 | LIB | 13 | SAG | 11 | CAP | 10 | AQU |
| 13 | LEO | 14 | LIB | 13 | SCO | 15 | CAP | 13 | AQU | 13 | PIS |
| 15 | VIR | 17 | SCO | 15 | SAG | 17 | AQU | 15 | PIS | 15 | ARI |
| 18 | LIB | 19 | SAG | 18 | CAP | 19 | PIS | 17 | ARI | 17 | TAU |
| 20 | SCO | 21 | CAP | 20 | AQU | 21 | ARI | 20 | TAU | 19 | GEM |
| 23 | SAG | 23 | AQU | 22 | PIS | 23 | TAU | 22 | GEM | 21 | CAN |
| 25 | CAP | 25 | PIS | 24 | ARI | 25 | GEM | 24 | CAN | 24 | LEO |
| 27 | AQU | 27 | ARI | 26 | TAU | 28 | CAN | 26 | LEO | 26 | VIR |
| 29 | PIS | 29 | TAU | 28 | GEM | 30 | LEO | 29 | VIR | 29 | LIB |
| 31 | ARI | | | 30 | CAN | | | | | 31 | SCO |

# Moon Signs 1945-2025

## 1962

| | JAN | | FEB | | MAR | | APR | | MAY | | JUN |
|---|---|---|---|---|---|---|---|---|---|---|---|
| 3 | SAG | 1 | CAP | 1 | CAP | 1 | PIS | 1 | ARI | 1 | GEM |
| 5 | CAP | 3 | AQU | 3 | AQU | 3 | ARI | 3 | TAU | 3 | CAN |
| 7 | AQU | 5 | PIS | 5 | PIS | 5 | TAU | 5 | GEM | 6 | LEO |
| 9 | PIS | 7 | ARI | 7 | ARI | 7 | GEM | 7 | CAN | 8 | VIR |
| 11 | ARI | 9 | TAU | 9 | TAU | 9 | CAN | 9 | LEO | 10 | LIB |
| 13 | TAU | 12 | GEM | 11 | GEM | 12 | LEO | 12 | VIR | 13 | SCO |
| 15 | GEM | 14 | CAN | 13 | CAN | 14 | VIR | 14 | LIB | 15 | SAG |
| 18 | CAN | 16 | LEO | 16 | LEO | 17 | LIB | 17 | SCO | 18 | CAP |
| 20 | LEO | 19 | VIR | 18 | VIR | 19 | SCO | 19 | SAG | 20 | AQU |
| 23 | VIR | 21 | LIB | 21 | LIB | 22 | SAG | 21 | CAP | 22 | PIS |
| 25 | LIB | 24 | SCO | 23 | SCO | 24 | CAP | 24 | AQU | 24 | ARI |
| 28 | SCO | 26 | SAG | 26 | SAG | 26 | AQU | 26 | PIS | 26 | TAU |
| 30 | SAG | | | 28 | CAP | 28 | PIS | 28 | ARI | 28 | GEM |

| | JUL | | AUG | | SEP | | OCT | | NOV | | DEC |
|---|---|---|---|---|---|---|---|---|---|---|---|
| 1 | CAN | 2 | VIR | 3 | SCO | 3 | SAG | 1 | CAP | 1 | AQU |
| 3 | LEO | 4 | LIB | 5 | SAG | 5 | CAP | 4 | AQU | 3 | PIS |
| 5 | VIR | 7 | SCO | 8 | CAP | 7 | AQU | 6 | PIS | 5 | ARI |
| 8 | LIB | 9 | SAG | 10 | AQU | 10 | PIS | 8 | ARI | 7 | TAU |
| 10 | SCO | 11 | CAP | 12 | PIS | 12 | ARI | 10 | TAU | 9 | GEM |
| 13 | SAG | 14 | AQU | 14 | ARI | 14 | TAU | 12 | GEM | 11 | CAN |
| 15 | CAP | 16 | PIS | 16 | TAU | 16 | GEM | 14 | CAN | 14 | LEO |
| 17 | AQU | 18 | ARI | 18 | GEM | 18 | CAN | 16 | LEO | 16 | VIR |
| 19 | PIS | 20 | TAU | 20 | CAN | 20 | LEO | 19 | VIR | 19 | LIB |
| 21 | ARI | 22 | GEM | 23 | LEO | 22 | VIR | 21 | LIB | 21 | SCO |
| 23 | TAU | 24 | CAN | 25 | VIR | 25 | LIB | 24 | SCO | 24 | SAG |
| 26 | GEM | 26 | LEO | 28 | LIB | 27 | SCO | 26 | SAG | 26 | CAP |
| 28 | CAN | 29 | VIR | 30 | SCO | 30 | SAG | 29 | CAP | 28 | AQU |
| 30 | LEO | 31 | LIB | | | | | | | 30 | PIS |

## 1963

| | JAN | | FEB | | MAR | | APR | | MAY | | JUN |
|---|---|---|---|---|---|---|---|---|---|---|---|
| 1 | ARI | 2 | GEM | 1 | GEM | 2 | LEO | 2 | VIR | 3 | SCO |
| 4 | TAU | 4 | CAN | 3 | CAN | 4 | VIR | 4 | LIB | 5 | SAG |
| 6 | GEM | 6 | LEO | 6 | LEO | 7 | LIB | 7 | SCO | 8 | CAP |
| 8 | CAN | 9 | VIR | 8 | VIR | 9 | SCO | 9 | SAG | 10 | AQU |
| 10 | LEO | 11 | LIB | 11 | LIB | 12 | SAG | 12 | CAP | 12 | PIS |
| 12 | VIR | 14 | SCO | 13 | SCO | 14 | CAP | 14 | AQU | 15 | ARI |
| 15 | LIB | 16 | SAG | 16 | SAG | 17 | AQU | 16 | PIS | 17 | TAU |
| 17 | SCO | 19 | CAP | 18 | CAP | 19 | PIS | 18 | ARI | 19 | GEM |
| 20 | SAG | 21 | AQU | 20 | AQU | 21 | ARI | 20 | TAU | 21 | CAN |
| 22 | CAP | 23 | PIS | 23 | PIS | 23 | TAU | 22 | GEM | 23 | LEO |
| 25 | AQU | 25 | ARI | 25 | ARI | 25 | GEM | 24 | CAN | 25 | VIR |
| 27 | PIS | 27 | TAU | 27 | TAU | 27 | CAN | 27 | LEO | 28 | LIB |
| 29 | ARI | | | 29 | GEM | 29 | LEO | 29 | VIR | 30 | SCO |
| 31 | TAU | | | 31 | CAN | | | 31 | LIB | | |

| | JUL | | AUG | | SEP | | OCT | | NOV | | DEC |
|---|---|---|---|---|---|---|---|---|---|---|---|
| 3 | SAG | 1 | CAP | 2 | PIS | 2 | ARI | 2 | GEM | 2 | CAN |
| 5 | CAP | 4 | AQU | 4 | ARI | 4 | TAU | 4 | CAN | 4 | LEO |
| 7 | AQU | 6 | PIS | 7 | TAU | 6 | GEM | 6 | LEO | 6 | VIR |
| 10 | PIS | 8 | ARI | 9 | GEM | 8 | CAN | 9 | VIR | 8 | LIB |
| 12 | ARI | 10 | TAU | 11 | CAN | 10 | LEO | 11 | LIB | 11 | SCO |
| 14 | TAU | 12 | GEM | 13 | LEO | 12 | VIR | 14 | SCO | 13 | SAG |
| 16 | GEM | 14 | CAN | 15 | VIR | 15 | LIB | 16 | SAG | 16 | CAP |
| 18 | CAN | 17 | LEO | 18 | LIB | 17 | SCO | 19 | CAP | 18 | AQU |
| 20 | LEO | 19 | VIR | 20 | SCO | 20 | SAG | 21 | AQU | 21 | PIS |
| 23 | VIR | 21 | LIB | 23 | SAG | 22 | CAP | 24 | PIS | 23 | ARI |
| 25 | LIB | 24 | SCO | 25 | CAP | 25 | AQU | 26 | ARI | 25 | TAU |
| 27 | SCO | 26 | SAG | 28 | AQU | 27 | PIS | 28 | TAU | 27 | GEM |
| 30 | SAG | 29 | CAP | 30 | PIS | 29 | ARI | 30 | GEM | 29 | CAN |
| | | 31 | AQU | | | 31 | TAU | | | | |

# Moon Signs 1945-2025

## 1964

| | JAN | | FEB | | MAR | | APR | | MAY | | JUN |
|---|---|---|---|---|---|---|---|---|---|---|---|
| 2 | VIR | 1 | LIB | 2 | SCO | 1 | SAG | 1 | CAP | 2 | PIS |
| 5 | LIB | 4 | SCO | 4 | SAG | 3 | CAP | 3 | AQU | 4 | ARI |
| 7 | SCO | 6 | SAG | 7 | CAP | 6 | AQU | 5 | PIS | 6 | TAU |
| 10 | SAG | 9 | CAP | 9 | AQU | 8 | PIS | 8 | ARI | 8 | GEM |
| 12 | CAP | 11 | AQU | 12 | PIS | 10 | ARI | 10 | TAU | 10 | CAN |
| 15 | AQU | 13 | PIS | 14 | ARI | 12 | TAU | 12 | GEM | 12 | LEO |
| 17 | PIS | 16 | ARI | 16 | TAU | 14 | GEM | 14 | CAN | 14 | VIR |
| 19 | ARI | 18 | TAU | 18 | GEM | 16 | CAN | 16 | LEO | 17 | LIB |
| 21 | TAU | 20 | GEM | 20 | CAN | 19 | LEO | 18 | VIR | 19 | SCO |
| 24 | GEM | 22 | CAN | 22 | LEO | 21 | VIR | 20 | LIB | 22 | SAG |
| 26 | CAN | 24 | LEO | 25 | VIR | 23 | LIB | 23 | SCO | 24 | CAP |
| 28 | LEO | 26 | VIR | 27 | LIB | 26 | SCO | 25 | SAG | 27 | AQU |
| 30 | VIR | 28 | LIB | 29 | SCO | 28 | SAG | 28 | CAP | 29 | PIS |
| | | | | | | | | 30 | AQU | | |

| | JUL | | AUG | | SEP | | OCT | | NOV | | DEC |
|---|---|---|---|---|---|---|---|---|---|---|---|
| 1 | ARI | 2 | GEM | 2 | LEO | 2 | VIR | 3 | SCO | 2 | SAG |
| 4 | TAU | 4 | CAN | 5 | VIR | 4 | LIB | 5 | SAG | 5 | CAP |
| 6 | GEM | 6 | LEO | 7 | LIB | 6 | SCO | 8 | CAP | 7 | AQU |
| 8 | CAN | 8 | VIR | 9 | SCO | 9 | SAG | 10 | AQU | 10 | PIS |
| 10 | LEO | 10 | LIB | 11 | SAG | 11 | CAP | 13 | PIS | 12 | ARI |
| 12 | VIR | 13 | SCO | 14 | CAP | 14 | AQU | 15 | ARI | 15 | TAU |
| 14 | LIB | 15 | SAG | 16 | AQU | 16 | PIS | 17 | TAU | 17 | GEM |
| 16 | SCO | 18 | CAP | 19 | PIS | 19 | ARI | 19 | GEM | 19 | CAN |
| 19 | SAG | 20 | AQU | 21 | ARI | 21 | TAU | 21 | CAN | 21 | LEO |
| 21 | CAP | 23 | PIS | 23 | TAU | 23 | GEM | 23 | LEO | 23 | VIR |
| 24 | AQU | 25 | ARI | 25 | GEM | 25 | CAN | 25 | VIR | 25 | LIB |
| 26 | PIS | 27 | TAU | 28 | CAN | 27 | LEO | 28 | LIB | 27 | SCO |
| 29 | ARI | 29 | GEM | 30 | LEO | 29 | VIR | 30 | SCO | 30 | SAG |
| 31 | TAU | 31 | CAN | | | 31 | LIB | | | | |

## 1965

| | JAN | | FEB | | MAR | | APR | | MAY | | JUN |
|---|---|---|---|---|---|---|---|---|---|---|---|
| 1 | CAP | 2 | PIS | 2 | PIS | 3 | TAU | 2 | GEM | 1 | CAN |
| 4 | AQU | 5 | ARI | 4 | ARI | 5 | GEM | 4 | CAN | 3 | LEO |
| 6 | PIS | 7 | TAU | 6 | TAU | 7 | CAN | 6 | LEO | 5 | VIR |
| 9 | ARI | 9 | GEM | 9 | GEM | 9 | LEO | 8 | VIR | 7 | LIB |
| 11 | TAU | 11 | CAN | 11 | CAN | 11 | VIR | 11 | LIB | 9 | SCO |
| 13 | GEM | 13 | LEO | 13 | LEO | 13 | LIB | 13 | SCO | 12 | SAG |
| 15 | CAN | 16 | VIR | 15 | VIR | 16 | SCO | 15 | SAG | 14 | CAP |
| 17 | LEO | 18 | LIB | 17 | LIB | 18 | SAG | 18 | CAP | 16 | AQU |
| 19 | VIR | 20 | SCO | 19 | SCO | 20 | CAP | 20 | AQU | 19 | PIS |
| 21 | LIB | 22 | SAG | 22 | SAG | 23 | AQU | 23 | PIS | 21 | ARI |
| 23 | SCO | 25 | CAP | 24 | CAP | 25 | PIS | 25 | ARI | 24 | TAU |
| 26 | SAG | 27 | AQU | 27 | AQU | 28 | ARI | 27 | TAU | 26 | GEM |
| 28 | CAP | | | 29 | PIS | 30 | TAU | 30 | GEM | 28 | CAN |
| 31 | AQU | | | 31 | ARI | | | | | 30 | LEO |

| | JUL | | AUG | | SEP | | OCT | | NOV | | DEC |
|---|---|---|---|---|---|---|---|---|---|---|---|
| 2 | VIR | 3 | SCO | 1 | SAG | 1 | CAP | 2 | PIS | 2 | ARI |
| 4 | LIB | 5 | SAG | 4 | CAP | 4 | AQU | 5 | ARI | 5 | TAU |
| 6 | SCO | 7 | CAP | 6 | AQU | 6 | PIS | 7 | TAU | 7 | GEM |
| 9 | SAG | 10 | AQU | 9 | PIS | 9 | ARI | 9 | GEM | 9 | CAN |
| 11 | CAP | 13 | PIS | 11 | ARI | 11 | TAU | 12 | CAN | 11 | LEO |
| 14 | AQU | 15 | ARI | 14 | TAU | 13 | GEM | 14 | LEO | 13 | VIR |
| 16 | PIS | 17 | TAU | 16 | GEM | 15 | CAN | 16 | VIR | 15 | LIB |
| 19 | ARI | 20 | GEM | 18 | CAN | 17 | LEO | 18 | LIB | 17 | SCO |
| 21 | TAU | 22 | CAN | 20 | LEO | 20 | VIR | 20 | SCO | 20 | SAG |
| 23 | GEM | 24 | LEO | 22 | VIR | 22 | LIB | 22 | SAG | 22 | CAP |
| 25 | CAN | 26 | VIR | 24 | LIB | 24 | SCO | 25 | CAP | 25 | AQU |
| 27 | LEO | 28 | LIB | 26 | SCO | 26 | SAG | 27 | AQU | 27 | PIS |
| 29 | VIR | 30 | SCO | 29 | SAG | 28 | CAP | 30 | PIS | 30 | ARI |
| 31 | LIB | | | | | 31 | AQU | | | | |

# Moon Signs 1945-2025

## 1966

| | JAN | | FEB | | MAR | | APR | | MAY | | JUN |
|---|---|---|---|---|---|---|---|---|---|---|---|
| 1 | TAU | 2 | CAN | 1 | CAN | 2 | VIR | 1 | LIB | 2 | SAG |
| 3 | GEM | 4 | LEO | 3 | LEO | 4 | LIB | 3 | SCO | 4 | CAP |
| 5 | CAN | 6 | VIR | 5 | VIR | 6 | SCO | 5 | SAG | 6 | AQU |
| 7 | LEO | 8 | LIB | 7 | LIB | 8 | SAG | 8 | CAP | 9 | PIS |
| 9 | VIR | 10 | SCO | 9 | SCO | 10 | CAP | 10 | AQU | 11 | ARI |
| 11 | LIB | 12 | SAG | 12 | SAG | 13 | AQU | 12 | PIS | 14 | TAU |
| 14 | SCO | 15 | CAP | 14 | CAP | 15 | PIS | 15 | ARI | 16 | GEM |
| 16 | SAG | 17 | AQU | 16 | AQU | 18 | ARI | 17 | TAU | 18 | CAN |
| 18 | CAP | 20 | PIS | 19 | PIS | 20 | TAU | 20 | GEM | 20 | LEO |
| 21 | AQU | 22 | ARI | 21 | ARI | 22 | GEM | 22 | CAN | 23 | VIR |
| 23 | PIS | 25 | TAU | 24 | TAU | 25 | CAN | 24 | LEO | 25 | LIB |
| 26 | ARI | 27 | GEM | 26 | GEM | 27 | LEO | 26 | VIR | 27 | SCO |
| 28 | TAU | | | 29 | CAN | 29 | VIR | 28 | LIB | 29 | SAG |
| 31 | GEM | | | 31 | LEO | | | 31 | SCO | | |

| | JUL | | AUG | | SEP | | OCT | | NOV | | DEC |
|---|---|---|---|---|---|---|---|---|---|---|---|
| 1 | CAP | 2 | PIS | 1 | ARI | 1 | TAU | 2 | CAN | 2 | LEO |
| 4 | AQU | 5 | ARI | 4 | TAU | 3 | GEM | 4 | LEO | 4 | VIR |
| 6 | PIS | 7 | TAU | 6 | GEM | 6 | CAN | 6 | VIR | 6 | LIB |
| 9 | ARI | 10 | GEM | 9 | CAN | 8 | LEO | 8 | LIB | 8 | SCO |
| 11 | TAU | 12 | CAN | 11 | LEO | 10 | VIR | 11 | SCO | 10 | SAG |
| 14 | GEM | 14 | LEO | 13 | VIR | 12 | LIB | 13 | SAG | 12 | CAP |
| 16 | CAN | 16 | VIR | 15 | LIB | 14 | SCO | 15 | CAP | 14 | AQU |
| 18 | LEO | 18 | LIB | 17 | SCO | 16 | SAG | 17 | AQU | 17 | PIS |
| 20 | VIR | 20 | SCO | 19 | SAG | 18 | CAP | 20 | PIS | 19 | ARI |
| 22 | LIB | 22 | SAG | 21 | CAP | 21 | AQU | 22 | ARI | 22 | TAU |
| 24 | SCO | 25 | CAP | 23 | AQU | 23 | PIS | 25 | TAU | 24 | GEM |
| 26 | SAG | 27 | AQU | 26 | PIS | 26 | ARI | 27 | GEM | 27 | CAN |
| 29 | CAP | 30 | PIS | 28 | ARI | 28 | TAU | 29 | CAN | 29 | LEO |
| 31 | AQU | | | | | 31 | GEM | | | 31 | VIR |

## 1967

| | JAN | | FEB | | MAR | | APR | | MAY | | JUN |
|---|---|---|---|---|---|---|---|---|---|---|---|
| 2 | LIB | 3 | SAG | 2 | SAG | 3 | AQU | 2 | PIS | 1 | ARI |
| 4 | SCO | 5 | CAP | 4 | CAP | 5 | PIS | 5 | ARI | 4 | TAU |
| 6 | SAG | 7 | AQU | 6 | AQU | 8 | ARI | 7 | TAU | 6 | GEM |
| 9 | CAP | 10 | PIS | 9 | PIS | 10 | TAU | 10 | GEM | 9 | CAN |
| 11 | AQU | 12 | ARI | 11 | ARI | 13 | GEM | 12 | CAN | 11 | LEO |
| 13 | PIS | 15 | TAU | 14 | TAU | 15 | CAN | 15 | LEO | 13 | VIR |
| 16 | ARI | 17 | GEM | 16 | GEM | 17 | LEO | 17 | VIR | 15 | LIB |
| 18 | TAU | 19 | CAN | 19 | CAN | 20 | VIR | 19 | LIB | 17 | SCO |
| 21 | GEM | 22 | LEO | 21 | LEO | 22 | LIB | 21 | SCO | 19 | SAG |
| 23 | CAN | 24 | VIR | 23 | VIR | 24 | SCO | 23 | SAG | 21 | CAP |
| 25 | LEO | 26 | LIB | 25 | LIB | 26 | SAG | 25 | CAP | 24 | AQU |
| 27 | VIR | 28 | SCO | 27 | SCO | 28 | CAP | 27 | AQU | 26 | PIS |
| 29 | LIB | | | 29 | SAG | 30 | AQU | 30 | PIS | 28 | ARI |
| 31 | SCO | | | 31 | CAP | | | | | | |

| | JUL | | AUG | | SEP | | OCT | | NOV | | DEC |
|---|---|---|---|---|---|---|---|---|---|---|---|
| 1 | TAU | 2 | CAN | 1 | LEO | 2 | LIB | 1 | SCO | 2 | CAP |
| 3 | GEM | 4 | LEO | 3 | VIR | 4 | SCO | 3 | SAG | 4 | AQU |
| 6 | CAN | 7 | VIR | 5 | LIB | 6 | SAG | 5 | CAP | 7 | PIS |
| 8 | LEO | 9 | LIB | 7 | SCO | 9 | CAP | 7 | AQU | 9 | ARI |
| 10 | VIR | 11 | SCO | 9 | SAG | 11 | AQU | 9 | PIS | 12 | TAU |
| 12 | LIB | 13 | SAG | 11 | CAP | 13 | PIS | 12 | ARI | 14 | GEM |
| 15 | SCO | 15 | CAP | 14 | AQU | 16 | ARI | 14 | TAU | 17 | CAN |
| 17 | SAG | 17 | AQU | 16 | PIS | 18 | TAU | 17 | GEM | 19 | LEO |
| 19 | CAP | 20 | PIS | 18 | ARI | 21 | GEM | 19 | CAN | 21 | VIR |
| 21 | AQU | 22 | ARI | 21 | TAU | 23 | CAN | 22 | LEO | 24 | LIB |
| 23 | PIS | 25 | TAU | 23 | GEM | 26 | LEO | 24 | VIR | 26 | SCO |
| 26 | ARI | 27 | GEM | 26 | CAN | 28 | VIR | 26 | LIB | 28 | SAG |
| 28 | TAU | 30 | CAN | 28 | LEO | 30 | LIB | 28 | SCO | 30 | CAP |
| 31 | GEM | | | 30 | VIR | | | 30 | SAG | | |

# Moon Signs 1945-2025

## 1968

| JAN | | FEB | | MAR | | APR | | MAY | | JUN | |
|---|---|---|---|---|---|---|---|---|---|---|---|
| 1 | AQU | 2 | ARI | 3 | TAU | 2 | GEM | 1 | CAN | 2 | VIR |
| 3 | PIS | 4 | TAU | 5 | GEM | 4 | CAN | 4 | LEO | 5 | LIB |
| 6 | ARI | 7 | GEM | 8 | CAN | 7 | LEO | 6 | VIR | 7 | SCO |
| 8 | TAU | 9 | CAN | 10 | LEO | 9 | VIR | 8 | LIB | 9 | SAG |
| 11 | GEM | 12 | LEO | 12 | VIR | 11 | LIB | 10 | SCO | 11 | CAP |
| 13 | CAN | 14 | VIR | 14 | LIB | 13 | SCO | 12 | SAG | 13 | AQU |
| 15 | LEO | 16 | LIB | 17 | SCO | 15 | SAG | 14 | CAP | 15 | PIS |
| 18 | VIR | 18 | SCO | 19 | SAG | 17 | CAP | 16 | AQU | 17 | ARI |
| 20 | LIB | 20 | SAG | 21 | CAP | 19 | AQU | 19 | PIS | 20 | TAU |
| 22 | SCO | 22 | CAP | 23 | AQU | 21 | PIS | 21 | ARI | 22 | GEM |
| 24 | SAG | 25 | AQU | 25 | PIS | 24 | ARI | 24 | TAU | 25 | CAN |
| 26 | CAP | 27 | PIS | 28 | ARI | 26 | TAU | 26 | GEM | 27 | LEO |
| 28 | AQU | 29 | ARI | 30 | TAU | 29 | GEM | 29 | CAN | 30 | VIR |
| 31 | PIS | | | | | | | 31 | LEO | | |

| JUL | | AUG | | SEP | | OCT | | NOV | | DEC | |
|---|---|---|---|---|---|---|---|---|---|---|---|
| 2 | LIB | 3 | SAG | 1 | CAP | 2 | PIS | 1 | ARI | 1 | TAU |
| 4 | SCO | 5 | CAP | 3 | AQU | 5 | ARI | 3 | TAU | 3 | GEM |
| 6 | SAG | 7 | AQU | 5 | PIS | 7 | TAU | 6 | GEM | 5 | CAN |
| 8 | CAP | 9 | PIS | 7 | ARI | 10 | GEM | 8 | CAN | 8 | LEO |
| 10 | AQU | 11 | ARI | 10 | TAU | 12 | CAN | 11 | LEO | 11 | VIR |
| 12 | PIS | 13 | TAU | 12 | GEM | 15 | LEO | 13 | VIR | 13 | LIB |
| 15 | ARI | 16 | GEM | 15 | CAN | 17 | VIR | 16 | LIB | 15 | SCO |
| 17 | TAU | 18 | CAN | 17 | LEO | 19 | LIB | 18 | SCO | 17 | SAG |
| 20 | GEM | 21 | LEO | 20 | VIR | 21 | SCO | 20 | SAG | 19 | CAP |
| 22 | CAN | 23 | VIR | 22 | LIB | 23 | SAG | 22 | CAP | 21 | AQU |
| 25 | LEO | 25 | LIB | 24 | SCO | 25 | CAP | 24 | AQU | 23 | PIS |
| 27 | VIR | 28 | SCO | 26 | SAG | 27 | AQU | 26 | PIS | 26 | ARI |
| 29 | LIB | 30 | SAG | 28 | CAP | 30 | PIS | 28 | ARI | 28 | TAU |
| 31 | SCO | | | 30 | AQU | | | | | 30 | GEM |

## 1969

| JAN | | FEB | | MAR | | APR | | MAY | | JUN | |
|---|---|---|---|---|---|---|---|---|---|---|---|
| 2 | CAN | 1 | LEO | 2 | VIR | 1 | LIB | 1 | SCO | 1 | CAP |
| 4 | LEO | 3 | VIR | 5 | LIB | 3 | SCO | 3 | SAG | 3 | AQU |
| 7 | VIR | 6 | LIB | 7 | SCO | 5 | SAG | 5 | CAP | 5 | PIS |
| 9 | LIB | 8 | SCO | 9 | SAG | 8 | CAP | 7 | AQU | 7 | ARI |
| 12 | SCO | 10 | SAG | 11 | CAP | 10 | AQU | 9 | PIS | 10 | TAU |
| 14 | SAG | 12 | CAP | 13 | AQU | 12 | PIS | 11 | ARI | 12 | GEM |
| 16 | CAP | 14 | AQU | 16 | PIS | 14 | ARI | 14 | TAU | 15 | CAN |
| 18 | AQU | 16 | PIS | 18 | ARI | 16 | TAU | 16 | GEM | 17 | LEO |
| 20 | PIS | 18 | ARI | 20 | TAU | 19 | GEM | 19 | CAN | 20 | VIR |
| 22 | ARI | 21 | TAU | 22 | GEM | 21 | CAN | 21 | LEO | 22 | LIB |
| 24 | TAU | 23 | GEM | 25 | CAN | 24 | LEO | 24 | VIR | 25 | SCO |
| 27 | GEM | 26 | CAN | 27 | LEO | 26 | VIR | 26 | LIB | 27 | SAG |
| 29 | CAN | 28 | LEO | 30 | VIR | 29 | LIB | 28 | SCO | 29 | CAP |
| | | | | | | | | 30 | SAG | | |

| JUL | | AUG | | SEP | | OCT | | NOV | | DEC | |
|---|---|---|---|---|---|---|---|---|---|---|---|
| 1 | AQU | 1 | ARI | 2 | GEM | 2 | CAN | 1 | LEO | 1 | VIR |
| 3 | PIS | 3 | TAU | 5 | CAN | 4 | LEO | 3 | VIR | 3 | LIB |
| 5 | ARI | 6 | GEM | 7 | LEO | 7 | VIR | 6 | LIB | 5 | SCO |
| 7 | TAU | 8 | CAN | 10 | VIR | 9 | LIB | 8 | SCO | 8 | SAG |
| 10 | GEM | 11 | LEO | 12 | LIB | 12 | SCO | 10 | SAG | 10 | CAP |
| 12 | CAN | 13 | VIR | 14 | SCO | 14 | SAG | 12 | CAP | 12 | AQU |
| 15 | LEO | 16 | LIB | 17 | SAG | 16 | CAP | 14 | AQU | 14 | PIS |
| 17 | VIR | 18 | SCO | 19 | CAP | 18 | AQU | 16 | PIS | 16 | ARI |
| 20 | LIB | 20 | SAG | 21 | AQU | 20 | PIS | 19 | ARI | 18 | TAU |
| 22 | SCO | 22 | CAP | 23 | PIS | 22 | ARI | 21 | TAU | 20 | GEM |
| 24 | SAG | 24 | AQU | 25 | ARI | 25 | TAU | 23 | GEM | 23 | CAN |
| 26 | CAP | 26 | PIS | 27 | TAU | 27 | GEM | 26 | CAN | 25 | LEO |
| 28 | AQU | 29 | ARI | 29 | GEM | 29 | CAN | 28 | LEO | 28 | VIR |
| 30 | PIS | 31 | TAU | | | | | | | 30 | LIB |

# Moon Signs 1945-2025

## 1970

| | JAN | | FEB | | MAR | | APR | | MAY | | JUN |
|---|---|---|---|---|---|---|---|---|---|---|---|
| 2 | SCO | 2 | CAP | 2 | CAP | 2 | PIS | 2 | ARI | 2 | GEM |
| 4 | SAG | 4 | AQU | 4 | AQU | 4 | ARI | 4 | TAU | 5 | CAN |
| 6 | CAP | 6 | PIS | 6 | PIS | 6 | TAU | 6 | GEM | 7 | LEO |
| 8 | AQU | 8 | ARI | 8 | ARI | 9 | GEM | 8 | CAN | 10 | VIR |
| 10 | PIS | 11 | TAU | 10 | TAU | 11 | CAN | 11 | LEO | 12 | LIB |
| 12 | ARI | 13 | GEM | 12 | GEM | 14 | LEO | 13 | VIR | 15 | SCO |
| 14 | TAU | 15 | CAN | 15 | CAN | 16 | VIR | 16 | LIB | 17 | SAG |
| 17 | GEM | 18 | LEO | 17 | LEO | 19 | LIB | 18 | SCO | 19 | CAP |
| 19 | CAN | 20 | VIR | 20 | VIR | 21 | SCO | 20 | SAG | 21 | AQU |
| 22 | LEO | 23 | LIB | 22 | LIB | 23 | SAG | 23 | CAP | 23 | PIS |
| 24 | VIR | 25 | SCO | 25 | SCO | 25 | CAP | 25 | AQU | 25 | ARI |
| 27 | LIB | 28 | SAG | 27 | SAG | 27 | AQU | 27 | PIS | 27 | TAU |
| 29 | SCO | | | 29 | CAP | 30 | PIS | 29 | ARI | 30 | GEM |
| 31 | SAG | | | 31 | AQU | | | 31 | TAU | | |

| | JUL | | AUG | | SEP | | OCT | | NOV | | DEC |
|---|---|---|---|---|---|---|---|---|---|---|---|
| 2 | CAN | 1 | LEO | 2 | LIB | 2 | SCO | 3 | CAP | 2 | AQU |
| 4 | LEO | 3 | VIR | 5 | SCO | 4 | SAG | 5 | AQU | 4 | PIS |
| 7 | VIR | 6 | LIB | 7 | SAG | 6 | CAP | 7 | PIS | 6 | ARI |
| 10 | LIB | 8 | SCO | 9 | CAP | 9 | AQU | 9 | ARI | 8 | TAU |
| 12 | SCO | 11 | SAG | 11 | AQU | 11 | PIS | 11 | TAU | 11 | GEM |
| 14 | SAG | 13 | CAP | 13 | PIS | 13 | ARI | 13 | GEM | 13 | CAN |
| 16 | CAP | 15 | AQU | 15 | ARI | 15 | TAU | 16 | CAN | 15 | LEO |
| 18 | AQU | 17 | PIS | 17 | TAU | 17 | GEM | 18 | LEO | 18 | VIR |
| 20 | PIS | 19 | ARI | 19 | GEM | 19 | CAN | 20 | VIR | 20 | LIB |
| 22 | ARI | 21 | TAU | 22 | CAN | 22 | LEO | 23 | LIB | 23 | SCO |
| 25 | TAU | 23 | GEM | 24 | LEO | 24 | VIR | 25 | SCO | 25 | SAG |
| 27 | GEM | 26 | CAN | 27 | VIR | 27 | LIB | 28 | SAG | 27 | CAP |
| 29 | CAN | 28 | LEO | 29 | LIB | 29 | SCO | 30 | CAP | 29 | AQU |
| | | 31 | VIR | | | 31 | SAG | | | 31 | PIS |

## 1971

| | JAN | | FEB | | MAR | | APR | | MAY | | JUN |
|---|---|---|---|---|---|---|---|---|---|---|---|
| 3 | ARI | 1 | TAU | 2 | GEM | 1 | CAN | 1 | LEO | 2 | LIB |
| 5 | TAU | 3 | GEM | 5 | CAN | 3 | LEO | 3 | VIR | 5 | SCO |
| 7 | GEM | 5 | CAN | 7 | LEO | 6 | VIR | 6 | LIB | 7 | SAG |
| 9 | CAN | 8 | LEO | 10 | VIR | 8 | LIB | 8 | SCO | 9 | CAP |
| 12 | LEO | 10 | VIR | 12 | LIB | 11 | SCO | 11 | SAG | 11 | AQU |
| 14 | VIR | 13 | LIB | 15 | SCO | 13 | SAG | 13 | CAP | 14 | PIS |
| 17 | LIB | 15 | SCO | 17 | SAG | 16 | CAP | 15 | AQU | 16 | ARI |
| 19 | SCO | 18 | SAG | 19 | CAP | 18 | AQU | 17 | PIS | 18 | TAU |
| 22 | SAG | 20 | CAP | 22 | AQU | 20 | PIS | 20 | ARI | 20 | GEM |
| 24 | CAP | 22 | AQU | 24 | PIS | 22 | ARI | 22 | TAU | 22 | CAN |
| 26 | AQU | 24 | PIS | 26 | ARI | 24 | TAU | 24 | GEM | 24 | LEO |
| 28 | PIS | 26 | ARI | 28 | TAU | 26 | GEM | 26 | CAN | 27 | VIR |
| 30 | ARI | 28 | TAU | 30 | GEM | 28 | CAN | 28 | LEO | 29 | LIB |
| | | | | | | | | 30 | VIR | | |

| | JUL | | AUG | | SEP | | OCT | | NOV | | DEC |
|---|---|---|---|---|---|---|---|---|---|---|---|
| 2 | SCO | 1 | SAG | 2 | AQU | 1 | PIS | 2 | TAU | 1 | GEM |
| 4 | SAG | 3 | CAP | 4 | PIS | 3 | ARI | 4 | GEM | 3 | CAN |
| 7 | CAP | 5 | AQU | 6 | ARI | 5 | TAU | 6 | CAN | 5 | LEO |
| 9 | AQU | 7 | PIS | 8 | TAU | 7 | GEM | 8 | LEO | 8 | VIR |
| 11 | PIS | 9 | ARI | 10 | GEM | 9 | CAN | 10 | VIR | 10 | LIB |
| 13 | ARI | 11 | TAU | 12 | CAN | 12 | LEO | 13 | LIB | 13 | SCO |
| 15 | TAU | 13 | GEM | 14 | LEO | 14 | VIR | 15 | SCO | 15 | SAG |
| 17 | GEM | 16 | CAN | 17 | VIR | 16 | LIB | 18 | SAG | 17 | CAP |
| 19 | CAN | 18 | LEO | 19 | LIB | 19 | SCO | 20 | CAP | 20 | AQU |
| 22 | LEO | 20 | VIR | 22 | SCO | 22 | SAG | 23 | AQU | 22 | PIS |
| 24 | VIR | 23 | LIB | 24 | SAG | 24 | CAP | 25 | PIS | 24 | ARI |
| 27 | LIB | 26 | SCO | 27 | CAP | 26 | AQU | 27 | ARI | 26 | TAU |
| 29 | SCO | 28 | SAG | 29 | AQU | 29 | PIS | 29 | TAU | 28 | GEM |
| | | 30 | CAP | | | 31 | ARI | | | 30 | CAN |

# Moon Signs 1945-2025

## 1972

| JAN | | FEB | | MAR | | APR | | MAY | | JUN | |
|---|---|---|---|---|---|---|---|---|---|---|---|
| 2 | LEO | 3 | LIB | 1 | LIB | 2 | SAG | 2 | CAP | 1 | AQU |
| 4 | VIR | 5 | SCO | 4 | SCO | 5 | CAP | 5 | AQU | 3 | PIS |
| 6 | LIB | 8 | SAG | 6 | SAG | 7 | AQU | 7 | PIS | 5 | ARI |
| 9 | SCO | 10 | CAP | 9 | CAP | 10 | PIS | 9 | ARI | 7 | TAU |
| 11 | SAG | 12 | AQU | 11 | AQU | 12 | ARI | 11 | TAU | 9 | GEM |
| 14 | CAP | 15 | PIS | 13 | PIS | 14 | TAU | 13 | GEM | 11 | CAN |
| 16 | AQU | 17 | ARI | 15 | ARI | 16 | GEM | 15 | CAN | 14 | LEO |
| 18 | PIS | 19 | TAU | 17 | TAU | 18 | CAN | 17 | LEO | 16 | VIR |
| 20 | ARI | 21 | GEM | 19 | GEM | 20 | LEO | 19 | VIR | 18 | LIB |
| 23 | TAU | 23 | CAN | 21 | CAN | 22 | VIR | 22 | LIB | 21 | SCO |
| 25 | GEM | 25 | LEO | 24 | LEO | 25 | LIB | 24 | SCO | 23 | SAG |
| 27 | CAN | 28 | VIR | 26 | VIR | 27 | SCO | 27 | SAG | 26 | CAP |
| 29 | LEO | | | 28 | LIB | 30 | SAG | 29 | CAP | 28 | AQU |
| 31 | VIR | | | 31 | SCO | | | | | 30 | PIS |

| JUL | | AUG | | SEP | | OCT | | NOV | | DEC | |
|---|---|---|---|---|---|---|---|---|---|---|---|
| 3 | ARI | 1 | TAU | 1 | CAN | 1 | LEO | 2 | LIB | 1 | SCO |
| 5 | TAU | 3 | GEM | 4 | LEO | 3 | VIR | 4 | SCO | 4 | SAG |
| 7 | GEM | 5 | CAN | 6 | VIR | 5 | LIB | 7 | SAG | 7 | CAP |
| 9 | CAN | 7 | LEO | 8 | LIB | 8 | SCO | 9 | CAP | 9 | AQU |
| 11 | LEO | 10 | VIR | 11 | SCO | 10 | SAG | 12 | AQU | 11 | PIS |
| 13 | VIR | 12 | LIB | 13 | SAG | 13 | CAP | 14 | PIS | 14 | ARI |
| 15 | LIB | 14 | SCO | 16 | CAP | 15 | AQU | 16 | ARI | 16 | TAU |
| 18 | SCO | 17 | SAG | 18 | AQU | 18 | PIS | 18 | TAU | 18 | GEM |
| 20 | SAG | 19 | CAP | 20 | PIS | 20 | ARI | 20 | GEM | 20 | CAN |
| 23 | CAP | 22 | AQU | 22 | ARI | 22 | TAU | 22 | CAN | 22 | LEO |
| 25 | AQU | 24 | PIS | 24 | TAU | 24 | GEM | 24 | LEO | 24 | VIR |
| 28 | PIS | 26 | ARI | 27 | GEM | 26 | CAN | 27 | VIR | 26 | LIB |
| 30 | ARI | 28 | TAU | 29 | CAN | 28 | LEO | 29 | LIB | 29 | SCO |
| | | 30 | GEM | | | 30 | VIR | | | | |

## 1973

| JAN | | FEB | | MAR | | APR | | MAY | | JUN | |
|---|---|---|---|---|---|---|---|---|---|---|---|
| 3 | CAP | 2 | AQU | 1 | AQU | 2 | ARI | 1 | TAU | 2 | CAN |
| 5 | AQU | 4 | PIS | 3 | PIS | 4 | TAU | 3 | GEM | 4 | LEO |
| 8 | PIS | 6 | ARI | 5 | ARI | 6 | GEM | 5 | CAN | 6 | VIR |
| 10 | ARI | 8 | TAU | 8 | TAU | 8 | CAN | 7 | LEO | 8 | LIB |
| 12 | TAU | 10 | GEM | 10 | GEM | 10 | LEO | 10 | VIR | 11 | SCO |
| 14 | GEM | 13 | CAN | 12 | CAN | 12 | VIR | 12 | LIB | 13 | SAG |
| 16 | CAN | 15 | LEO | 14 | LEO | 15 | LIB | 14 | SCO | 16 | CAP |
| 18 | LEO | 17 | VIR | 16 | VIR | 17 | SCO | 17 | SAG | 18 | AQU |
| 20 | VIR | 19 | LIB | 18 | LIB | 20 | SAG | 19 | CAP | 21 | PIS |
| 23 | LIB | 21 | SCO | 21 | SCO | 22 | CAP | 22 | AQU | 23 | ARI |
| 25 | SCO | 24 | SAG | 23 | SAG | 25 | AQU | 24 | PIS | 25 | TAU |
| 28 | SAG | 26 | CAP | 26 | CAP | 27 | PIS | 27 | ARI | 27 | GEM |
| 30 | CAP | | | 28 | AQU | 29 | ARI | 29 | TAU | 29 | CAN |
| | | | | 31 | PIS | | | 31 | GEM | | |

| JUL | | AUG | | SEP | | OCT | | NOV | | DEC | |
|---|---|---|---|---|---|---|---|---|---|---|---|
| 1 | LEO | 2 | LIB | 1 | SCO | 3 | CAP | 2 | AQU | 1 | PIS |
| 3 | VIR | 4 | SCO | 3 | SAG | 5 | AQU | 4 | PIS | 4 | ARI |
| 5 | LIB | 7 | SAG | 5 | CAP | 8 | PIS | 6 | ARI | 6 | TAU |
| 8 | SCO | 9 | CAP | 8 | AQU | 10 | ARI | 9 | TAU | 8 | GEM |
| 10 | SAG | 12 | AQU | 10 | PIS | 12 | TAU | 11 | GEM | 10 | CAN |
| 13 | CAP | 14 | PIS | 13 | ARI | 14 | GEM | 13 | CAN | 12 | LEO |
| 15 | AQU | 16 | ARI | 15 | TAU | 16 | CAN | 15 | LEO | 14 | VIR |
| 18 | PIS | 19 | TAU | 17 | GEM | 19 | LEO | 17 | VIR | 16 | LIB |
| 20 | ARI | 21 | GEM | 19 | CAN | 21 | VIR | 19 | LIB | 19 | SCO |
| 22 | TAU | 23 | CAN | 21 | LEO | 23 | LIB | 22 | SCO | 21 | SAG |
| 25 | GEM | 25 | LEO | 23 | VIR | 25 | SCO | 24 | SAG | 24 | CAP |
| 27 | CAN | 27 | VIR | 26 | LIB | 28 | SAG | 26 | CAP | 26 | AQU |
| 29 | LEO | 29 | LIB | 28 | SCO | 30 | CAP | 29 | AQU | 29 | PIS |
| 31 | VIR | | | 30 | SAG | | | | | 31 | ARI |

# Moon Signs 1945-2025

## 1974

| JAN | | FEB | | MAR | | APR | | MAY | | JUN | |
|---|---|---|---|---|---|---|---|---|---|---|---|
| 2 | TAU | 1 | GEM | 2 | CAN | 1 | LEO | 2 | LIB | 1 | SOO |
| 5 | GEM | 3 | CAN | 4 | LEO | 3 | VIR | 4 | SCO | 3 | SAG |
| 7 | CAN | 5 | LEO | 7 | VIR | 5 | LIB | 7 | SAG | 6 | CAP |
| 9 | LEO | 7 | VIR | 9 | LIB | 7 | SCO | 9 | CAP | 8 | AQU |
| 11 | VIR | 9 | LIB | 11 | SCO | 9 | SAG | 12 | AQU | 11 | PIS |
| 13 | LIB | 11 | SCO | 13 | SAG | 12 | CAP | 14 | PIS | 13 | ARI |
| 15 | SCO | 14 | SAG | 16 | CAP | 14 | AQU | 17 | ARI | 15 | TAU |
| 17 | SAG | 16 | CAP | 18 | AQU | 17 | PIS | 21 | GEM | 18 | GEM |
| 20 | CAP | 19 | AQU | 21 | PIS | 19 | ARI | 23 | CAN | 20 | CAN |
| 22 | AQU | 21 | PIS | 23 | ARI | 22 | TAU | 25 | LEO | 22 | LEO |
| 25 | PIS | 24 | ARI | 25 | TAU | 24 | GEM | 27 | VIR | 24 | VIR |
| 27 | ARI | 26 | TAU | 27 | GEM | 26 | CAN | 30 | LIB | 26 | LIB |
| 30 | TAU | 28 | GEM | 30 | CAN | 28 | LEO | | | 28 | SCO |
| | | | | | | 30 | VIR | | | 30 | SAG |

| JUL | | AUG | | SEP | | OCT | | NOV | | DEC | |
|---|---|---|---|---|---|---|---|---|---|---|---|
| 3 | CAP | 2 | AQU | 3 | ARI | 2 | TAU | 1 | GEM | 1 | CAN |
| 5 | AQU | 4 | PIS | 5 | TAU | 5 | GEM | 3 | CAN | 3 | LEO |
| 8 | PIS | 7 | ARI | 8 | GEM | 7 | CAN | 5 | LEO | 5 | VIR |
| 10 | ARI | 9 | TAU | 10 | CAN | 9 | LEO | 8 | VIR | 7 | LIB |
| 13 | TAU | 11 | GEM | 12 | LEO | 11 | VIR | 10 | LIB | 9 | SCO |
| 15 | GEM | 13 | CAN | 14 | VIR | 13 | LIB | 12 | SCO | 11 | SAG |
| 17 | CAN | 15 | LEO | 16 | LIB | 15 | SCO | 14 | SAG | 14 | CAP |
| 19 | LEO | 17 | VIR | 18 | SCO | 18 | SAG | 16 | CAP | 16 | AQU |
| 21 | VIR | 19 | LIB | 20 | SAG | 20 | CAP | 19 | AQU | 19 | PIS |
| 23 | LIB | 22 | SCO | 23 | CAP | 22 | AQU | 21 | PIS | 21 | ARI |
| 25 | SCO | 24 | SAG | 25 | AQU | 25 | PIS | 24 | ARI | 24 | TAU |
| 28 | SAG | 26 | CAP | 28 | PIS | 27 | ARI | 26 | TAU | 26 | GEM |
| 30 | CAP | 29 | AQU | 30 | ARI | 30 | TAU | 28 | GEM | 28 | CAN |
| | | 31 | PIS | | | | | | | 30 | LEO |

## 1975

| JAN | | FEB | | MAR | | APR | | MAY | | JUN | |
|---|---|---|---|---|---|---|---|---|---|---|---|
| 1 | VIR | 2 | SCO | 1 | SCO | 2 | CAP | 2 | AQU | 3 | ARI |
| 3 | LIB | 4 | SAG | 3 | SAG | 4 | AQU | 4 | PIS | 5 | TAU |
| 5 | SCO | 6 | CAP | 5 | CAP | 7 | PIS | 7 | ARI | 8 | GEM |
| 8 | SAG | 9 | AQU | 8 | AQU | 9 | ARI | 9 | TAU | 10 | CAN |
| 10 | CAP | 11 | PIS | 10 | PIS | 12 | TAU | 11 | GEM | 12 | LEO |
| 12 | AQU | 14 | ARI | 13 | ARI | 14 | GEM | 14 | CAN | 14 | VIR |
| 15 | PIS | 16 | TAU | 15 | TAU | 16 | CAN | 16 | LEO | 16 | LIB |
| 17 | ARI | 19 | GEM | 18 | GEM | 19 | LEO | 18 | VIR | 18 | SCO |
| 20 | TAU | 21 | CAN | 20 | CAN | 21 | VIR | 20 | LIB | 21 | SAG |
| 22 | GEM | 23 | LEO | 22 | LEO | 23 | LIB | 22 | SCO | 23 | CAP |
| 24 | CAN | 25 | VIR | 24 | VIR | 25 | SCO | 24 | SAG | 25 | AQU |
| 26 | LEO | 27 | LIB | 26 | LIB | 27 | SAG | 27 | CAP | 28 | PIS |
| 28 | VIR | | | 28 | SCO | 29 | CAP | 29 | AQU | 30 | ARI |
| 30 | LIB | | | 30 | SAG | | | 31 | PIS | | |

| JUL | | AUG | | SEP | | OCT | | NOV | | DEC | |
|---|---|---|---|---|---|---|---|---|---|---|---|
| 3 | TAU | 1 | GEM | 2 | LEO | 2 | VIR | 2 | SCO | 2 | SAG |
| 5 | GEM | 4 | CAN | 4 | VIR | 4 | LIB | 4 | SAG | 4 | CAP |
| 7 | CAN | 6 | LEO | 6 | LIB | 6 | SCO | 6 | CAP | 6 | AQU |
| 9 | LEO | 8 | VIR | 8 | SCO | 8 | SAG | 9 | AQU | 8 | PIS |
| 11 | VIR | 10 | LIB | 10 | SAG | 10 | CAP | 11 | PIS | 11 | ARI |
| 14 | LIB | 12 | SCO | 13 | CAP | 12 | AQU | 14 | ARI | 13 | TAU |
| 16 | SCO | 14 | SAG | 15 | AQU | 15 | PIS | 16 | TAU | 16 | GEM |
| 18 | SAG | 16 | CAP | 18 | PIS | 17 | ARI | 19 | GEM | 18 | CAN |
| 20 | CAP | 19 | AQU | 20 | ARI | 20 | TAU | 21 | CAN | 20 | LEO |
| 23 | AQU | 21 | PIS | 23 | TAU | 22 | GEM | 23 | LEO | 23 | VIR |
| 25 | PIS | 24 | ARI | 25 | GEM | 25 | CAN | 25 | VIR | 25 | LIB |
| 28 | ARI | 26 | TAU | 27 | CAN | 27 | LEO | 27 | LIB | 27 | SCO |
| 30 | TAU | 29 | GEM | 30 | LEO | 29 | VIR | 30 | SCO | 29 | SAG |
| | | 31 | CAN | | | 31 | LIB | | | 31 | CAP |

## 1976

| JAN | | FEB | | MAR | | APR | | MAY | | JUN | |
|---|---|---|---|---|---|---|---|---|---|---|---|
| 2 | AQU | 1 | PIS | 2 | ARI | 1 | TAU | 3 | CAN | 1 | LEO |
| 5 | PIS | 4 | ARI | 4 | TAU | 3 | GEM | 5 | LEO | 4 | VIR |
| 7 | ARI | 6 | TAU | 7 | GEM | 6 | CAN | 7 | VIR | 6 | LIB |
| 10 | TAU | 9 | GEM | 9 | CAN | 8 | LEO | 10 | LIB | 8 | SCO |
| 12 | GEM | 11 | CAN | 12 | LEO | 10 | VIR | 12 | SCO | 10 | SAG |
| 15 | CAN | 13 | LEO | 14 | VIR | 12 | LIB | 14 | SAG | 12 | CAP |
| 17 | LEO | 15 | VIR | 16 | LIB | 14 | SCO | 16 | CAP | 14 | AQU |
| 19 | VIR | 17 | LIB | 18 | SCO | 16 | SAG | 18 | AQU | 17 | PIS |
| 21 | LIB | 19 | SCO | 20 | SAG | 18 | CAP | 20 | PIS | 19 | ARI |
| 23 | SCO | 21 | SAG | 22 | CAP | 20 | AQU | 23 | ARI | 22 | TAU |
| 25 | SAG | 24 | CAP | 24 | AQU | 23 | PIS | 25 | TAU | 24 | GEM |
| 27 | CAP | 26 | AQU | 27 | PIS | 25 | ARI | 28 | GEM | 26 | CAN |
| 30 | AQU | 28 | PIS | 29 | ARI | 28 | TAU | 30 | CAN | 29 | LEO |
| | | | | | | 30 | GEM | | | | |

| JUL | | AUG | | SEP | | OCT | | NOV | | DEC | |
|---|---|---|---|---|---|---|---|---|---|---|---|
| 1 | VIR | 1 | SCO | 2 | CAP | 1 | AQU | 2 | ARI | 2 | TAU |
| 3 | LIB | 4 | SAG | 4 | AQU | 4 | PIS | 5 | TAU | 5 | GEM |
| 5 | SCO | 6 | CAP | 7 | PIS | 6 | ARI | 8 | GEM | 7 | CAN |
| 7 | SAG | 8 | AQU | 9 | ARI | 9 | TAU | 10 | CAN | 10 | LEO |
| 9 | CAP | 10 | PIS | 11 | TAU | 11 | GEM | 12 | LEO | 12 | VIR |
| 12 | AQU | 13 | ARI | 14 | GEM | 14 | CAN | 15 | VIR | 14 | LIB |
| 14 | PIS | 15 | TAU | 17 | CAN | 16 | LEO | 17 | LIB | 16 | SCO |
| 16 | ARI | 18 | GEM | 19 | LEO | 18 | VIR | 19 | SCO | 18 | SAG |
| 19 | TAU | 20 | CAN | 21 | VIR | 21 | LIB | 21 | SAG | 20 | CAP |
| 21 | GEM | 22 | LEO | 23 | LIB | 23 | SCO | 23 | CAP | 22 | AQU |
| 24 | CAN | 25 | VIR | 25 | SCO | 25 | SAG | 25 | AQU | 25 | PIS |
| 26 | LEO | 27 | LIB | 27 | SAG | 27 | CAP | 27 | PIS | 27 | ARI |
| 28 | VIR | 29 | SCO | 29 | CAP | 29 | AQU | 30 | ARI | 30 | TAU |
| 30 | LIB | 31 | SAG | | | 31 | PIS | | | | |

## 1977

| JAN | | FEB | | MAR | | APR | | MAY | | JUN | |
|---|---|---|---|---|---|---|---|---|---|---|---|
| 1 | GEM | 2 | LEO | 2 | LEO | 2 | LIB | 2 | SCO | 2 | CAP |
| 4 | CAN | 5 | VIR | 4 | VIR | 5 | SCO | 4 | SAG | 4 | AQU |
| 6 | LEO | 7 | LIB | 6 | LIB | 7 | SAG | 6 | CAP | 7 | PIS |
| 8 | VIR | 9 | SCO | 8 | SCO | 9 | CAP | 8 | AQU | 9 | ARI |
| 10 | LIB | 11 | SAG | 10 | SAG | 11 | AQU | 10 | PIS | 11 | TAU |
| 13 | SCO | 13 | CAP | 12 | CAP | 13 | PIS | 13 | ARI | 14 | GEM |
| 15 | SAG | 15 | AQU | 15 | AQU | 15 | ARI | 15 | TAU | 16 | CAN |
| 17 | CAP | 17 | PIS | 17 | PIS | 18 | TAU | 18 | GEM | 19 | LEO |
| 19 | AQU | 20 | ARI | 19 | ARI | 20 | GEM | 20 | CAN | 21 | VIR |
| 21 | PIS | 22 | TAU | 22 | TAU | 23 | CAN | 23 | LEO | 24 | LIB |
| 23 | ARI | 25 | GEM | 24 | GEM | 25 | LEO | 25 | VIR | 26 | SCO |
| 26 | TAU | 27 | CAN | 27 | CAN | 28 | VIR | 27 | LIB | 28 | SAG |
| 28 | GEM | | | 29 | LEO | 30 | LIB | 29 | SCO | 30 | CAP |
| 31 | CAN | | | 31 | VIR | | | 31 | SAG | | |

| JUL | | AUG | | SEP | | OCT | | NOV | | DEC | |
|---|---|---|---|---|---|---|---|---|---|---|---|
| 2 | AQU | 3 | ARI | 1 | TAU | 1 | GEM | 3 | LEO | 2 | VIR |
| 4 | PIS | 5 | TAU | 4 | GEM | 4 | CAN | 5 | VIR | 5 | LIB |
| 6 | ARI | 7 | GEM | 6 | CAN | 6 | LEO | 7 | LIB | 7 | SCO |
| 9 | TAU | 10 | CAN | 9 | LEO | 9 | VIR | 9 | SCO | 9 | SAG |
| 11 | GEM | 12 | LEO | 11 | VIR | 11 | LIB | 11 | SAG | 11 | CAP |
| 14 | CAN | 15 | VIR | 13 | LIB | 13 | SCO | 13 | CAP | 13 | AQU |
| 16 | LEO | 17 | LIB | 16 | SCO | 15 | SAG | 15 | AQU | 15 | PIS |
| 19 | VIR | 19 | SCO | 18 | SAG | 17 | CAP | 18 | PIS | 17 | ARI |
| 21 | LIB | 21 | SAG | 20 | CAP | 19 | AQU | 20 | ARI | 19 | TAU |
| 23 | SCO | 24 | CAP | 22 | AQU | 21 | PIS | 22 | TAU | 22 | GEM |
| 25 | SAG | 26 | AQU | 24 | PIS | 24 | ARI | 25 | GEM | 25 | CAN |
| 27 | CAP | 28 | PIS | 26 | ARI | 26 | TAU | 27 | CAN | 27 | LEO |
| 29 | AQU | 30 | ARI | 29 | TAU | 28 | GEM | 30 | LEO | 30 | VIR |
| 31 | PIS | | | | | 31 | CAN | | | | |

# Moon Signs 1945-2025

## 1978

| | JAN | | FEB | | MAR | | APR | | MAY | | JUN |
|---|---|---|---|---|---|---|---|---|---|---|---|
| 1 | LIB | 2 | SAG | 1 | SAG | 1 | AQU | 1 | PIS | 1 | TAU |
| 3 | SCO | 4 | CAP | 3 | CAP | 3 | PIS | 3 | ARI | 4 | GEM |
| 5 | SAG | 6 | AQU | 5 | AQU | 6 | ARI | 5 | TAU | 6 | CAN |
| 7 | CAP | 8 | PIS | 7 | PIS | 8 | TAU | 8 | GEM | 9 | LEO |
| 9 | AQU | 10 | ARI | 9 | ARI | 10 | GEM | 10 | CAN | 11 | VIR |
| 11 | PIS | 12 | TAU | 12 | TAU | 13 | CAN | 13 | LEO | 14 | LIB |
| 13 | ARI | 15 | GEM | 14 | GEM | 15 | LEO | 15 | VIR | 16 | SCO |
| 16 | TAU | 17 | CAN | 16 | CAN | 18 | VIR | 17 | LIB | 18 | SAG |
| 18 | GEM | 20 | LEO | 19 | LEO | 20 | LIB | 20 | SCO | 20 | CAP |
| 21 | CAN | 22 | VIR | 21 | VIR | 22 | SCO | 22 | SAG | 22 | AQU |
| 23 | LEO | 24 | LIB | 24 | LIB | 24 | SAG | 24 | CAP | 24 | PIS |
| 26 | VIR | 27 | SCO | 26 | SCO | 26 | CAP | 26 | AQU | 26 | ARI |
| 28 | LIB | | | 28 | SAG | 29 | AQU | 28 | PIS | 29 | TAU |
| 30 | SCO | | | 30 | CAP | | | 30 | ARI | | |

| | JUL | | AUG | | SEP | | OCT | | NOV | | DEC |
|---|---|---|---|---|---|---|---|---|---|---|---|
| 1 | GEM | 2 | LEO | 1 | VIR | 1 | LIB | 2 | SAG | 1 | CAP |
| 4 | CAN | 5 | VIR | 4 | LIB | 3 | SCO | 4 | CAP | 3 | AQU |
| 6 | LEO | 7 | LIB | 6 | SCO | 5 | SAG | 6 | AQU | 5 | PIS |
| 9 | VIR | 10 | SCO | 8 | SAG | 8 | CAP | 8 | PIS | 7 | ARI |
| 11 | LIB | 12 | SAG | 10 | CAP | 10 | AQU | 10 | ARI | 10 | TAU |
| 13 | SCO | 14 | CAP | 12 | AQU | 12 | PIS | 12 | TAU | 12 | GEM |
| 16 | SAG | 16 | AQU | 14 | PIS | 14 | ARI | 15 | GEM | 14 | CAN |
| 18 | CAP | 18 | PIS | 17 | ARI | 16 | TAU | 17 | CAN | 17 | LEO |
| 20 | AQU | 20 | ARI | 19 | TAU | 18 | GEM | 20 | LEO | 19 | VIR |
| 22 | PIS | 22 | TAU | 21 | GEM | 21 | CAN | 22 | VIR | 22 | LIB |
| 24 | ARI | 25 | GEM | 23 | CAN | 23 | LEO | 25 | LIB | 24 | SCO |
| 26 | TAU | 27 | CAN | 26 | LEO | 26 | VIR | 27 | SCO | 27 | SAG |
| 28 | GEM | 30 | LEO | 28 | VIR | 28 | LIB | 29 | SAG | 29 | CAP |
| 31 | CAN | | | | | 31 | SCO | | | 31 | AQU |

## 1979

| | JAN | | FEB | | MAR | | APR | | MAY | | JUN |
|---|---|---|---|---|---|---|---|---|---|---|---|
| 2 | PIS | 2 | TAU | 2 | TAU | 3 | CAN | 2 | LEO | 1 | VIR |
| 4 | ARI | 5 | GEM | 4 | GEM | 5 | LEO | 5 | VIR | 4 | LIB |
| 6 | TAU | 7 | CAN | 6 | CAN | 8 | VIR | 7 | LIB | 6 | SCO |
| 8 | GEM | 9 | LEO | 9 | LEO | 10 | LIB | 10 | SCO | 8 | SAG |
| 11 | CAN | 12 | VIR | 11 | VIR | 12 | SCO | 12 | SAG | 11 | CAP |
| 13 | LEO | 15 | LIB | 14 | LIB | 15 | SAG | 14 | CAP | 13 | AQU |
| 16 | VIR | 17 | SCO | 16 | SCO | 17 | CAP | 16 | AQU | 15 | PIS |
| 18 | LIB | 19 | SAG | 19 | SAG | 19 | AQU | 18 | PIS | 17 | ARI |
| 21 | SCO | 21 | CAP | 21 | CAP | 21 | PIS | 21 | ARI | 19 | TAU |
| 23 | SAG | 24 | AQU | 23 | AQU | 23 | ARI | 23 | TAU | 21 | GEM |
| 25 | CAP | 26 | PIS | 25 | PIS | 25 | TAU | 25 | GEM | 24 | CAN |
| 27 | AQU | 28 | ARI | 27 | ARI | 28 | GEM | 27 | CAN | 26 | LEO |
| 29 | PIS | | | 29 | TAU | 30 | CAN | 30 | LEO | 29 | VIR |
| 31 | ARI | | | 31 | GEM | | | | | | |

| | JUL | | AUG | | SEP | | OCT | | NOV | | DEC |
|---|---|---|---|---|---|---|---|---|---|---|---|
| 1 | LIB | 2 | SAG | 1 | CAP | 2 | PIS | 1 | ARI | 2 | GEM |
| 4 | SCO | 4 | CAP | 3 | AQU | 4 | ARI | 3 | TAU | 4 | CAN |
| 6 | SAG | 6 | AQU | 5 | PIS | 6 | TAU | 5 | GEM | 7 | LEO |
| 8 | CAP | 8 | PIS | 7 | ARI | 8 | GEM | 7 | CAN | 9 | VIR |
| 10 | AQU | 10 | ARI | 9 | TAU | 11 | CAN | 9 | LEO | 12 | LIB |
| 12 | PIS | 13 | TAU | 11 | GEM | 13 | LEO | 12 | VIR | 14 | SCO |
| 14 | ARI | 15 | GEM | 13 | CAN | 16 | VIR | 14 | LIB | 17 | SAG |
| 16 | TAU | 17 | CAN | 16 | LEO | 18 | LIB | 17 | SCO | 19 | CAP |
| 19 | GEM | 20 | LEO | 18 | VIR | 21 | SCO | 19 | SAG | 21 | AQU |
| 21 | CAN | 22 | VIR | 21 | LIB | 23 | SAG | 22 | CAP | 23 | PIS |
| 23 | LEO | 25 | LIB | 23 | SCO | 25 | CAP | 24 | AQU | 25 | ARI |
| 26 | VIR | 27 | SCO | 26 | SAG | 28 | AQU | 26 | PIS | 27 | TAU |
| 28 | LIB | 30 | SAG | 28 | CAP | 30 | PIS | 28 | ARI | 30 | GEM |
| 31 | SCO | | | 30 | AQU | | | 30 | TAU | | |

# Moon Signs 1945-2025

## 1980

| JAN | | FEB | | MAR | | APR | | MAY | | JUN | |
|---|---|---|---|---|---|---|---|---|---|---|---|
| 1 | CAN | 2 | VIR | 3 | LIB | 2 | SCO | 1 | SAG | 2 | AQU |
| 3 | LEO | 4 | LIB | 5 | SCO | 4 | SAG | 4 | CAP | 4 | PIS |
| 6 | VIR | 7 | SCO | 8 | SAG | 6 | CAP | 6 | AQU | 6 | ARI |
| 8 | LIB | 9 | SAG | 10 | CAP | 9 | AQU | 8 | PIS | 9 | TAU |
| 11 | SCO | 12 | CAP | 12 | AQU | 11 | PIS | 10 | ARI | 11 | GEM |
| 13 | SAG | 14 | AQU | 14 | PIS | 13 | ARI | 12 | TAU | 13 | CAN |
| 15 | CAP | 16 | PIS | 16 | ARI | 15 | TAU | 14 | GEM | 15 | LEO |
| 17 | AQU | 18 | ARI | 18 | TAU | 17 | GEM | 16 | CAN | 17 | VIR |
| 19 | PIS | 20 | TAU | 20 | GEM | 19 | CAN | 19 | LEO | 20 | LIB |
| 21 | ARI | 22 | GEM | 23 | CAN | 21 | LEO | 21 | VIR | 22 | SCO |
| 24 | TAU | 24 | CAN | 25 | LEO | 24 | VIR | 24 | LIB | 25 | SAG |
| 26 | GEM | 27 | LEO | 27 | VIR | 26 | LIB | 26 | SCO | 27 | CAP |
| 28 | CAN | 29 | VIR | 30 | LIB | 29 | SCO | 29 | SAG | 29 | AQU |
| 30 | LEO | | | | | | | 31 | CAP | | |

| JUL | | AUG | | SEP | | OCT | | NOV | | DEC | |
|---|---|---|---|---|---|---|---|---|---|---|---|
| 2 | PIS | 2 | TAU | 3 | CAN | 2 | LEO | 1 | VIR | 1 | LIB |
| 4 | ARI | 4 | GEM | 5 | LEO | 5 | VIR | 3 | LIB | 3 | SCO |
| 6 | TAU | 6 | CAN | 7 | VIR | 7 | LIB | 6 | SCO | 6 | SAG |
| 8 | GEM | 9 | LEO | 10 | LIB | 10 | SCO | 8 | SAG | 8 | CAP |
| 10 | CAN | 11 | VIR | 12 | SCO | 12 | SAG | 11 | CAP | 10 | AQU |
| 12 | LEO | 14 | LIB | 15 | SAG | 15 | CAP | 13 | AQU | 13 | PIS |
| 15 | VIR | 16 | SCO | 17 | CAP | 17 | AQU | 15 | PIS | 15 | ARI |
| 17 | LIB | 19 | SAG | 20 | AQU | 19 | PIS | 18 | ARI | 17 | TAU |
| 20 | SCO | 21 | CAP | 22 | PIS | 21 | ARI | 20 | TAU | 19 | GEM |
| 22 | SAG | 23 | AQU | 24 | ARI | 23 | TAU | 22 | GEM | 21 | CAN |
| 25 | CAP | 25 | PIS | 26 | TAU | 25 | GEM | 24 | CAN | 23 | LEO |
| 27 | AQU | 27 | ARI | 28 | GEM | 27 | CAN | 26 | LEO | 25 | VIR |
| 29 | PIS | 29 | TAU | 30 | CAN | 29 | LEO | 28 | VIR | 28 | LIB |
| 31 | ARI | 31 | GEM | | | | | | | 30 | SCO |

## 1981

| JAN | | FEB | | MAR | | APR | | MAY | | JUN | |
|---|---|---|---|---|---|---|---|---|---|---|---|
| 2 | SAG | 1 | CAP | 2 | AQU | 1 | PIS | 1 | ARI | 1 | GEM |
| 4 | CAP | 3 | AQU | 5 | PIS | 3 | ARI | 3 | TAU | 3 | CAN |
| 7 | AQU | 5 | PIS | 7 | ARI | 5 | TAU | 5 | GEM | 5 | LEO |
| 9 | PIS | 7 | ARI | 9 | TAU | 7 | GEM | 7 | CAN | 7 | VIR |
| 11 | ARI | 9 | TAU | 11 | GEM | 9 | CAN | 9 | LEO | 10 | LIB |
| 13 | TAU | 12 | GEM | 13 | CAN | 11 | LEO | 11 | VIR | 12 | SCO |
| 15 | GEM | 14 | CAN | 15 | LEO | 14 | VIR | 13 | LIB | 15 | SAG |
| 17 | CAN | 16 | LEO | 18 | VIR | 16 | LIB | 16 | SCO | 17 | CAP |
| 20 | LEO | 18 | VIR | 20 | LIB | 19 | SCO | 18 | SAG | 20 | AQU |
| 22 | VIR | 21 | LIB | 22 | SCO | 21 | SAG | 21 | CAP | 22 | PIS |
| 24 | LIB | 23 | SCO | 25 | SAG | 24 | CAP | 23 | AQU | 24 | ARI |
| 27 | SCO | 26 | SAG | 27 | CAP | 26 | AQU | 26 | PIS | 26 | TAU |
| 29 | SAG | 28 | CAP | 30 | AQU | 28 | PIS | 28 | ARI | 28 | GEM |
| | | | | | | | | 30 | TAU | 30 | CAN |

| JUL | | AUG | | SEP | | OCT | | NOV | | DEC | |
|---|---|---|---|---|---|---|---|---|---|---|---|
| 2 | LEO | 1 | VIR | 2 | SCO | 2 | SAG | 1 | CAP | 1 | AQU |
| 5 | VIR | 3 | LIB | 5 | SAG | 5 | CAP | 3 | AQU | 3 | PIS |
| 7 | LIB | 6 | SCO | 7 | CAP | 7 | AQU | 6 | PIS | 5 | ARI |
| 10 | SCO | 8 | SAG | 10 | AQU | 9 | PIS | 8 | ARI | 7 | TAU |
| 12 | SAG | 11 | CAP | 12 | PIS | 11 | ARI | 10 | TAU | 9 | GEM |
| 15 | CAP | 13 | AQU | 14 | ARI | 13 | TAU | 12 | GEM | 11 | CAN |
| 17 | AQU | 16 | PIS | 16 | TAU | 15 | GEM | 14 | CAN | 13 | LEO |
| 19 | PIS | 18 | ARI | 18 | GEM | 18 | CAN | 16 | LEO | 16 | VIR |
| 21 | ARI | 20 | TAU | 20 | CAN | 20 | LEO | 18 | VIR | 18 | LIB |
| 24 | TAU | 22 | GEM | 22 | LEO | 22 | VIR | 21 | LIB | 20 | SCO |
| 26 | GEM | 24 | CAN | 25 | VIR | 24 | LIB | 23 | SCO | 23 | SAG |
| 28 | CAN | 26 | LEO | 27 | LIB | 27 | SCO | 26 | SAG | 25 | CAP |
| 30 | LEO | 28 | VIR | 29 | SCO | 29 | SAG | 28 | CAP | 28 | AQU |
| | | 31 | LIB | | | | | | | 30 | PIS |

**1982**

| | JAN | | FEB | | MAR | | APR | | MAY | | JUN |
|---|---|---|---|---|---|---|---|---|---|---|---|
| 2 | ARI | 2 | GEM | 1 | GEM | 2 | LEO | 1 | VIR | 2 | SCO |
| 4 | TAU | 4 | CAN | 3 | CAN | 4 | VIR | 4 | LIB | 5 | SAG |
| 6 | GEM | 6 | LEO | 6 | LEO | 6 | LIB | 6 | SCO | 7 | CAP |
| 8 | CAN | 8 | VIR | 8 | VIR | 9 | SCO | 8 | SAG | 10 | AQU |
| 10 | LEO | 11 | LIB | 10 | LIB | 11 | SAG | 11 | CAP | 12 | PIS |
| 12 | VIR | 13 | SCO | 12 | SCO | 14 | CAP | 13 | AQU | 15 | ARI |
| 14 | LIB | 15 | SAG | 15 | SAG | 16 | AQU | 16 | PIS | 17 | TAU |
| 17 | SCO | 18 | CAP | 17 | CAP | 19 | PIS | 18 | ARI | 19 | GEM |
| 19 | SAG | 20 | AQU | 20 | AQU | 21 | ARI | 20 | TAU | 21 | CAN |
| 22 | CAP | 23 | PIS | 22 | PIS | 23 | TAU | 22 | GEM | 23 | LEO |
| 24 | AQU | 25 | ARI | 24 | ARI | 25 | GEM | 24 | CAN | 25 | VIR |
| 26 | PIS | 27 | TAU | 27 | TAU | 27 | CAN | 26 | LEO | 27 | LIB |
| 29 | ARI | | | 29 | GEM | 29 | LEO | 29 | VIR | 29 | SCO |
| 31 | TAU | | | 31 | CAN | | | 31 | LIB | | |

| | JUL | | AUG | | SEP | | OCT | | NOV | | DEC |
|---|---|---|---|---|---|---|---|---|---|---|---|
| 2 | SAG | 1 | CAP | 2 | PIS | 2 | ARI | 2 | GEM | 2 | CAN |
| 4 | CAP | 3 | AQU | 4 | ARI | 4 | TAU | 4 | CAN | 4 | LEO |
| 7 | AQU | 6 | PIS | 7 | TAU | 6 | GEM | 6 | LEO | 6 | VIR |
| 9 | PIS | 8 | ARI | 9 | GEM | 8 | CAN | 9 | VIR | 8 | LIB |
| 12 | ARI | 10 | TAU | 11 | CAN | 10 | LEO | 11 | LIB | 10 | SCO |
| 14 | TAU | 13 | GEM | 13 | LEO | 12 | VIR | 13 | SCO | 13 | SAG |
| 16 | GEM | 15 | CAN | 15 | VIR | 15 | LIB | 15 | SAG | 15 | CAP |
| 18 | CAN | 17 | LEO | 17 | LIB | 17 | SCO | 18 | CAP | 18 | AQU |
| 20 | LEO | 19 | VIR | 19 | SCO | 19 | SAG | 21 | AQU | 20 | PIS |
| 22 | VIR | 21 | LIB | 22 | SAG | 22 | CAP | 23 | PIS | 23 | ARI |
| 24 | LIB | 23 | SCO | 24 | CAP | 24 | AQU | 25 | ARI | 25 | TAU |
| 27 | SCO | 25 | SAG | 27 | AQU | 27 | PIS | 28 | TAU | 27 | GEM |
| 29 | SAG | 28 | CAP | 29 | PIS | 29 | ARI | 30 | GEM | 29 | CAN |
| | | 31 | AQU | | | 31 | TAU | | | 31 | LEO |

**1963**

| | JAN | | FEB | | MAR | | APR | | MAY | | JUN |
|---|---|---|---|---|---|---|---|---|---|---|---|
| 2 | VIR | 1 | LIB | 2 | SCO | 1 | SAG | 1 | CAP | 2 | PIS |
| 4 | LIB | 3 | SCO | 5 | SAG | 3 | CAP | 3 | AQU | 5 | ARI |
| 7 | SCO | 5 | SAG | 7 | CAP | 6 | AQU | 6 | PIS | 7 | TAU |
| 9 | SAG | 8 | CAP | 10 | AQU | 8 | PIS | 8 | ARI | 9 | GEM |
| 12 | CAP | 10 | AQU | 12 | PIS | 11 | ARI | 11 | TAU | 11 | CAN |
| 14 | AQU | 13 | PIS | 15 | ARI | 13 | TAU | 13 | GEM | 13 | LEO |
| 17 | PIS | 15 | ARI | 17 | TAU | 15 | GEM | 15 | CAN | 15 | VIR |
| 19 | ARI | 18 | TAU | 19 | GEM | 18 | CAN | 17 | LEO | 17 | LIB |
| 21 | TAU | 20 | GEM | 21 | CAN | 20 | LEO | 19 | VIR | 20 | SCO |
| 24 | GEM | 22 | CAN | 23 | LEO | 22 | VIR | 21 | LIB | 22 | SAG |
| 25 | CAN | 24 | LEO | 26 | VIR | 24 | LIB | 23 | SCO | 24 | CAP |
| 28 | LEO | 26 | VIR | 28 | LIB | 26 | SCO | 26 | SAG | 27 | AQU |
| 30 | VIR | 28 | LIB | 30 | SCO | 28 | SAG | 28 | CAP | 29 | PIS |
| | | | | | | | | 31 | AQU | | |

| | JUL | | AUG | | SEP | | OCT | | NOV | | DEC |
|---|---|---|---|---|---|---|---|---|---|---|---|
| 2 | ARI | 1 | TAU | 1 | CAN | 1 | LEO | 1 | LIB | 1 | SCO |
| 4 | TAU | 3 | GEM | 3 | LEO | 3 | VIR | 3 | SCO | 3 | SAG |
| 7 | GEM | 5 | CAN | 5 | VIR | 5 | LIB | 6 | SAG | 5 | CAP |
| 9 | CAN | 7 | LEO | 7 | LIB | 7 | SCO | 8 | CAP | 8 | AQU |
| 11 | LEO | 9 | VIR | 10 | SCO | 9 | SAG | 10 | AQU | 10 | PIS |
| 13 | VIR | 11 | LIB | 12 | SAG | 11 | CAP | 13 | PIS | 13 | ARI |
| 15 | LIB | 13 | SCO | 14 | CAP | 14 | AQU | 15 | ARI | 15 | TAU |
| 17 | SCO | 15 | SAG | 17 | AQU | 16 | PIS | 18 | TAU | 17 | GEM |
| 19 | SAG | 18 | CAP | 19 | PIS | 19 | ARI | 20 | GEM | 20 | CAN |
| 22 | CAP | 20 | AQU | 22 | ARI | 21 | TAU | 22 | CAN | 22 | LEO |
| 24 | AQU | 23 | PIS | 24 | TAU | 24 | GEM | 24 | LEO | 24 | VIR |
| 27 | PIS | 25 | ARI | 26 | GEM | 26 | CAN | 26 | VIR | 26 | LIB |
| 29 | ARI | 28 | TAU | 29 | CAN | 28 | LEO | 29 | LIB | 28 | SCO |
| | | 30 | GEM | | | 30 | VIR | | | 30 | SAG |

## 1984

| JAN | | FEB | | MAR | | APR | | MAY | | JUN | |
|---|---|---|---|---|---|---|---|---|---|---|---|
| 2 | CAP | 3 | PIS | 1 | PIS | 2 | TAU | 2 | GEM | 1 | CAN |
| 4 | AQU | 5 | ARI | 4 | ARI | 5 | GEM | 4 | CAN | 3 | LEO |
| 6 | PIS | 8 | TAU | 6 | TAU | 7 | CAN | 6 | LEO | 5 | VIR |
| 9 | ARI | 10 | GEM | 8 | GEM | 9 | LEO | 9 | VIR | 7 | LIB |
| 11 | TAU | 12 | CAN | 11 | CAN | 11 | VIR | 11 | LIB | 9 | SCO |
| 14 | GEM | 15 | LEO | 13 | LEO | 13 | LIB | 13 | SCO | 11 | SAG |
| 16 | CAN | 17 | VIR | 15 | VIR | 15 | SCO | 15 | SAG | 13 | CAP |
| 18 | LEO | 19 | LIB | 17 | LIB | 17 | SAG | 17 | CAP | 16 | AQU |
| 20 | VIR | 21 | SCO | 19 | SCO | 20 | CAP | 19 | AQU | 18 | PIS |
| 22 | LIB | 23 | SAG | 21 | SAG | 22 | AQU | 22 | PIS | 21 | ARI |
| 24 | SCO | 25 | CAP | 23 | CAP | 25 | PIS | 24 | ARI | 23 | TAU |
| 26 | SAG | 28 | AQU | 26 | AQU | 27 | ARI | 27 | TAU | 25 | GEM |
| 29 | CAP | | | 28 | PIS | 30 | TAU | 29 | GEM | 28 | CAN |
| 31 | AQU | | | 31 | ARI | | | | | 30 | LEO |

| JUL | | AUG | | SEP | | OCT | | NOV | | DEC | |
|---|---|---|---|---|---|---|---|---|---|---|---|
| 2 | VIR | 3 | SCO | 1 | SAG | 1 | CAP | 2 | PIS | 1 | ARI |
| 4 | LIB | 5 | SAG | 3 | CAP | 3 | AQU | 4 | ARI | 4 | TAU |
| 6 | SCO | 7 | CAP | 6 | AQU | 5 | PIS | 7 | TAU | 6 | GEM |
| 9 | SAG | 9 | AQU | 8 | PIS | 8 | ARI | 9 | GEM | 9 | CAN |
| 11 | CAP | 12 | PIS | 11 | ARI | 10 | TAU | 12 | CAN | 11 | LEO |
| 13 | AQU | 14 | ARI | 13 | TAU | 13 | GEM | 14 | LEO | 13 | VIR |
| 16 | PIS | 17 | TAU | 16 | GEM | 15 | CAN | 16 | VIR | 15 | LIB |
| 18 | ARI | 19 | GEM | 18 | CAN | 18 | LEO | 18 | LIB | 17 | SCO |
| 21 | TAU | 22 | CAN | 20 | LEO | 20 | VIR | 20 | SCO | 20 | SAG |
| 23 | GEM | 24 | LEO | 22 | VIR | 22 | LIB | 22 | SAG | 22 | CAP |
| 25 | CAN | 26 | VIR | 24 | LIB | 24 | SCO | 24 | CAP | 24 | AQU |
| 27 | LEO | 28 | LIB | 26 | SCO | 26 | SAG | 27 | AQU | 26 | PIS |
| 29 | VIR | 30 | SCO | 28 | SAG | 28 | CAP | 29 | PIS | 29 | ARI |
| 31 | LIB | | | | | 30 | AQU | | | 31 | TAU |

## 1985

| JAN | | FEB | | MAR | | APR | | MAY | | JUN | |
|---|---|---|---|---|---|---|---|---|---|---|---|
| 3 | GEM | 2 | CAN | 1 | CAN | 2 | VIR | 1 | LIB | 2 | SAG |
| 5 | CAN | 4 | LEO | 3 | LEO | 4 | LIB | 3 | SCO | 4 | CAP |
| 7 | LEO | 6 | VIR | 5 | VIR | 6 | SCO | 5 | SAG | 6 | AQU |
| 9 | VIR | 8 | LIB | 7 | LIB | 8 | SAG | 7 | CAP | 8 | PIS |
| 12 | LIB | 10 | SCO | 9 | SCO | 10 | CAP | 9 | AQU | 11 | ARI |
| 14 | SCO | 12 | SAG | 11 | SAG | 12 | AQU | 12 | PIS | 13 | TAU |
| 16 | SAG | 14 | CAP | 14 | CAP | 14 | PIS | 14 | ARI | 16 | GEM |
| 18 | CAP | 17 | AQU | 16 | AQU | 17 | ARI | 17 | TAU | 18 | CAN |
| 20 | AQU | 19 | PIS | 18 | PIS | 20 | TAU | 19 | GEM | 20 | LEO |
| 23 | PIS | 21 | ARI | 21 | ARI | 22 | GEM | 22 | CAN | 23 | VIR |
| 25 | ARI | 24 | TAU | 23 | TAU | 25 | CAN | 24 | LEO | 25 | LIB |
| 28 | TAU | 27 | GEM | 26 | GEM | 27 | LEO | 26 | VIR | 27 | SCO |
| 30 | GEM | | | 28 | CAN | 29 | VIR | 29 | LIB | 29 | SAG |
| | | | | 31 | LEO | | | 31 | SCO | | |

| JUL | | AUG | | SEP | | OCT | | NOV | | DEC | |
|---|---|---|---|---|---|---|---|---|---|---|---|
| 1 | CAP | 2 | PIS | 1 | ARI | 3 | GEM | 2 | CAN | 1 | LEO |
| 3 | AQU | 4 | ARI | 3 | TAU | 5 | CAN | 4 | LEO | 4 | VIR |
| 5 | PIS | 7 | TAU | 6 | GEM | 8 | LEO | 6 | VIR | 6 | LIB |
| 8 | ARI | 9 | GEM | 8 | CAN | 10 | VIR | 9 | LIB | 8 | SCO |
| 10 | TAU | 12 | CAN | 10 | LEO | 12 | LIB | 11 | SCO | 10 | SAG |
| 13 | GEM | 14 | LEO | 13 | VIR | 14 | SCO | 13 | SAG | 12 | CAP |
| 15 | CAN | 16 | VIR | 15 | LIB | 16 | SAG | 15 | CAP | 14 | AQU |
| 18 | LEO | 18 | LIB | 17 | SCO | 18 | CAP | 17 | AQU | 16 | PIS |
| 20 | VIR | 20 | SCO | 19 | SAG | 20 | AQU | 19 | PIS | 19 | ARI |
| 22 | LIB | 22 | SAG | 21 | CAP | 23 | PIS | 21 | ARI | 21 | TAU |
| 24 | SCO | 25 | CAP | 23 | AQU | 25 | ARI | 24 | TAU | 24 | GEM |
| 26 | SAG | 27 | AQU | 25 | PIS | 28 | TAU | 26 | GEM | 26 | CAN |
| 28 | CAP | 29 | PIS | 28 | ARI | 30 | GEM | 29 | CAN | 29 | LEO |
| 31 | AQU | | | 30 | TAU | | | | | 31 | VIR |

# Moon Signs 1945-2025

## 1986

| | JAN | | FEB | | MAR | | APR | | MAY | | JUN |
|---|---|---|---|---|---|---|---|---|---|---|---|
| 2 | LIB | 1 | SCO | 2 | SAG | 2 | AQU | 2 | PIS | 3 | TAU |
| 4 | SCO | 3 | SAG | 4 | CAP | 5 | PIS | 4 | ARI | 5 | GEM |
| 6 | SAG | 5 | CAP | 6 | AQU | 7 | ARI | 7 | TAU | 8 | CAN |
| 8 | CAP | 7 | AQU | 8 | PIS | 9 | TAU | 9 | GEM | 11 | LEO |
| 11 | AQU | 9 | PIS | 11 | ARI | 12 | GEM | 12 | CAN | 13 | VIR |
| 13 | PIS | 11 | ARI | 13 | TAU | 14 | CAN | 14 | LEO | 15 | LIB |
| 15 | ARI | 14 | TAU | 16 | GEM | 17 | LEO | 17 | VIR | 17 | SCO |
| 17 | TAU | 16 | GEM | 18 | CAN | 19 | VIR | 19 | LIB | 19 | SAG |
| 20 | GEM | 19 | CAN | 21 | LEO | 21 | LIB | 21 | SCO | 21 | CAP |
| 22 | CAN | 21 | LEO | 23 | VIR | 24 | SCO | 23 | SAG | 23 | AQU |
| 25 | LEO | 24 | VIR | 25 | LIB | 26 | SAG | 25 | CAP | 26 | PIS |
| 27 | VIR | 26 | LIB | 27 | SCO | 28 | CAP | 27 | AQU | 28 | ARI |
| 29 | LIB | 28 | SCO | 29 | SAG | 30 | AQU | 29 | PIS | 30 | TAU |
| | | | | 31 | CAP | | | 31 | ARI | | |

| | JUL | | AUG | | SEP | | OCT | | NOV | | DEC |
|---|---|---|---|---|---|---|---|---|---|---|---|
| 3 | GEM | 2 | CAN | 3 | VIR | 2 | LIB | 1 | SCO | 2 | CAP |
| 5 | CAN | 4 | LEO | 5 | LIB | 4 | SCO | 3 | SAG | 4 | AQU |
| 8 | LEO | 6 | VIR | 7 | SCO | 7 | SAG | 5 | CAP | 6 | PIS |
| 10 | VIR | 9 | LIB | 9 | SAG | 9 | CAP | 7 | AQU | 9 | ARI |
| 12 | LIB | 11 | SCO | 11 | CAP | 11 | AQU | 9 | PIS | 11 | TAU |
| 15 | SCO | 13 | SAG | 14 | AQU | 13 | PIS | 11 | ARI | 14 | GEM |
| 17 | SAG | 15 | CAP | 16 | PIS | 15 | ARI | 14 | TAU | 16 | CAN |
| 19 | CAP | 17 | AQU | 18 | ARI | 18 | TAU | 16 | GEM | 19 | LEO |
| 21 | AQU | 19 | PIS | 20 | TAU | 20 | GEM | 19 | CAN | 21 | VIR |
| 23 | PIS | 22 | ARI | 23 | GEM | 23 | CAN | 21 | LEO | 24 | LIB |
| 25 | ARI | 24 | TAU | 25 | CAN | 25 | LEO | 24 | VIR | 26 | SCO |
| 28 | TAU | 26 | GEM | 28 | LEO | 27 | VIR | 26 | LIB | 28 | SAG |
| 30 | GEM | 29 | CAN | 30 | VIR | 30 | LIB | 28 | SCO | 30 | CAP |
| | | 31 | LEO | | | | | 30 | SAG | | |

## 1987

| | JAN | | FEB | | MAR | | APR | | MAY | | JUN |
|---|---|---|---|---|---|---|---|---|---|---|---|
| 1 | AQU | 1 | ARI | 1 | ARI | 2 | GEM | 2 | CAN | 3 | VIR |
| 3 | PIS | 4 | TAU | 3 | TAU | 4 | CAN | 4 | LEO | 5 | LIB |
| 5 | ARI | 6 | GEM | 5 | GEM | 7 | LEO | 7 | VIR | 8 | SCO |
| 7 | TAU | 9 | CAN | 8 | CAN | 9 | VIR | 9 | LIB | 10 | SAG |
| 10 | GEM | 11 | LEO | 10 | LEO | 12 | LIB | 11 | SCO | 12 | CAP |
| 12 | CAN | 14 | VIR | 13 | VIR | 14 | SCO | 13 | SAG | 14 | AQU |
| 15 | LEO | 16 | LIB | 15 | LIB | 16 | SAG | 15 | CAP | 16 | PIS |
| 17 | VIR | 18 | SCO | 18 | SCO | 18 | CAP | 17 | AQU | 18 | ARI |
| 20 | LIB | 21 | SAG | 20 | SAG | 20 | AQU | 20 | PIS | 20 | TAU |
| 22 | SCO | 23 | CAP | 22 | CAP | 22 | PIS | 22 | ARI | 23 | GEM |
| 24 | SAG | 25 | AQU | 24 | AQU | 25 | ARI | 24 | TAU | 25 | CAN |
| 26 | CAP | 27 | PIS | 26 | PIS | 27 | TAU | 26 | GEM | 28 | LEO |
| 28 | AQU | | | 28 | ARI | 29 | GEM | 29 | CAN | 30 | VIR |
| 30 | PIS | | | 30 | TAU | | | 31 | LEO | | |

| | JUL | | AUG | | SEP | | OCT | | NOV | | DEC |
|---|---|---|---|---|---|---|---|---|---|---|---|
| 3 | LIB | 1 | SCO | 2 | CAP | 1 | AQU | 2 | ARI | 1 | TAU |
| 5 | SCO | 4 | SAG | 4 | AQU | 3 | PIS | 4 | TAU | 4 | GEM |
| 7 | SAG | 6 | CAP | 6 | PIS | 6 | ARI | 6 | GEM | 6 | CAN |
| 9 | CAP | 8 | AQU | 8 | ARI | 8 | TAU | 9 | CAN | 8 | LEO |
| 11 | AQU | 10 | PIS | 10 | TAU | 10 | GEM | 11 | LEO | 11 | VIR |
| 13 | PIS | 12 | ARI | 13 | GEM | 12 | CAN | 14 | VIR | 14 | LIB |
| 15 | ARI | 14 | TAU | 15 | CAN | 15 | LEO | 16 | LIB | 16 | SCO |
| 18 | TAU | 16 | GEM | 17 | LEO | 17 | VIR | 18 | SCO | 18 | SAG |
| 20 | GEM | 19 | CAN | 20 | VIR | 20 | LIB | 21 | SAG | 20 | CAP |
| 22 | CAN | 21 | LEO | 22 | LIB | 22 | SCO | 23 | CAP | 22 | AQU |
| 25 | LEO | 24 | VIR | 25 | SCO | 24 | SAG | 25 | AQU | 24 | PIS |
| 27 | VIR | 26 | LIB | 27 | SAG | 26 | CAP | 27 | PIS | 26 | ARI |
| 30 | LIB | 29 | SCO | 29 | CAP | 29 | AQU | 29 | ARI | 29 | TAU |
| | | 31 | SAG | | | 31 | PIS | | | 31 | GEM |

# Moon Signs 1945-2025

## 1988

| | JAN | | FEB | | MAR | | APR | | MAY | | JUN |
|---|---|---|---|---|---|---|---|---|---|---|---|
| 2 | CAN | 1 | LEO | 2 | VIR | 1 | LIB | 3 | SAG | 1 | CAP |
| 5 | LEO | 4 | VIR | 4 | LIB | 3 | SCO | 5 | CAP | 3 | AQU |
| 7 | VIR | 6 | LIB | 7 | SCO | 5 | SAG | 7 | AQU | 5 | PIS |
| 10 | LIB | 9 | SCO | 9 | SAG | 8 | CAP | 9 | PIS | 8 | ARI |
| 12 | SCO | 11 | SAG | 11 | CAP | 10 | AQU | 11 | ARI | 10 | TAU |
| 15 | SAG | 13 | CAP | 14 | AQU | 12 | PIS | 13 | TAU | 12 | GEM |
| 17 | CAP | 15 | AQU | 16 | PIS | 14 | ARI | 16 | GEM | 14 | CAN |
| 19 | AQU | 17 | PIS | 18 | ARI | 16 | TAU | 18 | CAN | 17 | LEO |
| 21 | PIS | 19 | ARI | 20 | TAU | 18 | GEM | 20 | LEO | 19 | VIR |
| 23 | ARI | 21 | TAU | 22 | GEM | 20 | CAN | 23 | VIR | 22 | LIB |
| 25 | TAU | 23 | GEM | 24 | CAN | 23 | LEO | 25 | LIB | 24 | SCO |
| 27 | GEM | 26 | CAN | 27 | LEO | 25 | VIR | 28 | SCO | 26 | SAG |
| 30 | CAN | 28 | LEO | 29 | VIR | 28 | LIB | 30 | SAG | 29 | CAP |
| | | | | | | 30 | SCO | | | | |

| | JUL | | AUG | | SEP | | OCT | | NOV | | DEC |
|---|---|---|---|---|---|---|---|---|---|---|---|
| 1 | AQU | 1 | ARI | 2 | GEM | 1 | CAN | 2 | VIR | 2 | LIB |
| 3 | PIS | 3 | TAU | 4 | CAN | 4 | LEO | 5 | LIB | 5 | SCO |
| 5 | ARI | 5 | GEM | 6 | LEO | 6 | VIR | 7 | SCO | 7 | SAG |
| 7 | TAU | 8 | CAN | 9 | VIR | 9 | LIB | 10 | SAG | 9 | CAP |
| 9 | GEM | 10 | LEO | 11 | LIB | 11 | SCO | 12 | CAP | 12 | AQU |
| 11 | CAN | 13 | VIR | 14 | SCO | 14 | SAG | 14 | AQU | 14 | PIS |
| 14 | LEO | 15 | LIB | 16 | SAG | 16 | CAP | 17 | PIS | 16 | ARI |
| 16 | VIR | 18 | SCO | 19 | CAP | 18 | AQU | 19 | ARI | 18 | TAU |
| 19 | LIB | 20 | SAG | 21 | AQU | 20 | PIS | 21 | TAU | 20 | GEM |
| 21 | SCO | 22 | CAP | 23 | PIS | 22 | ARI | 23 | GEM | 22 | CAN |
| 24 | SAG | 24 | AQU | 25 | ARI | 24 | TAU | 25 | CAN | 25 | LEO |
| 26 | CAP | 26 | PIS | 27 | TAU | 26 | GEM | 27 | LEO | 27 | VIR |
| 28 | AQU | 28 | ARI | 29 | GEM | 29 | CAN | 30 | VIR | 30 | LIB |
| 30 | PIS | 30 | TAU | | | 31 | LEO | | | | |

## 1989

| | JAN | | FEB | | MAR | | APR | | MAY | | JUN |
|---|---|---|---|---|---|---|---|---|---|---|---|
| 1 | SCO | 2 | CAP | 2 | CAP | 2 | PIS | 2 | ARI | 2 | GEM |
| 4 | SAG | 4 | AQU | 4 | AQU | 4 | ARI | 4 | TAU | 4 | CAN |
| 6 | CAP | 6 | PIS | 6 | PIS | 6 | TAU | 6 | GEM | 7 | LEO |
| 8 | AQU | 8 | ARI | 8 | ARI | 8 | GEM | 8 | CAN | 9 | VIR |
| 10 | PIS | 11 | TAU | 10 | TAU | 11 | CAN | 10 | LEO | 11 | LIB |
| 12 | ARI | 13 | GEM | 12 | GEM | 13 | LEO | 13 | VIR | 14 | SCO |
| 14 | TAU | 15 | CAN | 14 | CAN | 15 | VIR | 15 | LIB | 16 | SAG |
| 16 | GEM | 17 | LEO | 17 | LEO | 18 | LIB | 18 | SCO | 19 | CAP |
| 19 | CAN | 20 | VIR | 19 | VIR | 20 | SCO | 20 | SAG | 21 | AQU |
| 21 | LEO | 22 | LIB | 22 | LIB | 23 | SAG | 22 | CAP | 23 | PIS |
| 23 | VIR | 25 | SCO | 24 | SCO | 25 | CAP | 25 | AQU | 25 | ARI |
| 26 | LIB | 27 | SAG | 27 | SAG | 28 | AQU | 27 | PIS | 27 | TAU |
| 29 | SCO | | | 29 | CAP | 30 | PIS | 29 | ARI | 30 | GEM |
| 31 | SAG | | | 31 | AQU | | | 31 | TAU | | |

| | JUL | | AUG | | SEP | | OCT | | NOV | | DEC |
|---|---|---|---|---|---|---|---|---|---|---|---|
| 2 | CAN | 3 | VIR | 1 | LIB | 1 | SCO | 2 | CAP | 2 | AQU |
| 4 | LEO | 5 | LIB | 4 | SCO | 4 | SAG | 5 | AQU | 4 | PIS |
| 6 | VIR | 8 | SCO | 6 | SAG | 6 | CAP | 7 | PIS | 7 | ARI |
| 9 | LIB | 10 | SAG | 9 | CAP | 9 | AQU | 9 | ARI | 9 | TAU |
| 11 | SCO | 12 | CAP | 11 | AQU | 11 | PIS | 11 | TAU | 11 | GEM |
| 14 | SAG | 15 | AQU | 13 | PIS | 13 | ARI | 13 | GEM | 13 | CAN |
| 16 | CAP | 17 | PIS | 15 | ARI | 15 | TAU | 15 | CAN | 15 | LEO |
| 18 | AQU | 19 | ARI | 17 | TAU | 17 | GEM | 17 | LEO | 17 | VIR |
| 20 | PIS | 21 | TAU | 19 | GEM | 19 | CAN | 20 | VIR | 19 | LIB |
| 23 | ARI | 23 | GEM | 21 | CAN | 21 | LEO | 22 | LIB | 22 | SCO |
| 25 | TAU | 25 | CAN | 24 | LEO | 23 | VIR | 25 | SCO | 24 | SAG |
| 27 | GEM | 28 | LEO | 26 | VIR | 26 | LIB | 27 | SAG | 27 | CAP |
| 29 | CAN | 30 | VIR | 29 | LIB | 28 | SCO | 30 | CAP | 29 | AQU |
| 31 | LEO | | | | | 31 | SAG | | | | |

# Moon Signs 1945-2025

## 1990

| | JAN | | FEB | | MAR | | APR | | MAY | | JUN |
|---|---|---|---|---|---|---|---|---|---|---|---|
| 1 | PIS | 1 | TAU | 2 | GEM | 1 | CAN | 3 | VIR | 1 | LIB |
| 3 | ARI | 3 | GEM | 5 | CAN | 3 | LEO | 5 | LIB | 4 | SCO |
| 5 | TAU | 5 | CAN | 7 | LEO | 5 | VIR | 8 | SCO | 6 | SAG |
| 7 | GEM | 8 | LEO | 9 | VIR | 8 | LIB | 10 | SAG | 9 | CAP |
| 9 | CAN | 10 | VIR | 12 | LIB | 10 | SCO | 13 | CAP | 11 | AQU |
| 11 | LEO | 12 | LIB | 14 | SCO | 13 | SAG | 15 | AQU | 14 | PIS |
| 13 | VIR | 15 | SCO | 16 | SAG | 15 | CAP | 17 | PIS | 16 | ARI |
| 16 | LIB | 17 | SAG | 19 | CAP | 18 | AQU | 20 | ARI | 18 | TAU |
| 18 | SCO | 20 | CAP | 21 | AQU | 20 | PIS | 22 | TAU | 20 | GEM |
| 21 | SAG | 22 | AQU | 24 | PIS | 22 | ARI | 24 | GEM | 22 | CAN |
| 23 | CAP | 24 | PIS | 26 | ARI | 24 | TAU | 26 | CAN | 24 | LEO |
| 26 | AQU | 26 | ARI | 28 | TAU | 26 | GEM | 28 | LEO | 26 | VIR |
| 28 | PIS | 28 | TAU | 30 | GEM | 28 | CAN | 30 | VIR | 29 | LIB |
| 30 | ARI | | | | | 30 | LEO | | | | |

| | JUL | | AUG | | SEP | | OCT | | NOV | | DEC |
|---|---|---|---|---|---|---|---|---|---|---|---|
| 1 | SCO | 2 | CAP | 1 | AQU | 1 | PIS | 2 | TAU | 1 | GEM |
| 4 | SAG | 5 | AQU | 3 | PIS | 3 | ARI | 4 | GEM | 3 | CAN |
| 6 | CAP | 7 | PIS | 6 | ARI | 5 | TAU | 6 | CAN | 5 | LEO |
| 9 | AQU | 9 | ARI | 9 | TAU | 7 | GEM | 8 | LEO | 7 | VIR |
| 11 | PIS | 12 | TAU | 10 | GEM | 9 | CAN | 10 | VIR | 9 | LIB |
| 13 | ARI | 14 | GEM | 12 | CAN | 11 | LEO | 12 | LIB | 12 | SCO |
| 15 | TAU | 16 | CAN | 14 | LEO | 14 | VIR | 15 | SCO | 14 | SAG |
| 17 | GEM | 18 | LEO | 16 | VIR | 16 | LIB | 17 | SAG | 17 | CAP |
| 19 | CAN | 20 | VIR | 19 | LIB | 18 | SCO | 20 | CAP | 19 | AQU |
| 21 | LEO | 22 | LIB | 21 | SCO | 21 | SAG | 22 | AQU | 22 | PIS |
| 24 | VIR | 25 | SCO | 24 | SAG | 23 | CAP | 25 | PIS | 24 | ARI |
| 26 | LIB | 27 | SAG | 26 | CAP | 26 | AQU | 27 | ARI | 26 | TAU |
| 28 | SCO | 30 | CAP | 29 | AQU | 28 | PIS | 29 | TAU | 28 | GEM |
| 31 | SAG | | | | | 30 | ARI | | | 30 | CAN |

## 1991

| | JAN | | FEB | | MAR | | APR | | MAY | | JUN |
|---|---|---|---|---|---|---|---|---|---|---|---|
| 1 | LEO | 2 | LIB | 2 | LIB | 3 | SAG | 2 | CAP | 1 | AQU |
| 4 | VIR | 4 | SCO | 4 | SCO | 5 | CAP | 5 | AQU | 4 | PIS |
| 6 | LIB | 7 | SAG | 6 | SAG | 8 | AQU | 7 | PIS | 6 | ARI |
| 8 | SCO | 9 | CAP | 9 | CAP | 10 | PIS | 10 | ARI | 8 | TAU |
| 11 | SAG | 12 | AQU | 11 | AQU | 12 | ARI | 12 | TAU | 10 | GEM |
| 13 | CAP | 14 | PIS | 14 | PIS | 15 | TAU | 14 | GEM | 12 | CAN |
| 16 | AQU | 17 | ARI | 16 | ARI | 17 | GEM | 16 | CAN | 14 | LEO |
| 18 | PIS | 19 | TAU | 18 | TAU | 19 | CAN | 18 | LEO | 16 | VIR |
| 20 | ARI | 21 | GEM | 20 | GEM | 21 | LEO | 20 | VIR | 19 | LIB |
| 23 | TAU | 23 | CAN | 22 | CAN | 23 | VIR | 22 | LIB | 21 | SCO |
| 25 | GEM | 25 | LEO | 25 | LEO | 25 | LIB | 25 | SCO | 23 | SAG |
| 27 | CAN | 27 | VIR | 27 | VIR | 28 | SCO | 27 | SAG | 26 | CAP |
| 29 | LEO | | | 29 | LIB | 30 | SAG | 30 | CAP | 29 | AQU |
| 31 | VIR | | | 31 | SCO | | | | | | |

| | JUL | | AUG | | SEP | | OCT | | NOV | | DEC |
|---|---|---|---|---|---|---|---|---|---|---|---|
| 1 | PIS | 2 | TAU | 3 | CAN | 2 | LEO | 2 | LIB | 2 | SCO |
| 3 | ARI | 4 | GEM | 5 | LEO | 4 | VIR | 5 | SCO | 4 | SAG |
| 6 | TAU | 5 | CAN | 7 | VIR | 6 | LIB | 7 | SAG | 7 | CAP |
| 8 | GEM | 8 | LEO | 9 | LIB | 8 | SCO | 10 | CAP | 9 | AQU |
| 10 | CAN | 10 | VIR | 11 | SCO | 11 | SAG | 12 | AQU | 12 | PIS |
| 12 | LEO | 12 | LIB | 13 | SAG | 13 | CAP | 15 | PIS | 14 | ARI |
| 14 | VIR | 15 | SCO | 16 | CAP | 16 | AQU | 17 | ARI | 17 | TAU |
| 16 | LIB | 17 | SAG | 18 | AQU | 18 | PIS | 19 | TAU | 19 | GEM |
| 18 | SCO | 20 | CAP | 21 | PIS | 21 | ARI | 21 | GEM | 21 | CAN |
| 21 | SAG | 22 | AQU | 23 | ARI | 23 | TAU | 23 | CAN | 23 | LEO |
| 23 | CAP | 25 | PIS | 25 | TAU | 25 | GEM | 25 | LEO | 25 | VIR |
| 26 | AQU | 27 | ARI | 28 | GEM | 27 | CAN | 28 | VIR | 27 | LIB |
| 28 | PIS | 29 | TAU | 30 | CAN | 29 | LEO | 30 | LIB | 29 | SCO |
| 31 | ARI | 31 | GEM | | | 31 | VIR | | | | |

# Moon Signs 1945-2025

## 1992

| JAN | | FEB | | MAR | | APR | | MAY | | JUN | |
|---|---|---|---|---|---|---|---|---|---|---|---|
| 1 | SAG | 2 | AQU | 3 | PIS | 1 | ARI | 1 | TAU | 2 | CAN |
| 3 | CAP | 4 | PIS | 5 | ARI | 4 | TAU | 3 | GEM | 4 | LEO |
| 6 | AQU | 7 | ARI | 8 | TAU | 6 | GEM | 5 | CAN | 6 | VIR |
| 8 | PIS | 9 | TAU | 10 | GEM | 8 | CAN | 8 | LEO | 8 | LIB |
| 11 | ARI | 12 | GEM | 12 | CAN | 10 | LEO | 10 | VIR | 10 | SCO |
| 13 | TAU | 14 | CAN | 14 | LEO | 12 | VIR | 12 | LIB | 13 | SAG |
| 15 | GEM | 16 | LEO | 16 | VIR | 15 | LIB | 14 | SCO | 15 | CAP |
| 17 | CAN | 18 | VIR | 18 | LIB | 17 | SCO | 16 | SAG | 17 | AQU |
| 19 | LEO | 20 | LIB | 20 | SCO | 19 | SAG | 19 | CAP | 20 | PIS |
| 21 | VIR | 22 | SCO | 23 | SAG | 21 | CAP | 21 | AQU | 22 | ARI |
| 23 | LIB | 24 | SAG | 25 | CAP | 24 | AQU | 24 | PIS | 25 | TAU |
| 25 | SCO | 27 | CAP | 27 | AQU | 26 | PIS | 26 | ARI | 27 | GEM |
| 28 | SAG | 29 | AQU | 30 | PIS | 29 | ARI | 28 | TAU | 29 | CAN |
| 30 | CAP | | | | | | | 31 | GEM | | |

| JUL | | AUG | | SEP | | OCT | | NOV | | DEC | |
|---|---|---|---|---|---|---|---|---|---|---|---|
| 1 | LEO | 2 | LIB | 2 | SAG | 2 | CAP | 1 | AQU | 1 | PIS |
| 3 | VIR | 4 | SCO | 5 | CAP | 5 | AQU | 3 | PIS | 3 | ARI |
| 5 | LIB | 6 | SAG | 7 | AQU | 7 | PIS | 6 | ARI | 6 | TAU |
| 7 | SCO | 8 | CAP | 10 | PIS | 10 | ARI | 8 | TAU | 8 | GEM |
| 10 | SAG | 11 | AQU | 12 | ARI | 12 | TAU | 11 | GEM | 10 | CAN |
| 12 | CAP | 13 | PIS | 15 | TAU | 14 | GEM | 13 | CAN | 12 | LEO |
| 15 | AQU | 16 | ARI | 17 | GEM | 17 | CAN | 15 | LEO | 14 | VIR |
| 17 | PIS | 18 | TAU | 19 | CAN | 19 | LEO | 17 | VIR | 16 | LIB |
| 20 | ARI | 21 | GEM | 21 | LEO | 21 | VIR | 19 | LIB | 19 | SCO |
| 22 | TAU | 23 | CAN | 24 | VIR | 23 | LIB | 21 | SCO | 21 | SAG |
| 24 | GEM | 25 | LEO | 26 | LIB | 25 | SCO | 24 | SAG | 23 | CAP |
| 27 | CAN | 27 | VIR | 28 | SCO | 27 | SAG | 26 | CAP | 26 | AQU |
| 29 | LEO | 29 | LIB | 30 | SAG | 29 | CAP | 28 | AQU | 28 | PIS |
| 31 | VIR | 31 | SCO | | | | | | | 31 | ARI |

## 1993

| JAN | | FEB | | MAR | | APR | | MAY | | JUN | |
|---|---|---|---|---|---|---|---|---|---|---|---|
| 2 | TAU | 1 | GEM | 2 | CAN | 1 | LEO | 2 | LIB | 1 | SCO |
| 4 | GEM | 3 | CAN | 5 | LEO | 3 | VIR | 4 | SCO | 3 | SAG |
| 7 | CAN | 5 | LEO | 7 | VIR | 5 | LIB | 6 | SAG | 5 | CAP |
| 9 | LEO | 7 | VIR | 9 | LIB | 7 | SCO | 9 | CAP | 7 | AQU |
| 11 | VIR | 9 | LIB | 11 | SCO | 9 | SAG | 11 | AQU | 10 | PIS |
| 13 | LIB | 11 | SCO | 13 | SAG | 11 | CAP | 13 | PIS | 12 | ARI |
| 15 | SCO | 13 | SAG | 15 | CAP | 14 | AQU | 16 | ARI | 15 | TAU |
| 17 | SAG | 16 | CAP | 17 | AQU | 16 | PIS | 18 | TAU | 17 | GEM |
| 19 | CAP | 18 | AQU | 20 | PIS | 19 | ARI | 21 | GEM | 19 | CAN |
| 22 | AQU | 21 | PIS | 22 | ARI | 21 | TAU | 23 | CAN | 22 | LEO |
| 24 | PIS | 23 | ARI | 25 | TAU | 24 | GEM | 25 | LEO | 24 | VIR |
| 27 | ARI | 26 | TAU | 27 | GEM | 26 | CAN | 28 | VIR | 26 | LIB |
| 29 | TAU | 28 | GEM | 30 | CAN | 28 | LEO | 30 | LIB | 28 | SCO |
| | | | | | | 30 | VIR | | | 30 | SAG |

| JUL | | AUG | | SEP | | OCT | | NOV | | DEC | |
|---|---|---|---|---|---|---|---|---|---|---|---|
| 2 | CAP | 1 | AQU | 2 | ARI | 2 | TAU | 1 | GEM | 3 | LEO |
| 5 | AQU | 3 | PIS | 5 | TAU | 4 | GEM | 3 | CAN | 5 | VIR |
| 7 | PIS | 6 | ARI | 7 | GEM | 7 | CAN | 5 | LEO | 7 | LIB |
| 10 | ARI | 8 | TAU | 10 | CAN | 9 | LEO | 8 | VIR | 9 | SCO |
| 12 | TAU | 11 | GEM | 12 | LEO | 11 | VIR | 10 | LIB | 11 | SAG |
| 15 | GEM | 13 | CAN | 14 | VIR | 13 | LIB | 12 | SCO | 13 | CAP |
| 17 | CAN | 15 | LEO | 16 | LIB | 15 | SCO | 14 | SAG | 15 | AQU |
| 19 | LEO | 17 | VIR | 18 | SCO | 17 | SAG | 16 | CAP | 18 | PIS |
| 21 | VIR | 19 | LIB | 20 | SAG | 19 | CAP | 18 | AQU | 20 | ARI |
| 23 | LIB | 21 | SCO | 22 | CAP | 22 | AQU | 20 | PIS | 23 | TAU |
| 25 | SCO | 24 | SAG | 24 | AQU | 24 | PIS | 23 | ARI | 25 | GEM |
| 27 | SAG | 26 | CAP | 27 | PIS | 27 | ARI | 26 | TAU | 28 | CAN |
| 30 | CAP | 28 | AQU | 29 | ARI | 29 | TAU | 28 | GEM | 30 | LEO |
| | | 31 | PIS | | | | | 30 | CAN | | |

# Moon Signs 1945-2025

## 1994

| JAN | | FEB | | MAR | | APR | | MAY | | JUN | |
|---|---|---|---|---|---|---|---|---|---|---|---|
| 1 | VIR | 2 | SCO | 1 | SCO | 1 | CAP | 1 | AQU | 2 | ARI |
| 3 | LIB | 4 | SAG | 3 | SAG | 4 | AQU | 3 | PIS | 5 | TAU |
| 5 | SCO | 6 | CAP | 5 | CAP | 6 | PIS | 6 | ARI | 7 | GEM |
| 8 | SAG | 8 | AQU | 7 | AQU | 9 | ARI | 8 | TAU | 10 | CAN |
| 10 | CAP | 11 | PIS | 10 | PIS | 11 | TAU | 11 | GEM | 12 | LEO |
| 12 | AQU | 13 | ARI | 12 | ARI | 14 | GEM | 13 | CAN | 14 | VIR |
| 14 | PIS | 16 | TAU | 15 | TAU | 16 | CAN | 16 | LEO | 16 | LIB |
| 17 | ARI | 18 | GEM | 17 | GEM | 18 | LEO | 18 | VIR | 19 | SCO |
| 19 | TAU | 20 | CAN | 20 | CAN | 21 | VIR | 20 | LIB | 21 | SAG |
| 22 | GEM | 23 | LEO | 22 | LEO | 23 | LIB | 22 | SCO | 23 | CAP |
| 24 | CAN | 25 | VIR | 24 | VIR | 25 | SCO | 24 | SAG | 25 | AQU |
| 26 | LEO | 27 | LIB | 26 | LIB | 27 | SAG | 26 | CAP | 27 | PIS |
| 28 | VIR | | | 28 | SCO | 29 | CAP | 28 | AQU | 29 | ARI |
| 31 | LIB | | | 30 | SAG | | | 31 | PIS | | |

| JUL | | AUG | | SEP | | OCT | | NOV | | DEC | |
|---|---|---|---|---|---|---|---|---|---|---|---|
| 2 | TAU | 1 | GEM | 2 | LEO | 2 | VIR | 2 | SCO | 2 | SAG |
| 4 | GEM | 3 | CAN | 4 | VIR | 4 | LIB | 4 | SAG | 4 | CAP |
| 7 | CAN | 6 | LEO | 6 | LIB | 6 | SCO | 6 | CAP | 6 | AQU |
| 9 | LEO | 8 | VIR | 8 | SCO | 8 | SAG | 8 | AQU | 8 | PIS |
| 11 | VIR | 10 | LIB | 10 | SAG | 10 | CAP | 11 | PIS | 10 | ARI |
| 14 | LIB | 12 | SCO | 13 | CAP | 12 | AQU | 13 | ARI | 13 | TAU |
| 16 | SCO | 14 | SAG | 15 | AQU | 14 | PIS | 15 | TAU | 15 | GEM |
| 18 | SAG | 16 | CAP | 17 | PIS | 17 | ARI | 18 | GEM | 18 | CAN |
| 20 | CAP | 18 | AQU | 19 | ARI | 19 | TAU | 20 | CAN | 20 | LEO |
| 22 | AQU | 21 | PIS | 22 | TAU | 22 | GEM | 23 | LEO | 23 | VIR |
| 24 | PIS | 23 | ARI | 24 | GEM | 24 | CAN | 25 | VIR | 25 | LIB |
| 27 | ARI | 26 | TAU | 27 | CAN | 27 | LEO | 28 | LIB | 27 | SCO |
| 29 | TAU | 28 | GEM | 29 | LEO | 29 | VIR | 30 | SCO | 29 | SAG |
| | | 31 | CAN | | | 31 | LIB | | | 31 | CAP |

## 1995

| JAN | | FEB | | MAR | | APR | | MAY | | JUN | |
|---|---|---|---|---|---|---|---|---|---|---|---|
| 2 | AQU | 1 | PIS | 2 | ARI | 1 | TAU | 1 | GEM | 2 | LEO |
| 4 | PIS | 3 | ARI | 5 | TAU | 3 | GEM | 3 | CAN | 5 | VIR |
| 7 | ARI | 5 | TAU | 7 | GEM | 6 | CAN | 6 | LEO | 7 | LIB |
| 9 | TAU | 8 | GEM | 10 | CAN | 9 | LEO | 8 | VIR | 9 | SCO |
| 12 | GEM | 10 | CAN | 12 | LEO | 11 | VIR | 10 | LIB | 11 | SAG |
| 14 | CAN | 13 | LEO | 14 | VIR | 13 | LIB | 13 | SCO | 13 | CAP |
| 16 | LEO | 15 | VIR | 17 | LIB | 15 | SCO | 15 | SAG | 15 | AQU |
| 19 | VIR | 17 | LIB | 19 | SCO | 17 | SAG | 17 | CAP | 17 | PIS |
| 21 | LIB | 19 | SCO | 21 | SAG | 19 | CAP | 19 | AQU | 19 | ARI |
| 23 | SCO | 22 | SAG | 23 | CAP | 21 | AQU | 21 | PIS | 22 | TAU |
| 25 | SAG | 24 | CAP | 25 | AQU | 24 | PIS | 23 | ARI | 24 | GEM |
| 27 | CAP | 26 | AQU | 27 | PIS | 26 | ARI | 26 | TAU | 27 | CAN |
| 30 | AQU | 28 | PIS | 30 | ARI | 28 | TAU | 28 | GEM | 29 | LEO |
| | | | | | | | | 31 | CAN | | |

| JUL | | AUG | | SEP | | OCT | | NOV | | DEC | |
|---|---|---|---|---|---|---|---|---|---|---|---|
| 2 | VIR | 3 | SCO | 1 | SAG | 2 | AQU | 1 | PIS | 3 | TAU |
| 4 | LIB | 5 | SAG | 3 | CAP | 5 | PIS | 3 | ARI | 5 | GEM |
| 6 | SCO | 7 | CAP | 5 | AQU | 7 | ARI | 5 | TAU | 8 | CAN |
| 8 | SAG | 9 | AQU | 7 | PIS | 9 | TAU | 8 | GEM | 10 | LEO |
| 10 | CAP | 11 | PIS | 9 | ARI | 12 | GEM | 10 | CAN | 13 | VIR |
| 12 | AQU | 13 | ARI | 12 | TAU | 14 | CAN | 13 | LEO | 15 | LIB |
| 14 | PIS | 15 | TAU | 14 | GEM | 17 | LEO | 15 | VIR | 17 | SCO |
| 17 | ARI | 18 | GEM | 17 | CAN | 19 | VIR | 18 | LIB | 19 | SAG |
| 19 | TAU | 20 | CAN | 19 | LEO | 21 | LIB | 20 | SCO | 21 | CAP |
| 22 | GEM | 23 | LEO | 22 | VIR | 23 | SCO | 22 | SAG | 23 | AQU |
| 24 | CAN | 25 | VIR | 24 | LIB | 26 | SAG | 24 | CAP | 25 | PIS |
| 27 | LEO | 28 | LIB | 26 | SCO | 28 | CAP | 26 | AQU | 28 | ARI |
| 29 | VIR | 30 | SCO | 28 | SAG | 30 | AQU | 28 | PIS | 30 | TAU |
| 31 | LIB | | | 30 | CAP | | | 30 | ARI | | |

# Moon Signs 1945-2025

## 1996

| | JAN | | FEB | | MAR | | APR | | MAY | | JUN |
|---|---|---|---|---|---|---|---|---|---|---|---|
| 1 | GEM | 3 | LEO | 1 | LEO | 2 | LIB | 2 | SCO | 2 | CAP |
| 4 | CAN | 5 | VIR | 3 | VIR | 4 | SCO | 4 | SAG | 4 | AQU |
| 6 | LEO | 8 | LIB | 6 | LIB | 7 | SAG | 6 | CAP | 6 | PIS |
| 9 | VIR | 10 | SCO | 8 | SCO | 9 | CAP | 8 | AQU | 9 | ARI |
| 11 | LIB | 12 | SAG | 10 | SAG | 11 | AQU | 10 | PIS | 11 | TAU |
| 14 | SCO | 14 | CAP | 13 | CAP | 13 | PIS | 12 | ARI | 13 | GEM |
| 16 | SAG | 16 | AQU | 15 | AQU | 15 | ARI | 15 | TAU | 15 | CAN |
| 18 | CAP | 18 | PIS | 17 | PIS | 17 | TAU | 17 | GEM | 18 | LEO |
| 20 | AQU | 20 | ARI | 19 | ARI | 20 | GEM | 19 | CAN | 21 | VIR |
| 22 | PIS | 23 | TAU | 21 | TAU | 22 | CAN | 22 | LEO | 23 | LIB |
| 24 | ARI | 25 | GEM | 23 | GEM | 25 | LEO | 25 | VIR | 26 | SCO |
| 26 | TAU | 27 | CAN | 26 | CAN | 27 | VIR | 27 | LIB | 28 | SAG |
| 29 | GEM | | | 28 | LEO | 30 | LIB | 29 | SCO | 30 | CAP |
| 31 | CAN | | | 31 | VIR | | | 31 | SAG | | |

| | JUL | | AUG | | SEP | | OCT | | NOV | | DEC |
|---|---|---|---|---|---|---|---|---|---|---|---|
| 2 | AQU | 2 | ARI | 1 | TAU | 3 | CAN | 2 | LEO | 2 | VIR |
| 4 | PIS | 4 | TAU | 3 | GEM | 5 | LEO | 4 | VIR | 4 | LIB |
| 6 | ARI | 7 | GEM | 6 | CAN | 8 | VIR | 7 | LIB | 6 | SCO |
| 8 | TAU | 9 | CAN | 8 | LEO | 10 | LIB | 9 | SCO | 9 | SAG |
| 11 | GEM | 12 | LEO | 11 | VIR | 13 | SCO | 11 | SAG | 11 | CAP |
| 13 | CAN | 14 | VIR | 13 | LIB | 15 | SAG | 13 | CAP | 13 | AQU |
| 16 | LEO | 17 | LIB | 15 | SCO | 17 | CAP | 16 | AQU | 15 | PIS |
| 18 | VIR | 19 | SCO | 18 | SAG | 19 | AQU | 18 | PIS | 17 | ARI |
| 21 | LIB | 21 | SAG | 20 | CAP | 21 | PIS | 20 | ARI | 19 | TAU |
| 23 | SCO | 24 | CAP | 22 | AQU | 23 | ARI | 22 | TAU | 22 | GEM |
| 25 | SAG | 26 | AQU | 24 | PIS | 26 | TAU | 24 | GEM | 24 | CAN |
| 27 | CAP | 28 | PIS | 26 | ARI | 28 | GEM | 27 | CAN | 26 | LEO |
| 29 | AQU | 30 | ARI | 28 | TAU | 30 | CAN | 29 | LEO | 29 | VIR |
| 31 | PIS | | | 30 | GEM | | | | | 31 | LIB |

---

## 1997

| | JAN | | FEB | | MAR | | APR | | MAY | | JUN |
|---|---|---|---|---|---|---|---|---|---|---|---|
| 3 | SCO | 1 | SAG | 1 | SAG | 1 | AQU | 1 | PIS | 1 | TAU |
| 5 | SAG | 4 | CAP | 3 | CAP | 4 | PIS | 3 | ARI | 4 | GEM |
| 7 | CAP | 6 | AQU | 5 | AQU | 6 | ARI | 5 | TAU | 6 | CAN |
| 9 | AQU | 8 | PIS | 7 | PIS | 8 | TAU | 7 | GEM | 8 | LEO |
| 11 | PIS | 10 | ARI | 9 | ARI | 10 | GEM | 9 | CAN | 11 | VIR |
| 13 | ARI | 12 | TAU | 11 | TAU | 12 | CAN | 12 | LEO | 13 | LIB |
| 15 | TAU | 14 | GEM | 13 | GEM | 14 | LEO | 14 | VIR | 16 | SCO |
| 18 | GEM | 16 | CAN | 16 | CAN | 17 | VIR | 17 | LIB | 18 | SAG |
| 20 | CAN | 19 | LEO | 18 | LEO | 19 | LIB | 19 | SCO | 20 | CAP |
| 23 | LEO | 21 | VIR | 21 | VIR | 22 | SCO | 22 | SAG | 22 | AQU |
| 25 | VIR | 24 | LIB | 23 | LIB | 24 | SAG | 24 | CAP | 24 | PIS |
| 28 | LIB | 26 | SCO | 26 | SCO | 27 | CAP | 26 | AQU | 26 | ARI |
| 30 | SCO | | | 28 | SAG | 29 | AQU | 28 | PIS | 29 | TAU |
| | | | | 30 | CAP | | | 30 | ARI | | |

| | JUL | | AUG | | SEP | | OCT | | NOV | | DEC |
|---|---|---|---|---|---|---|---|---|---|---|---|
| 1 | GEM | 2 | LEO | 3 | LIB | 3 | SCO | 1 | SAG | 1 | CAP |
| 3 | CAN | 4 | VIR | 6 | SCO | 5 | SAG | 4 | CAP | 3 | AQU |
| 5 | LEO | 7 | LIB | 8 | SAG | 8 | CAP | 6 | AQU | 5 | PIS |
| 8 | VIR | 9 | SCO | 10 | CAP | 10 | AQU | 8 | PIS | 8 | ARI |
| 10 | LIB | 12 | SAG | 12 | AQU | 12 | PIS | 10 | ARI | 10 | TAU |
| 13 | SCO | 14 | CAP | 15 | PIS | 14 | ARI | 12 | TAU | 12 | GEM |
| 15 | SAG | 16 | AQU | 17 | ARI | 16 | TAU | 14 | GEM | 14 | CAN |
| 18 | CAP | 18 | PIS | 19 | TAU | 18 | GEM | 17 | CAN | 16 | LEO |
| 20 | AQU | 20 | ARI | 21 | GEM | 20 | CAN | 19 | LEO | 19 | VIR |
| 22 | PIS | 22 | TAU | 23 | CAN | 23 | LEO | 21 | VIR | 21 | LIB |
| 24 | ARI | 24 | GEM | 25 | LEO | 25 | VIR | 24 | LIB | 24 | SCO |
| 26 | TAU | 27 | CAN | 28 | VIR | 28 | LIB | 26 | SCO | 26 | SAG |
| 28 | GEM | 29 | LEO | 30 | LIB | 30 | SCO | 29 | SAG | 28 | CAP |
| 30 | CAN | 31 | VIR | | | | | | | 31 | AQU |

## 1998

| JAN | | FEB | | MAR | | APR | | MAY | | JUN | |
|---|---|---|---|---|---|---|---|---|---|---|---|
| 2 | PIS | 2 | TAU | 2 | TAU | 2 | CAN | 2 | LEO | 3 | LIB |
| 4 | ARI | 4 | GEM | 4 | GEM | 4 | LEO | 4 | VIR | 5 | SCO |
| 6 | TAU | 7 | CAN | 6 | CAN | 7 | VIR | 7 | LIB | 8 | SAG |
| 8 | GEM | 9 | LEO | 8 | LEO | 9 | LIB | 9 | SCO | 10 | CAP |
| 10 | cAN | 11 | VIR | 11 | VIR | 12 | SCO | 12 | SAG | 13 | AQU |
| 13 | LEO | 14 | LIB | 13 | LIB | 14 | SAG | 14 | CAP | 15 | PIS |
| 15 | VIR | 16 | SCO | 16 | SCO | 17 | CAP | 16 | AQU | 17 | ARI |
| 18 | LIB | 19 | SAG | 18 | SAG | 19 | AQU | 19 | PIS | 19 | TAU |
| 20 | SCO | 21 | CAP | 21 | CAP | 21 | PIS | 21 | ARI | 21 | GEM |
| 23 | SAG | 23 | AQU | 23 | AQU | 23 | ARI | 23 | TAU | 23 | CAN |
| 25 | CAP | 25 | PIS | 25 | PIS | 25 | TAU | 25 | GEM | 25 | LEO |
| 27 | AQU | 27 | ARI | 27 | ARI | 27 | GEM | 27 | CAN | 28 | VIR |
| 29 | PIS | | | 29 | TAU | 29 | CAN | 29 | LEO | 30 | LIB |
| 31 | ARI | | | 31 | GEM | | | 31 | VIR | | |

| JUL | | AUG | | SEP | | OCT | | NOV | | DEC | |
|---|---|---|---|---|---|---|---|---|---|---|---|
| 3 | SCO | 2 | SAG | 3 | AQU | 2 | PIS | 1 | ARI | 2 | GEM |
| 5 | SAG | 4 | CAP | 5 | PIS | 4 | ARI | 3 | TAU | 4 | CAN |
| 8 | CAP | 6 | AQU | 7 | ARI | 6 | TAU | 5 | GEM | 6 | LEO |
| 10 | AQU | 8 | PIS | 9 | TAU | 8 | GEM | 7 | CAN | 9 | VIR |
| 12 | PIS | 11 | ARI | 11 | GEM | 10 | CAN | 9 | LEO | 11 | LIB |
| 14 | ARI | 13 | TAU | 13 | CAN | 13 | LEO | 11 | VIR | 14 | SCO |
| 16 | TAU | 15 | GEM | 15 | LEO | 15 | VIR | 14 | LIB | 16 | SAG |
| 18 | GEM | 17 | CAN | 18 | VIR | 17 | LIB | 16 | SCO | 19 | CAP |
| 21 | CAN | 19 | LEO | 20 | LIB | 20 | SCO | 19 | SAG | 21 | AQU |
| 23 | LEO | 21 | VIR | 23 | SCO | 23 | SAG | 21 | CAP | 23 | PIS |
| 25 | VIR | 24 | LIB | 25 | SAG | 25 | CAP | 24 | AQU | 25 | ARI |
| 28 | LIB | 26 | SCO | 28 | CAP | 27 | AQU | 26 | PIS | 28 | TAU |
| 30 | SCO | 29 | SAG | 30 | AQU | 30 | PIS | 28 | ARI | 30 | GEM |
| | | 31 | CAP | | | | | 30 | TAU | | |

## 1999

| JAN | | FEB | | MAR | | APR | | MAY | | JUN | |
|---|---|---|---|---|---|---|---|---|---|---|---|
| 1 | CAN | 1 | VIR | 1 | VIR | 2 | SCO | 2 | SAG | 3 | AQU |
| 3 | LEO | 4 | LIB | 3 | LIB | 4 | SAG | 4 | CAP | 5 | PIS |
| 5 | VIR | 6 | SCO | 6 | SCO | 7 | CAP | 7 | AQU | 8 | ARI |
| 7 | LIB | 9 | SAG | 8 | SAG | 9 | AQU | 9 | PIS | 10 | TAU |
| 10 | SCO | 11 | CAP | 11 | CAP | 12 | PIS | 11 | ARI | 12 | GEM |
| 12 | SAG | 14 | AQU | 13 | AQU | 14 | ARI | 13 | TAU | 14 | CAN |
| 15 | CAP | 16 | PIS | 15 | PIS | 16 | TAU | 15 | GEM | 16 | LEO |
| 17 | AQU | 18 | ARI | 17 | ARI | 18 | GEM | 17 | CAN | 18 | VIR |
| 19 | PIS | 20 | TAU | 19 | TAU | 20 | CAN | 19 | LEO | 20 | LIB |
| 22 | ARI | 22 | GEM | 21 | GEM | 22 | LEO | 21 | VIR | 23 | SCO |
| 24 | TAU | 24 | CAN | 23 | CAN | 24 | VIR | 24 | LIB | 25 | SAG |
| 26 | GEM | 26 | LEO | 26 | LEO | 27 | LIB | 26 | SCO | 28 | CAP |
| 28 | CAN | | | 28 | VIR | 29 | SCO | 29 | SAG | 30 | AQU |
| 30 | LEO | | | 30 | LIB | | | 31 | CAP | | |

| JUL | | AUG | | SEP | | OCT | | NOV | | DEC | |
|---|---|---|---|---|---|---|---|---|---|---|---|
| 2 | PIS | 1 | ARI | 2 | GEM | 1 | CAN | 1 | VIR | 1 | LIB |
| 5 | ARI | 3 | TAU | 4 | CAN | 3 | LEO | 4 | LIB | 3 | SCO |
| 7 | TAU | 5 | GEM | 6 | LEO | 5 | VIR | 6 | SCO | 6 | SAG |
| 9 | GEM | 7 | CAN | 8 | VIR | 8 | LIB | 9 | SAG | 8 | CAP |
| 11 | CAN | 9 | LEO | 10 | LIB | 10 | SCO | 11 | CAP | 11 | AQU |
| 13 | LEO | 12 | VIR | 13 | SCO | 12 | SAG | 14 | AQU | 13 | PIS |
| 15 | VIR | 14 | LIB | 15 | SAG | 15 | CAP | 16 | PIS | 16 | ARI |
| 17 | LIB | 16 | SCO | 18 | CAP | 17 | AQU | 18 | ARI | 18 | TAU |
| 20 | SCO | 19 | SAG | 20 | AQU | 20 | PIS | 21 | TAU | 20 | GEM |
| 22 | SAG | 21 | CAP | 22 | PIS | 22 | ARI | 23 | GEM | 22 | CAN |
| 25 | CAP | 24 | AQU | 25 | ARI | 24 | TAU | 25 | CAN | 24 | LEO |
| 27 | AQU | 26 | PIS | 27 | TAU | 26 | GEM | 27 | LEO | 26 | VIR |
| 30 | PIS | 28 | ARI | 29 | GEM | 28 | CAN | 29 | VIR | 28 | LIB |
| | | 30 | TAU | | | 30 | LEO | | | 31 | SCO |

# Moon Signs 1945-2025

## 2000

| | JAN | | FEB | | MAR | | APR | | MAY | | JUN |
|---|---|---|---|---|---|---|---|---|---|---|---|
| 3 | SAG | 1 | CAP | 2 | AQU | 1 | PIS | 3 | TAU | 1 | GEM |
| 5 | CAP | 4 | AQU | 4 | PIS | 3 | ARI | 5 | GEM | 3 | CAN |
| 7 | AQU | 6 | PIS | 7 | ARI | 5 | TAU | 7 | CAN | 5 | LEO |
| 10 | PIS | 8 | ARI | 9 | TAU | 7 | GEM | 9 | LEO | 7 | VIR |
| 12 | ARI | 11 | TAU | 11 | GEM | 9 | CAN | 11 | VIR | 9 | LIB |
| 14 | TAU | 13 | GEM | 13 | CAN | 11 | LEO | 13 | LIB | 12 | SCO |
| 16 | GEM | 15 | CAN | 15 | LEO | 14 | VIR | 15 | SCO | 14 | SAG |
| 18 | CAN | 17 | LEO | 17 | viR | 16 | LIB | 18 | SAG | 17 | CAP |
| 20 | LEO | 19 | VIR | 20 | LIB | 18 | SCO | 20 | CAP | 19 | AQU |
| 23 | VIR | 21 | LIB | 22 | SCO | 21 | SAG | 23 | AQU | 22 | PIS |
| 25 | LIB | 23 | SCO | 24 | SAG | 23 | CAP | 25 | PIS | 24 | ARI |
| 27 | SCO | 26 | SAG | 27 | CAP | 26 | AQU | 28 | ARI | 26 | TAU |
| 29 | SAG | 28 | CAP | 29 | AQU | 28 | PIS | 30 | TAU | 28 | GEM |
| | | | | | | 30 | ARI | | | 30 | CAN |

| | JUL | | AUG | | SEP | | OCT | | NOV | | DEC |
|---|---|---|---|---|---|---|---|---|---|---|---|
| 2 | LEO | 1 | VIR | 2 | SCO | 1 | SAG | 3 | AQU | 2 | PIS |
| 4 | VIR | 3 | LIB | 4 | SAG | 4 | CAP | 5 | PIS | 5 | ARI |
| 7 | LIB | 5 | SCO | 6 | CAP | 6 | AQU | 8 | ARI | 7 | TAU |
| 9 | SCO | 8 | SAG | 9 | AQU | 9 | PIS | 10 | TAU | 9 | GEM |
| 11 | SAG | 10 | CAP | 11 | PIS | 11 | ARI | 12 | GEM | 11 | CAN |
| 14 | CAP | 13 | AQU | 14 | ARI | 13 | TAU | 14 | CAN | 13 | LEO |
| 16 | AQU | 15 | PIS | 16 | TAU | 16 | GEM | 16 | LEO | 15 | VIR |
| 19 | PIS | 18 | ARI | 18 | GEM | 18 | CAN | 18 | VIR | 18 | LIB |
| 21 | ARI | 20 | TAU | 20 | CAN | 20 | LEO | 20 | LIB | 20 | SCO |
| 24 | TAU | 22 | GEM | 23 | LEO | 22 | VIR | 23 | SCO | 22 | SAG |
| 26 | GEM | 24 | CAN | 25 | VIR | 24 | LIB | 25 | SAG | 25 | CAP |
| 28 | CAN | 26 | LEO | 27 | LIB | 26 | SCO | 27 | CAP | 27 | AQU |
| 30 | LEO | 28 | VIR | 29 | SCO | 29 | SAG | 30 | AQU | 30 | PIS |
| | | 30 | LIB | | | 31 | CAP | | | | |

## 2001

| | JAN | | FEB | | MAR | | APR | | MAY | | JUN |
|---|---|---|---|---|---|---|---|---|---|---|---|
| 1 | ARI | 2 | GEM | 1 | GEM | 2 | LEO | 1 | VIR | 2 | SCO |
| 4 | TAU | 4 | CAN | 4 | CAN | 4 | VIR | 3 | LIB | 4 | SAG |
| 6 | GEM | 6 | LEO | 6 | LEO | 6 | LIB | 6 | SCO | 7 | CAP |
| 8 | CAN | 8 | VIR | 8 | VIR | 8 | SCO | 8 | SAG | 9 | AQU |
| 10 | LEO | 10 | LIB | 10 | LIB | 10 | SAG | 10 | CAP | 11 | PIS |
| 12 | VIR | 12 | SCO | 12 | SCO | 13 | CAP | 13 | AQU | 14 | ARI |
| 14 | LIB | 15 | SAG | 14 | SAG | 15 | AQU | 15 | PIS | 16 | TAU |
| 16 | SCO | 17 | CAP | 16 | CAP | 18 | PIS | 18 | ARI | 19 | GEM |
| 18 | SAG | 20 | AQU | 19 | AQU | 20 | ARI | 20 | TAU | 21 | CAN |
| 21 | CAP | 22 | PIS | 22 | PIS | 23 | TAU | 22 | GEM | 23 | LEO |
| 23 | AQU | 25 | ARI | 24 | ARI | 25 | GEM | 24 | CAN | 25 | VIR |
| 26 | PIS | 27 | TAU | 26 | TAU | 27 | CAN | 27 | LEO | 27 | LIB |
| 28 | ARI | | | 29 | GEM | 29 | LEO | 29 | VIR | 29 | SCO |
| 31 | TAU | | | 31 | CAN | | | 31 | LIB | | |

| | JUL | | AUG | | SEP | | OCT | | NOV | | DEC |
|---|---|---|---|---|---|---|---|---|---|---|---|
| 1 | SAG | 3 | AQU | 1 | PIS | 1 | ARI | 2 | GEM | 2 | CAN |
| 4 | CAP | 5 | PIS | 4 | ARI | 4 | TAU | 4 | CAN | 4 | LEO |
| 6 | AQU | 8 | ARI | 6 | TAU | 6 | GEM | 7 | LEO | 6 | VIR |
| 9 | PIS | 10 | TAU | 9 | GEM | 8 | CAN | 9 | VIR | 8 | LIB |
| 11 | ARI | 12 | GEM | 11 | CAN | 10 | LEO | 11 | LIB | 10 | SCO |
| 14 | TAU | 15 | CAN | 13 | LEO | 13 | VIR | 13 | SCO | 12 | SAG |
| 16 | GEM | 17 | LEO | 15 | VIR | 15 | LIB | 15 | SAG | 15 | CAP |
| 18 | CAN | 19 | VIR | 17 | LIB | 17 | SCO | 17 | CAP | 17 | AQU |
| 20 | LEO | 21 | LIB | 19 | SCO | 19 | SAG | 20 | AQU | 20 | PIS |
| 22 | VIR | 23 | SCO | 21 | SAG | 21 | CAP | 22 | PIS | 22 | ARI |
| 24 | LIB | 25 | SAG | 24 | CAP | 23 | AQU | 25 | ARI | 25 | TAU |
| 26 | SCO | 27 | CAP | 26 | AQU | 26 | PIS | 27 | TAU | 27 | GEM |
| 29 | SAG | 30 | AQU | 29 | PIS | 28 | ARI | 30 | GEM | 29 | CAN |
| 31 | CAP | | | | | 31 | TAU | | | 31 | LEO |

| 2002 | JAN | | FEB | | MAR | | APR | | MAY | | JUN | |
|---|---|---|---|---|---|---|---|---|---|---|---|---|
| | 2 | VIR | 1 | LIB | 1 | SCO | 1 | SAG | 2 | AQU | 1 | PIS |
| | 4 | LIB | 3 | SCO | 4 | SAG | 3 | CAP | 5 | PIS | 4 | ARI |
| | 6 | SCO | 5 | SAG | 6 | CAP | 5 | AQU | 7 | ARI | 6 | TAU |
| | 9 | SAG | 7 | CAP | 9 | AQU | 8 | PIS | 10 | TAU | 9 | GEM |
| | 11 | CAP | 10 | AQU | 11 | PIS | 10 | ARI | 12 | GEM | 11 | CAN |
| | 13 | AQU | 12 | PIS | 14 | ARI | 13 | TAU | 15 | CAN | 13 | LEO |
| | 16 | PIS | 15 | ARI | 16 | TAU | 15 | GEM | 17 | LEO | 15 | VIR |
| | 18 | ARI | 17 | TAU | 19 | GEM | 18 | CAN | 19 | VIR | 18 | LIB |
| | 21 | TAU | 20 | GEM | 21 | CAN | 20 | LEO | 21 | LIB | 20 | SCO |
| | 23 | GEM | 22 | CAN | 24 | LEO | 22 | VIR | 23 | SCO | 22 | SAG |
| | 26 | CAN | 24 | LEO | 26 | VIR | 24 | LIB | 25 | SAG | 24 | CAP |
| | 28 | LEO | 26 | VIR | 28 | LIB | 26 | SCO | 28 | CAP | 26 | AQU |
| | 30 | VIR | 28 | LIB | 30 | SCO | 28 | SAG | 30 | AQU | 29 | PIS |
| | | | | | | | 30 | CAP | | | | |

| | JUL | | AUG | | SEP | | OCT | | NOV | | DEC | |
|---|---|---|---|---|---|---|---|---|---|---|---|---|
| | 1 | ARI | 2 | GEM | 1 | CAN | 1 | LEO | 1 | LIB | 1 | SCO |
| | 4 | TAU | 5 | CAN | 3 | LEO | 3 | VIR | 3 | SCO | 3 | SAG |
| | 6 | GEM | 7 | LEO | 5 | VIR | 5 | LIB | 5 | SAG | 5 | CAP |
| | 8 | CAN | 9 | VIR | 7 | LIB | 7 | SCO | 7 | CAP | 7 | AQU |
| | 11 | LEO | 11 | LIB | 9 | SCO | 9 | SAG | 10 | AQU | 9 | PIS |
| | 13 | VIR | 13 | SCO | 12 | SAG | 11 | CAP | 12 | PIS | 12 | ARI |
| | 15 | LIB | 15 | SAG | 14 | CAP | 13 | AQU | 15 | ARI | 14 | TAU |
| | 17 | SCO | 18 | CAP | 16 | AQU | 16 | PIS | 17 | TAU | 17 | GEM |
| | 19 | SAG | 20 | AQU | 19 | PIS | 18 | ARI | 20 | GEM | 19 | CAN |
| | 21 | CAP | 22 | PIS | 21 | ARI | 21 | TAU | 22 | CAN | 22 | LEO |
| | 24 | AQU | 25 | ARI | 24 | TAU | 23 | GEM | 24 | LEO | 24 | VIR |
| | 26 | PIS | 27 | TAU | 26 | GEM | 25 | CAN | 27 | VIR | 26 | LIB |
| | 28 | ARI | 30 | GEM | 29 | CAN | 28 | LEO | 29 | LIB | 28 | SCO |
| | 31 | TAU | | | | | 30 | VIR | | | 30 | SAG |

| 2003 | JAN | | FEB | | MAR | | APR | | MAY | | JUN | |
|---|---|---|---|---|---|---|---|---|---|---|---|---|
| | 1 | CAP | 2 | PIS | 1 | PIS | 3 | TAU | 2 | GEM | 1 | CAN |
| | 3 | AQU | 5 | ARI | 4 | ARI | 5 | GEM | 5 | CAN | 4 | LEO |
| | 6 | PIS | 7 | TAU | 6 | TAU | 8 | CAN | 7 | LEO | 6 | VIR |
| | 8 | ARI | 10 | GEM | 9 | GEM | 10 | LEO | 10 | VIR | 8 | LIB |
| | 11 | TAU | 12 | CAN | 11 | CAN | 12 | VIR | 12 | LIB | 10 | SCO |
| | 13 | GEM | 14 | LEO | 14 | LEO | 14 | LIB | 14 | SCO | 12 | SAG |
| | 16 | CAN | 16 | VIR | 16 | VIR | 16 | SCO | 16 | SAG | 14 | CAP |
| | 18 | LEO | 18 | LIB | 18 | LIB | 18 | SAG | 18 | CAP | 16 | AQU |
| | 20 | VIR | 21 | SCO | 20 | SCO | 20 | CAP | 20 | AQU | 19 | PIS |
| | 22 | LIB | 23 | SAG | 22 | SAG | 23 | AQU | 22 | PIS | 21 | ARI |
| | 24 | SCO | 25 | CAP | 24 | CAP | 25 | PIS | 25 | ARI | 23 | TAU |
| | 26 | SAG | 27 | AQU | 26 | AQU | 27 | ARI | 27 | TAU | 26 | GEM |
| | 29 | CAP | | | 29 | PIS | 30 | TAU | 30 | GEM | 28 | CAN |
| | 31 | AQU | | | 31 | ARI | | | | | | |

| | JUL | | AUG | | SEP | | OCT | | NOV | | DEC | |
|---|---|---|---|---|---|---|---|---|---|---|---|---|
| | 1 | LEO | 2 | LIB | 2 | SAG | 1 | CAP | 2 | PIS | 2 | ARI |
| | 3 | VIR | 4 | SCO | 4 | CAP | 4 | AQU | 5 | ARI | 4 | TAU |
| | 5 | LIB | 6 | SAG | 6 | AQU | 6 | PIS | 7 | TAU | 7 | GEM |
| | 7 | SCO | 8 | CAP | 9 | PIS | 8 | ARI | 10 | GEM | 9 | CAN |
| | 10 | SAG | 10 | AQU | 11 | ARI | 11 | TAU | 12 | CAN | 12 | LEO |
| | 12 | CAP | 12 | PIS | 13 | TAU | 13 | GEM | 15 | LEO | 14 | VIR |
| | 14 | AQU | 15 | ARI | 16 | GEM | 16 | CAN | 17 | VIR | 16 | LIB |
| | 16 | PIS | 17 | TAU | 18 | CAN | 18 | LEO | 19 | LIB | 19 | SCO |
| | 18 | ARI | 20 | GEM | 21 | LEO | 21 | VIR | 21 | SCO | 21 | SAG |
| | 21 | TAU | 22 | CAN | 23 | VIR | 23 | LIB | 23 | SAG | 23 | CAP |
| | 23 | GEM | 24 | LEO | 25 | LIB | 25 | SCO | 25 | CAP | 25 | AQU |
| | 26 | CAN | 27 | VIR | 27 | SCO | 27 | SAG | 27 | AQU | 27 | PIS |
| | 28 | LEO | 29 | LIB | 29 | SAG | 29 | CAP | 29 | PIS | 29 | ARI |
| | 30 | VIR | 31 | SCO | | | 31 | AQU | | | | |

# Moon Signs 1945-2025

## 2004

| JAN | | FEB | | MAR | | APR | | MAY | | JUN | |
|---|---|---|---|---|---|---|---|---|---|---|---|
| 1 | TAU | 2 | CAN | 3 | LEO | 1 | VIR | 1 | LIB | 2 | SAG |
| 3 | GEM | 4 | LEO | 5 | VIR | 4 | LIB | 3 | SCO | 4 | CAP |
| 6 | CAN | 7 | VIR | 7 | LIB | 6 | SCO | 5 | SAG | 6 | AQU |
| 8 | LEO | 9 | LIB | 9 | SCO | 8 | SAG | 7 | CAP | 8 | PIS |
| 10 | VIR | 11 | SCO | 12 | SAG | 10 | CAP | 9 | AQU | 10 | ARI |
| 13 | LIB | 13 | SAG | 14 | CAP | 12 | AQU | 11 | PIS | 12 | TAU |
| 15 | SCO | 15 | CAP | 16 | AQU | 14 | PIS | 14 | ARI | 15 | GEM |
| 17 | SAG | 17 | AQU | 18 | PIS | 16 | ARI | 16 | TAU | 17 | CAN |
| 19 | CAP | 20 | PIS | 20 | ARI | 19 | TAU | 19 | GEM | 20 | LEO |
| 21 | AQU | 22 | ARI | 23 | TAU | 21 | GEM | 21 | CAN | 22 | VIR |
| 23 | PIS | 24 | TAU | 25 | GEM | 24 | CAN | 24 | LEO | 25 | LIB |
| 25 | ARI | 27 | GEM | 28 | CAN | 26 | LEO | 26 | VIR | 27 | SCO |
| 28 | TAU | 29 | CAN | 30 | LEO | 29 | VIR | 28 | LIB | 29 | SAG |
| 30 | GEM | | | | | | | 31 | SCO | | |

| JUL | | AUG | | SEP | | OCT | | NOV | | DEC | |
|---|---|---|---|---|---|---|---|---|---|---|---|
| 1 | CAP | 1 | PIS | 2 | TAU | 2 | GEM | 1 | CAN | 1 | LEO |
| 3 | AQU | 4 | ARI | 5 | GEM | 5 | CAN | 3 | LEO | 3 | VIR |
| 5 | PIS | 6 | TAU | 7 | CAN | 7 | LEO | 6 | VIR | 6 | LIB |
| 7 | ARI | 8 | GEM | 10 | LEO | 10 | VIR | 8 | LIB | 8 | SCO |
| 10 | TAU | 11 | CAN | 12 | VIR | 12 | LIB | 10 | SCO | 10 | SAG |
| 12 | GEM | 13 | LEO | 14 | LIB | 14 | SCO | 13 | SAG | 12 | CAP |
| 15 | CAN | 16 | VIR | 17 | SCO | 16 | SAG | 15 | CAP | 14 | AQU |
| 17 | LEO | 18 | LIB | 19 | SAG | 18 | CAP | 17 | AQU | 16 | PIS |
| 20 | VIR | 20 | SCO | 21 | CAP | 20 | AQU | 19 | PIS | 18 | ARI |
| 22 | LIB | 23 | SAG | 23 | AQU | 23 | PIS | 21 | ARI | 21 | TAU |
| 24 | SCO | 25 | CAP | 25 | PIS | 25 | ARI | 23 | TAU | 23 | GEM |
| 26 | SAG | 27 | AQU | 27 | ARI | 27 | TAU | 26 | GEM | 25 | CAN |
| 28 | CAP | 29 | PIS | 30 | TAU | 29 | GEM | 28 | CAN | 28 | LEO |
| 30 | AQU | 31 | ARI | | | | | | | 31 | VIR |

## 2005

| JAN | | FEB | | MAR | | APR | | MAY | | JUN | |
|---|---|---|---|---|---|---|---|---|---|---|---|
| 2 | LIB | 1 | SCO | 2 | SAG | 3 | AQU | 2 | PIS | 3 | TAU |
| 4 | SCO | 3 | SAG | 4 | CAP | 5 | PIS | 4 | ARI | 5 | GEM |
| 6 | SAG | 5 | CAP | 6 | AQU | 7 | ARI | 6 | TAU | 7 | CAN |
| 8 | CAP | 7 | AQU | 8 | PIS | 9 | TAU | 9 | GEM | 10 | LEO |
| 10 | AQU | 9 | PIS | 10 | ARI | 11 | GEM | 11 | CAN | 12 | VIR |
| 12 | PIS | 11 | ARI | 13 | TAU | 14 | CAN | 14 | LEO | 15 | LIB |
| 15 | ARI | 13 | TAU | 15 | GEM | 16 | LEO | 16 | VIR | 17 | SCO |
| 17 | TAU | 16 | GEM | 17 | CAN | 19 | VIR | 18 | LIB | 19 | SAG |
| 19 | GEM | 18 | CAN | 20 | LEO | 21 | LIB | 21 | SCO | 21 | CAP |
| 22 | CAN | 21 | LEO | 22 | VIR | 23 | SCO | 23 | SAG | 23 | AQU |
| 24 | LEO | 23 | VIR | 25 | LIB | 26 | SAG | 25 | CAP | 25 | PIS |
| 27 | VIR | 25 | LIB | 27 | SCO | 28 | CAP | 27 | AQU | 28 | ARI |
| 29 | LIB | 28 | SCO | 29 | SAG | 30 | AQU | 29 | PIS | 30 | TAU |
| | | | | 31 | CAP | | | 31 | ARI | | |

| JUL | | AUG | | SEP | | OCT | | NOV | | DEC | |
|---|---|---|---|---|---|---|---|---|---|---|---|
| 2 | GEM | 1 | CAN | 2 | VIR | 2 | LIB | 1 | SCO | 2 | CAP |
| 5 | CAN | 3 | LEO | 5 | SCO | 4 | SCO | 3 | SAG | 4 | AQU |
| 7 | LEO | 6 | VIR | 7 | SCO | 7 | SAG | 5 | CAP | 7 | PIS |
| 10 | VIR | 8 | LIB | 9 | SAG | 9 | CAP | 7 | AQU | 9 | ARI |
| 12 | LIB | 11 | SCO | 12 | CAP | 11 | AQU | 9 | PIS | 11 | TAU |
| 15 | SCO | 13 | SAG | 14 | AQU | 13 | PIS | 11 | ARI | 13 | GEM |
| 17 | SAG | 15 | CAP | 16 | PIS | 15 | ARI | 14 | TAU | 15 | CAN |
| 19 | CAP | 17 | AQU | 18 | ARI | 17 | TAU | 16 | GEM | 18 | LEO |
| 21 | AQU | 19 | PIS | 20 | TAU | 19 | GEM | 18 | CAN | 20 | VIR |
| 23 | PIS | 21 | ARI | 22 | GEM | 22 | CAN | 21 | LEO | 23 | LIB |
| 25 | ARI | 23 | TAU | 24 | CAN | 24 | LEO | 23 | VIR | 25 | SCO |
| 27 | TAU | 26 | GEM | 27 | LEO | 27 | VIR | 26 | LIB | 28 | SAG |
| 29 | GEM | 28 | CAN | 29 | VIR | 29 | LIB | 28 | SCO | 30 | CAP |
| | | 31 | LEO | | | | | 30 | SAG | | |

# Moon Signs 1945-2025

## 2006

| JAN | | FEB | | MAR | | APR | | MAY | | JUN | |
|---|---|---|---|---|---|---|---|---|---|---|---|
| 1 | AQU | 1 | ARI | 1 | ARI | 1 | GEM | 1 | CAN | 2 | VIR |
| 3 | PIS | 3 | TAU | 3 | TAU | 4 | CAN | 3 | LEO | 5 | LIB |
| 5 | ARI | 6 | GEM | 5 | GEM | 6 | LEO | 6 | VIR | 7 | SCO |
| 7 | TAU | 8 | CAN | 7 | CAN | 9 | VIR | 8 | LIB | 10 | SAG |
| 9 | GEM | 10 | LEO | 10 | LEO | 11 | LIB | 11 | SCO | 12 | CAP |
| 12 | CAN | 13 | VIR | 12 | VIR | 14 | SCO | 13 | SAG | 14 | AQU |
| 14 | LEO | 16 | LIB | 15 | LIB | 16 | SAG | 15 | CAP | 16 | PIS |
| 17 | VIR | 18 | SCO | 17 | SCO | 18 | CAP | 18 | AQU | 18 | ARI |
| 19 | LIB | 20 | SAG | 20 | SAG | 20 | AQU | 20 | PIS | 20 | TAU |
| 22 | SCO | 23 | CAP | 22 | CAP | 22 | PIS | 22 | ARI | 22 | GEM |
| 24 | SAG | 25 | AQU | 24 | AQU | 25 | ARI | 24 | TAU | 25 | CAN |
| 25 | CAP | 27 | PIS | 26 | PIS | 27 | TAU | 26 | GEM | 27 | LEO |
| 28 | AQU | | | 28 | ARI | 29 | GEM | 28 | CAN | 29 | VIR |
| 30 | PIS | | | 30 | TAU | | | 31 | LEO | | |

| JUL | | AUG | | SEP | | OCT | | NOV | | DEC | |
|---|---|---|---|---|---|---|---|---|---|---|---|
| 2 | LIB | 1 | SCO | 2 | CAP | 1 | AQU | 2 | ARI | 1 | TAU |
| 5 | SCO | 3 | SAG | 4 | AQU | 4 | PIS | 4 | TAU | 3 | GEM |
| 7 | SAG | 5 | CAP | 6 | PIS | 6 | ARI | 6 | GEM | 6 | CAN |
| 9 | CAP | 8 | AQU | 8 | ARI | 8 | TAU | 8 | CAN | 8 | LEO |
| 11 | AQU | 10 | PIS | 10 | TAU | 10 | GEM | 10 | LEO | 10 | VIR |
| 13 | PIS | 12 | ARI | 12 | GEM | 12 | CAN | 13 | VIR | 13 | LIB |
| 15 | ARI | 14 | TAU | 14 | CAN | 14 | LEO | 15 | LIB | 15 | SCO |
| 17 | TAU | 16 | GEM | 17 | LEO | 17 | VIR | 18 | SCO | 18 | SAG |
| 20 | GEM | 18 | CAN | 19 | VIR | 19 | LIB | 20 | SAG | 20 | CAP |
| 22 | CAN | 21 | LEO | 22 | LIB | 22 | SCO | 23 | CAP | 22 | AQU |
| 24 | LEO | 23 | VIR | 24 | SCO | 24 | SAG | 25 | AQU | 24 | PIS |
| 27 | VIR | 26 | LIB | 27 | SAG | 26 | CAP | 27 | PIS | 27 | ARI |
| 29 | LIB | 28 | SCO | 29 | CAP | 29 | AQU | 29 | ARI | 29 | TAU |
| | | 31 | SAG | | | 31 | PIS | | | 31 | GEM |

## 2007

| JAN | | FEB | | MAR | | APR | | MAY | | JUN | |
|---|---|---|---|---|---|---|---|---|---|---|---|
| 2 | CAN | 1 | LEO | 2 | VIR | 1 | LIB | 1 | SCO | 2 | CAP |
| 4 | LEO | 3 | VIR | 5 | LIB | 3 | SCO | 3 | SAG | 4 | AQU |
| 7 | VIR | 5 | LIB | 7 | SCO | 6 | SAG | 6 | CAP | 7 | PIS |
| 9 | LIB | 8 | SCO | 10 | SAG | 8 | CAP | 8 | AQU | 9 | ARI |
| 12 | SCO | 10 | SAG | 12 | CAP | 11 | AQU | 10 | PIS | 11 | TAU |
| 14 | SAG | 13 | CAP | 14 | AQU | 13 | PIS | 12 | ARI | 13 | GEM |
| 16 | CAP | 15 | AQU | 17 | PIS | 15 | ARI | 14 | TAU | 15 | CAN |
| 19 | AQU | 17 | PIS | 19 | ARI | 17 | TAU | 16 | GEM | 17 | LEO |
| 21 | PIS | 19 | ARI | 21 | TAU | 19 | GEM | 18 | CAN | 19 | VIR |
| 23 | ARI | 21 | TAU | 23 | GEM | 21 | CAN | 21 | LEO | 22 | LIB |
| 25 | TAU | 23 | GEM | 25 | CAN | 23 | LEO | 23 | VIR | 24 | SCO |
| 27 | GEM | 25 | CAN | 27 | LEO | 26 | VIR | 25 | LIB | 27 | SAG |
| 29 | CAN | 28 | LEO | 29 | VIR | 28 | LIB | 28 | SCO | 29 | CAP |
| | | | | | | | | 31 | SAG | | |

| JUL | | AUG | | SEP | | OCT | | NOV | | DEC | |
|---|---|---|---|---|---|---|---|---|---|---|---|
| 2 | AQU | 2 | ARI | 1 | TAU | 2 | CAN | 3 | VIR | 3 | LIB |
| 4 | PIS | 4 | TAU | 3 | GEM | 4 | LEO | 5 | LIB | 5 | SCO |
| 6 | ARI | 6 | GEM | 5 | CAN | 7 | VIR | 8 | SCO | 8 | SAG |
| 8 | TAU | 9 | CAN | 7 | LEO | 9 | LIB | 10 | SAG | 10 | CAP |
| 10 | GEM | 11 | LEO | 9 | VIR | 12 | SCO | 13 | CAP | 13 | AQU |
| 12 | CAN | 13 | VIR | 12 | LIB | 14 | SAG | 15 | AQU | 15 | PIS |
| 14 | LEO | 15 | LIB | 14 | SCO | 17 | CAP | 18 | PIS | 17 | ARI |
| 17 | VIR | 18 | SCO | 17 | SAG | 19 | AQU | 20 | ARI | 19 | TAU |
| 19 | LIB | 20 | SAG | 19 | CAP | 21 | PIS | 22 | TAU | 21 | GEM |
| 22 | SCO | 23 | CAP | 22 | AQU | 23 | ARI | 24 | GEM | 23 | CAN |
| 24 | SAG | 25 | AQU | 24 | PIS | 25 | TAU | 26 | CAN | 25 | LEO |
| 27 | CAP | 27 | PIS | 26 | ARI | 27 | GEM | 28 | LEO | 27 | VIR |
| 29 | AQU | 29 | ARI | 28 | TAU | 29 | CAN | 30 | VIR | 30 | LIB |
| 31 | PIS | | | 30 | GEM | 31 | LEO | | | | |

## 2008

| JAN | | FEB | | MAR | | APR | | MAY | | JUN | |
|---|---|---|---|---|---|---|---|---|---|---|---|
| 1 | SCO | 3 | CAP | 1 | CAP | 2 | PIS | 2 | ARI | 2 | GEM |
| 4 | SAG | 5 | AQU | 3 | AQU | 4 | ARI | 4 | TAU | 4 | CAN |
| 6 | CAP | 7 | PIS | 6 | PIS | 6 | TAU | 6 | GEM | 6 | LEO |
| 9 | AQU | 10 | ARI | 8 | ARI | 8 | GEM | 8 | CAN | 8 | VIR |
| 11 | PIS | 12 | TAU | 10 | TAU | 10 | CAN | 10 | LEO | 11 | LIB |
| 13 | ARI | 14 | GEM | 12 | GEM | 13 | LEO | 12 | VIR | 13 | SCO |
| 15 | TAU | 16 | CAN | 14 | CAN | 15 | VIR | 14 | LIB | 15 | SAG |
| 18 | GEM | 18 | LEO | 16 | LEO | 17 | LIB | 17 | SCO | 18 | CAP |
| 20 | CAN | 20 | VIR | 19 | VIR | 20 | SCO | 19 | SAG | 21 | AQU |
| 22 | LEO | 23 | LIB | 21 | LIB | 22 | SAG | 22 | CAP | 23 | PIS |
| 24 | VIR | 25 | SCO | 23 | SCO | 25 | CAP | 24 | AQU | 25 | ARI |
| 26 | LIB | 28 | SAG | 26 | SAG | 27 | AQU | 27 | PIS | 28 | TAU |
| 29 | SCO | | | 28 | CAP | 30 | PIS | 29 | ARI | 30 | GEM |
| 31 | SAG | | | 31 | AQU | | | 31 | TAU | | |

| JUL | | AUG | | SEP | | OCT | | NOV | | DEC | |
|---|---|---|---|---|---|---|---|---|---|---|---|
| 2 | CAN | 2 | VIR | 1 | LIB | 3 | SAG | 2 | CAP | 2 | AQU |
| 4 | LEO | 4 | LIB | 3 | SCO | 5 | CAP | 4 | AQU | 4 | PIS |
| 6 | VIR | 7 | SCO | 6 | SAG | 8 | AQU | 7 | PIS | 6 | ARI |
| 8 | LIB | 9 | SAG | 8 | CAP | 10 | PIS | 9 | ARI | 9 | TAU |
| 10 | SCO | 12 | CAP | 11 | AQU | 13 | ARI | 11 | TAU | 11 | GEM |
| 13 | SAG | 14 | AQU | 13 | PIS | 15 | TAU | 13 | GEM | 13 | CAN |
| 15 | CAP | 17 | PIS | 15 | ARI | 17 | GEM | 15 | CAN | 15 | LEO |
| 18 | AQU | 19 | ARI | 17 | TAU | 19 | CAN | 17 | LEO | 17 | VIR |
| 20 | PIS | 21 | TAU | 19 | GEM | 21 | LEO | 19 | VIR | 19 | LIB |
| 23 | ARI | 23 | GEM | 22 | CAN | 23 | VIR | 22 | LIB | 21 | SCO |
| 25 | TAU | 25 | CAN | 24 | LEO | 25 | LIB | 24 | SCO | 24 | SAG |
| 27 | GEM | 27 | LEO | 26 | VIR | 28 | SCO | 27 | SAG | 26 | CAP |
| 29 | CAN | 30 | VIR | 28 | LIB | 30 | SAG | 29 | CAP | 29 | AQU |
| 31 | LEO | | | 30 | SCO | | | | | 31 | PIS |

## 2009

| JAN | | FEB | | MAR | | APR | | MAY | | JUN | |
|---|---|---|---|---|---|---|---|---|---|---|---|
| 3 | ARI | 1 | TAU | 3 | GEM | 1 | CAN | 2 | VIR | 1 | LIB |
| 5 | TAU | 3 | GEM | 5 | CAN | 3 | LEO | 5 | LIB | 3 | SCO |
| 7 | GEM | 5 | CAN | 7 | LEO | 5 | VIR | 7 | SCO | 6 | SAG |
| 9 | CAN | 7 | LEO | 9 | VIR | 7 | LIB | 9 | SAG | 8 | CAP |
| 11 | LEO | 10 | VIR | 11 | LIB | 10 | SCO | 12 | CAP | 11 | AQU |
| 13 | VIR | 12 | LIB | 13 | SCO | 12 | SAG | 14 | AQU | 13 | PIS |
| 15 | LIB | 14 | SCO | 16 | SAG | 15 | CAP | 17 | PIS | 16 | ARI |
| 18 | SCO | 16 | SAG | 18 | CAP | 17 | AQU | 19 | ARI | 18 | TAU |
| 20 | SAG | 19 | CAP | 21 | AQU | 20 | PIS | 21 | TAU | 20 | GEM |
| 23 | CAP | 21 | AQU | 23 | PIS | 22 | ARI | 24 | GEM | 22 | CAN |
| 25 | AQU | 24 | PIS | 26 | ARI | 24 | TAU | 26 | CAN | 24 | LEO |
| 28 | PIS | 26 | ARI | 28 | TAU | 26 | GEM | 28 | LEO | 26 | VIR |
| 30 | ARI | 28 | TAU | 30 | GEM | 28 | CAN | 30 | VIR | 28 | LIB |
| | | | | | | 30 | LEO | | | 30 | SCO |

| JUL | | AUG | | SEP | | OCT | | NOV | | DEC | |
|---|---|---|---|---|---|---|---|---|---|---|---|
| 3 | SAG | 2 | CAP | 3 | PIS | 3 | ARI | 1 | TAU | 1 | GEM |
| 5 | CAP | 4 | AQU | 5 | ARI | 5 | TAU | 4 | GEM | 3 | CAN |
| 8 | AQU | 7 | PIS | 8 | TAU | 7 | GEM | 6 | CAN | 5 | LEO |
| 10 | PIS | 9 | ARI | 10 | GEM | 9 | CAN | 8 | LEO | 7 | VIR |
| 13 | ARI | 11 | TAU | 12 | CAN | 12 | LEO | 10 | VIR | 9 | LIB |
| 15 | TAU | 14 | GEM | 14 | LEO | 14 | VIR | 12 | LIB | 11 | SCO |
| 17 | GEM | 16 | CAN | 16 | VIR | 16 | LIB | 14 | SCO | 14 | SAG |
| 19 | CAN | 18 | LEO | 18 | LIB | 18 | SCO | 17 | SAG | 16 | CAP |
| 21 | LEO | 20 | VIR | 20 | SCO | 20 | SAG | 19 | CAP | 19 | AQU |
| 23 | VIR | 22 | LIB | 23 | SAG | 23 | CAP | 21 | AQU | 21 | PIS |
| 26 | LIB | 24 | SCO | 25 | CAP | 25 | AQU | 24 | PIS | 24 | ARI |
| 28 | SCO | 26 | SAG | 28 | AQU | 28 | PIS | 26 | ARI | 26 | TAU |
| 30 | SAG | 29 | CAP | 30 | PIS | 30 | ARI | 29 | TAU | 28 | GEM |
| | | 31 | AQU | | | | | | | 30 | CAN |

# Moon Signs 1945-2025

## 2010

| JAN | | FEB | | MAR | | APR | | MAY | | JUN | |
|---|---|---|---|---|---|---|---|---|---|---|---|
| 1 | LEO | 2 | LIB | 1 | LIB | 2 | SAG | 2 | CAP | 1 | AQU |
| 3 | VIR | 4 | SCO | 3 | SCO | 4 | CAP | 4 | AQU | 3 | PIS |
| 6 | LIB | 6 | SAG | 6 | SAG | 7 | AQU | 7 | PIS | 6 | ARI |
| 8 | SCO | 9 | CAP | 8 | CAP | 9 | PIS | 9 | ARI | 8 | TAU |
| 10 | SAG | 11 | AQU | 11 | AQU | 12 | ARI | 12 | TAU | 10 | GEM |
| 13 | CAP | 14 | PIS | 13 | PIS | 14 | TAU | 14 | GEM | 12 | CAN |
| 15 | AQU | 16 | ARI | 16 | ARI | 17 | GEM | 16 | CAN | 14 | LEO |
| 18 | PIS | 19 | TAU | 18 | TAU | 19 | CAN | 18 | LEO | 17 | VIR |
| 20 | ARI | 21 | GEM | 20 | GEM | 21 | LEO | 20 | VIR | 19 | LIB |
| 22 | TAU | 23 | CAN | 23 | CAN | 23 | VIR | 22 | LIB | 21 | SCO |
| 25 | GEM | 25 | LEO | 25 | LEO | 25 | LIB | 25 | SCO | 23 | SAG |
| 27 | CAN | 27 | VIR | 27 | VIR | 27 | SCO | 27 | SAG | 25 | CAP |
| 29 | LEO | | | 29 | LIB | 29 | SAG | 29 | CAP | 28 | AQU |
| 31 | VIR | | | 31 | SCO | | | | | 30 | PIS |

| JUL | | AUG | | SEP | | OCT | | NOV | | DEC | |
|---|---|---|---|---|---|---|---|---|---|---|---|
| 3 | ARI | 2 | TAU | 3 | CAN | 2 | LEO | 3 | LIB | 2 | SCO |
| 5 | TAU | 4 | GEM | 5 | LEO | 4 | VIR | 5 | SCO | 4 | SAG |
| 8 | GEM | 6 | CAN | 7 | VIR | 6 | LIB | 7 | SAG | 6 | CAP |
| 10 | CAN | 8 | LEO | 9 | LIB | 8 | SCO | 9 | CAP | 9 | AQU |
| 12 | LEO | 10 | VIR | 11 | SCO | 10 | SAG | 11 | AQU | 11 | PIS |
| 14 | VIR | 12 | LIB | 13 | SAG | 12 | CAP | 14 | PIS | 14 | ARI |
| 16 | LIB | 14 | SCO | 15 | CAP | 15 | AQU | 16 | ARI | 16 | TAU |
| 18 | SCO | 17 | SAG | 18 | AQU | 17 | PIS | 19 | TAU | 18 | GEM |
| 20 | SAG | 19 | CAP | 20 | PIS | 20 | ARI | 21 | GEM | 21 | CAN |
| 23 | CAP | 21 | AQU | 23 | ARI | 22 | TAU | 23 | CAN | 23 | LEO |
| 25 | AQU | 24 | PIS | 25 | TAU | 25 | GEM | 26 | LEO | 25 | VIR |
| 28 | PIS | 26 | ARI | 28 | GEM | 27 | CAN | 28 | VIR | 27 | LIB |
| 30 | ARI | 29 | TAU | 30 | CAN | 29 | LEO | 30 | LIB | 29 | SCO |
| | | 31 | GEM | | | 31 | VIR | | | 31 | SAG |

## 2011

| JAN | | FEB | | MAR | | APR | | MAY | | JUN | |
|---|---|---|---|---|---|---|---|---|---|---|---|
| 3 | CAP | 1 | AQU | 1 | AQU | 2 | ARI | 2 | TAU | 3 | CAN |
| 5 | AQU | 4 | PIS | 3 | PIS | 4 | TAU | 4 | GEM | 5 | LEO |
| 7 | PIS | 6 | ARI | 6 | ARI | 7 | GEM | 6 | CAN | 7 | VIR |
| 10 | ARI | 9 | TAU | 8 | TAU | 9 | CAN | 9 | LEO | 9 | LIB |
| 12 | TAU | 11 | GEM | 11 | GEM | 11 | LEO | 11 | VIR | 11 | SCO |
| 15 | GEM | 14 | CAN | 13 | CAN | 14 | VIR | 13 | LIB | 13 | SAG |
| 17 | CAN | 16 | LEO | 15 | LEO | 16 | LIB | 15 | SCO | 16 | CAP |
| 19 | LEO | 18 | VIR | 17 | VIR | 18 | SCO | 17 | SAG | 18 | AQU |
| 21 | VIR | 20 | LIB | 19 | LIB | 20 | SAG | 19 | CAP | 20 | PIS |
| 23 | LIB | 22 | SCO | 21 | SCO | 22 | CAP | 21 | AQU | 23 | ARI |
| 25 | SCO | 24 | SAG | 23 | SAG | 24 | AQU | 24 | PIS | 25 | TAU |
| 28 | SAG | 26 | CAP | 25 | CAP | 27 | PIS | 26 | ARI | 28 | GEM |
| 30 | CAP | | | 28 | AQU | 29 | ARI | 29 | TAU | 30 | CAN |
| | | | | 30 | PIS | | | 31 | GEM | | |

| JUL | | AUG | | SEP | | OCT | | NOV | | DEC | |
|---|---|---|---|---|---|---|---|---|---|---|---|
| 2 | LEO | 1 | VIR | 1 | SCO | 1 | SAG | 1 | AQU | 1 | PIS |
| 4 | VIR | 3 | LIB | 3 | SAG | 3 | CAP | 4 | PIS | 3 | ARI |
| 6 | LIB | 5 | SCO | 5 | CAP | 5 | AQU | 6 | ARI | 6 | TAU |
| 9 | SCO | 7 | SAG | 8 | AQU | 7 | PIS | 9 | TAU | 8 | GEM |
| 11 | SAG | 9 | CAP | 10 | PIS | 10 | ARI | 11 | GEM | 11 | CAN |
| 13 | CAP | 11 | AQU | 13 | ARI | 12 | TAU | 14 | CAN | 13 | LEO |
| 15 | AQU | 14 | PIS | 15 | TAU | 15 | GEM | 16 | LEO | 15 | VIR |
| 18 | PIS | 16 | ARI | 18 | GEM | 17 | CAN | 18 | VIR | 18 | LIB |
| 20 | ARI | 19 | TAU | 20 | CAN | 20 | LEO | 20 | LIB | 20 | SCO |
| 23 | TAU | 21 | GEM | 22 | LEO | 22 | VIR | 22 | SCO | 22 | SAG |
| 25 | GEM | 24 | CAN | 24 | VIR | 24 | LIB | 24 | SAG | 24 | CAP |
| 27 | CAN | 26 | LEO | 27 | LIB | 26 | SCO | 26 | CAP | 26 | AQU |
| 30 | LEO | 28 | VIR | 29 | SCO | 28 | SAG | 29 | AQU | 28 | PIS |
| | | 30 | LIB | | | 30 | CAP | | | 31 | ARI |

# Moon Signs 1945-2025

## 2012

| JAN | | FEB | | MAR | | APR | | MAY | | JUN | |
|---|---|---|---|---|---|---|---|---|---|---|---|
| 2 | TAU | 1 | GEM | 2 | CAN | 1 | LEO | 2 | LIB | 1 | SCO |
| 5 | GEM | 4 | CAN | 4 | LEO | 3 | VIR | 4 | SCO | 3 | SAG |
| 7 | CAN | 6 | LEO | 6 | VIR | 5 | LIB | 6 | SAG | 5 | CAP |
| 9 | LEO | 8 | VIR | 8 | LIB | 7 | SCO | 8 | CAP | 7 | AQU |
| 12 | VIR | 10 | LIB | 11 | SCO | 9 | SAG | 11 | AQU | 9 | PIS |
| 14 | LIB | 12 | SCO | 13 | SAG | 11 | CAP | 13 | PIS | 11 | ARI |
| 16 | SCO | 14 | SAG | 15 | CAP | 13 | AQU | 15 | ARI | 14 | TAU |
| 18 | SAG | 17 | CAP | 17 | AQU | 16 | PIS | 18 | TAU | 17 | GEM |
| 20 | CAP | 19 | AQU | 19 | PIS | 18 | ARI | 20 | GEM | 19 | CAN |
| 22 | AQU | 21 | PIS | 22 | ARI | 20 | TAU | 23 | CAN | 21 | LEO |
| 25 | PIS | 23 | ARI | 24 | TAU | 23 | GEM | 25 | LEO | 24 | VIR |
| 27 | ARI | 26 | TAU | 27 | GEM | 26 | CAN | 28 | VIR | 26 | LIB |
| 30 | TAU | 28 | GEM | 29 | CAN | 28 | LEO | 30 | LIB | 28 | SCO |
| | | | | | | 30 | VIR | | | 30 | SAG |

| JUL | | AUG | | SEP | | OCT | | NOV | | DEC | |
|---|---|---|---|---|---|---|---|---|---|---|---|
| 2 | CAP | 1 | AQU | 2 | ARI | 1 | TAU | 3 | CAN | 2 | LEO |
| 4 | AQU | 3 | PIS | 4 | TAU | 4 | GEM | 5 | LEO | 5 | VIR |
| 6 | PIS | 5 | ARI | 6 | GEM | 6 | CAN | 7 | VIR | 7 | LIB |
| 9 | ARI | 8 | TAU | 9 | CAN | 9 | LEO | 10 | LIB | 9 | SCO |
| 11 | TAU | 10 | GEM | 11 | LEO | 11 | VIR | 12 | SCO | 11 | SAG |
| 14 | GEM | 13 | CAN | 14 | VIR | 13 | LIB | 14 | SAG | 13 | CAP |
| 16 | CAN | 15 | LEO | 16 | LIB | 15 | SCO | 16 | CAP | 15 | AQU |
| 19 | LEO | 17 | VIR | 18 | SCO | 17 | SAG | 18 | AQU | 17 | PIS |
| 21 | VIR | 19 | LIB | 20 | SAG | 19 | CAP | 20 | PIS | 20 | ARI |
| 23 | LIB | 22 | SCO | 22 | CAP | 22 | AQU | 22 | ARI | 22 | TAU |
| 25 | SCO | 24 | SAG | 24 | AQU | 24 | PIS | 25 | TAU | 25 | GEM |
| 28 | SAG | 26 | CAP | 27 | PIS | 26 | ARI | 27 | GEM | 27 | CAN |
| 30 | CAP | 28 | AQU | 29 | ARI | 29 | TAU | 30 | CAN | 30 | LEO |
| | | 30 | PIS | | | 31 | GEM | | | | |

## 2013

| JAN | | FEB | | MAR | | APR | | MAY | | JUN | |
|---|---|---|---|---|---|---|---|---|---|---|---|
| 1 | VIR | 2 | SCO | 1 | SCO | 2 | CAP | 1 | AQU | 2 | ARI |
| 3 | LIB | 4 | SAG | 3 | SAG | 4 | AQU | 3 | PIS | 4 | TAU |
| 6 | SCO | 6 | CAP | 5 | CAP | 6 | PIS | 5 | ARI | 6 | GEM |
| 8 | SAG | 8 | AQU | 7 | AQU | 8 | ARI | 8 | TAU | 9 | CAN |
| 10 | CAP | 10 | PIS | 10 | PIS | 10 | TAU | 10 | GEM | 12 | LEO |
| 12 | AQU | 12 | ARI | 12 | ARI | 13 | GEM | 13 | CAN | 14 | VIR |
| 14 | PIS | 15 | TAU | 14 | TAU | 15 | CAN | 15 | LEO | 16 | LIB |
| 16 | ARI | 17 | GEM | 17 | GEM | 18 | LEO | 18 | VIR | 19 | SCO |
| 18 | TAU | 20 | CAN | 19 | CAN | 20 | VIR | 20 | LIB | 21 | SAG |
| 21 | GEM | 22 | LEO | 22 | LEO | 23 | LIB | 22 | SCO | 23 | CAP |
| 23 | CAN | 25 | VIR | 24 | VIR | 25 | SCO | 24 | SAG | 25 | AQU |
| 26 | LEO | 27 | LIB | 26 | LIB | 27 | SAG | 26 | CAP | 27 | PIS |
| 28 | VIR | | | 28 | SCO | 29 | CAP | 28 | AQU | 29 | ARI |
| 31 | LIB | | | 30 | SAG | | | 30 | PIS | | |

| JUL | | AUG | | SEP | | OCT | | NOV | | DEC | |
|---|---|---|---|---|---|---|---|---|---|---|---|
| 1 | TAU | 2 | CAN | 1 | LEO | 1 | VIR | 2 | SCO | 2 | SAG |
| 4 | GEM | 5 | LEO | 4 | VIR | 3 | LIB | 4 | SAG | 4 | CAP |
| 6 | CAN | 7 | VIR | 6 | LIB | 6 | SCO | 6 | CAP | 6 | AQU |
| 9 | LEO | 10 | LIB | 8 | SCO | 8 | SAG | 8 | AQU | 8 | PIS |
| 11 | VIR | 12 | SCO | 11 | SAG | 10 | CAP | 10 | PIS | 10 | ARI |
| 14 | LIB | 14 | SAG | 13 | CAP | 12 | AQU | 13 | ARI | 12 | TAU |
| 16 | SCO | 16 | CAP | 15 | AQU | 14 | PIS | 15 | TAU | 15 | GEM |
| 18 | SAG | 18 | AQU | 17 | PIS | 16 | ARI | 17 | GEM | 17 | CAN |
| 20 | CAP | 20 | PIS | 19 | ARI | 19 | TAU | 20 | CAN | 20 | LEO |
| 22 | AQU | 23 | ARI | 21 | TAU | 21 | GEM | 22 | LEO | 22 | VIR |
| 24 | PIS | 25 | TAU | 24 | GEM | 23 | CAN | 25 | VIR | 25 | LIB |
| 26 | ARI | 27 | GEM | 26 | CAN | 26 | LEO | 27 | LIB | 27 | SCO |
| 28 | TAU | 30 | CAN | 29 | LEO | 28 | VIR | 29 | SCO | 29 | SAG |
| 31 | GEM | | | | | 31 | LIB | | | 31 | CAP |

# Moon Signs 1945-2025

## 2014

| | JAN | | FEB | | MAR | | APR | | MAY | | JUN |
|---|---|---|---|---|---|---|---|---|---|---|---|
| 2 | AQU | 1 | PIS | 2 | ARI | 1 | TAU | 3 | CAN | 1 | LEO |
| 4 | PIS | 3 | ARI | 4 | TAU | 3 | GEM | 5 | LEO | 4 | VIR |
| 6 | ARI | 5 | TAU | 6 | GEM | 5 | CAN | 8 | VIR | 6 | LIB |
| 8 | TAU | 7 | GEM | 9 | CAN | 8 | LEO | 10 | LIB | 9 | SCO |
| 11 | GEM | 10 | CAN | 11 | LEO | 10 | VIR | 12 | SCO | 11 | SAG |
| 13 | CAN | 12 | LEO | 14 | VIR | 13 | LIB | 15 | SAG | 13 | CAP |
| 16 | LEO | 15 | VIR | 16 | LIB | 15 | SCO | 17 | CAP | 15 | AQU |
| 18 | VIR | 17 | LIB | 19 | SCO | 17 | SAG | 19 | AQU | 17 | PIS |
| 21 | LIB | 19 | SCO | 21 | SAG | 19 | CAP | 21 | PIS | 19 | ARI |
| 23 | SCO | 22 | SAG | 23 | CAP | 21 | AQU | 23 | ARI | 21 | TAU |
| 25 | GEM | 24 | CAP | 25 | AQU | 24 | PIS | 25 | TAU | 24 | GEM |
| 28 | CAP | 26 | AQU | 27 | PIS | 26 | ARI | 27 | GEM | 26 | CAN |
| 30 | AQU | 28 | PIS | 29 | ARI | 28 | TAU | 30 | CAN | 29 | LEO |
| | | | | | | 30 | GEM | | | | |

| | JUL | | AUG | | SEP | | OCT | | NOV | | DEC |
|---|---|---|---|---|---|---|---|---|---|---|---|
| 1 | VIR | 2 | SCO | 1 | SAG | 3 | AQU | 1 | PIS | 3 | TAU |
| 4 | LIB | 5 | SAG | 3 | CAP | 5 | PIS | 3 | ARI | 5 | GEM |
| 6 | SCO | 7 | CAP | 5 | AQU | 7 | ARI | 5 | TAU | 7 | CAN |
| 8 | SAG | 9 | AQU | 7 | PIS | 9 | TAU | 7 | GEM | 9 | LEO |
| 10 | CAP | 11 | PIS | 9 | ARI | 11 | GEM | 10 | CAN | 12 | VIR |
| 12 | AQU | 13 | ARI | 11 | TAU | 13 | CAN | 12 | LEO | 14 | LIB |
| 14 | PIS | 15 | TAU | 14 | GEM | 16 | LEO | 15 | VIR | 17 | SCO |
| 16 | ARI | 17 | GEM | 16 | CAN | 18 | VIR | 17 | LIB | 19 | SAG |
| 19 | TAU | 20 | CAN | 18 | LEO | 21 | LIB | 20 | SCO | 21 | CAP |
| 21 | GEM | 22 | LEO | 21 | VIR | 23 | SCO | 22 | SAG | 23 | AQU |
| 23 | CAN | 25 | VIR | 23 | LIB | 25 | SAG | 24 | CAP | 25 | PIS |
| 26 | LEO | 27 | LIB | 26 | SCO | 28 | CAP | 26 | AQU | 28 | ARI |
| 28 | VIR | 30 | SCO | 28 | SAG | 30 | AQU | 28 | PIS | 30 | TAU |
| 31 | LIB | | | 30 | CAP | | | 30 | ARI | | |

## 2015

| | JAN | | FEB | | MAR | | APR | | MAY | | JUN |
|---|---|---|---|---|---|---|---|---|---|---|---|
| 1 | GEM | 2 | LEO | 1 | LEO | 3 | LIB | 2 | SCO | 1 | SAG |
| 3 | CAN | 5 | VIR | 4 | VIR | 5 | SCO | 5 | SAG | 3 | CAP |
| 6 | LEO | 7 | LIB | 6 | LIB | 8 | SAG | 7 | CAP | 6 | AQU |
| 8 | VIR | 10 | SCO | 9 | SCO | 10 | CAP | 9 | AQU | 8 | PIS |
| 11 | LIB | 12 | SAG | 11 | SAG | 12 | AQU | 11 | PIS | 10 | ARI |
| 13 | SCO | 14 | CAP | 14 | CAP | 14 | PIS | 14 | ARI | 12 | TAU |
| 16 | SAG | 16 | AQU | 16 | AQU | 16 | ARI | 16 | TAU | 14 | GEM |
| 18 | CAP | 18 | PIS | 18 | PIS | 18 | TAU | 18 | GEM | 16 | CAN |
| 20 | AQU | 20 | ARI | 20 | ARI | 20 | GEM | 20 | CAN | 19 | LEO |
| 22 | PIS | 22 | TAU | 22 | TAU | 22 | CAN | 22 | LEO | 21 | VIR |
| 24 | ARI | 25 | GEM | 24 | GEM | 25 | LEO | 25 | VIR | 24 | LIB |
| 26 | TAU | 27 | CAN | 26 | CAN | 27 | VIR | 27 | LIB | 25 | SCO |
| 28 | GEM | | | 29 | LEO | 30 | LIB | 30 | SCO | 28 | SAG |
| 31 | CAN | | | 31 | VIR | | | | | | |

| | JUL | | AUG | | SEP | | OCT | | NOV | | DEC |
|---|---|---|---|---|---|---|---|---|---|---|---|
| 1 | CAP | 1 | PIS | 2 | TAU | 1 | GEM | 2 | LEO | 2 | VIR |
| 3 | AQU | 3 | ARI | 4 | GEM | 3 | CAN | 4 | VIR | 4 | LIB |
| 5 | PIS | 5 | TAU | 6 | CAN | 6 | LEO | 7 | LIB | 7 | SCO |
| 7 | ARI | 8 | GEM | 8 | LEO | 8 | VIR | 9 | SCO | 9 | SAG |
| 9 | TAU | 10 | CAN | 11 | VIR | 11 | LIB | 12 | SAG | 12 | CAP |
| 11 | GEM | 12 | LEO | 13 | LIB | 13 | SCO | 14 | CAP | 14 | AQU |
| 14 | CAN | 15 | VIR | 16 | SCO | 16 | SAG | 17 | AQU | 16 | PIS |
| 16 | LEO | 17 | LIB | 18 | SAG | 18 | CAP | 19 | PIS | 18 | ARI |
| 18 | VIR | 20 | SCO | 21 | CAP | 20 | AQU | 21 | ARI | 20 | TAU |
| 21 | LIB | 22 | SAG | 23 | AQU | 23 | PIS | 23 | TAU | 22 | GEM |
| 23 | SCO | 24 | CAP | 25 | PIS | 25 | ARI | 25 | GEM | 25 | CAN |
| 26 | SAG | 27 | AQU | 27 | ARI | 27 | TAU | 27 | CAN | 27 | LEO |
| 28 | CAP | 29 | PIS | 29 | TAU | 29 | GEM | 29 | LEO | 29 | VIR |
| 30 | AQU | 31 | ARI | | | 31 | CAN | | | | |

# Moon Signs 1945-2025

## 2016

| JAN | | FEB | | MAR | | APR | | MAY | | JUN | |
|---|---|---|---|---|---|---|---|---|---|---|---|
| 1 | LIB | 2 | SAG | 3 | CAP | 1 | AQU | 1 | PIS | 1 | TAU |
| 3 | SCO | 4 | CAP | 5 | AQU | 4 | PIS | 3 | ARI | 3 | GEM |
| 6 | SAG | 7 | AQU | 7 | PIS | 6 | ARI | 5 | TAU | 5 | CAN |
| 8 | CAP | 9 | PIS | 9 | ARI | 8 | TAU | 7 | GEM | 8 | LEO |
| 10 | AQU | 11 | ARI | 11 | TAU | 10 | GEM | 9 | CAN | 10 | VIR |
| 12 | PIS | 13 | TAU | 13 | GEM | 12 | CAN | 11 | LEO | 12 | LIB |
| 14 | ARI | 15 | GEM | 15 | CAN | 14 | LEO | 14 | VIR | 15 | SCO |
| 19 | GEM | 19 | LEO | 20 | VIR | 19 | LIB | 19 | SCO | 20 | CAP |
| 21 | CAN | 22 | VIR | 23 | LIB | 21 | SCO | 21 | SAG | 22 | AQU |
| 23 | LEO | 24 | LIB | 25 | SCO | 24 | SAG | 24 | CAP | 24 | PIS |
| 25 | VIR | 27 | SCO | 28 | SAG | 26 | CAP | 26 | AQU | 27 | ARI |
| 28 | LIB | 29 | SAG | 30 | CAP | 29 | AQU | 28 | PIS | 29 | TAU |
| 30 | SCO | | | | | | | 30 | ARI | | |

| JUL | | AUG | | SEP | | OCT | | NOV | | DEC | |
|---|---|---|---|---|---|---|---|---|---|---|---|
| 1 | GEM | 1 | LEO | 2 | LIB | 2 | SCO | 1 | SAG | 1 | CAP |
| 3 | CAN | 4 | VIR | 5 | SCO | 5 | SAG | 3 | CAP | 3 | AQU |
| 5 | LEO | 6 | LIB | 7 | SAG | 7 | CAP | 6 | AQU | 5 | PIS |
| 7 | VIR | 9 | SCO | 10 | CAP | 10 | AQU | 8 | PIS | 8 | ARI |
| 10 | LIB | 11 | SAG | 12 | AQU | 12 | PIS | 10 | ARI | 10 | TAU |
| 12 | SCO | 13 | CAP | 14 | PIS | 14 | ARI | 12 | TAU | 12 | GEM |
| 15 | SAG | 16 | AQU | 16 | ARI | 16 | TAU | 14 | GEM | 14 | CAN |
| 17 | CAP | 18 | PIS | 19 | TAU | 18 | GEM | 16 | CAN | 16 | LEO |
| 19 | AQU | 20 | ARI | 21 | GEM | 20 | CAN | 18 | LEO | 18 | VIR |
| 22 | PIS | 22 | TAU | 23 | CAN | 22 | LEO | 21 | VIR | 20 | LIB |
| 24 | ARI | 24 | GEM | 25 | LEO | 24 | VIR | 23 | LIB | 23 | SCO |
| 26 | TAU | 26 | CAN | 27 | VIR | 27 | LIB | 25 | SCO | 25 | SAG |
| 28 | GEM | 29 | LEO | 30 | LIB | 29 | SCO | 28 | SAG | 28 | CAP |
| 30 | CAN | 31 | VIR | | | | | | | 30 | AQU |

## 2017

| JAN | | FEB | | MAR | | APR | | MAY | | JUN | |
|---|---|---|---|---|---|---|---|---|---|---|---|
| 2 | PIS | 2 | TAU | 2 | TAU | 2 | CAN | 1 | LEO | 2 | LIB |
| 4 | ARI | 4 | GEM | 4 | GEM | 4 | LEO | 4 | VIR | 5 | SCO |
| 6 | TAU | 7 | CAN | 6 | CAN | 6 | VIR | 6 | LIB | 7 | SAG |
| 8 | GEM | 9 | LEO | 8 | LEO | 9 | LIB | 9 | SCO | 10 | CAP |
| 10 | CAN | 11 | VIR | 10 | VIR | 11 | SCO | 11 | SAG | 12 | AQU |
| 12 | LEO | 13 | LIB | 13 | LIB | 14 | SAG | 14 | CAP | 15 | PIS |
| 14 | VIR | 16 | SCO | 15 | SCO | 16 | CAP | 16 | AQU | 17 | ARI |
| 17 | LIB | 18 | SAG | 17 | SAG | 19 | AQU | 18 | PIS | 19 | TAU |
| 19 | SCO | 21 | CAP | 20 | CAP | 21 | PIS | 21 | ARI | 21 | GEM |
| 22 | SAG | 23 | AQU | 22 | AQU | 23 | ARI | 23 | TAU | 23 | CAN |
| 24 | CAP | 25 | PIS | 25 | PIS | 25 | TAU | 25 | GEM | 25 | LEO |
| 27 | AQU | 28 | ARI | 27 | ARI | 27 | GEM | 27 | CAN | 27 | VIR |
| 29 | PIS | | | 29 | TAU | 29 | CAN | 29 | LEO | 30 | LIB |
| 31 | ARI | | | 31 | GEM | | | 31 | VIR | | |

| JUL | | AUG | | SEP | | OCT | | NOV | | DEC | |
|---|---|---|---|---|---|---|---|---|---|---|---|
| 2 | SCO | 1 | SAG | 2 | AQU | 2 | PIS | 1 | ARI | 2 | GEM |
| 5 | SAG | 3 | CAP | 5 | PIS | 4 | ARI | 3 | TAU | 4 | CAN |
| 7 | CAP | 6 | AQU | 7 | ARI | 6 | TAU | 5 | GEM | 6 | LEO |
| 10 | AQU | 8 | PIS | 9 | TAU | 8 | GEM | 7 | CAN | 8 | VIR |
| 12 | PIS | 11 | ARI | 11 | GEM | 10 | CAN | 9 | LEO | 11 | LIB |
| 14 | ARI | 13 | TAU | 13 | CAN | 13 | LEO | 11 | VIR | 13 | SCO |
| 17 | TAU | 15 | GEM | 15 | LEO | 15 | VIR | 13 | LIB | 15 | SAG |
| 19 | GEM | 17 | CAN | 18 | VIR | 17 | LIB | 16 | SCO | 18 | CAP |
| 21 | CAN | 19 | LEO | 20 | LIB | 19 | SCO | 18 | SAG | 20 | AQU |
| 23 | LEO | 21 | VIR | 22 | SCO | 22 | SAG | 21 | CAP | 23 | PIS |
| 25 | VIR | 23 | LIB | 24 | SAG | 24 | CAP | 23 | AQU | 25 | ARI |
| 27 | LIB | 26 | SCO | 27 | CAP | 27 | AQU | 26 | PIS | 28 | TAU |
| 29 | SCO | 28 | SAG | 29 | AQU | 29 | PIS | 28 | ARI | 30 | GEM |
| | | 31 | CAP | | | | | 30 | TAU | | |

# Moon Signs 1945-2025

## 2018

| | JAN | | FEB | | MAR | | APR | | MAY | | JUN |
|---|---|---|---|---|---|---|---|---|---|---|---|
| 1 | CAN | 1 | VIR | 1 | VIR | 1 | SCO | 1 | SAG | 2 | AQU |
| 3 | LEO | 3 | LIB | 3 | LIB | 4 | SAG | 3 | CAP | 5 | PIS |
| 5 | VIR | 5 | SCO | 5 | SCO | 6 | CAP | 6 | AQU | 7 | ARI |
| 7 | LIB | 8 | SAG | 7 | SAG | 9 | AQU | 8 | PIS | 9 | TAU |
| 9 | SCO | 10 | CAP | 10 | CAP | 11 | PIS | 11 | ARI | 12 | GEM |
| 12 | SAG | 13 | AQU | 12 | AQU | 13 | ARI | 13 | TAU | 14 | CAN |
| 14 | CAP | 15 | PIS | 15 | PIS | 16 | TAU | 15 | GEM | 16 | LEO |
| 17 | AQU | 18 | ARI | 17 | ARI | 18 | GEM | 17 | CAN | 18 | VIR |
| 19 | PIS | 20 | TAU | 19 | TAU | 20 | CAN | 19 | LEO | 20 | LIB |
| 22 | ARI | 22 | GEM | 22 | GEM | 22 | LEO | 21 | VIR | 22 | SCO |
| 24 | TAU | 24 | CAN | 24 | CAN | 24 | VIR | 24 | LIB | 24 | SAG |
| 26 | GEM | 26 | LEO | 26 | LEO | 26 | LIB | 26 | SCO | 27 | CAP |
| 28 | CAN | | | 28 | VIR | 29 | SCO | 28 | SAG | 29 | AQU |
| 30 | LEO | | | 30 | LIB | | | 31 | CAP | | |

| | JUL | | AUG | | SEP | | OCT | | NOV | | DEC |
|---|---|---|---|---|---|---|---|---|---|---|---|
| 2 | PIS | 1 | ARI | 2 | GEM | 1 | CAN | 2 | VIR | 1 | LIB |
| 4 | ARI | 3 | TAU | 4 | CAN | 3 | LEO | 4 | LIB | 3 | SCO |
| 7 | TAU | 5 | GEM | 6 | LEO | 5 | VIR | 6 | SCO | 5 | SAG |
| 9 | GEM | 7 | CAN | 8 | VIR | 7 | LIB | 8 | SAG | 8 | CAP |
| 11 | CAN | 9 | LEO | 10 | LIB | 9 | SCO | 10 | CAP | 10 | AQU |
| 13 | LEO | 11 | VIR | 12 | SCO | 12 | SAG | 13 | AQU | 13 | PIS |
| 15 | VIR | 14 | LIB | 14 | SAG | 14 | CAP | 15 | PIS | 15 | ARI |
| 17 | LIB | 16 | SCO | 17 | CAP | 17 | AQU | 18 | ARI | 18 | TAU |
| 19 | SCO | 18 | SAG | 19 | AQU | 19 | PIS | 20 | TAU | 20 | GEM |
| 22 | SAG | 20 | CAP | 22 | PIS | 22 | ARI | 22 | GEM | 22 | CAN |
| 24 | CAP | 23 | AQU | 24 | ARI | 24 | TAU | 25 | CAN | 24 | LEO |
| 27 | AQU | 26 | PIS | 27 | TAU | 26 | GEM | 27 | LEO | 26 | VIR |
| 29 | PIS | 28 | ARI | 29 | GEM | 28 | CAN | 29 | VIR | 28 | LIB |
| | | 30 | TAU | | | 30 | LEO | | | 30 | SCO |

## 2019

| | JAN | | FEB | | MAR | | APR | | MAY | | JUN |
|---|---|---|---|---|---|---|---|---|---|---|---|
| 2 | SAG | 3 | AQU | 2 | AQU | 1 | PIS | 1 | ARI | 2 | GEM |
| 4 | CAP | 5 | PIS | 5 | PIS | 3 | ARI | 3 | TAU | 4 | CAN |
| 7 | AQU | 8 | ARI | 7 | ARI | 6 | TAU | 5 | GEM | 6 | LEO |
| 9 | PIS | 10 | TAU | 10 | TAU | 8 | GEM | 8 | CAN | 8 | VIR |
| 12 | ARI | 13 | GEM | 12 | GEM | 10 | CAN | 10 | LEO | 10 | LIB |
| 14 | TAU | 15 | CAN | 14 | CAN | 13 | LEO | 12 | VIR | 12 | SCO |
| 16 | GEM | 17 | LEO | 16 | LEO | 15 | VIR | 14 | LIB | 15 | SAG |
| 18 | CAN | 19 | VIR | 18 | VIR | 17 | LIB | 16 | SCO | 17 | CAP |
| 20 | LEO | 21 | LIB | 20 | LIB | 19 | SCO | 18 | SAG | 19 | AQU |
| 22 | VIR | 23 | SCO | 22 | SCO | 21 | SAG | 21 | CAP | 22 | PIS |
| 24 | LIB | 25 | SAG | 25 | SAG | 23 | CAP | 23 | AQU | 24 | ARI |
| 27 | SCO | 28 | CAP | 27 | CAP | 26 | AQU | 26 | PIS | 27 | TAU |
| 29 | SAG | | | 29 | AQU | 28 | PIS | 28 | ARI | 29 | GEM |
| 31 | CAP | | | | | | | 30 | TAU | | |

| | JUL | | AUG | | SEP | | OCT | | NOV | | DEC |
|---|---|---|---|---|---|---|---|---|---|---|---|
| 1 | CAN | 2 | VIR | 2 | SCO | 2 | SAG | 3 | AQU | 3 | PIS |
| 3 | LEO | 4 | LIB | 4 | SAG | 4 | CAP | 5 | PIS | 5 | ARI |
| 5 | VIR | 6 | SCO | 7 | CAP | 6 | AQU | 8 | ARI | 8 | TAU |
| 8 | LIB | 8 | SAG | 9 | AQU | 9 | PIS | 10 | TAU | 10 | GEM |
| 10 | SCO | 11 | CAP | 12 | PIS | 11 | ARI | 13 | GEM | 12 | CAN |
| 12 | SAG | 13 | AQU | 14 | ARI | 14 | TAU | 15 | CAN | 14 | LEO |
| 14 | CAP | 15 | PIS | 17 | TAU | 16 | GEM | 17 | LEO | 17 | VIR |
| 17 | AQU | 18 | ARI | 19 | GEM | 19 | CAN | 19 | VIR | 19 | LIB |
| 19 | PIS | 20 | TAU | 22 | CAN | 21 | LEO | 21 | LIB | 21 | SCO |
| 22 | ARI | 23 | GEM | 24 | LEO | 23 | VIR | 24 | SCO | 23 | SAG |
| 24 | TAU | 25 | CAN | 26 | VIR | 25 | LIB | 26 | SAG | 25 | CAP |
| 27 | GEM | 27 | LEO | 28 | LIB | 27 | SCO | 28 | CAP | 28 | AQU |
| 29 | CAN | 29 | VIR | 30 | SCO | 29 | SAG | 30 | AQU | 30 | PIS |
| 31 | LEO | 31 | LIB | | | 31 | CAP | | | | |

# Moon Signs 1945-2025

## 2020

| | JAN | | FEB | | MAR | | APR | | MAY | | JUN |
|---|---|---|---|---|---|---|---|---|---|---|---|
| 1 | ARI | 3 | GEM | 1 | GEM | 2 | LEO | 2 | VIR | 2 | SCO |
| 4 | TAU | 5 | CAN | 3 | CAN | 4 | VIR | 4 | LIB | 4 | SAG |
| 6 | GEM | 7 | LEO | 6 | LEO | 6 | LIB | 6 | SCO | 6 | CAP |
| 9 | CAN | 9 | VIR | 8 | VIR | 8 | SCO | 8 | SAG | 8 | AQU |
| 11 | LEO | 11 | LIB | 10 | LIB | 10 | SAG | 10 | CAP | 11 | PIS |
| 13 | VIR | 13 | SCO | 12 | SCO | 12 | CAP | 12 | AQU | 13 | ARI |
| 15 | LIB | 15 | SAG | 14 | SAG | 15 | AQU | 14 | PIS | 16 | TAU |
| 17 | SCO | 18 | CAP | 16 | CAP | 17 | PIS | 17 | ARI | 18 | GEM |
| 19 | SAG | 20 | AQU | 18 | AQU | 20 | ARI | 19 | TAU | 21 | CAN |
| 22 | CAP | 23 | PIS | 21 | PIS | 22 | TAU | 22 | GEM | 23 | LEO |
| 24 | AQU | 25 | ARI | 23 | ARI | 25 | GEM | 24 | CAN | 25 | VIR |
| 26 | PIS | 28 | TAU | 26 | TAU | 27 | CAN | 27 | LEO | 27 | LIB |
| 29 | ARI | | | 28 | GEM | 29 | LEO | 29 | VIR | 29 | SCO |
| 31 | TAU | | | 31 | CAN | | | 31 | LIB | | |

| | JUL | | AUG | | SEP | | OCT | | NOV | | DEC |
|---|---|---|---|---|---|---|---|---|---|---|---|
| 1 | SAG | 2 | AQU | 1 | PIS | 3 | TAU | 2 | GEM | 1 | CAN |
| 3 | CAP | 4 | PIS | 3 | ARI | 5 | GEM | 4 | CAN | 4 | LEO |
| 6 | AQU | 7 | ARI | 6 | TAU | 8 | CAN | 7 | LEO | 6 | VIR |
| 8 | PIS | 9 | TAU | 8 | GEM | 10 | LEO | 9 | VIR | 8 | LIB |
| 11 | ARI | 12 | GEM | 11 | CAN | 13 | VIR | 11 | LIB | 10 | SCO |
| 13 | TAU | 14 | CAN | 13 | LEO | 15 | LIB | 13 | SCO | 12 | SAG |
| 16 | GEM | 17 | LEO | 15 | VIR | 17 | SCO | 15 | SAG | 14 | CAP |
| 18 | CAN | 19 | VIR | 17 | LIB | 19 | SAG | 17 | CAP | 17 | AQU |
| 20 | LEO | 21 | LIB | 19 | SCO | 21 | CAP | 19 | AQU | 19 | PIS |
| 22 | VIR | 23 | SCO | 21 | SAG | 23 | AQU | 21 | PIS | 21 | ARI |
| 24 | LIB | 25 | SAG | 23 | CAP | 25 | PIS | 24 | ARI | 24 | TAU |
| 26 | SCO | 27 | CAP | 26 | AQU | 28 | ARI | 26 | TAU | 26 | GEM |
| 29 | SAG | 29 | AQU | 28 | PIS | 30 | TAU | 29 | GEM | 29 | CAN |
| 31 | CAP | | | 30 | ARI | | | | | 31 | LEO |

## 2021

| | JAN | | FEB | | MAR | | APR | | MAY | | JUN |
|---|---|---|---|---|---|---|---|---|---|---|---|
| 2 | VIR | 1 | LIB | 2 | SCO | 1 | SAG | 2 | AQU | 1 | PIS |
| 5 | LIB | 3 | SCO | 4 | SAG | 3 | CAP | 4 | PIS | 3 | ARI |
| 7 | SCO | 5 | SAG | 6 | CAP | 5 | AQU | 7 | ARI | 6 | TAU |
| 9 | SAG | 7 | CAP | 9 | AQU | 7 | PIS | 9 | TAU | 8 | GEM |
| 11 | CAP | 9 | AQU | 11 | PIS | 10 | ARI | 12 | GEM | 11 | CAN |
| 13 | AQU | 12 | PIS | 13 | ARI | 12 | TAU | 14 | CAN | 13 | LEO |
| 15 | PIS | 14 | ARI | 16 | TAU | 15 | GEM | 17 | LEO | 15 | VIR |
| 18 | ARI | 16 | TAU | 18 | GEM | 17 | CAN | 19 | VIR | 18 | LIB |
| 20 | TAU | 19 | GEM | 21 | CAN | 20 | LEO | 21 | LIB | 20 | SCO |
| 23 | GEM | 21 | CAN | 23 | LEO | 22 | VIR | 23 | SCO | 22 | SAG |
| 25 | CAN | 24 | LEO | 25 | VIR | 24 | LIB | 25 | SAG | 24 | CAP |
| 27 | LEO | 26 | VIR | 28 | LIB | 26 | SCO | 27 | CAP | 26 | AQU |
| 30 | VIR | 28 | LIB | 30 | SCO | 28 | SAG | 29 | AQU | 28 | PIS |
| | | | | | | 30 | CAP | | | 30 | ARI |

| | JUL | | AUG | | SEP | | OCT | | NOV | | DEC |
|---|---|---|---|---|---|---|---|---|---|---|---|
| 3 | TAU | 2 | GEM | 1 | CAN | 3 | VIR | 1 | LIB | 1 | SCO |
| 5 | GEM | 4 | CAN | 3 | LEO | 5 | LIB | 3 | SCO | 3 | SAG |
| 8 | CAN | 7 | LEO | 5 | VIR | 7 | SCO | 5 | SAG | 5 | CAP |
| 10 | LEO | 9 | VIR | 7 | LIB | 9 | SAG | 7 | CAP | 7 | AQU |
| 13 | VIR | 11 | LIB | 10 | SCO | 11 | CAP | 9 | AQU | 9 | PIS |
| 15 | LIB | 13 | SCO | 12 | SAG | 13 | AQU | 12 | PIS | 11 | ARI |
| 17 | SCO | 15 | SAG | 14 | CAP | 15 | PIS | 14 | ARI | 14 | TAU |
| 19 | SAG | 18 | CAP | 16 | AQU | 18 | ARI | 16 | TAU | 16 | GEM |
| 21 | CAP | 20 | AQU | 18 | PIS | 20 | TAU | 19 | GEM | 19 | CAN |
| 23 | AQU | 22 | PIS | 20 | ARI | 23 | GEM | 21 | CAN | 21 | LEO |
| 25 | PIS | 24 | ARI | 23 | TAU | 25 | CAN | 24 | LEO | 24 | VIR |
| 28 | ARI | 26 | TAU | 25 | GEM | 28 | LEO | 26 | VIR | 26 | LIB |
| 30 | TAU | 29 | GEM | 28 | CAN | 30 | VIR | 29 | LIB | 28 | SCO |
| | | | | 30 | LEO | | | | | 30 | SAG |

# Moon Signs 1945-2025

## 2022

| JAN | | FEB | | MAR | | APR | | MAY | | JUN | |
|---|---|---|---|---|---|---|---|---|---|---|---|
| 1 | CAP | 2 | PIS | 1 | PIS | 2 | TAU | 2 | GEM | 1 | CAN |
| 3 | AQU | 4 | ARI | 3 | ARI | 4 | GEM | 4 | CAN | 3 | LEO |
| 5 | PIS | 6 | TAU | 6 | TAU | 7 | CAN | 7 | LEO | 6 | VIR |
| 8 | ARI | 9 | GEM | 8 | GEM | 9 | LEO | 9 | VIR | 8 | LIB |
| 10 | TAU | 11 | CAN | 11 | CAN | 12 | VIR | 12 | LIB | 10 | SCO |
| 12 | GEM | 14 | LEO | 13 | LEO | 14 | LIB | 14 | SCO | 12 | SAG |
| 15 | CAN | 16 | VIR | 16 | VIR | 16 | SCO | 16 | SAG | 14 | CAP |
| 17 | LEO | 18 | LIB | 18 | LIB | 18 | SAG | 18 | CAP | 16 | AQU |
| 20 | VIR | 21 | SCO | 20 | SCO | 20 | CAP | 20 | AQU | 18 | PIS |
| 22 | LIB | 23 | SAG | 22 | SAG | 23 | AQU | 22 | PIS | 20 | ARI |
| 24 | SCO | 25 | CAP | 24 | CAP | 25 | PIS | 24 | ARI | 23 | TAU |
| 27 | SAG | 27 | AQU | 26 | AQU | 27 | ARI | 27 | TAU | 25 | GEM |
| 29 | CAP | | | 28 | PIS | 29 | TAU | 29 | GEM | 28 | CAN |
| 31 | AQU | | | 31 | ARI | | | | | 30 | LEO |

| JUL | | AUG | | SEP | | OCT | | NOV | | DEC | |
|---|---|---|---|---|---|---|---|---|---|---|---|
| 3 | VIR | 1 | LIB | 2 | SAG | 2 | CAP | 2 | PIS | 1 | ARI |
| 5 | LIB | 4 | SCO | 4 | CAP | 4 | AQU | 4 | ARI | 4 | TAU |
| 8 | SCO | 6 | SAG | 6 | AQU | 6 | PIS | 7 | TAU | 6 | GEM |
| 10 | SAG | 8 | CAP | 8 | PIS | 8 | ARI | 9 | GEM | 9 | CAN |
| 12 | CAP | 10 | AQU | 11 | ARI | 10 | TAU | 11 | CAN | 11 | LEO |
| 14 | AQU | 12 | PIS | 13 | TAU | 13 | GEM | 14 | LEO | 14 | VIR |
| 16 | PIS | 14 | ARI | 15 | GEM | 15 | CAN | 16 | VIR | 16 | LIB |
| 18 | ARI | 16 | TAU | 18 | CAN | 17 | LEO | 19 | LIB | 18 | SCO |
| 20 | TAU | 19 | GEM | 20 | LEO | 20 | VIR | 21 | SCO | 21 | SAG |
| 23 | GEM | 21 | CAN | 23 | VIR | 22 | LIB | 23 | SAG | 23 | CAP |
| 25 | CAN | 24 | LEO | 25 | LIB | 25 | SCO | 25 | CAP | 25 | AQU |
| 28 | LEO | 26 | VIR | 27 | SCO | 27 | SAG | 27 | AQU | 27 | PIS |
| 30 | VIR | 29 | LIB | 29 | SAG | 29 | CAP | 29 | PIS | 29 | ARI |
| | | 31 | SCO | | | 31 | AQU | | | 31 | TAU |

## 2023

| JAN | | FEB | | MAR | | APR | | MAY | | JUN | |
|---|---|---|---|---|---|---|---|---|---|---|---|
| 2 | GEM | 1 | CAN | 3 | LEO | 2 | VIR | 2 | LIB | 3 | SAG |
| 5 | CAN | 4 | LEO | 5 | VIR | 4 | LIB | 4 | SCO | 5 | CAP |
| 7 | LEO | 6 | VIR | 8 | LIB | 7 | SCO | 6 | SAG | 7 | AQU |
| 10 | VIR | 9 | LIB | 10 | SCO | 9 | SAG | 8 | CAP | 9 | PIS |
| 12 | LIB | 11 | SCO | 13 | SAG | 11 | CAP | 10 | AQU | 11 | ARI |
| 15 | SCO | 13 | SAG | 15 | CAP | 13 | AQU | 12 | PIS | 13 | TAU |
| 17 | SAG | 16 | CAP | 17 | AQU | 15 | PIS | 15 | ARI | 15 | GEM |
| 19 | CAP | 18 | AQU | 19 | PIS | 17 | ARI | 17 | TAU | 18 | CAN |
| 21 | AQU | 20 | PIS | 21 | ARI | 19 | TAU | 19 | GEM | 20 | LEO |
| 23 | PIS | 22 | ARI | 23 | TAU | 22 | GEM | 21 | CAN | 23 | VIR |
| 25 | ARI | 24 | TAU | 25 | GEM | 24 | CAN | 24 | LEO | 25 | LIB |
| 27 | TAU | 26 | GEM | 28 | CAN | 27 | LEO | 26 | VIR | 28 | SCO |
| 30 | GEM | 28 | CAN | 30 | LEO | 29 | VIR | 29 | LIB | 30 | SAG |
| | | | | | | | | 31 | SCO | | |

| JUL | | AUG | | SEP | | OCT | | NOV | | DEC | |
|---|---|---|---|---|---|---|---|---|---|---|---|
| 2 | CAP | 2 | PIS | 1 | ARI | 3 | GEM | 1 | CAN | 1 | LEO |
| 4 | AQU | 4 | ARI | 3 | TAU | 5 | CAN | 4 | LEO | 3 | VIR |
| 6 | PIS | 7 | TAU | 5 | GEM | 7 | LEO | 6 | VIR | 6 | LIB |
| 8 | ARI | 9 | GEM | 8 | CAN | 10 | VIR | 9 | LIB | 8 | SCO |
| 10 | TAU | 11 | CAN | 10 | LEO | 12 | LIB | 11 | SCO | 11 | SAG |
| 13 | GEM | 14 | LEO | 13 | VIR | 15 | SCO | 13 | SAG | 13 | CAP |
| 15 | CAN | 16 | VIR | 15 | LIB | 17 | SAG | 16 | CAP | 15 | AQU |
| 17 | LEO | 19 | LIB | 18 | SCO | 19 | CAP | 18 | AQU | 17 | PIS |
| 20 | VIR | 21 | SCO | 20 | SAG | 22 | AQU | 20 | PIS | 19 | ARI |
| 23 | LIB | 24 | SAG | 22 | CAP | 24 | PIS | 22 | ARI | 21 | TAU |
| 25 | SCO | 26 | CAP | 24 | AQU | 26 | ARI | 24 | TAU | 24 | GEM |
| 27 | SAG | 28 | AQU | 26 | PIS | 28 | TAU | 26 | GEM | 26 | CAN |
| 29 | CAP | 30 | PIS | 28 | ARI | 30 | GEM | 29 | CAN | 28 | LEO |
| 31 | AQU | | | 30 | TAU | | | | | 31 | VIR |

# Moon Signs 1945-2025

## 2024

| | JAN | | FEB | | MAR | | APR | | MAY | | JUN |
|---|---|---|---|---|---|---|---|---|---|---|---|
| 2 | LIB | 1 | SCO | 2 | SAG | 3 | AQU | 2 | PIS | 3 | TAU |
| 5 | SCO | 4 | SAG | 4 | CAP | 5 | PIS | 4 | ARI | 5 | GEM |
| 7 | SAG | 6 | CAP | 6 | AQU | 7 | ARI | 6 | TAU | 7 | CAN |
| 9 | CAP | 8 | AQU | 8 | PIS | 9 | TAU | 8 | GEM | 9 | LEO |
| 11 | AQU | 10 | PIS | 10 | ARI | 11 | GEM | 10 | CAN | 12 | VIR |
| 13 | PIS | 12 | ARI | 12 | TAU | 13 | CAN | 13 | LEO | 14 | LIB |
| 16 | ARI | 14 | TAU | 14 | GEM | 15 | LEO | 15 | VIR | 17 | SCO |
| 18 | TAU | 16 | GEM | 17 | CAN | 18 | VIR | 18 | LIB | 19 | SAG |
| 20 | GEM | 18 | CAN | 19 | LEO | 20 | LIB | 20 | SCO | 21 | CAP |
| 22 | CAN | 21 | LEO | 22 | VIR | 23 | SCO | 23 | SAG | 23 | AQU |
| 25 | LEO | 23 | VIR | 24 | LIB | 25 | SAG | 25 | CAP | 26 | PIS |
| 27 | VIR | 26 | LIB | 27 | SCO | 28 | CAP | 27 | AQU | 28 | ARI |
| 30 | LIB | 28 | SCO | 29 | SAG | 30 | AQU | 29 | PIS | 30 | TAU |
| | | | | 31 | CAP | | | 31 | ARI | | |

| | JUL | | AUG | | SEP | | OCT | | NOV | | DEC |
|---|---|---|---|---|---|---|---|---|---|---|---|
| 2 | GEM | 3 | LEO | 1 | VIR | 1 | LIB | 3 | SAG | 2 | CAP |
| 4 | CAN | 5 | VIR | 4 | LIB | 3 | SCO | 5 | CAP | 4 | AQU |
| 6 | LEO | 8 | LIB | 7 | SCO | 6 | SAG | 7 | AQU | 7 | PIS |
| 9 | VIR | 10 | SCO | 9 | SAG | 9 | CAP | 9 | PIS | 9 | ARI |
| 11 | LIB | 13 | SAG | 11 | CAP | 11 | AQU | 12 | ARI | 11 | TAU |
| 14 | SCO | 15 | CAP | 14 | AQU | 13 | PIS | 14 | TAU | 13 | GEM |
| 16 | SAG | 17 | AQU | 16 | PIS | 15 | ARI | 16 | GEM | 15 | CAN |
| 19 | CAP | 19 | PIS | 18 | ARI | 17 | TAU | 18 | CAN | 17 | LEO |
| 21 | AQU | 21 | ARI | 20 | TAU | 19 | GEM | 20 | LEO | 20 | VIR |
| 23 | PIS | 23 | TAU | 22 | GEM | 21 | CAN | 22 | VIR | 22 | LIB |
| 25 | ARI | 25 | GEM | 24 | CAN | 24 | LEO | 25 | LIB | 25 | SCO |
| 27 | TAU | 28 | CAN | 26 | LEO | 26 | VIR | 27 | SCO | 27 | SAG |
| 29 | GEM | 30 | LEO | 29 | VIR | 28 | LIB | 30 | SAG | 29 | CAP |
| 31 | CAN | | | | | 31 | SCO | | | | |

## 2025

| | JAN | | FEB | | MAR | | APR | | MAY | | JUN |
|---|---|---|---|---|---|---|---|---|---|---|---|
| 1 | AQU | 1 | ARI | 1 | ARI | 1 | GEM | 1 | CAN | 1 | VIR |
| 3 | PIS | 3 | TAU | 3 | TAU | 3 | CAN | 3 | LEO | 4 | LIB |
| 5 | ARI | 6 | GEM | 5 | GEM | 5 | LEO | 5 | VIR | 6 | SCO |
| 7 | TAU | 8 | CAN | 7 | CAN | 8 | VIR | 8 | LIB | 9 | SAG |
| 9 | GEM | 10 | LEO | 9 | LEO | 10 | LIB | 10 | SCO | 11 | CAP |
| 11 | CAN | 12 | VIR | 12 | VIR | 13 | SCO | 13 | SAG | 14 | AQU |
| 14 | LEO | 15 | LIB | 14 | LIB | 15 | SAG | 15 | CAP | 16 | PIS |
| 16 | VIR | 17 | SCO | 17 | SCO | 18 | CAP | 18 | AQU | 18 | ARI |
| 18 | LIB | 20 | SAG | 19 | SAG | 20 | AQU | 20 | PIS | 20 | TAU |
| 21 | SCO | 22 | CAP | 22 | CAP | 23 | PIS | 22 | ARI | 22 | GEM |
| 23 | SAG | 25 | AQU | 24 | AQU | 25 | ARI | 24 | TAU | 24 | CAN |
| 26 | CAP | 27 | PIS | 26 | PIS | 27 | TAU | 26 | GEM | 27 | LEO |
| 28 | AQU | | | 28 | ARI | 29 | GEM | 28 | CAN | 29 | VIR |
| 30 | PIS | | | 30 | TAU | | | 30 | LEO | | |

| | JUL | | AUG | | SEP | | OCT | | NOV | | DEC |
|---|---|---|---|---|---|---|---|---|---|---|---|
| 1 | LIB | 3 | SAG | 1 | CAP | 1 | AQU | 2 | ARI | 1 | TAU |
| 4 | SCO | 5 | CAP | 4 | AQU | 3 | PIS | 4 | TAU | 3 | GEM |
| 6 | SAG | 7 | AQU | 6 | PIS | 6 | ARI | 6 | GEM | 5 | CAN |
| 9 | CAP | 10 | PIS | 8 | ARI | 8 | TAU | 8 | CAN | 7 | LEO |
| 11 | AQU | 12 | ARI | 10 | TAU | 10 | GEM | 10 | LEO | 10 | VIR |
| 13 | PIS | 14 | TAU | 12 | GEM | 12 | CAN | 12 | VIR | 12 | LIB |
| 15 | ARI | 16 | GEM | 14 | CAN | 14 | LEO | 15 | LIB | 14 | SCO |
| 18 | TAU | 18 | CAN | 17 | LEO | 16 | VIR | 17 | SCO | 17 | SAG |
| 20 | GEM | 20 | LEO | 19 | VIR | 18 | LIB | 20 | SAG | 20 | CAP |
| 22 | CAN | 23 | VIR | 21 | LIB | 21 | SCO | 22 | CAP | 22 | AQU |
| 24 | LEO | 25 | LIB | 24 | SCO | 23 | SAG | 25 | AQU | 24 | PIS |
| 26 | VIR | 27 | SCO | 26 | SAG | 26 | CAP | 27 | PIS | 27 | ARI |
| 29 | LIB | 30 | SAG | 29 | CAP | 28 | AQU | 29 | ARI | 29 | TAU |
| 31 | SCO | | | | | 31 | PIS | | | 31 | GEM |

# How to Use Mercury Tables

Find the year of birth on the following pages. Next locate the month under than year. The dates listed indicate the day Mercury moves into a sign. It stays in that sign until the next date with a different sign  is listed. **Example**: In the year  1951, on February 1,  Mercury was in Capricorn (CAP). Mercury continued in Capricorn through February 9, and then at some time during February 10, Mercury entered Aquarius (AQU)

The D and R after the sign indicates whether Mercury was Direct or Retrograde. When the R appears it means Mercury turned retrograde on that day and will remain in retrograde motion until the next date that a D appears after the sign.  Example: On January 1, 1951, Mercury is retrograde (R) in Capricorn and continued in retrograde motion until turning direct (D) at some time during January 11. Mercury then travels direct (D) through the rest of Capricorn, on into Aquarius (on February 10, as stated above), then on through Aquaruis then Pisces and Aries, and steadily onward into Taurus through April 13. At some time during April 14, Mercury (in Taurus) turns retrograde (R) again.

You can find the exact UT times of the retrograde and direct stations from an ephemeris that includes a daily aspectarian. The various editions of *The American Ephemeris* include an Astrodata box at the bottom of each page that lists the time that planets change signs (ingress) and the time of retrograde and direct stations. For the current year, you may be able to purchase an astrological calendar set for your own time zone that includes the exact times of retrograde and direct stations

## Mercury Signs 1945-2025

| 1945 | 1946 | 1947 |
|---|---|---|
| JAN 15 CAP-D | JAN 10 CAP-D | JAN 4 CAP-D |
| FEB 6 AQU-D | JAN 30 AQU-D | JAN 22 AQU-D |
| FEB 24 PIC-D | FEB 16 PIC-D | FEB 9 PIC-D |
| MAR 12 ARI-D | MAR 5 ARI-D | FEB 27 PIC-R |
| APR 3 ARI-R | MAR 16 ARI-R | MAR 22 PIC-D |
| APR 27 ARI-D | APR 2 PIC-R | APR 17 ARI-D |
| MAY 17 TAU-D | APR 9 PIC-D | MAY 5 TAU-D |
| JUN 5 GEM-D | APR 17 ARI-D | MAY 19 GEM-D |
| JUN 19 CAN-D | MAY 12 TAU-D | JUN 3 CAN-D |
| JUL 4 LEO-D | MAY 28 GEM-D | JUL 2 CAN-R |
| JUL 28 VIR-D | JUN 11 CAN-D | JUL 25 CAN-D |
| AUG 6 VIR-R | JUN 28 LEO-D | AUG 11 LEO-D |
| AUG 18 LEO-R | JUL 19 LEO-R | AUG 27 VIR-D |
| AUG 30 LEO-D | AUG 12 LEO-D | SEP 12 LIB-D |
| SEP 11 VIR-D | SEP 4 VIR-D | OCT 2 SCO-D |
| SEP 28 LIB-D | SEP 20 LIB-D | OCT 25 SCO-R |
| OCT 16 SCO-D | OCT 8 SCO-D | NOV 15 SCO-D |
| NOV 4 SAG-D | OCT 31 SAG-D | DEC 8 SAG-D |
| NOV 27 SAG-R | NOV 11 SAG-R | DEC 27 CAP-D |
| DEC 17 SAG-D | NOV 21 SCO-R | |
| | DEC 1 SCO-D | |
| | DEC 14 SAG-D | |

## Sign Abbreviations

| ARI | Aries | Can | Cancer | LIB | Libra | CAP | Capricorn |
|---|---|---|---|---|---|---|---|
| TAU | Taurus | LEO | Leo | SCO | Scorpio | AQU | Aquarius |
| GEM | Gemini | VIR | Virgo | SAG | Sagittarius | PISC | Pisces |

# Mercury Signs 1945-2025

| 1948 | 1949 | 1950 | 1951 | 1952 | 1953 |
|---|---|---|---|---|---|
| JAN 15 AQU-D | JAN 7 AQU-D | JAN 2 AQU-D | JAN 12 CAP-R | JAN 14 CAP-D | JAN 7 CAP-D |
| FEB 3 PIC-D | JAN 24 AQU-R | JAN 8 AQU-R | FEB 10 AQU-D | FEB 4 AQU-D | JAN 26 AQU-D |
| FEB 11 PIC-R | FEB 14 AQU-D | JAN 16 CAP-R | MAR 1 PIC-D | FEB 21 PIC-D | FEB 12 PIC-D |
| FEB 21 AQU-R | MAR 15 PIC-D | JAN 29 CAP-D | MAR 17 ARI-D | MAR 8 ARI-D | MAR 3 ARI-D |
| MAR 4 AQU-D | APR 17 TAU-D | FEB 15 AQU-D | APR 3 TAU-D | MAR 26 ARI-R | MAR 9 ARI-R |
| MAR 19 PIC-D | MAY 3 GEM-D | MAR 8 PIC-D | APR 14 TAU-R | APR 19 ARI-D | MAR 16 PIC-R |
| APR 10 ARI-D | MAY 23 GEM-R | MAR 25 ARI-D | MAY 2 ARI-R | MAY 15 TAU-D | APR 1 PIC-D |
| APR 26 TAU-D | JUN 16 GEM-D | APR 9 TAU-D | MAY 8 ARI-D | JUN 1 GEM-D | APR 18 ARI-D |
| MAY 10 GEM-D | JUL 11 CAN-D | MAY 3 TAU-R | MAY 16 TAU-D | JUN 12 CAN-D | MAY 9 TAU-D |
| MAY 29 CAN-D | JUL 26 LEO-D | MAY 27 TAU-D | JUN 10 GEM-D | JUL 1 LEO-D | MAY 24 GEM-D |
| JUN 11 CAN-R | AUG 10 VIR-D | JUN 15 GEM-D | JUN 25 CAN-D | JUL 29 LEO-R | JUN 7 CAN-D |
| JUN 29 GEM-R | AUG 29 LIB-D | JUL 17 LEO-D | JUL 9 LEO-D | AUG 22 LEO-D | JUN 27 LEO-D |
| JUL 5 GEM-D | SEP 21 LIB-R | AUG 3 VIR-D | JUL 28 VIR-D | SEP 8 VIR-D | JUL 11 LEO-R |
| JUL 12 CAN-D | SEP 12 LIB-D | AUG 28 LIB-D | AUG 17 VIR-R | SEP 25 LIB-D | JUL 29 CAN-R |
| AUG 3 LEO-D | NOV 4 SCO-D | SEP 4 LIB-R | SEP 9 VIR-D | OCT 12 SCO-D | AUG 4 CAN-D |
| AUG 18 VIR-D | NOV 23 SAG-D | SEP 11 VIR-R | OCT 3 LIB-D | NOV 2 SAG-D | AUG 12 LEO-D |
| SEP 4 LIB-D | DEC 12 CAP-D | SEP 26 VIR-D | OCT 20 SCO-D | NOV 20 SAG-R | AUG 31 VIR-D |
| SEP 28 SCO-D | | OCT 10 LIB-D | NOV 9 SAG-D | DEC 10 SAG-D | SEP 16 LIB-D |
| OCT 8 SCO-R | | OCT 28 SCO-D | DEC 2 CAP-D | | OCT 5 SCO-D |
| OCT 18 LIB-D | | NOV 16 SAG-D | DEC 7 CAP-R | | NOV 1 SAG-D |
| NOV 11 SCO-D | | DEC 6 CAP-D | DEC 13 SAG-R | | NOV 3 SAG-D |
| NOV 30 SAG-D | | DEC 23 CAP-R | DEC 27 SAG-D | | NOV 7 SCO-R |
| DEC 19 CAP-D | | | | | NOV 23 SCO-D |
| | | | | | DEC 11 SAG-D |
| | | | | | DEC 31 CAP-D |

| 1954 | 1955 | 1956 | 1957 | 1958 | 1959 |
|---|---|---|---|---|---|
| JAN 19 AQU-D | JAN 11 AQU-D | JAN 5 AQU-D | JAN 2 CAP-R | JAN 5 SAG-D | JAN 11 CAP-D |
| FEB 5 PIC-D | FEB 3 AQU-R | JAN 18 AQU-R | JAN 21 CAP-D | JAN 15 CAP-D | JAN 31 AQU-D |
| FEB 20 PIC-R | FEB 25 AQU-D | FEB 3 CAP-R | FEB 13 AQU-D | FEB 7 AQU-D | FEB 18 PIC-D |
| MAR 14 PIC-D | MAR 18 PIC-D | FEB 8 CAP-D | MAR 5 PIC-D | FEB 25 PIC-D | MAR 6 ARI-D |
| APR 14 ARI-D | APR 7 ARI-D | FEB 16 AQU-D | MAR 21 ARI-D | MAR 13 ARI-D | MAR 19 ARI-R |
| MAY 1 TAU-D | APR 23 TAU-D | MAR 12 PIC-D | APR 5 TAU-D | APR 3 TAU-D | APR 12 ARI-D |
| MAY 15 GEM-D | MAY 7 GEM-D | MAR 29 ARI-D | APR 25 TAU-R | APR 6 TAU-R | MAY 13 TAU-D |
| MAY 31 CAN-D | JUN 3 GEM-R | APR 13 TAU-D | MAY 19 TAU-D | APR 11 ARI-R | MAY 29 GEM-D |
| JUN 23 CAN-R | JUN 27 GEM-D | APR 30 GEM-D | JUN 13 GEM-D | APR 30 ARI-D | JUN 12 CAN-D |
| JUL 17 CAN-D | JUL 14 CAN-D | MAY 14 GEM-R | JUN 29 CAN-D | MAY 18 TAU-D | JUN 29 LEO-D |
| AUG 8 LEO-D | JUL 31 LEO-D | JUN 7 GEM-D | JUL 13 LEO-D | JUN 6 GEM-D | JUL 22 LEO-R |
| AUG 23 VIR-D | AUG 15 VIR-D | JUL 7 CAN-D | JUL 31 VIR-D | JUN 21 CAN-D | AUG 15 LEO-D |
| SEP 9 LIB-D | SEP 2 LIB-D | JUL 22 LEO-D | AUG 27 VIR-R | JUL 5 LEO-D | SEP 6 VIR-D |
| SEP 30 SCO-D | OCT 2 LIB-R | AUG 6 VIR-D | SEP 19 VIR-D | JUL 27 VIR-D | SEP 22 LIB-D |
| OCT 18 SCO-R | OCT 22 LIB-D | AUG 27 LIB-D | OCT 7 LIB-D | AUG 9 VIR-R | OCT 10 SCO-D |
| NOV 12 SCO-D | NOV 9 SCO-D | SEP 13 LIB-R | OCT 24 LIB-D | AUG 24 LEO-D | NOV 1 SAG-D |
| DEC 5 SAG-D | NOV 28 SAG-D | SEP 30 VIR-R | NOV 12 SAG-D | SEP 2 LEO-D | NOV 14 SAG-R |
| DEC 24 CAP-D | DEC 17 CAP-D | OCT 5 VIR-D | DEC 3 CAP-D | SEP 12 VIR-D | NOV 26 SCO-R |
| | | OCT 12 LIB-D | DEC 16 CAP-R | SEP 29 LIB-D | DEC 3 SCO-D |
| | | NOV 1 SCO-D | DEC 29 SAG-D | OCT 17 SCO-D | DEC 14 SAG-D |
| | | NOV 19 SAG-D | | NOV 6 SAG-D | |
| | | DEC 9 CAP-D | | NOV 30 SAG-R | |
| | | | | DEC 20 SAG-D | |

# Mercury Signs 1945-2025

| 1960 | 1961 | 1962 | 1963 | 1964 | 1965 |
|------|------|------|------|------|------|
| JAN 5 CAP-D | JAN 15 AQU-D | JAN 8 AQU-D | JAN 3 AQU-D | JAN 15 CAP-D | JAN 14 CAP-D |
| JAN 24 AQU-D | FEB 2 PIC-D | JAN 27 AQU-R | JAN 11 AQU-R | FEB 11 AQU-D | FEB 4 AQU-D |
| FEB 10 PIC-D | FEB 12 PIC-R | FEB 17 AQU-D | JAN 21 CAP-R | MAR 17 PIC-D | FEB 22 PIC-D |
| MAR 2 PIC-R | FEB 25 AQU-R | MAR 16 PIC-D | FEB 1 CAP-D | APR 3 TAU-D | MAR 10 ARI-D |
| MAR 24 PIC-D | MAR 6 AQU-D | APR 4 ARI-D | FEB 16 AQU-D | APR 17 TAU-R | MAR 29 ARI-R |
| APR 17 ARI-D | MAR 19 PIC-D | APR 19 TAU-D | MAR 10 PIC-D | MAY 10 TAU-D | APR 22 ARI-D |
| MAY 5 TAU-D | APR 11 ARI-D | MAY 4 GEM-D | MAR 27 ARI-D | JUN 10 GEM-D | MAY 16 TAU-D |
| MAY 20 GEM-D | APR 27 TAU-D | MAY 26 GEM-R | APR 10 TAU-D | JUN 25 CAN-D | JUN 3 GEM-D |
| JUN 3 CAN-D | MAY 11 GEM-D | JUN 19 GEM-D | MAY 4 GEM-D | JUL 10 LEO-D | JUN 17 CAN-D |
| JUL 2 LEO-D | MAY 29 CAN-D | JUL 12 CAN-D | MAY 7 GEM-R | JUL 28 VIR-D | AUG 1 VIR-D |
| JUL 4 LEO-R | JUN 14 CAN-R | JUL 27 LEO-D | MAY 11 TAU-R | AUG 19 VIR-R | AUG 2 VIR-R |
| JUL 7 CAN-R | JUL 8 CAN-D | AUG 11 VIR-D | MAY 30 TAU-D | SEP 11 VIR-D | AUG 4 LEO-R |
| JUL 27 CAN-D | AUG 5 LEO-D | AUG 30 LIB-D | JUN 15 GEM-D | OCT 4 LIB-D | AUG 25 VEO-D |
| AUG 11 LEO-D | AUG 19 VIR-D | SEP 24 LIB-R | JUL 5 CAN-D | OCT 21 SCO-D | SEP 9 VIR-D |
| AUG 28 VIR-D | SEP 5 LIB-D | OCT 15 LIB-D | JUL 19 LEO-D | NOV 9 SAG-D | SEP 26 LIB-D |
| SEP 13 LIB-D | SEP 28 SCO-D | NOV 6 SCO-D | AUG 4 VIR-D | DEC 1 CAP-D | OCT 13 SCO-D |
| OCT 2 SCO-D | OCT 10 SCO-R | NOV 24 SAG-D | AUG 27 LIB-D | DEC 9 CAP-R | NOV 3 SAG-D |
| OCT 27 SCO-R | OCT 23 LIB-R | DEC 13 CAP-D | SEP 6 LIB-R | DEC 17 SAG-R | NOV 23 SAG-R |
| NOV 16 SCO-D | OCT 31 LIB-D | | SEP 18 VIR-D | DEC 29 SAG-D | DEC 12 SAG-D |
| DEC 8 SAG-D | NOV 11 SCO-D | | SEP 29 VIR-D | | |
| DEC 28 CAP-D | DEC 1 SAG-D | | OCT 11 LIB-D | | |
| | DEC 21 CAP-D | | OCT 29 SCO-D | | |
| | | | NOV 17 SAG-D | | |
| | | | DEC 7 CAP-D | | |
| | | | DEC 26 CAP-R | | |

| 1966 | 1967 | 1968 | 1969 | 1970 | 1971 |
|------|------|------|------|------|------|
| JAN 8 CAP-D | JAN 2 CAP-D | JAN 13 AQU-D | JAN 5 AQU-D | JAN 4 CAP-R | JAN 3 SAG-R |
| JAN 29 AQU-D | JAN 20 AQU-D | FEB 2 PIC-D | JAN 20 AQU-R | JAN 24 CAP-D | JAN 8 SAG-R |
| FEB 14 PIC-D | FEB 7 PIC-D | FEB 6 PIC-R | FEB 10 AQU-D | FEB 14 AQU-D | JAN 15 CAP-D |
| MAR 4 ARI-D | FEB 24 PIC-R | FEB 12 AQU-D | MAR 13 PIC-D | MAR 5 PIC-D | FEB 8 AQU-D |
| MAR 12 ARI-R | MAR 17 PIC-D | FEB 28 AQU-D | MAR 31 ARI-D | MAR 23 ARI-D | FEB 27 PIC-D |
| MAR 23 PIC-R | APR 15 ARI-D | MAR 18 PIC-D | APR 15 TAU-D | APR 7 TAU-D | MAR 15 ARI-D |
| APR 4 PIC-D | MAY 2 TAU-D | APR 8 ARI-D | MAY 1 GEM-D | APR 28 TAU-R | APR 2 TAU-D |
| APR 18 ARI-D | MAY 17 GEM-D | APR 23 TAU-D | MAY 17 GEM-R | MAY 22 TAU-D | APR 9 TAU-R |
| MAY 10 TAU-D | JUN 1 CAN-D | MAY 7 GEM-D | JUN 10 GEM-D | JUN 14 GEM-D | APR 19 ARI-R |
| MAY 25 GEM-D | JUN 26 CAN-R | MAY 30 CAN-D | JUL 9 CAN-D | JUL 1 CAN-D | MAY 3 ARI-D |
| JUN 8 CAN-D | JUL 20 CAN-D | JUN 6 CAN-R | JUL 23 LEO-D | JUL 15 LEO-D | MAY 18 TAU-D |
| JUN 27 LEO-D | AUG 9 LEO-D | JUN 14 GEM-R | AUG 8 VIR-D | AUG 1 VIR-D | JUN 8 GEM-D |
| JUL 14 LEO-R | AUG 25 VIR-D | JUN 30 GEM-D | AUG 28 LIB-D | AUG 30 VIR-R | JUN 22 CAN-D |
| AUG 7 LEO-D | SEP 10 LIB-D | JUL 14 CAN-D | SEP 16 LIB-R | SEP 22 VIR-D | JUL 6 LEO-D |
| SEP 2 VIR-D | OCT 1 SCO-D | AUG 1 LEO-D | OCT 8 SCO-R | OCT 8 LIB-D | JUL 27 VIR-D |
| SEP 18 LIB-D | OCT 21 SCO-R | AUG 16 VIR-D | OCT 9 SCO-D | OCT 25 SCO-D | AUG 12 VIR-R |
| OCT 6 SCO-D | NOV 10 SCO-D | SEP 3 LIB-D | OCT 10 LIB-D | NOV 14 SAG-D | AUG 30 LEO-R |
| OCT 31 SAG-D | DEC 6 SAG-D | SEP 27 SCO-D | NOV 2 SCO-D | DEC 4 CAP-D | SEP 5 LEO-D |
| NOV 6 SAG-R | DEC 25 CAP-D | OCT 3 SCO-D | NOV 21 SAG-D | DEC 19 CAP-R | SEP 12 VIR-D |
| NOV 14 SCO-R | | OCT 8 LIB-R | DEC 10 CAP-D | | OCT 2 LIB-D |
| NOV 26 SCO-D | | OCT 24 LIB-D | | | OCT 18 SCO-D |
| DEC 12 SAG-D | | NOV 9 SCO-D | | | NOV 7 SAG-D |
| | | NOV 28 SAG-D | | | DEC 3 SAG-R |
| | | DEC 17 CAP-D | | | DEC 22 SAG-D |

# Mercury Signs 1945-2025

| 1972 | 1973 | 1974 | 1975 | 1976 | 1977 |
|------|------|------|------|------|------|
| JAN 12 CAP-D | JAN 5 CAP-D | JAN 17 AQU-D | JAN 9 AQU-D | JAN 3 AQU-D | JAN 17 CAP-D |
| FEB 1 AQU-D | JAN 24 AQU-D | FEB 3 PIC-D | JAN 30 AQU-R | JAN 14 AQU-R | FEB 11 AQU-D |
| FEB 19 PIC-D | FEB 10 PIC-D | FEB 15 PIC-R | FEB 20 AQU-D | JAN 26 CAP-R | MAR 3 PIC-D |
| MAR 6 ARI-D | MAR 4 PIC-R | MAR 3 AQU-R | MAR 17 PIC-D | FEB 3 CAP-D | MAR 19 ARI-D |
| MAR 21 ARI-R | MAR 27 PIC-D | MAR 9 AQU-D | APR 5 ARI-D | FEB 16 AQU-D | APR 4 TAU-D |
| APR 13 ARI-D | APR 17 ARI-D | MAR 18 PIC-D | APR 20 TAU-D | MAR 9 PIC-D | APR 20 TAU-R |
| MAY 13 TAU-D | MAY 7 TAU-D | APR 12 ARI-D | MAY 6 GEM-D | MAR 27 ARI-D | MAY 13 TAU-D |
| MAY 30 GEM-D | MAY 21 GEM-D | MAY 13 GEM-D | MAY 29 GEM-R | APR 11 TAU-D | JUN 11 GEM-D |
| JUN 13 CAN-D | JUN 5 CAN-D | MAY 30 CAN-D | JUN 22 GEM-D | APR 30 GEM-D | JUN 28 CAN-D |
| JUN 29 LEO-D | JUN 28 LEO-D | JUN 17 CAN-R | JUL 13 CAN-D | MAY 9 GEM-R | JUL 11 LEO-D |
| JUL 24 LEO-R | JUL 6 LEO-R | JUL 12 CAN-D | JUL 29 LEO-D | MAY 20 TAU-D | JUL 29 VIR-D |
| AUG 17 LEO-D | JUL 17 CAN-R | AUG 6 LEO-D | AUG 13 VIR-D | JUN 2 TAU-D | AUG 22 VIR-R |
| SEP 6 VIR-D | JUL 30 CAN-D | AUG 21 VIR-D | AUG 31 LIB-D | JUN 14 GEM-D | SEP 14 VIR-D |
| SEP 22 LIB-D | AUG 12 LEO-D | SEP 7 LIB-D | SEP 27 LIB-R | JUL 5 CAN-D | OCT 5 LIB-D |
| OCT 10 SCO-D | AUG 29 VIR-D | SEP 29 SCO-D | OCT 18 LIB-D | JUL 19 LEO-D | OCT 22 SCO-D |
| OCT 31 SAG-R | SEP 14 LIB-D | OCT 13 SCO-D | NOV 7 SCO-D | AUG 4 VIR-D | NOV 10 SAG-D |
| NOV 15 SAG-R | OCT 3 SCO-D | OCT 27 LIB-R | NOV 26 SAG-D | AUG 25 LIB-D | DEC 2 CAP-D |
| NOV 30 SCO-D | OCT 30 SCO-R | NOV 3 LIB-D | DEC 15 CAP-D | SEP 8 LIB-R | DEC 12 CAP-R |
| DEC 5 SCO-D | NOV 19 SCO-D | NOV 12 SCO-D | | SEP 22 VIR-R | DEC 22 SAG-R |
| DEC 13 SAG-D | DEC 9 SAG-D | DEC 3 SAG-D | | OCT 1 VIR-D | DEC 31 SAG-D |
| | DEC 29 CAP-D | DEC 22 CAP-D | | OCT 11 LIB-D | |
| | | | | OCT 30 SCO-D | |
| | | | | NOV 17 SAG-D | |
| | | | | DEC 7 CAP-D | |
| | | | | DEC 28 CAP-R | |

| 1978 | 1979 | 1980 | 1981 | 1982 | 1983 |
|------|------|------|------|------|------|
| JAN 14 CAP-D | JAN 9 CAP-D | JAN 3 CAP-D | JAN 13 AQU-D | JAN 6 AQU-D | JAN 2 AQU-D |
| FEB 5 AQU-D | JAN 29 AQU-D | JAN 22 AQU-D | FEB 1 PIC-D | JAN 23 AQU-R | JAN 7 AQU-R |
| MAR 11 ARI-D | FEB 15 PIC-D | FEB 8 PIC-D | FEB 8 PIC-R | FEB 13 AQU-D | JAN 13 CAP-R |
| APR 2 ARI-R | MAR 4 ARI-D | FEB 26 PIC-R | FEB 17 AQU-R | MAR 14 PIC-D | JAN 27 CAP-D |
| APR 25 ARI-D | MAR 15 ARI-R | MAR 19 PIC-D | MAR 2 AQU-D | APR 1 ARI-D | FEB 15 AQU-D |
| MAY 17 TAU-D | MAR 29 PIC-R | APR 15 ARI-D | MAR 19 PIC-D | APR 16 TAU-D | MAR 8 PIC-D |
| JUN 4 GEM-D | APR 7 PIC-D | MAY 17 GEM-D | APR 9 PIC-D | MAY 3 GEM-D | MAR 24 ARI-D |
| JUN 18 CAN-D | APR 18 ARI-D | JUN 28 CAN-D | APR 25 TAU-D | MAY 21 GEM-R | APR 8 TAU-D |
| JUL 3 LEO-D | MAY 11 TAU-D | JUL 22 CAN-D | MAY 9 GEM-D | JUN 13 GEM-D | MAY 2 TAU-R |
| JUL 28 VIR-D | MAY 27 GEM-D | AUG 10 LEO-D | MAY 29 CAN-D | JUL 10 CAN-D | MAY 26 TAU-D |
| AUG 4 VIR-R | JUN 10 CAN-D | AUG 25 VIR-D | JUN 9 CAN-R | JUL 25 LEO-D | JUN 15 GEM-D |
| AUG 14 LEO-R | JUN 28 LEO-D | SEP 11 LIB-D | JUN 23 GEM-R | AUG 9 VIR-D | JUL 2 CAN-D |
| AUG 28 LEO-D | JUL 17 LEO-R | OCT 1 SCO-D | JUL 4 GEM-D | AUG 29 LIB-D | JUL 16 LEO-D |
| SEP 10 VIR-D | AUG 11 LEO-D | OCT 23 SCO-R | JUL 13 CAN-D | SEP 19 LIB-R | AUG 2 VIR-D |
| SEP 27 LIB-D | SEP 3 VIR-D | NOV 12 SCO-D | AUG 2 LEO-D | OCT 11 LIB-D | AUG 30 VIR-D |
| OCT 15 SCO-D | SEP 19 LIB-D | DEC 6 SAG-D | AUG 17 VIR-D | NOV 4 SCO-D | SEP 2 LIB-R |
| NOV 4 SAG-D | OCT 8 SCO-D | DEC 25 CAP-D | SEP 3 LIB-D | NOV 22 SAG-D | SEP 7 VIR-R |
| NOV 25 SAG-R | OCT 31 SAG-D | | SEP 28 SCO-D | DEC 11 CAP-D | SEP 24 VIR-D |
| DEC 15 SAG-D | NOV 9 SAG-R | | OCT 6 SCO-R | | OCT 9 LIB-D |
| | NOV 19 SCO-R | | OCT 15 LIB-R | | OCT 27 SCO-D |
| | NOV 29 SCO-D | | OCT 27 LIB-D | | NOV 15 SAG-D |
| | DEC 13 SAG-D | | NOV 10 SCO-D | | DEC 5 CAP-D |
| | | | NOV 29 SAG-D | | DEC 22 CAP-R |
| | | | DEC 18 CAP-D | | |

# Mercury Signs 1945-2025

| 1984 | 1985 | 1986 | 1987 | 1988 | 1989 |
|---|---|---|---|---|---|
| JAN 11 CAP-D | JAN 12 CAP-D | JAN 6 CAP-D | JAN 18 AQU-D | JAN 11 AQU-D | JAN 3 AQU-D |
| FEB 10 AQU-D | FEB 2 AQU-D | JAN 26 AQU-D | FEB 5 PIC-D | FEB 2 AQU-R | JAN 16 AQU-R |
| FEB 28 PIC-D | FEB 19 PIC-D | FEB 12 PIC-D | FEB 16 PIC-R | FEB 23 AQU-D | JAN 30 CAP-R |
| MAR 15 ARI-D | MAR 8 ARI-D | MAR 4 ARI-D | MAR 12 AQU-R | MAR 17 PIC-D | FEB 5 CAP-D |
| APR 1 TAU-D | MAR 24 ARI-R | MAR 7 ARI-R | MAR 13 AQU-D | APR 5 ARI-D | FEB 15 AQU-D |
| APR 11 TAU-R | APR 17 ARI-D | MAR 12 PIC-R | APR 14 PIC-D | APR 21 TAU-D | MAR 11 PIC-D |
| APR 26 ARI-R | MAY 15 TAU-D | MAR 30 PIC-D | APR 12 ARI-D | MAY 5 GEM-D | MAR 29 ARI-D |
| MAY 6 ARI-D | MAY 31 GEM-D | APR 18 ARI-D | APR 30 TAU-D | MAY 31 GEM-R | APR 12 TAU-D |
| MAY 16 TAU-D | JUN 14 CAN-D | MAY 8 TAU-D | MAY 14 GEM-D | JUN 24 GEM-D | APR 30 GEM-D |
| JUN 8 GEM-D | JUN 30 LEO-D | MAY 23 GEM-D | MAY 31 CAN-D | JUL 13 CAN-D | MAY 12 GEM-R |
| JUN 23 CAN-D | JUL 28 LEO-R | JUN 6 CAN-D | JUN 21 CAN-R | JUL 29 LEO-D | MAY 29 TAU-R |
| JUL 7 LEO-D | AUG 20 LEO-D | JUN 27 LEO-D | JUL 15 CAN-D | AUG 13 VIR-D | JUN 5 TAU-D |
| JUL 27 VIR-D | SEP 7 VIR-D | JUL 9 LEO-R | AUG 7 LEO-D | AUG 31 LIB-D | JUN 13 GEM-D |
| AUG 14 LEO-D | SEP 23 LIB-D | JUL 24 CAN-R | AUG 22 VIR-D | SEP 28 LIB-R | JUL 7 CAN-D |
| SEP 7 VIR-D | OCT 11 SCO-D | AUG 3 CAN-D | SEP 9 LIB-D | OCT 20 LIB-D | JUL 21 LEO-D |
| OCT 1 LIB-D | NOV 1 SAG-D | AUG 12 LEO-D | SEP 30 SCO-D | NOV 7 SCO-D | AUG 6 VIR-D |
| OCT 19 SCO-D | NOV 18 SAG-R | AUG 31 VIR-D | OCT 16 SCO-R | NOV 26 SAG-D | AUG 27 LIB-D |
| NOV 7 SAG-D | DEC 5 SCO-R | SEP 16 LIB-D | NOV 2 LIB-R | DEC 15 CAP-D | SEP 11 LIB-R |
| DEC 2 CAP-D | DEC 8 SCO-D | OCT 5 SCO-D | NOV 6 LIB-D | | SEP 27 VIR-R |
| DEC 4 CAP-R | DEC 13 SAG-D | NOV 2 SCO-R | NOV 12 SCO-D | | OCT 4 VIR-D |
| DEC 8 SAG-R | | NOV 22 SCO-D | DEC 4 SAG-D | | OCT 12 LIB-D |
| DEC 24 SAG-D | | DEC 11 SAG-D | DEC 23 CAP-D | | OCT 31 SCO-D |
| | | DEC 30 CAP-D | | | NOV 19 SAG-D |
| | | | | | DEC 8 CAP-D |
| | | | | | DEC 30 CAP-R |

| 1990 | 1991 | 1992 | 1993 | 1994 | 1995 |
|---|---|---|---|---|---|
| JAN 20 CAP-D | JAN 4 SAG-D | JAN 11 CAP-D | JAN 3 CAP-D | JAN 15 AQU-D | JAN 7 AQU-D |
| FEB 13 AQU-D | JAN 15 CAP-D | JAN 30 AQU-D | JAN 22 AQU-D | FEB 2 PIC-D | JAN 26 AQU-R |
| MAR 4 PIC-D | FEB 6 AQU-D | FEB 17 PIC-D | FEB 8 PIC-D | FEB 11 PIC-R | FEB 16 AQU-D |
| MAR 21 ARI-D | FEB 25 PIC-D | MAR 4 ARI-D | FEB 27 PIC-R | FEB 22 AQU-R | MAR 15 PIC-D |
| APR 5 TAU-D | MAR 12 ARI-D | MAR 17 ARI-R | MAR 22 PIC-D | MAR 5 AQU-D | APR 3 ARI-D |
| APR 23 TAU-R | APR 4 ARI-R | APR 4 PIC-R | APR 16 ARI-D | MAR 19 PIC-D | APR 18 TAU-D |
| MAY 17 TAU-D | APR 28 ARI-D | APR 9 PIC-D | MAY 4 TAU-D | APR 10 ARI-D | MAY 3 GEM-D |
| JUN 13 GEM-D | MAY 17 TAU-D | APR 15 ARI-D | MAY 19 GEM-D | APR 26 TAU-D | MAY 24 GEM-R |
| JUN 28 CAN-D | JUN 6 GEM-D | MAY 12 TAU-D | JUN 3 CAN-D | MAY 10 GEM-D | JUN 17 GEM-D |
| JUL 12 LEO-D | JUN 20 CAN-D | MAY 27 GEM-D | JUL 1 CAN-R | MAY 29 CAN-D | JUL 11 CAN-D |
| JUL 30 VIR-D | JUL 5 LEO-D | JUN 10 CAN-D | JUL 25 CAN-D | JUN 12 CAN-R | JUL 26 LEO-D |
| AUG 25 VIR-R | JUL 27 VIR-D | JUN 28 LEO-D | AUG 11 LEO-D | JUL 3 GEM-R | AUG 11 VIR-D |
| SEP 17 VIR-D | AUG 7 VIR-R | JUL 20 LEO-R | AUG 27 VIR-D | JUL 6 GEM-D | AUG 30 LIB-D |
| OCT 6 LIB-D | AUG 20 LEO-R | AUG 13 LEO-D | SEP 12 LIB-D | JUL 11 CAN-D | SEP 22 LIB-R |
| OCT 24 SCO-D | AUG 31 LEO-D | SEP 4 VIR-D | OCT 2 SCO-D | AUG 4 LEO-D | OCT 14 LIB-D |
| NOV 12 SAG-D | SEP 11 VIR-D | SEP 20 LIB-D | OCT 25 SCO-R | AUG 19 VIR-D | NOV 5 SCO-D |
| DEC 3 CAP-D | SEP 29 LIB-D | OCT 8 SCO-D | NOV 15 SCO-D | SEP 5 LIB-D | NOV 23 SAG-D |
| DEC 14 CAP-R | OCT 16 SCO-D | OCT 30 SAG-D | DEC 8 SAG-D | SEP 28 SCO-D | DEC 13 CAP-D |
| DEC 26 SAG-R | NOV 5 SAG-D | NOV 11 SAG-R | DEC 27 CAP-D | OCT 9 SCO-R | |
| | NOV 28 SAG-R | NOV 22 SCO-R | | OCT 20 LIB-R | |
| | DEC 18 SAG-D | DEC 1 SCO-D | | OCT 30 LIB-D | |
| | | DEC 13 SAG-D | | NOV 11 SCO-D | |
| | | | | DEC 1 SAG-D | |
| | | | | DEC 20 CAP-D | |

# Mercury Signs 1945-2025

| 1996 | 1997 | 1998 | 1999 | 2000 | 2001 |
|------|------|------|------|------|------|
| JAN 2 AQU-D | JAN 12 CAP-D | JAN 13 CAP-D | JAN 8 CAP-D | JAN 1 CAP-D | JAN 11 AQU-D |
| JAN 9 AQU-R | FEB 10 AQU-D | FEB 3 AQU-D | JAN 27 AQU-D | JAN 19 AQU-D | FEB 2 PIC-D |
| JAN 18 CAP-R | MAR 1 PIC-D | FEB 21 PIC-D | FEB 13 PIC-D | FEB 6 PIC-D | FEB 7 AQU-R |
| JAN 30 CAP-D | MAR 17 ARI-D | MAR 9 ARI-D | MAR 3 ARI-D | FEB 21 PIC-R | FEB 25 AQU-D |
| FEB 16 AQU-D | APR 2 TAU-D | MAR 27 ARI-R | MAR 10 ARI-R | MAR 14 PIC-D | MAR 18 PIC-D |
| MAR 8 PIC-D | APR 14 TAU-R | APR 20 ARI-D | MAR 19 PIC-R | APR 14 ARI-D | APR 7 ARI-D |
| MAR 25 ARI-D | MAY 6 ARI-R | MAY 16 TAU-D | APR 2 PIC-D | MAY 1 TAU-D | APR 22 TAU-D |
| APR 9 TAU-D | MAY 8 ARI-D | JUN 2 GEM-D | APR 18 ARI-D | MAY 15 GEM-D | MAY 7 GEM-D |
| MAY 3 TAU-R | MAY 13 TAU-D | JUN 15 CAN-D | MAY 9 TAU-D | MAY 31 CAN-D | JUN 4 GEM-R |
| MAY 27 TAU-D | JUN 9 GEM-D | JUL 1 LEO-D | MAY 24 GEM-D | JUL 17 CAN-D | JUN 28 GEM-D |
| JUN 14 GEM-D | JUN 24 CAN-D | JUL 31 LEO-R | JUN 8 CAN-D | AUG 8 LEO-D | JUL 13 CAN-D |
| JUL 3 CAN-D | JUL 9 LEO-D | AUG 23 LEO-D | JUN 27 LEO-D | AUG 23 VIR-D | JUL 31 LEO-D |
| JUL 17 LEO-D | JUL 28 VIR-D | SEP 9 VIR-D | JUL 12 LEO-R | SEP 8 LIB-D | AUG 15 VIR-D |
| AUG 2 VIR-D | AUG 17 VIR-R | SEP 25 LIB-D | AUG 1 CAN-R | SEP 29 SCO-D | SEP 2 LIB-D |
| AUG 27 LIB-D | SEP 10 VIR-D | OCT 13 SCO-D | AUG 6 CAN-D | OCT 18 SCO-R | OCT 2 LIB-R |
| SEP 4 LIB-R | OCT 3 LIB-D | NOV 2 SAG-D | AUG 12 LEO-D | NOV 8 LIB-R | OCT 23 LIB-D |
| SEP 13 VIR-R | OCT 20 SCO-D | NOV 21 SAG-R | SEP 1 VIR-D | NOV 9 SCO-D | NOV 8 SCO-D |
| SEP 26 VIR-D | NOV 8 SAG-D | DEC 11 SAG-D | SEP 17 LIB-D | DEC 4 SAG-D | NOV 27 SAG-D |
| OCT 10 LIB-D | DEC 1 CAP-D | | OCT 6 SCO-D | DEC 24 CAP-D | DEC 16 CAP-D |
| OCT 28 SCO-D | DEC 7 CAP-R | | OCT 31 SAG-D | | |
| NOV 15 SAG-D | DEC 14 SAG-R | | NOV 5 SAG-R | | |
| DEC 5 CAP-D | DEC 27 SAG-D | | NOV 10 SCO-R | | |
| DEC 23 CAP-R | | | NOV 25 SCO-D | | |
| | | | DEC 12 SAG-D | | |

| 2002 | 2003 | 2004 | 2005 | 2006 | 2007 |
|------|------|------|------|------|------|
| JAN 4 AQU-D | JAN 14 AQU-D | JAN 6 SAG-D | JAN 11 CAP-D | JAN 4 CAP-D | JAN 16 AQU-D |
| JAN 18 AQU-R | FEB 6 PIC-D | JAN 15 CAP-D | JAN 31 AQU-D | JAN 23 AQU-D | FEB 3 PIC-D |
| FEB 5 CAP-R | MAR 22 ARI-D | FEB 8 AQU-D | FEB 17 PIC-D | FEB 10 PIC-D | FEB 14 PIC-R |
| FEB 8 CAP-D | APR 6 TAU-D | FEB 26 PIC-D | MAR 6 ARI-D | MAR 3 PIC-R | FEB 28 AQU-R |
| FEB 14 AQU-D | APR 26 TAU-R | MAR 13 ARI-D | MAR 20 ARI-R | MAR 25 PIC-D | MAR 8 AQU-D |
| MAR 12 PIC-D | MAY 20 TAU-D | APR 2 TAU-D | APR 12 ARI-D | APR 17 ARI-D | MAR 19 PIC-D |
| MAR 30 ARI-D | JUN 14 GEM-D | APR 6 TAU-R | MAY 13 TAU-D | MAY 6 TAU-D | APR 11 ARI-D |
| APR 14 TAU-D | JUN 30 CAN-D | APR 14 ARI-R | MAY 29 GEM-D | MAY 20 GEM-D | APR 28 TAU-D |
| MAY 1 GEM-D | JUL 14 LEO-D | APR 30 ARI-D | JUN 12 CAN-D | JUN 4 CAN-D | MAY 12 GEM-D |
| MAY 15 GEM-R | JUL 31 VIR-D | MAY 17 TAU-D | JUN 29 LEO-D | JUN 29 LEO-D | MAY 30 CAN-D |
| JUN 8 GEM-D | AUG 28 VIR-R | JUN 6 GEM-D | JUL 23 LEO-R | JUL 4 LEO-R | JUN 15 CAN-R |
| JUL 8 CAN-D | SEP 20 VIR-D | JUN 20 CAN-D | AUG 16 LEO-D | JUL 11 CAN-R | JUL 10 CAN-D |
| JUL 22 LEO-D | OCT 8 LIB-D | JUL 5 LEO-D | SEP 5 VIR-D | JUL 29 CAN-D | AUG 5 LEO-D |
| AUG 7 VIR-D | OCT 25 SCO-D | JUL 26 VIR-D | SEP 21 LIB-D | AUG 12 LEO-D | AUG 20 VIR-D |
| AUG 27 LIB-D | NOV 13 SAG-D | AUG 10 VIR-R | OCT 9 SCO-D | AUG 28 VIR-D | SEP 6 LIB-D |
| SEP 14 LIB-R | DEC 3 CAP-D | AUG 26 LEO-D | OCT 31 SAG-D | SEP 13 LIB-D | SEP 28 SCO-D |
| OCT 3 VIR-R | DEC 17 CAP-R | SEP 3 LEO-D | NOV 14 SAG-R | OCT 3 SCO-D | OCT 12 SCO-R |
| OCT 6 VIR-D | DEC 31 SAG-R | SEP 11 VIR-D | NOV 27 SCO-R | OCT 28 SCO-R | OCT 25 LIB-R |
| OCT 12 LIB-D | | SEP 29 LIB-D | DEC 4 SCO-D | NOV 18 SCO-D | NOV 2 LIB-D |
| NOV 1 SCO-D | | OCT 16 SCO-D | DEC 13 SAG-D | DEC 9 SAG-D | NOV 12 SCO-D |
| NOV 20 SAG-D | | NOV 5 SAG-D | | DEC 28 CAP-D | DEC 2 SAG-D |
| DEC 9 CAP-D | | NOV 30 SAG-R | | | DEC 21 CAP-D |
| DEC 13 CAP-R | | DEC 20 SAG-D | | | |
| DEC 23 CAP-D | | | | | |

# Mercury Signs 1945-2025

| 2008 | 2009 | 2010 | 2011 | 2012 | 2013 |
|---|---|---|---|---|---|
| JAN 9 AQU-D | JAN 2 AQU-D | JAN 15 CAP-D | JAN 14 CAP-D | JAN 9 CAP-D | JAN 1 CAP-D |
| JAN 28 AQU-R | JAN 11 AQU-R | FEB 11 AQU-D | FEB 4 AQU-D | JAN 28 AQU-D | JAN 20 AQU-D |
| FEB 19 AQU-D | JAN 22 CAP-R | MAR 2 PIC-D | FEB 22 PIC-D | FEB 15 PIC-D | FEB 6 PIC-D |
| MAR 15 PIC-D | FEB 1 CAP-D | MAR 18 ARI-D | MAR 10 ARI-D | MAR 3 ARI-D | FEB 23 PIC-R |
| APR 3 ARI-D | FEB 15 AQU-D | APR 3 TAU-D | MAR 30 ARI-R | MAR 12 ARI-R | MAR 17 PIC-D |
| APR 18 TAU-D | MAR 9 PIC-D | APR 18 TAU-R | APR 23 ARI-D | MAR 24 PIC-R | APR 15 ARI-D |
| MAY 3 GEM-D | MAR 26 ARI-D | MAY 11 TAU-D | MAY 16 TAU-D | APR 4 PIC-D | MAY 2 TAU-D |
| MAY 26 GEM-R | APR 11 TAU-D | JUN 11 GEM-D | JUN 3 GEM-D | APR 17 ARI-D | MAY 16 GEM-D |
| JUN 19 GEM-D | MAY 1 GEM-D | JUN 26 CAN-D | JUN 17 CAN-D | MAY 10 TAU-D | JUN 1 CAN-D |
| JUL 11 CAN-D | MAY 7 GEM-R | JUL 10 LEO-D | JUL 3 LEO-D | MAY 25 GEM-D | JUN 26 CAN-R |
| JUL 27 LEO-D | MAY 14 TAU-R | JUL 28 VIR-D | JUL 29 VIR-D | JUN 8 CAN-D | JUL 20 CAN-D |
| AUG 11 VIR-D | MAY 31 TAU-D | AUG 20 VIR-R | AUG 3 VIR-R | JUN 27 LEO-D | AUG 9 LEO-D |
| AUG 30 LIB-D | JUN 15 GEM-D | SEP 12 VIR-D | AUG 9 LEO-R | JUL 15 LEO-D | AUG 24 VIR-D |
| SEP 24 LIB-R | JUL 4 CAN-D | OCT 4 LIB-D | AUG 26 LEO-D | AUG 8 LEO-D | SEP 10 LIB-D |
| OCT 15 LIB-D | JUL 18 LEO-D | OCT 21 SCO-D | SEP 10 VIR-D | SEP 2 VIR-D | SEP 30 SCO-D |
| NOV 5 SCO-D | AUG 3 VIR-D | NOV 9 SAG-D | SEP 26 LIB-D | SEP 17 LIB-D | OCT 21 SCO-R |
| NOV 24 SAG-D | AUG 26 LIB-D | DEC 2 CAP-D | OCT 14 SCO-D | OCT 5 SCO-D | NOV 10 SCO-D |
| DEC 13 CAP-D | SEP 7 LIB-R | DEC 11 CAP-R | NOV 3 SAG-D | OCT 30 SAG-D | DEC 6 SAG-D |
|  | SEP 19 VIR-R | DEC 19 SAG-R | NOV 24 SAG-R | NOV 6 SAG-R | DEC 25 CAP-D |
|  | SEP 29 VIR-D | DEC 30 SAG-D | DEC 14 SAG-D | NOV 15 SCO-R |  |
|  | OCT 11 LIB-D |  |  | NOV 26 SCO-D |  |
|  | OCT 29 SCO-D |  |  | DEC 12 SAG-D |  |
|  | NOV 17 SAG-D |  |  |  |  |
|  | DEC 6 CAP-D |  |  |  |  |
|  | DEC 26 CAP-R |  |  |  |  |

| 2014 | 2015 | 2016 | 2017 | 2018 | 2019 |
|---|---|---|---|---|---|
| JAN 12 AQU-D | JAN 6 AQU-D | JAN 3 AQU-D | JAN 5 SAG-R | JAN 12 CAP-D | JAN 6 CAP-D |
| FEB 1 PIC-D | JAN 21 AQU-R | JAN 5 AQU-R | JAN 8 SAG-D | FEB 1 AQU-D | JAN 25 AQU-D |
| FEB 6 PIC-R | FEB 11 AQU-D | JAN 25 AQU-D | JAN 13 CAP-D | FEB 19 PIC-D | FEB 11 PIC-D |
| FEB 14 AQU-R | MAR 14 PIC-D | FEB 14 AQU-D | FEB 8 AQU-D | MAR 7 ARI-D | MAR 5 PIC-R |
| FEB 28 AQU-D | APR 1 ARI-D | MAR 6 PIC-D | FEB 26 PIC-D | MAR 23 ARI-R | MAR 28 PIC-D |
| MAR 18 PIC-D | APR 15 TAU-D | MAR 23 ARI-D | MAR 14 ARI-D | APR 15 ARI-D | APR 18 ARI-D |
| APR 8 ARI-D | MAY 2 GEM-D | APR 6 TAU-D | APR 1 TAU-D | MAY 14 TAU-D | MAY 7 TAU-D |
| APR 24 TAU-D | MAY 19 GEM-R | APR 28 TAU-R | APR 9 TAU-R | MAY 30 GEM-D | MAY 22 GEM-D |
| MAY 8 GEM-D | JUN 11 GEM-D | MAY 22 TAU-D | APR 21 ARI-R | JUN 13 CAN-D | JUN 5 CAN-D |
| MAY 30 CAN-D | JUL 9 CAN-D | JUN 13 GEM-D | MAY 3 ARI-D | JUN 30 LEO-D | JUN 26 CAN-D |
| JUN 7 CAN-R | JUL 24 LEO-D | JUN 30 CAN-D | MAY 17 TAU-D | JUL 26 LEO-R | JUL 7 LEO-R |
| JUN 18 GEM-R | AUG 8 VIR-D | JUL 15 LEO-D | JUN 7 GEM-D | AUG 19 LEO-D | JUL 20 CAN-R |
| JUL 2 GEM-D | AUG 28 LIB-D | JUL 31 VIR-D | JUN 22 CAN-D | SEP 7 VIR-D | AUG 2 CAN-D |
| JUL 14 CAN-D | SEP 17 LIB-R | AUG 30 VIR-R | JUL 7 LEO-D | SEP 23 LIB-D | AUG 12 LEO-D |
| AUG 1 LEO-D | OCT 9 LIB-D | SEP 22 VIR-D | JUL 26 VIR-D | OCT 11 SCO-D | AUG 30 VIR-D |
| AUG 16 VIR-D | NOV 3 SCO-D | OCT 8 LIB-D | AUG 13 VIR-R | NOV 1 SAG-D | SEP 15 LIB-D |
| SEP 3 LIB-D | NOV 21 SAG-D | OCT 25 SCO-D | SEP 1 LEO-R | NOV 17 SAG-R | OCT 4 SCO-D |
| SEP 28 SCO-D | DEC 11 CAP-D | NOV 13 SAG-D | SEP 5 LEO-D | DEC 2 SCO-R | OCT 31 SCO-R |
| OCT 4 SCO-R |  | DEC 3 CAP-D | SEP 11 VIR-D | DEC 6 SCO-D | NOV 20 SCO-D |
| OCT 11 LIB-R |  | DEC 19 CAP-R | OCT 1 LIB-D | DEC 13 SAG-D | DEC 10 SAG-D |
| OCT 25 LIB-D |  |  | OCT 18 SCO-D |  | DEC 30 CAP-D |
| NOV 9 SCO-D |  |  | NOV 6 SAG-D |  |  |
| NOV 29 SAG-D |  |  | DEC 3 SAG-R |  |  |
| DEC 18 CAP-D |  |  | DEC 23 SAG-D |  |  |

# Mercury Signs 1945-2025

| 2020 | 2021 | 2022 | 2023 | 2024 | 2025 |
|---|---|---|---|---|---|
| JAN 17 AQU-D | JAN 9 AQU-D | JAN 3 AQU-D | JAN 18 CAP-D | JAN 2 SAG-D | JAN 9 CAP-D |
| FEB 4 PIC-D | JAN 30 AQU-R | JAN 14 AQU-R | FEB 12 AQU-D | JAN 15 CAP-D | JAN 29 AQU-D |
| FEB 17 PIC-R | FEB 21 AQU-D | JAN 28 CAP-D | MAR 3 PIC-D | FEB 6 AQU-D | FEB 15 PIC-D |
| MAR 5 AQU-R | MAR 16 PIC-D | FEB 4 CAP-D | MAR 20 ARI-D | FEB 24 PIC-D | MAR 4 ARI-D |
| MAR 10 AQU-D | APR 5 ARI-D | FEB 15 AQU-D | APR 4 TAU-D | MAR 11 ARI-D | MAR 15 ARI-R |
| MAR 17 PIC-D | APR 20 TAU-D | MAR 11 PIC-D | APR 21 TAU-R | APR 2 ARI-R | MAR 31 PIC-R |
| APR 12 ARI-D | MAY 5 GEM-D | MAR 28 ARI-D | MAY 14 TAU-D | APR 25 ARI-D | APR 7 PIC-D |
| APR 28 TAU-D | MAY 29 GEM-R | APR 12 TAU-D | JUN 12 GEM-D | MAY 16 TAU-D | APR 17 ARI-D |
| MAY 12 GEM-D | JUN 22 GEM-D | APR 30 GEM-D | JUN 28 CAN-D | JUN 4 GEM-D | MAY 11 TAU-D |
| MAY 29 CAN-D | JUL 12 CAN-D | MAY 10 GEM-R | JUL 12 LEO-D | JUN 18 CAN-D | MAY 27 GEM-D |
| JUN 18 CAN-R | AUG 12 VIR-D | MAY 24 TAU-D | JUL 29 VIR-D | JUL 3 LEO-D | JUN 9 CAN-D |
| JUL 12 CAN-D | AUG 31 LIB-D | JUN 3 TAU-D | AUG 23 VIR-R | JUL 26 VIR-D | JUN 27 LEO-D |
| AUG 6 LEO-D | SEP 27 LIB-R | JUN 14 GEM-D | SEP 15 VIR-D | AUG 5 VIR-R | JUL 18 LEO-R |
| AUG 21 VIR-D | OCT 18 LIB-D | JUL 6 CAN-D | OCT 5 LIB-D | AUG 16 LEO-R | AUG 11 LEO-D |
| SEP 6 LIB-D | NOV 6 SCO-D | JUL 20 LEO-D | OCT 23 SCO-D | AUG 28 LEO-D | SEP 3 VIR-D |
| SEP 28 SCO-D | NOV 25 SAG-D | AUG 5 VIR-D | NOV 11 SAG-D | SEP 10 VIR-D | SEP 19 LIB-D |
| OCT 14 SCO-R | DEC 14 CAP-D | AUG 27 LIB-D | DEC 2 CAP-D | SEP 27 LIB-R | OCT 7 SCO-D |
| OCT 29 LIB-R | | SEP 10 LIB-R | DEC 13 CAP-R | OCT 14 SCO-D | OCT 30 SCO-D |
| NOV 3 LIB-D | | SEP 24 VIR-R | DEC 24 SAG-R | NOV 3 SAG-D | NOV 9 SAG-R |
| NOV 11 SCO-D | | OCT 2 VIR-D | | NOV 26 SAG-R | NOV 20 SCO-R |
| DEC 2 SAG-D | | OCT 11 LIB-D | | DEC 15 SAG-D | NOV 29 SCO-D |
| DEC 21 CAP-D | | OCT 30 SCO-D | | | DEC 12 SAG-D |
| | | NOV 18 SAG-D | | | |
| | | DEC 7 CAP-D | | | |
| | | DEC 29 CAP-R | | | |

# How to Use Venus Tables

Find the year and month of birth below and on the following pages, then the day of birth (or the day listed prior to it). The sign listed is your Venus sign. It stays in that sign until the next date listed. **Example:** For a birth on Oct .30, 1945, scan to the closest day prior. Note that Oct. 18 lists LIB-D. This means that Venus is in Libra. The next day of change is Nov. 13, SCO. So, for Oct. 30, Venus is definitely in Libra. The D after the date means that Venus is Direct in motion. An R after the date means that Venus is Retrograde. (Learn about Venus Retrograde, pg.104.)

ARI Aries
TAU Taurus
GEM Gemini
CAN Cancer
LEO Leo
VIR Virgo
LIB Libra
SCO Scorpio
SAG Sagittarius
CAP Capricorn
AQU Aquarius
PISC Pisces

# Venus Signs 1945-2025

| 1945 | 1946 | 1947 |
|---|---|---|
| JAN 6 PIS-D | JAN 23 AQU-D | JAN 6 SAG-D |
| FEB 3 ARI-D | FEB 16 PIS-D | FEB 7 CAP-D |
| MAR 12 TAU-D | MAR 12 ARI-D | MAR 5 AQU-D |
| MAR 25 TAU-R | APR 5 TAU-D | MAR 31 PIS-D |
| APR 8 ARI-R | APR 30 GEM-D | APR 25 ARI-D |
| MAY 6 ARI-D | MAY 24 CAN-D | MAY 20 TAU-D |
| JUN 5 TAU-D | JUN 19 LEO-D | JUN 14 GEM-D |
| JUL 8 GEM-D | JUL 14 VIR-D | JUL 9 CAN-D |
| AUG 5 CAN-D | AUG 10 LIB-D | AUG 2 LEO-D |
| AUG 31 LEO-D | SEP 7 SCO-D | AUG 27 VIR-D |
| OCT 18 LIB-D | OCT 17 SAG-D | SEP 19 LIB-D |
| NOV 13 SCO-D | OCT 28 SAG-R | OCT 14 SCO-D |
| DEC 7 SAG-D | NOV 9 SCO-R | NOV 7 SAG-D |
| DEC 30 CAP-D | DEC 8 SCO-D | DEC 1 CAP-D |
| | | DEC 24 AQU-D |

# Venus Signs 1945-2025

| 1948 | | | 1949 | | | 1950 | | | 1951 | | |
|---|---|---|---|---|---|---|---|---|---|---|---|
| JAN | 18 | PIS-D | JAN | 14 | CAP-D | JAN | 10 | AQU-R | JAN | 8 | AQU-D |
| FEB | 12 | ARI-D | FEB | 7 | AQU-D | FEB | 20 | AQU-D | FEB | 1 | PIS-D |
| MAR | 9 | TAU-D | MAR | 3 | PIS-D | APR | 7 | PIS-D | FEB | 25 | ARI-D |
| APR | 5 | GEM-D | MAR | 27 | ARI-D | MAY | 6 | ARI-D | MAR | 22 | TAU-D |
| MAY | 8 | CAN-D | APR | 20 | TAU-D | JUN | 2 | TAU-D | APR | 16 | GEM-D |
| JUN | 3 | CAN-R | MAY | 14 | GEM-D | JUN | 28 | GEM-D | MAY | 11 | CAN-D |
| JUN | 30 | GEM-R | JUN | 8 | CAN-D | JUL | 23 | CAN-D | JUN | 8 | LEO-D |
| JUL | 16 | GEM-D | JUL | 2 | LEO-D | AUG | 17 | LEO-D | JUL | 8 | VIR-D |
| AUG | 3 | CAN-D | JUL | 27 | VIR-D | SEP | 10 | VIR-D | AUG | 13 | VIR-R |
| SEP | 9 | LEO-D | AUG | 21 | LIB-D | OCT | 5 | LIB-D | SEP | 25 | VIR-D |
| OCT | 7 | VIR-D | SEP | 15 | SCO-D | OCT | 29 | SCO-D | NOV | 10 | LIB-D |
| NOV | 2 | LIB-D | OCT | 11 | SAG-D | NOV | 21 | SAG-D | DEC | 8 | SCO-D |
| NOV | 26 | SCO-D | NOV | 6 | CAP-D | DEC | 15 | CAP-D | | | |
| DEC | 21 | SAG-D | DEC | 7 | AQU-D | | | | | | |

| 1952 | | | 1953 | | | 1954 | | | 1955 | | |
|---|---|---|---|---|---|---|---|---|---|---|---|
| JAN | 3 | SAG-D | JAN | 6 | PIS-D | JAN | 23 | AQU-D | JAN | 7 | SAG-D |
| JAN | 28 | CAP-D | FEB | 3 | ARI-D | FEB | 16 | PIS-D | FEB | 6 | CAP-D |
| FEB | 21 | AQU-D | MAR | 15 | TAU-D | MAR | 12 | ARI-D | MAR | 5 | AQU-D |
| MAR | 17 | PIS-D | MAR | 23 | TAU-D | APR | 5 | TAU-D | MAR | 31 | PIS-D |
| APR | 10 | ARI-D | APR | 1 | ARI-D | APR | 29 | GEM-D | APR | 25 | ARI-D |
| MAY | 5 | TAU-D | JUN | 6 | TAU-D | MAY | 24 | CAN-D | MAY | 20 | TAU-D |
| MAY | 29 | GEM-D | JUL | 8 | GEM-D | JUN | 18 | LEO-D | JUN | 14 | GEM-D |
| JUN | 23 | CAN-D | AUG | 4 | CAN-D | JUL | 14 | VIR-D | JUL | 8 | CAN-D |
| JUL | 17 | LEO-D | AUG | 30 | LEO-D | AUG | 9 | LIB-D | AUG | 2 | LEO-D |
| AUG | 10 | VIR-D | SEP | 24 | VIR-D | SEP | 7 | SCO-D | AUG | 26 | VIR-D |
| SEP | 4 | LIB-D | OCT | 19 | LIB-D | OCT | 25 | SAG-R | SEP | 19 | LIB-D |
| SEP | 28 | SCO-D | NOV | 11 | SCO-D | OCT | 28 | SCO-R | OCT | 13 | SCO-D |
| OCT | 22 | SAG-D | DEC | 6 | SAG-D | DEC | 5 | SCO-D | NOV | 6 | SAG-D |
| NOV | 16 | CAP-D | DEC | 30 | CAP-D | | | | NOV | 20 | CAP-D |
| DEC | 11 | AQU-D | | | | | | | DEC | 25 | AQU-D |

| 1956 | | | 1957 | | | 1958 | | | 1959 | | |
|---|---|---|---|---|---|---|---|---|---|---|---|
| JAN | 18 | PIS-D | JAN | 13 | CAP-D | JAN | 8 | AQU-R | JAN | 8 | AQU-D |
| FEB | 12 | ARI-D | FEB | 6 | AQU-D | FEB | 18 | AQU-D | FEB | 1 | PIS-D |
| MAR | 8 | TAU-D | MAR | 2 | PIS-D | APR | 7 | PIS-D | FEB | 25 | ARI-D |
| APR | 5 | GEM-D | MAR | 26 | ARI-D | MAY | 6 | ARI-D | MAR | 21 | TAU-D |
| MAY | 9 | CAN-D | APR | 19 | TAU-D | JUN | 1 | TAU-D | APR | 15 | GEM-D |
| MAY | 31 | CAN-R | MAY | 14 | GEM-D | JUN | 27 | GEM-D | MAY | 11 | CAN-D |
| JUN | 23 | GEM-R | JUN | 7 | CAN-D | JUL | 23 | CAN-D | JUN | 7 | LEO-D |
| JUL | 13 | GEM-D | JUL | 2 | LEO-D | AUG | 16 | LEO-D | JUL | 9 | VIR-D |
| AUG | 5 | CAN-D | JUL | 26 | VIR-D | SEP | 10 | VIR-D | AUG | 10 | VIR-R |
| SEP | 9 | LEO-D | AUG | 20 | LIB-D | OCT | 4 | LIB-D | SEP | 21 | LEO-R |
| OCT | 6 | VIR-D | SEP | 15 | SCO-D | OCT | 28 | SCO-D | SEP | 22 | LEO-D |
| NOV | 1 | LIB-D | OCT | 10 | SAG-D | NOV | 21 | SAG-D | SEP | 25 | VIR-D |
| NOV | 26 | SCO-D | NOV | 6 | CAP-D | DEC | 15 | CAP-D | NOV | 10 | LIB-D |
| DEC | 20 | SAG-D | DEC | 7 | AQU-D | | | | DEC | 8 | SCO-D |

| 1960 | | | 1961 | | | 1962 | | | 1963 | | |
|---|---|---|---|---|---|---|---|---|---|---|---|
| JAN | 3 | SAG-D | JAN | 5 | PIS-D | JAN | 22 | AQU-D | JAN | 7 | SAG-D |
| JAN | 27 | CAP-D | FEB | 2 | ARI-D | FEB | 15 | PIS-D | FEB | 6 | CAP-D |
| FEB | 21 | AQU-D | MAR | 20 | ARI-R | MAR | 11 | ARI-D | MAR | 5 | AQU-D |
| MAR | 16 | PIS-D | MAY | 2 | ARI-D | APR | 4 | TAU-D | MAR | 30 | PIS-D |
| APR | 10 | ARI-D | JUN | 6 | TAU-D | APR | 29 | GEM-D | APR | 24 | ARI-D |
| MAY | 4 | TAU-D | JUL | 7 | GEM-D | MAY | 23 | CAN-D | MAY | 19 | TAU-D |
| MAY | 29 | GEM-D | AUG | 4 | CAN-D | JUN | 18 | LEO-D | JUN | 13 | GEM-D |
| JUN | 22 | CAN-D | AUG | 29 | LEO-D | JUL | 13 | VIR-D | JUL | 8 | CAN-D |
| JUL | 16 | LEO-D | OCT | 18 | LIB-D | AUG | 9 | LIB-D | AUG | 1 | LEO-D |
| AUG | 10 | VIR-D | NOV | 12 | SCO-D | SEP | 6 | SCO-D | AUG | 26 | VIR-D |
| SEP | 3 | LIB-D | DEC | 5 | SAG-D | OCT | 23 | SCO-R | SEP | 19 | LIB-D |
| SEP | 27 | SCO-D | DEC | 29 | CAP-D | DEC | 3 | SCO-D | OCT | 13 | SCO-D |
| OCT | 22 | SAG-D | | | | | | | NOV | 6 | SAG-D |
| NOV | 15 | CAP-D | | | | | | | NOV | 30 | CAP-D |
| DEC | 10 | AQU-D | | | | | | | DEC | 24 | AQU-D |

# Venus Signs 1945-2025

| 1964 | | | 1965 | | | 1966 | | | 1967 | | |
|------|-----|-------|------|-----|-------|------|-----|-------|------|-----|-------|
| JAN | 17 | PIS-D | JAN | 13 | CAP-D | JAN | 5 | AQU-R | JAN | 7 | AQU-D |
| FEB | 11 | ARI-D | FEB | 6 | AQU-D | JAN | 15 | CAP-R | JAN | 31 | PIS-D |
| MAR | 8 | TAU-D | MAR | 2 | PIS-D | FEB | 7 | CAP-D | FEB | 24 | ARI-D |
| APR | 4 | GEM-D | MAR | 26 | ARI-D | FEB | 26 | AQU-D | MAR | 21 | TAU-D |
| MAY | 9 | CAN-D | APR | 19 | TAU-D | APR | 7 | PIS-D | APR | 15 | GEM-D |
| MAY | 29 | CAN-R | MAY | 13 | GEM-D | MAY | 5 | ARI-D | MAY | 11 | CAN-D |
| JUN | 18 | GEM-R | JUN | 7 | CAN-D | JUN | 1 | TAU-D | JUN | 7 | LEO-D |
| JUL | 11 | GEM-D | JUL | 1 | LEO-D | JUN | 27 | GEM-D | JUL | 9 | VIR-D |
| AUG | 6 | CAN-D | JUL | 26 | VIR-D | JUL | 22 | CAN-D | AUG | 8 | VIR-R |
| SEP | 8 | LEO-D | AUG | 20 | LIB-D | AUG | 16 | LEO-D | SEP | 9 | LEO-R |
| OCT | 6 | VIR-D | SEP | 14 | SCO-D | SEP | 9 | VIR-D | SEP | 21 | LEO-D |
| NOV | 1 | LIB-D | OCT | 10 | SAG-D | OCT | 3 | LIB-D | OCT | 2 | LIB-D |
| NOV | 25 | SCO-D | NOV | 6 | CAP-D | OCT | 27 | SCO-D | NOV | 10 | LIB-D |
| DEC | 20 | SAG-D | DEC | 7 | AQU-D | NOV | 20 | SAG-D | DEC | 8 | SCO-D |
| | | | | | | DEC | 14 | CAP-D | | | |

| 1968 | | | 1969 | | | 1970 | | | 1971 | | |
|------|-----|-------|------|-----|-------|------|-----|-------|------|-----|-------|
| JAN | 2 | SAG-D | JAN | 5 | PIS-D | JAN | 22 | AQU-D | JAN | 7 | SAG-D |
| JAN | 27 | CAP-D | FEB | 2 | ARI-D | FEB | 14 | PIS-D | FEB | 6 | CAP-D |
| FEB | 20 | AQU-D | MAR | 18 | ARI-R | MAR | 11 | ARI-D | MAR | 4 | AQU-D |
| MAR | 16 | PIS-D | APR | 29 | ARI-D | APR | 4 | TAU-D | MAR | 30 | PIS-D |
| APR | 9 | ARI-D | JUN | 6 | TAU-D | APR | 28 | GEM-D | APR | 24 | ARI-D |
| MAY | 4 | TAU-D | JUL | 7 | GEM-D | MAY | 23 | CAN-D | MAY | 19 | TAU-D |
| MAY | 28 | GEM-D | AUG | 4 | CAN-D | JUN | 17 | LEO-D | JUN | 13 | GEM-D |
| JUN | 21 | CAN-D | AUG | 29 | LEO-D | JUL | 13 | VIR-D | JUL | 7 | CAN-D |
| JUL | 16 | LEO-D | SEP | 23 | VIR-D | AUG | 9 | LIB-D | AUG | 1 | LEO-D |
| AUG | 9 | VIR-D | OCT | 18 | LIB-D | SEP | 7 | SCO-D | AUG | 25 | VIR-D |
| SEP | 3 | LIB-D | NOV | 11 | SCO-D | OCT | 20 | SCO-R | SEP | 18 | LIB-D |
| SEP | 27 | SCO-D | DEC | 5 | SAG-D | DEC | 2 | SCO-D | OCT | 12 | SCO-D |
| OCT | 22 | SAG-D | DEC | 29 | CAP-D | | | | NOV | 5 | SAG-D |
| NOV | 15 | CAP-D | | | | | | | NOV | 29 | CAP-D |
| DEC | 10 | AQU-D | | | | | | | DEC | 24 | AQU-D |

| 1972 | | | 1973 | | | 1974 | | | 1975 | | |
|------|-----|-------|------|-----|-------|------|-----|-------|------|-----|-------|
| JAN | 17 | PIS-D | JAN | 12 | CAP-D | JAN | 3 | AQU-R | JAN | 7 | AQU-D |
| FEB | 11 | ARI-D | FEB | 5 | AQU-D | JAN | 30 | CAP-R | JAN | 31 | PIS-D |
| MAR | 7 | TAU-D | MAR | 1 | PIS-D | FEB | 13 | CAP-D | FEB | 24 | ARI-D |
| APR | 4 | GEM-D | MAR | 25 | ARI-D | MAR | 1 | AQU-D | MAR | 20 | TAU-D |
| MAY | 10 | CAN-D | APR | 18 | TAU-D | APR | 7 | PIS-D | APR | 14 | GEM-D |
| MAY | 27 | CAN-R | MAY | 13 | GEM-D | MAY | 5 | ARI-D | MAY | 10 | CAN-D |
| JUN | 12 | GEM-R | JUN | 6 | CAN-D | JUN | 1 | TAU-D | JUN | 7 | LEO-D |
| JUL | 9 | GEM-D | JUL | 1 | LEO-D | JUN | 26 | GEM-D | JUL | 10 | VIR-D |
| AUG | 6 | CAN-D | JUL | 25 | VIR-D | JUL | 21 | CAN-D | AUG | 6 | VIR-R |
| SEP | 8 | LEO-D | AUG | 19 | LIB-D | AUG | 15 | LEO-D | SEP | 3 | LEO-R |
| OCT | 6 | VIR-D | SEP | 14 | SCO-D | SEP | 9 | VIR-D | SEP | 18 | LEO-D |
| OCT | 31 | LIB-D | OCT | 10 | SAG-D | OCT | 3 | LIB-D | OCT | 5 | VIR-D |
| NOV | 25 | SCO-D | NOV | 6 | CAP-D | OCT | 27 | SCO-D | NOV | 10 | LIB-D |
| DEC | 19 | SAG-D | DEC | 7 | AQU-D | NOV | 20 | SAG-D | DEC | 7 | SCO-D |
| | | | | | | DEC | 14 | CAP-D | | | |

| 1976 | | | 1977 | | | 1978 | | | 1979 | | |
|------|-----|-------|------|-----|-------|------|-----|-------|------|-----|-------|
| JAN | 2 | SAG-D | JAN | 5 | PIS-D | JAN | 21 | AQU-D | JAN | 8 | SAG-D |
| JAN | 27 | CAP-D | FEB | 3 | ARI-D | FEB | 14 | PIS-D | FEB | 6 | CAP-D |
| FEB | 20 | AQU-D | MAR | 16 | ARI-R | MAR | 10 | ARI-D | MAR | 4 | AQU-D |
| MAR | 15 | PIS-D | APR | 27 | ARI-D | APR | 3 | TAU-D | MAR | 29 | PIS-D |
| APR | 9 | ARI-D | JUN | 7 | TAU-D | APR | 28 | GEM-D | APR | 23 | ARI-D |
| MAY | 3 | TAU-D | JUL | 7 | GEM-D | MAY | 22 | CAN-D | MAY | 18 | TAU-D |
| MAY | 27 | GEM-D | AUG | 3 | CAN-D | JUN | 17 | LEO-D | JUN | 12 | GEM-D |
| JUN | 21 | CAN-D | AUG | 29 | LEO-D | JUL | 12 | VIR-D | JUL | 7 | CAN-D |
| JUL | 14 | LEO-D | SEP | 23 | VIR-D | AUG | 8 | LIB-D | JUL | 31 | LEO-D |
| AUG | 9 | VIR-D | OCT | 17 | LIB-D | SEP | 8 | SCO-D | AUG | 24 | VIR-D |
| SEP | 2 | LIB-D | NOV | 10 | SCO-D | OCT | 18 | SCO-R | SEP | 18 | LIB-D |
| OCT | 21 | SAG-D | DEC | 4 | SAG-D | NOV | 28 | SCO-D | OCT | 12 | SCO-D |
| NOV | 15 | CAP-D | DEC | 28 | CAP-D | | | | NOV | 5 | SAG-D |
| DEC | 10 | AQU-D | | | | | | | NOV | 29 | CAP-D |
| | | | | | | | | | DEC | 23 | AQU-D |

# Venus Signs 1945-2025

| 1980 | | | 1981 | | | 1982 | | | 1983 | | |
|---|---|---|---|---|---|---|---|---|---|---|---|
| | JAN 16 | PIS-D | | JAN 11 | CAP-D | | JAN 24 | CAP-R | | JAN 6 | AQU-D |
| | FEB 10 | ARI-D | | FEB 5 | AQU-D | | FEB 10 | CAP-D | | JAN 30 | PIS-D |
| | MAR 7 | TAU-D | | MAR 1 | PIS-D | | MAR 3 | AQU-D | | FEB 23 | ARI-D |
| | APR 4 | GEM-D | | MAR 25 | ARI-D | | APR 7 | PIS-D | | MAR 20 | TAU-D |
| | MAY 13 | CAN-D | | APR 18 | TAU-D | | MAY 5 | ARI-D | | APR 14 | GEM-D |
| | MAY 24 | CAN-R | | MAY 12 | GEM-D | | MAY 31 | TAU-D | | MAY 10 | CAN-D |
| | JUN 6 | CAN-D | | JUN 6 | CAN-D | | JUN 26 | GEM-D | | JUN 7 | LEO-D |
| | JUL 6 | GEM-D | | JUN 30 | LEO-D | | JUL 21 | CAN-D | | JUL 11 | VIR-D |
| | AUG 7 | CAN-D | | JUL 25 | VIR-D | | AUG 15 | LEO-D | | AUG 3 | VIR-R |
| | SEP 8 | LEO-D | | AUG 19 | LIB-D | | SEP 8 | VIR-D | | AUG 27 | LEO-R |
| | OCT 5 | VIR-D | | SEP 13 | SCO-D | | OCT 2 | LIB-D | | SEP 15 | LEO-D |
| | OCT 31 | LIB-D | | OCT 9 | SAG-D | | NOV 19 | SAG-D | | OCT 6 | VIR-D |
| | NOV 24 | SCO-D | | NOV 6 | CAP-D | | DEC 13 | CAP-D | | NOV 10 | LIB-D |
| | DEC 19 | SAG-D | | DEC 9 | AQU-D | | | | | DEC 7 | SCO-D |
| | | | | DEC 31 | AQU-R | | | | | | |

| 1984 | | | 1985 | | | 1986 | | | 1987 | | |
|---|---|---|---|---|---|---|---|---|---|---|---|
| | JAN 1 | SAG-D | | JAN 5 | PIS-D | | JAN 21 | AQU-D | | JAN 8 | SAG-D |
| | JAN 26 | CAP-D | | FEB 3 | ARI-D | | FEB 13 | PIS-D | | FEB 5 | CAP-D |
| | FEB 19 | AQU-D | | MAR 13 | ARI-R | | MAR 9 | ARI-D | | MAR 4 | AQU-D |
| | MAR 15 | PIS-D | | APR 25 | ARI-D | | APR 3 | TAU-D | | MAR 29 | PIS-D |
| | APR 8 | ARI-D | | JUN 7 | TAU-D | | APR 27 | GEM-D | | APR 23 | ARI-D |
| | MAY 2 | TAU-D | | JUL 7 | GEM-D | | MAY 21 | CAN-D | | MAY 18 | TAU-D |
| | MAY 27 | GEM-D | | AUG 3 | CAN-D | | JUN 16 | LEO-D | | JUN 12 | GEM-D |
| | JUN 20 | CAN-D | | AUG 28 | LEO-D | | JUL 12 | VIR-D | | JUL 6 | CAN-D |
| | JUL 15 | LEO-D | | SEP 22 | VIR-D | | AUG 8 | LIB-D | | JUL 31 | LEO-D |
| | AUG 8 | VIR-D | | OCT 17 | LIB-D | | SEP 8 | SCO-D | | AUG 24 | VIR-D |
| | SEP 1 | LIB-D | | NOV 10 | SCO-D | | OCT 15 | SCO-R | | SEP 17 | LIB-D |
| | SEP 26 | SCO-D | | DEC 4 | SAG-D | | NOV 26 | SCO-D | | OCT 11 | SCO-D |
| | OCT 21 | SAG-D | | DEC 28 | CAP-D | | | | | NOV 4 | SAG-D |
| | NOV 14 | CAP-D | | | | | | | | NOV 28 | CAP-D |
| | DEC 9 | AQU-D | | | | | | | | DEC 23 | AQU-D |

| 1988 | | | 1989 | | | 1990 | | | 1991 | | |
|---|---|---|---|---|---|---|---|---|---|---|---|
| | JAN 16 | PIS-D | | JAN 11 | CAP-D | | JAN 17 | CAP-R | | JAN 5 | AQU-D |
| | FEB 10 | ARI-D | | FEB 4 | AQU-D | | FEB 8 | CAP-D | | JAN 29 | PIS-D |
| | MAR 7 | TAU-D | | FEB 28 | PIS-D | | MAR 4 | AQU-D | | FEB 23 | ARI-D |
| | APR 4 | GEM-D | | MAR 24 | ARI-D | | APR 7 | PIS-D | | MAR 19 | TAU-D |
| | MAY 18 | CAN-D | | APR 17 | TAU-D | | MAY 4 | ARI-D | | APR 13 | GEM-D |
| | MAY 22 | CAN-R | | MAY 12 | GEM-D | | MAY 31 | TAU-D | | MAY 9 | CAN-D |
| | MAY 28 | GEM-R | | JUN 5 | CAN-D | | JUN 25 | GEM-D | | JUN 6 | LEO-D |
| | JUL 4 | GEM-D | | JUN 30 | LEO-D | | JUL 20 | CAN-D | | JUL 12 | VIR-D |
| | AUG 7 | CAN-D | | JUL 24 | VIR-D | | AUG 14 | LEO-D | | AUG 1 | VIR-R |
| | SEP 8 | LEO-D | | AUG 18 | LIB-D | | SEP 8 | VIR-D | | AUG 22 | LEO-R |
| | OCT 5 | VIR-D | | SEP 13 | SCO-D | | OCT 2 | LIB-D | | SEP 13 | LEO-D |
| | OCT 30 | LIB-D | | OCT 9 | SAG-D | | OCT 26 | SCO-D | | OCT 7 | VIR-D |
| | NOV 24 | SCO-D | | NOV 6 | CAP-D | | NOV 19 | SAG-D | | NOV 10 | LIB-D |
| | DEC 18 | SAG-D | | DEC 10 | AQU-D | | DEC 13 | CAP-D | | DEC 7 | SCO-D |
| | | | | DEC 29 | AQU-R | | | | | | |

| 1992 | | | 1993 | | | 1994 | | | 1995 | | |
|---|---|---|---|---|---|---|---|---|---|---|---|
| | JAN 1 | SAG-D | | JAN 4 | PIS-D | | JAN 20 | AQU-D | | JAN 8 | SAG-D |
| | JAN 26 | CAP-D | | FEB 3 | ARI-D | | FEB 13 | PIS-D | | FEB 5 | CAP-D |
| | FEB 19 | AQU-D | | MAR 11 | ARI-R | | MAR 9 | ARI-D | | MAR 3 | AQU-D |
| | MAR 14 | PIS-D | | APR 22 | ARI-D | | APR 2 | TAU-D | | MAR 29 | PIS-D |
| | APR 8 | ARI-D | | JUN 6 | TAU-D | | APR 27 | GEM-D | | APR 22 | ARI-D |
| | MAY 2 | TAU-D | | JUL 6 | GEM-D | | MAY 21 | CAN-D | | MAY 17 | TAU-D |
| | MAY 26 | GEM-D | | AUG 2 | CAN-D | | JUN 16 | LEO-D | | JUN 11 | GEM-D |
| | JUN 20 | CAN-D | | AUG 28 | LEO-D | | JUL 12 | VIR-D | | JUN 6 | CAN-D |
| | JUL 14 | LEO-D | | SEP 22 | VIR-D | | AUG 8 | LIB-D | | JUL 30 | LEO-D |
| | AUG 8 | VIR-D | | OCT 16 | LIB-D | | SEP 8 | SCO-D | | AUG 23 | VIR-D |
| | SEP 1 | LIB-D | | NOV 9 | SCO-D | | OCT 13 | SCO-R | | SEP 16 | LIB-D |
| | SEP 25 | SCO-D | | DEC 3 | SAG-D | | NOV 23 | SCO-D | | OCT 11 | SCO-D |
| | OCT 20 | SAG-D | | DEC 27 | CAP-D | | | | | NOV 4 | SAG-D |
| | NOV 14 | CAP-D | | | | | | | | NOV 28 | CAP-D |
| | DEC 9 | AQU-D | | | | | | | | DEC 22 | AQU-D |

# Venus Signs 1945-2025

| 1996 | | | 1997 | | | 1998 | | | 1999 | | |
|---|---|---|---|---|---|---|---|---|---|---|---|
| JAN | 15 | PIS-D | JAN | 11 | CAP-D | JAN | 10 | CAP-R | JAN | 5 | AQU-D |
| FEB | 9 | ARI-D | FEB | 3 | AQU-D | FEB | 5 | CAP-D | JAN | 29 | PIS-D |
| MAR | 6 | TAU-D | FEB | 27 | PIS-D | MAR | 5 | AQU-D | FEB | 22 | ARI-D |
| APR | 4 | GEM-D | MAR | 24 | ARI-D | APR | 7 | PIS-D | MAR | 19 | TAU-D |
| MAY | 20 | GEM-R | APR | 17 | TAU-D | MAY | 4 | ARI-D | APR | 13 | GEM-D |
| JUL | 2 | GEM-D | MAY | 11 | GEM-D | MAY | 30 | TAU-D | MAY | 9 | CAN-D |
| AUG | 8 | CAN-D | JUN | 4 | CAN-D | JUN | 25 | GEM-D | JUN | 6 | LEO-D |
| SEP | 7 | LEO-D | JUN | 29 | LEO-D | JUL | 20 | CAN-D | JUL | 13 | VIR-D |
| OCT | 4 | VIR-D | JUL | 24 | VIR-D | AUG | 14 | LEO-D | JUL | 30 | VIR-R |
| OCT | 30 | LIB-D | AUG | 18 | LIB-D | SEP | 7 | VIR-D | AUG | 16 | LEO-R |
| NOV | 23 | SCO-D | SEP | 12 | SCO-D | OCT | 1 | LIB-D | SEP | 11 | LEO-D |
| DEC | 18 | SAG-D | OCT | 9 | SAG-D | OCT | 25 | SCO-D | OCT | 8 | VIR-D |
| | | | NOV | 6 | CAP-D | NOV | 18 | SAG-D | NOV | 9 | LIB-D |
| | | | DEC | 12 | AQU-D | DEC | 12 | CAP-D | DEC | 6 | SCO-D |
| | | | DEC | 26 | AQU-R | | | | DEC | 31 | SAG-D |

| 2000 | | | 2001 | | | 2002 | | | 2003 | | |
|---|---|---|---|---|---|---|---|---|---|---|---|
| JAN | 25 | CAP-D | JAN | 4 | PIS-D | JAN | 19 | AQU-D | JAN | 8 | SAG-D |
| FEB | 18 | AQU-D | FEB | 3 | ARI-D | FEB | 12 | PIS-D | FEB | 5 | CAP-D |
| MAR | 14 | PIS-D | MAR | 9 | ARI-R | MAR | 8 | ARI-D | MAR | 3 | AQU-D |
| APR | 7 | ARI-D | APR | 20 | ARI-D | APR | 2 | TAU-D | MAR | 28 | PIS-D |
| MAY | 1 | TAU-D | JUN | 7 | TAU-D | APR | 26 | GEM-D | APR | 22 | ARI-D |
| MAY | 26 | GEM-D | JUL | 6 | GEM-D | MAY | 21 | CAN-D | MAY | 17 | TAU-D |
| JUN | 19 | CAN-D | AUG | 2 | CAN-D | JUN | 15 | LEO-D | JUN | 10 | GEM-D |
| JUL | 14 | LEO-D | AUG | 27 | LEO-D | JUL | 11 | VIR-D | JUL | 5 | CAN-D |
| AUG | 7 | VIR-D | SEP | 21 | VIR-D | AUG | 8 | LIB-D | JUL | 29 | LEO-D |
| AUG | 31 | LIB-D | OCT | 16 | LIB-D | SEP | 8 | SCO-D | UG | 23 | VIR-D |
| SEP | 25 | SCO-D | NOV | 9 | SCO-D | OCT | 10 | SCO-R | SEP | 16 | LIB-D |
| OCT | 20 | SAG-D | DEC | 3 | SAG-D | NOV | 21 | SCO-D | OCT | 10 | SCO-D |
| NOV | 13 | CAP-D | DEC | 27 | CAP-D | | | | NOV | 3 | SAG-D |
| DEC | 9 | AQU-D | | | | | | | NOV | 27 | CAP-D |
| | | | | | | | | | DEC | 22 | AQU-D |

| 2004 | | | 2005 | | | 2006 | | | 2007 | | |
|---|---|---|---|---|---|---|---|---|---|---|---|
| JAN | 15 | PIS-D | JAN | 10 | CAP-D | JAN | 2 | CAP-R | JAN | 4 | AQU-D |
| FEB | 9 | ARI-D | FEB | 3 | AQU-D | FEB | 3 | CAP-D | JAN | 28 | PIS-D |
| MAR | 6 | TAU-D | FEB | 27 | PIS-D | MAR | 5 | AQU-D | FEB | 22 | ARI-D |
| APR | 4 | GEM-D | MAR | 23 | ARI-D | APR | 6 | PIS-D | MAR | 18 | TAU-D |
| MAY | 17 | GEM-R | APR | 16 | TAU-D | MAY | 4 | ARI-D | APR | 12 | GEM-D |
| JUN | 29 | GEM-D | MAY | 10 | GEM-D | MAY | 30 | TAU-D | MAY | 9 | CAN-D |
| AUG | 8 | CAN-D | JUN | 4 | CAN-D | JUN | 24 | GEM-D | JUN | 6 | LEO-D |
| SEP | 7 | LEO-D | JUN | 29 | LEO-D | JUL | 19 | CAN-D | JUL | 15 | VIR-D |
| OCT | 4 | VIR-D | JUL | 23 | VIR-D | AUG | 13 | LEO-D | JUL | 27 | VIR-R |
| OCT | 29 | LIB-D | AUG | 17 | LIB-D | SEP | 7 | VIR-D | AUG | 9 | LEO-R |
| NOV | 23 | SCO-D | SEP | 12 | SCO-D | OCT | 1 | LIB-D | SEP | 8 | LEO-D |
| DEC | 17 | SAG-D | OCT | 8 | SAG-D | OCT | 25 | SCO-D | OCT | 9 | VIR-D |
| | | | NOV | 6 | CAP-D | NOV | 18 | SAG-D | NOV | 9 | LIB-D |
| | | | DEC | 15 | AQU-D | DEC | 12 | cAP-D | DEC | 6 | SCO-D |
| | | | DEC | 24 | AQU-R | | | | DEC | 31 | SAG-D |

| 2008 | | | 2009 | | | 2010 | | | 2011 | | |
|---|---|---|---|---|---|---|---|---|---|---|---|
| JAN | 25 | CAP-D | JAN | 4 | PIS-D | JAN | 19 | AQU-D | JAN | 8 | SAG-D |
| FEB | 18 | AQU-D | FEB | 3 | ARI-D | FEB | 12 | PIS-D | FEB | 5 | CAP-D |
| MAR | 13 | PIS-D | MAR | 6 | ARI-R | MAR | 8 | ARI-D | MAR | 2 | AQU-D |
| APR | 7 | ARI-D | APR | 12 | PIS-R | APR | 1 | TAU-D | MAR | 28 | PIS-D |
| MAY | 1 | TAU-D | APR | 17 | PIS-D | APR | 25 | GEM-D | APR | 21 | ARI-D |
| MAY | 25 | GEM-D | APR | 25 | ARI-D | MAY | 20 | CAN-D | MAY | 15 | TAU-D |
| JUN | 19 | CAN-D | JUN | 7 | TAU-D | JUN | 15 | LEO-D | JUN | 10 | GEM-D |
| JUL | 13 | LEO-D | JUL | 6 | GEM-D | JUL | 11 | VIR-D | JUL | 4 | CAN-D |
| AUG | 6 | VIR-D | AUG | 1 | CAN-D | AUG | 7 | LIB-D | JUL | 29 | LEO-D |
| AUG | 31 | LIB-D | AUG | 27 | LEO-D | SEP | 9 | SCO-D | AUG | 22 | VIR-D |
| SEP | 24 | SCO-D | SEP | 21 | VIR-D | OCT | 8 | SCO-R | SEP | 15 | LIB-D |
| OCT | 19 | SAG-D | OCT | 15 | LIB-D | NOV | 8 | LIB-R | OCT | 10 | SCO-D |
| NOV | 13 | CAP-D | NOV | 8 | SCO-D | NOV | 18 | LIB-D | NOV | 3 | SAG-D |
| DEC | 8 | AQU-D | DEC | 2 | SAG-D | NOV | 30 | SCO-D | NOV | 27 | CAP-D |
| | | | DEC | 26 | CAP-D | | | | DEC | 21 | AQU-D |

# Venus Signs 1945-2025

| 2012 | | | | 2013 | | | | 2014 | | | | 2015 | | | |
|------|-----|----|-------|------|-----|----|-------|------|-----|----|-------|------|-----|----|-------|
| | JAN | 15 | PIS-D | | JAN | 9 | CAP-D | | JAN | 31 | CAP-D | | JAN | 4 | AQU-D |
| | FEB | 9 | ARI-D | | FEB | 2 | AQU-D | | MAR | 6 | AQU-D | | JAN | 28 | PIS-D |
| | MAR | 6 | TAU-D | | FEB | 26 | PIS-D | | APR | 6 | PIS-D | | FEB | 21 | ARI-D |
| | APR | 4 | GEM-D | | MAR | 22 | ARI-D | | MAY | 3 | ARI-D | | MAR | 18 | TAU-D |
| | MAY | 15 | GEM-R | | APR | 16 | TAU-D | | MAY | 29 | TAU-D | | APR | 12 | GEM-D |
| | JUN | 27 | GEM-D | | MAY | 10 | GEM-D | | JUN | 24 | GEM-D | | MAY | 8 | CAN-D |
| | AUG | 8 | CAN-D | | JUN | 3 | CAN-D | | JUL | 19 | CAN-D | | JUN | 6 | LEO-D |
| | SEP | 7 | LEO-D | | JUN | 28 | LEO-D | | AUG | 13 | LEO-D | | JUL | 19 | VIR-D |
| | OCT | 4 | VIR-D | | JUL | 23 | VIR-D | | SEP | 6 | VIR-D | | JUL | 25 | VIR-R |
| | OCT | 29 | LIB-D | | AUG | 17 | LIB-D | | SEP | 30 | LIB-D | | AUG | 1 | LEO-R |
| | NOV | 22 | SCO-D | | SEP | 12 | SCO-D | | OCT | 24 | SCO-D | | SEP | 6 | LEO-D |
| | DEC | 16 | SAG-D | | OCT | 8 | SAG-D | | NOV | 17 | SAG-D | | OCT | 9 | VIR-D |
| | | | | | NOV | 6 | CAP-D | | DEC | 11 | CAP-D | | NOV | 9 | LIB-D |
| | | | | | DEC | 21 | CAP-R | | | | | | DEC | 5 | SCO-D |
| | | | | | | | | | | | | | DEC | 31 | SAG-D |

| 2016 | | | | 2017 | | | | 2018 | | | | 2019 | | | |
|------|-----|----|-------|------|-----|----|-------|------|-----|----|-------|------|-----|----|-------|
| | JAN | 24 | CAP-D | | JAN | 4 | PIS-D | | JAN | 18 | AQU-D | | JAN | 8 | SAG-D |
| | FEB | 17 | AQU-D | | FEB | 4 | ARI-D | | FEB | 11 | PIS-D | | FEB | 4 | CAP-D |
| | MAR | 13 | PIS-D | | MAR | 4 | ARI-R | | MAR | 7 | ARI-D | | MAR | 2 | AQU-D |
| | APR | 6 | ARI-D | | APR | 3 | PIS-R | | MAR | 31 | TAU-D | | MAR | 27 | PIS-D |
| | APR | 30 | TAU-D | | APR | 15 | PIS-D | | APR | 25 | GEM-D | | APR | 21 | ARI-D |
| | MAY | 25 | GEM-D | | APR | 29 | ARI-D | | MAY | 20 | CAN-D | | MAY | 16 | TAU-D |
| | JUN | 18 | CAN-D | | JUN | 7 | TAU-D | | JUN | 14 | LEO-D | | JUN | 9 | GEM-D |
| | JUL | 13 | LEO-D | | JUL | 5 | GEM-D | | JUL | 10 | VIR-D | | JUL | 4 | CAN-D |
| | AUG | 6 | VIR-D | | AUG | 1 | CAN-D | | AUG | 7 | LIB-D | | JUL | 28 | LEO-D |
| | AUG | 30 | LIB-D | | AUG | 26 | LEO-D | | SEP | 10 | SCO-D | | AUG | 22 | VIR-D |
| | SEP | 24 | SCO-D | | SEP | 20 | VIR-D | | OCT | 5 | SCO-R | | SEP | 15 | LIB-D |
| | OCT | 19 | SAG-D | | OCT | 15 | LIB-D | | NOV | 1 | LIB-R | | OCT | 9 | SCO-D |
| | NOV | 12 | CAP-D | | NOV | 8 | SCO-D | | NOV | 16 | LIB-D | | NOV | 2 | SAG-D |
| | DEC | 8 | AQU-D | | DEC | 2 | SAG-D | | DEC | 3 | SCO-D | | NOV | 26 | CAP-D |
| | | | | | DEC | 26 | CAP-D | | | | | | DEC | 21 | AQU-D |

| 2020 | | | | 2021 | | | | 2022 | | | | 2023 | | | |
|------|-----|----|-------|------|-----|----|-------|------|-----|----|-------|------|-----|----|-------|
| | JAN | 14 | PIS-D | | JAN | 9 | CAP-D | | JAN | 30 | CAP-D | | JAN | 3 | AQU-D |
| | FEB | 8 | ARI-D | | FEB | 2 | AQU-D | | MAR | 7 | AQU-D | | JAN | 27 | PIS-D |
| | MAR | 5 | TAU-D | | FEB | 26 | PIS-D | | APR | 6 | PIS-D | | FEB | 21 | ARI-D |
| | APR | 4 | GEM-D | | MAR | 22 | ARI-D | | MAY | 3 | ARI-D | | MAR | 17 | TAU-D |
| | MAY | 13 | GEM-R | | APR | 15 | TAU-D | | MAY | 29 | TAU-D | | APR | 11 | GEM-D |
| | JUN | 25 | GEM-D | | MAY | 9 | GEM-D | | JUN | 23 | GEM-D | | MAY | 8 | CAN-D |
| | AUG | 8 | cAN-D | | JUN | 3 | CAN-D | | JUL | 18 | CAN-D | | JUN | 6 | LEO-D |
| | SEP | 7 | LEO-D | | JUN | 27 | LEO-D | | AUG | 12 | LEO-D | | JUL | 23 | LEO-R |
| | OCT | 3 | VIR-D | | JUL | 22 | VIR-D | | SEP | 5 | VIR-D | | SEP | 4 | LEO-D |
| | OCT | 28 | LIB-D | | AUG | 16 | LIB-D | | SEP | 30 | LIB-D | | OCT | 9 | VIR-D |
| | NOV | 22 | SCO-D | | SEP | 11 | SCO-D | | OCT | 24 | SCO-D | | NOV | 9 | LIB-D |
| | DEC | 16 | SAG-D | | OCT | 8 | SAG-D | | NOV | 17 | SAG-D | | DEC | 5 | SCO-D |
| | | | | | NOV | 6 | CAP-D | | DEC | 10 | CAP-D | | DEC | 30 | SAG-D |
| | | | | | DEC | 19 | CAP-R | | | | | | | | |

| 2024 | | | | 2025 | | | |
|------|-----|----|-------|------|-----|----|-------|
| | JAN | 24 | CAP-D | | JAN | 3 | PIS-D |
| | FEB | 17 | AQU-D | | FEB | 5 | ARI-D |
| | MAR | 12 | PIS-D | | MAR | 2 | ARI-R |
| | APR | 5 | ARI-D | | MAR | 28 | PIS-R |
| | APR | 30 | TAU-D | | APR | 13 | PIS-D |
| | MAY | 24 | GEM-D | | MAY | 1 | ARI-D |
| | JUN | 18 | CAN-D | | JUN | 6 | TAU-D |
| | JUL | 12 | LEO-D | | JUL | 5 | GEM-D |
| | AUG | 5 | VIR-D | | JUL | 31 | CAN-D |
| | AUG | 30 | LIB-D | | AUG | 26 | LEO-D |
| | SEP | 23 | SCO-D | | SEP | 20 | VIR-D |
| | OCT | 18 | SAG-D | | OCT | 14 | LIB-D |
| | NOV | 12 | CAP-D | | NOV | 7 | SCO-D |
| | DEC | 8 | AQU-D | | DEC | 1 | SAG-D |
| | | | | | DEC | 25 | CAP-D |

# How to Use Mars Tables

Find the page among the Mars Tables for the year of birth, then the month. The dates listed show when Mars moves into a sign. Mars stays in that sign until the next date listed. You will need to have your chart fully calculated by computer to know for sure just what time of day Mars changes signs, or turns retrograde or direct.

**Example:** In the year 1945, as shown below, Mars was in LEO-D on Nov. 12 (D meaning direct in motion). Mars turns R (retrograde) on Dec. 3, and continues retrograde until re-entering CAN Cancer on Dec. 27. So, Mars is in Leo from Nov. 12 to sometime during the day of Dec. 27. Mars continues in Cancer until APR April 23, 1946 when it re-enters Leo. Again, if the birthday you are looking up is on the day that Mars changes signs, the only way you can be absolutely sure of the correct Mars sign is to have an accurately calculated chart for based on the date, time and location of birth.

## Mars Signs 1945-2025

### Sign Abbreviations

| | | | |
|---|---|---|---|
| ARI | Aries | LIB | Libra |
| TAU | Taurus | SCO | Scorpio |
| GEM | Gemini | SAG | Sagittarius |
| CAN | Cancer | CAP | Capricorn |
| LEO | Leo | AQU | Aquarius |
| VIR | Virgo | PISC | Pisces |

| 1945 | 1946 | 1947 |
|---|---|---|
| JAN 5 CAP-D | FEB 21 CAN-D | JAN 26 AQU-D |
| FEB 15 AQU-D | APR 23 LEO-D | MAR 5 PIS-D |
| MAR 25 PIS-D | JUN 21 VIR-D | APR 12 ARI-D |
| MAY 3 ARI-D | AUG 10 LIB-D | MAY 22 TAU-D |
| JUN 12 TAU-D | SEP 25 SCO-D | JUL 2 GEM-D |
| JUL 24 GEM-D | NOV 7 SAG-D | AUG 14 CAN-D |
| SEP 8 CAN-D | DEC 18 CAP-D | OCT 2 LEO-D |
| NOV 12 LEO-D | | DEC 2 VIR-D |
| DEC 3 LEO-R | | |
| DEC 27 CAN-R | | |

| 1948 | 1949 | 1950 | 1951 | 1952 | 1953 |
|---|---|---|---|---|---|
| JAN 7 VIR-R | JAN 5 AQU-D | FEB 11 LIB-R | JAN 23 PIS-D | JAN 21 SCO-D | FEB 9 ARI-D |
| FEB 13 LEO-R | FEB 12 PIS-D | MAR 29 VIR-R | MAR 2 ARI-D | MAR 24 SCO-R | MAR 21 TAU-D |
| MAR 28 LEO-D | MAR 22 ARI-D | MAY 2 VIR-D | APR 11 TAU-D | JUN 9 SCO-D | MAY 2 GEM-D |
| MAY 19 VIR-D | MAY 1 TAU-D | JUN 12 LIB-D | MAY 22 GEM-D | AUG 28 SAG-D | JUN 15 CAN-D |
| JUL 18 LIB-D | JUN 11 GEM-D | AUG 11 SCO-D | JUL 4 CAN-D | OCT 13 CAP-D | JUL 30 LEO-D |
| SEP 4 SCO-D | JUL 24 CAN-D | SEP 26 SAG-D | AUG 19 LEO-D | NOV 22 AQU-D | SEP 15 VIR-D |
| OCT 18 SAG-D | SEP 8 LEO-D | NOV 7 CAP-D | OCT 6 VIR-D | DEC 31 PIS-D | NOV 2 LIB-D |
| NOV 27 CAP-D | OCT 28 VIR-D | DEC 16 AQU-D | NOV 25 LIB-D | | DEC 21 SCO-D |
| | DEC 27 LIB-D | | | | |

| 1954 | 1955 | 1956 | 1957 | 1958 | 1959 |
|---|---|---|---|---|---|
| FEB 10 SAG-D | JAN 16 ARI-D | JAN 15 SAG-D | JAN 29 TAU-D | FEB 4 CAP-D | FEB 11 GEM-D |
| APR 13 CAP-D | FEB 27 TAU-D | MAR 1 CAP-D | MAR 18 GEM-D | MAR 18 AQU-D | APR 11 CAN-D |
| MAY 22 CAP-R | APR 11 GEM-D | APR 15 AQU-D | MAY 5 CAN-D | APR 28 PIS-D | JUN 2 LEO-D |
| JUL 4 SAG-R | MAY 27 CAN-D | JUN 4 PIS-D | JUN 22 LEO-D | JUN 8 ARI-D | JUL 21 VIR-D |
| JUL 28 SAG-D | JUL 12 LEO-D | AUG 9 PIS-R | AUG 9 VIR-D | JUL 22 TAU-D | SEP 6 LIB-D |
| AUG 25 CAP-D | AUG 28 VIR-D | OCT 9 PIS-D | SEP 25 LIB-D | SEP 22 GEM-D | OCT 22 SCO-D |
| OCT 22 AQU-D | OCT 14 LIB-D | DEC 7 ARI-D | NOV 9 SCO-D | OCT 9 GEM-R | DEC 4 SAG-D |
| DEC 5 PIS-D | NOV 30 SCO-D | | DEC 24 SAG-D | OCT 30 TAU-R | |
| | | | | DEC 19 TAU-D | |

# Mars Signs 1945-2025

| 1960 | 1961 | 1962 | 1963 | 1964 | 1965 |
|------|------|------|------|------|------|
| JAN 15 CAP-D | FEB 5 GEM-R | FEB 2 AQU-D | MAR 15 LEO-D | JAN 14 AQU-D | JAN 27 VIR-R |
| FEB 24 AQU-D | FEB 6 GEM-D | MAR 13 PIS-D | JUN 4 VIR-D | FEB 21 PIS-D | APR 18 VIR-D |
| APR 3 PIS-D | FEB 8 CAN-D | APR 20 ARI-D | JUL 28 LIB-D | MAR 30 ARI-D | JUN 30 LIB-D |
| MAY 12 ARI-D | MAY 7 LEO-D | MAY 29 TAU-D | SEP 13 SCO-D | MAY 8 TAU-D | AUG 21 SCO-D |
| JUN 21 TAU-D | JUN 29 VIR-D | JUL 10 GEM-D | OCT 26 SAG-D | JUN 18 GEM-D | OCT 5 SAG-D |
| AUG 3 GEM-D | AUG 18 LIB-D | AUG 23 CAN-D | DEC 6 CAP-D | JUL 31 CAN-D | NOV 15 CAP-D |
| SEP 22 CAN-D | OCT 2 SCO-D | OCT 12 LEO-D | | SEP 16 LEO-D | DEC 24 AQU-D |
| NOV 19 CAN-R | NOV 14 SAG-D | DEC 25 LEO-R | | NOV 7 VIR-D | |
| | DEC 25 CAPD | | | | |

| 1966 | 1967 | 1968 | 1969 | 1970 | 1971 |
|------|------|------|------|------|------|
| JAN 31 PIS-D | FEB 13 SCO-D | JAN 10 PIS-D | FEB 26 SAG-D | JAN 25 ARI-D | JAN 24 SAG-D |
| MAR 10 ARI-D | MAR 7 SCO-R | FEB 18 ARI-D | APR 26 SAG-R | MAR 8 TAU-D | MAR 13 CAP-D |
| APR 18 TAU-D | APR 1 LIB-R | MAR 28 TAU-D | JUL 7 SAG-D | APR 19 GEM-D | MAY 4 AQU-D |
| MAY 29 GEM-D | MAY 27 LIB-D | MAY 9 GEM-D | SEP 22 CAP-D | JUN 3 CAN-D | JUL 10 AQU-R |
| JUL 12 CAN-D | JUL 20 SCO-D | JUN 22 CAN-D | NOV 5 AQU-D | JUL 19 LEO-D | SEP 8 AQU-D |
| AUG 26 LEO-D | SEP 11 SAG-D | AUG 6 LEO-D | DEC 16 PIS-D | SEP 4 VIR-D | NOV 7 PIS-D |
| OCT 13 VIR-D | OCT 24 CAP-D | SEP 22 VIR-D | | OCT 21 LIB-D | DEC 27 ARI-D |
| DEC 5 LIB-D | DEC 2 AQU-D | NOV 10 LIB-D | | DEC 7 SCO-D | |
| | | DEC 30 SCO-D | | | |

| 1972 | 1973 | 1974 | 1975 | 1976 | 1977 |
|------|------|------|------|------|------|
| FEB 11 TAU-D | FEB 13 CAP-D | FEB 28 GEM-D | JAN 22 CAP-D | JAN 19 GEM-D | JAN 2 CAP-D |
| MAR 28 GEM-D | MAR 27 AQU-D | APR 21 CAN-D | MAR 4 AQU-D | MAR 19 CAN-D | FEB 10 AQU-D |
| MAY 12 CAN-D | MAY 9 PIS-D | JUN 10 LEO-D | APR 12 PIS-D | MAY 17 LEO-D | MAR 21 PIS-D |
| JUN 29 LEO-D | JUN 21 ARI-D | JUL 28 VIR-D | MAY 22 ARI-D | JUL 7 VIR-D | APR 28 ARI-D |
| AUG 16 VIR-D | AUG 13 TAU-D | SEP 13 LIB-D | JUL 2 TAU-D | AUG 25 LIB-D | JUN 7 TAU-D |
| OCT 1 LIB-D | SEP 18 TAU-R | OCT 29 SCO-D | AUG 14 GEM-D | OCT 9 SCO-D | JUL 18 GEM-D |
| NOV 16 SCO-D | OCT 30 ARI-R | DEC 11 SAG-D | OCT 18 CAN-D | NOV 21 SAG-D | SEP 2 CAN-D |
| DEC 31 SAG-D | NOV 25 ARI-D | | NOV 5 CAN-R | | OCT 27 LEO-D |
| | DEC 25 TAU-D | | NOV 26 GEM-R | | DEC 11 LEO-R |

| 1978 | 1979 | 1980 | 1981 | 1982 | 1983 |
|------|------|------|------|------|------|
| JAN 27 CAN-R | JAN 21 AQU-D | JAN 15 VIR-R | FEB 7 PIS-D | FEB 19 LIB-R | JAN 18 PIS-D |
| MAR 1 CAN-D | FEB 28 PIS-D | MAR 12 LEO-R | MAR 18 ARI-D | MAY 10 LIB-D | FEB 26 ARI-D |
| APR 11 LEO-D | APR 8 ARI-D | APR 5 LEO-D | APR 26 TAU-D | AUG 4 SCO-D | APR 6 TAU-D |
| JUN 15 VIR-D | MAY 17 TAU-D | MAY 5 VIR-D | JUN 6 GEM-D | SEP 21 SAG-D | MAY 17 GEM-D |
| AUG 5 LIB-D | JUN 27 GEM-D | JUL 11 LIB-D | JUL 18 CAN-D | NOV 1 CAP-D | JUN 30 CAN-D |
| SEP 20 SCO-D | AUG 9 CAN-D | AUG 30 SCO-D | SEP 3 LEO-D | DEC 11 AQU-D | AUG 14 LEO-D |
| NOV 3 SAG-D | SEP 25 LEO-D | OCT 13 SAG-D | OCT 22 VIR-D | | OCT 1 VIR-D |
| DEC 13 CAP-D | NOV 20 VIR-D | NOV 23 CAP-D | DEC 17 LIB-D | | NOV 19 LIB-D |
| | | DEC 31 AQU-D | | | |

| 1984 | 1985 | 1986 | 1987 | 1988 | 1989 |
|------|------|------|------|------|------|
| JAN 12 SCO-D | FEB 3 ARI-D | FEB 3 SAG-D | JAN 9 ARI-D | JAN 9 SAG-D | JAN 20 TAU-D |
| APR 4 SCO-R | MAR 15 TAU-D | MAR 29 CAP-D | FEB 21 TAU-D | FEB 23 CAP-D | MAR 12 GEM-D |
| JUN 18 SCO-D | APR 27 GEM-D | JUN 7 CAP-R | APR 6 GEM-D | APR 7 AQU-D | APR 30 CAN-D |
| AUG 18 SAG-D | JUN 10 CAN-D | AUG 11 CAP-D | MAY 22 CAN-D | MAY 23 PIS-D | JUN 17 LEO-D |
| OCT 6 CAP-D | JUL 26 LEO-D | OCT 10 AQU-D | JUL 7 LEO-D | JUL 14 ARI-D | AUG 4 VIR-D |
| NOV 16 AQU-D | SEP 11 VIR-D | NOV 27 PIS-D | AUG 23 VIR-D | AUG 25 ARI-R | SEP 20 LIB-D |
| DEC 26 PIS-D | OCT 28 LIB-D | | OCT 9 LIB-D | OCT 24 PIS-R | NOV 5 SCO-D |
| | DEC 15 SCO-D | | NOV 25 SCO-D | OCT 27 PIS-D | DEC 19 SAG-D |
| | | | | NOV 2 ARI-D | |

# Mars Signs 1945-2025

| 1990 | 1991 | 1992 | 1993 | 1994 | 1995 |
|---|---|---|---|---|---|
| JAN 30 CAP-D | JAN 1 TAU-D | JAN 10 CAP-D | FEB 14 CAN-D | JAN 29 AQU-D | JAN 1 VIR-R |
| MAR 12 AQU-D | JAN 21 GEM-D | FEB 19 AQU-D | APR 28 LEO-D | MAR 8 PIS-D | JAN 23 LEO-R |
| APR 21 PIS-D | APR 4 CAN-D | MAR 29 PIS-D | JUN 24 VIR-D | APR 15 ARI-D | MAR 23 LEO-D |
| JUN 1 ARI-D | MAY 27 LEO-D | MAY 6 ARI-D | AUG 13 LIB-D | MAY 24 TAU-D | MAY 26 VIR-D |
| JUL 14 TAU-D | JUL 16 VIR-D | JUN 15 TAU-D | SEP 28 SCO-D | JUL 4 GEM-D | JUL 22 LIB-D |
| SEP 1 GEM-D | SEP 2 LIB-D | JUL 27 GEM-D | NOV 10 SAG-D | AUG 17 CAN-D | SEP 8 SCO-D |
| OCT 19 GEM-R | OCT 17 SCO-D | SEP 13 CAN-D | DEC 21 CAP-D | OCT 5 LEO-D | OCT 21 SAG-D |
| DEC 15 TAU-R | NOV 30 SAG-D | NOV 26 CAN-R | | DEC 13 VIR-D | DEC 1 CAP-D |

| 1996 | 1997 | 1998 | 1999 | 2000 | 2001 |
|---|---|---|---|---|---|
| JAN 9 AQU-D | JAN 4 LIB-D | JAN 26 PIS-D | JAN 27 SCO-D | JAN 5 PIS-D | FEB 14 SAG-D |
| FEB 16 PIS-D | FEB 5 LIB-R | MAR 5 ARI-D | MAR 17 SCO-R | FEB 13 ARI-D | MAY 10 SAG-R |
| MAR 25 ARI-D | MAR 9 VIR-R | APR 14 TAU-D | MAY 6 LIB-R | MAR 24 TAU-D | JUL 18 SAG-D |
| MAY 3 TAU-D | APR 26 VIR-D | MAY 25 GEM-D | JUN 3 LIB-D | MAY 4 GEM-D | SEP 8 CAP-D |
| JUN 13 GEM-D | JUN 20 LIB-D | JUL 7 CAN-D | JUL 6 SCO-D | JUN 17 CAN-D | OCT 27 AQU-D |
| JUL 26 CAN-D | AUG 15 SCO-D | AUG 21 LEO-D | SEP 3 SAG-D | AUG 2 LEO-D | DEC 8 PIS-D |
| SEP 10 LEO-D | SEP 29 SAG-D | OCT 8 VIR-D | OCT 18 CAP-D | SEP 18 VIR-D | |
| OCT 31 VIR-D | NOV 10 CAP-D | NOV 28 LIB-D | NOV 27 AQU-D | NOV 5 LIB-D | |
| | DEC 19 AQU-D | | | DEC 24 SCO-D | |

| 2002 | 2003 | 2004 | 2005 | 2006 | 2007 |
|---|---|---|---|---|---|
| JAN 18 ARI-D | JAN 16 SAG-D | FEB 3 TAU-D | FEB 6 CAP-D | FEB 17 GEM-D | JAN 15 CAP-D |
| MAR 2 TAU-D | MAR 4 CAP-D | MAR 21 GEM-D | MAR 20 AQU-D | APR 13 CAN-D | FEB 25 AQU-D |
| APR 13 GEM-D | APR 21 AQU-D | MAY 7 CAN-D | APR 30 PIS-D | JUN 3 LEO-D | APR 6 PIS-D |
| MAY 28 CAN-D | JUN 16 PIS-D | JUN 23 LEO-D | JUN 11 ARI-D | JUL 22 VIR-D | MAY 15 ARI-D |
| JUL 13 LEO-D | JUL 29 PIS-R | AUG 10 VIR-D | JUL 27 TAU-D | SEP 7 LIB-D | JUN 24 TAU-D |
| AUG 29 VIR-D | SEP 27 PIS-D | SEP 26 LIB-D | OCT 1 TAU-R | OCT 23 SCO-D | SEP 28 CAN-D |
| OCT 15 LIB-D | DEC 16 ARI-D | NOV 10 SCO-D | DEC 9 TAU-D | DEC 5 SAG-D | NOV 14 CAN-R |
| DEC 1 SCO-D | | DEC 25 SAG-D | | | DEC 31 GEM-R |

| 2008 | 2009 | 2010 | 2011 | 2012 | 2013 |
|---|---|---|---|---|---|
| JAN 30 GEM-D | FEB 4 AQU-D | MAR 9 LEO-D | JAN 15 AQU-D | JAN 23 VIR-R | FEB 1 PIS-D |
| MAR 4 CAN-D | MAR 14 PIS-D | JUN 7 VIR-D | FEB 22 PIS-D | APR 13 VIR-D | MAR 12 ARI-D |
| MAY 9 LEO-D | APR 22 ARI-D | JUL 29 LIB-D | APR 1 ARI-D | JUL 3 LIB-D | APR 31 GEM-D |
| JUL 1 VIR-D | MAY 31 TAU-D | SEP 14 SCO-D | MAY 11 TAU-D | AUG 23 SCO-D | JUL 13 CAN-D |
| AUG 19 LIB-D | JUL 11 GEM-D | OCT 28 SAG-D | JUN 20 GEM-D | OCT 6 SAG-D | AUG 27 LEO-D |
| OCT 3 SCO-D | AUG 25 CAN-D | DEC 7 CAP-D | AUG 3 CAN-D | NOV 16 CAP-D | OCT 15 VIR-D |
| NOV 16 SAG-D | OCT 16 LEO-D | | SEP 18 LEO-D | DEC 25 AQU-D | DEC 7 LIB-D |
| DEC 31 CAP-D | DEC 19 LEO-R | | NOV 10 VIR-D | | |

| 2014 | 2015 | 2016 | 2017 | 2018 | 2019 |
|---|---|---|---|---|---|
| MAR 1 LIB-R | JAN 12 PIS-D | JAN 3 SCO-D | JAN 28 ARI-D | JAN 26 SAG-D | FEB 14 TAU-D |
| MAY 19 LIB-D | FEB 19 ARI-D | MAR 6 SAG-D | MAR 9 TAU-D | MAR 17 CAP-D | MAR 31 GEM-D |
| JUL 25 SCO-D | MAR 31 TAU-D | APR 16 SAG-R | APR 21 GEM-D | MAY 15 AQU-D | MAY 15 CAN-D |
| SEP 13 SAG-D | MAY 11 GEM-D | MAY 27 SCO-R | JUN 4 CAN-D | JUN 25 AQU-R | JUL 1 LEO-D |
| OCT 26 CAP-D | JUN 24 CAN-D | JUN 28 SCO-D | JUL 20 LEO-D | AUG 12 CAP-R | AUG 17 VIR-D |
| DEC 4 AQU-D | AUG 8 LEO-D | AUG 2 SAG-D | SEP 5 VIR-D | AUG 27 CAP-D | OCT 3 LIB-D |
| | SEP 24 VIR-D | SEP 27 CAP-D | OCT 22 LIB-D | SEP 10 AQU-D | NOV 19 SCO-D |
| | NOV 12 LIB-D | NOV 9 AQU-D | DEC 9 SCO-D | NOV 15 PIS-D | |
| | | DEC 19 PIS-D | | DEC 31 ARI-D | |

# Mars Signs 1945-2025

| 2020 | 2021 | 2022 | 2023 | 2024 | 2025 |
|---|---|---|---|---|---|
| JAN 3 SAG-D | JAN 5 TAU-D | JAN 24 CAP-D | JAN 11 GEM-D | JAN 4 CAP-D | JAN 6 CAN-R |
| FEB 16 CAP-D | MAR 3 GEM-D | MAR 6 AQU-D | MAR 25 CAN-D | FEB 13 AQU-D | FEB 23 CAN-D |
| MAR 30 AQU-D | APR 23 CAN-D | APR 14 PIS-D | MAY 20 LEO-D | MAR 22 PIS-D | APR 17 LEO-D |
| MAY 12 PIS-D | JUN 11 LEO-D | MAY 24 ARI-D | JUL 10 VIR-D | APR 30 ARI-D | JUN 17 VIR-D |
| JUN 27 ARI-D | JUL 29 VIR-D | JUL 5 TAU-D | AUG 27 LIB-D | JUN 8 TAU-D | AUG 6 LIB-D |
| SEP 8 ARI-R | SEP 14 LIB-D | AUG 20 GEM-D | OCT 11 SCO-D | JUL 20 GEM-D | SEP 22 SCO-D |
| NOV 14 ARI-D | OCT 30 SCO-D | OCT 29 GEM-R | NOV 24 SAG-D | SEP 4 CAN-D | NOV 4 SAG-D |
| | DEC 13 SAG-D | | | NOV 3 LEO-D | DEC 15 CAP-D |
| | | | | DEC 5 LEO-R | |

# Jupiter Signs 1945-2025


1945
JAN 01—VIR-D
JAN 12—VIR-R
MAY 14—VIR-D
AUG 26—LIB-D
1946
FEB 11—LIB-R
JUN 14-LIB-D
SEP 26—SCO-D
1947
MAR14—SCO-R
JUL 15—SCO-D
OCT 25—AG-D
1948
APR 15—SAG-R
AUG 16—SAG-D
NOV 16—CAP-D
1949
APR 13—AQU-D
MAY 20—AQU-R
SEP 18—CAP-D
DEC 01—AQU-D
1950
APR 16—PIS-D
JUN 26-PIS-R
SEP 16—AQU-R
OCT 24—AQU-D
DEC 02—PIS-D
1951
APR 33—ARI-D
AUG 04—ARI-D
NOV 30—ARI-D
1952
APR 29—TAU-D
SEP 14—TAU-R
1954
JAN 05—TAU-D
MAY 10—GEM-D
OCT 14—GEM-R
1955
FEB 10—GEM-D
MAY 25—CAN-D
NOV 17—CAN-R
MAR 16—CAN-D
JUN 14—LEO-D
NOV 18—VIR-D
DEC 18—VIR-R
1956
JAN 19—LEO-R
APR 17—LEO-D
JUL 08—VIR-D
DEC 14-LIB-D
1957
JAN 16—LIB-R
FEB 20—VIR-D
MAY 19—VIR-D
AUG 03—LIB-D
1958
JAN 14—SCO-D
FEB 15—SCO-R
MAR 22—LIB-R
JUN 19—LIB-D
SEP 03—SCO-D
1959
FEB 11—SAG-D
MAR 18—SAG-R
APR 25—SCO-R
JUL 20—SCO-D
OCT 06—SAG-D
1960
MAR 02—CAP-D
APR 19—CAP-R
JUN 11—SAG-R
AUG 20—AUG-D


OCT 27—CAP-D
1961
MAR 16—AQU-D
MAY 25—AQU-R
AUG 13—CAP-D
SEP 23—CAP-D
NOV 25—AQU-D
1962
MAR 26—PIS-D
JUL 02—PIS-R
OCT 27—PIS-D
1963
APR 04—ARI-D
AUG 09—ARI-R
DEC 04—ARI-D
1964
APR 14—TAU-D
SEP 14—TAU-R
1965
JAN 10—TAU-D
APR 23—GEM-D
SEP 22—CAN-D
OCT 19—CAN-R
NOV 18—GEM-R
1966
FEB 15—GEM-D
MAY 06—CAN-D
SEP 28—LEO-D
NOV 20—LEO-R
1967
JAN 16—CAN-R
MAR 21—CAN-D
MAY 24—LEO-D
OCT 19—VIR-R
DEC 22—VIR-R
1968
FEB 28—LEO-R
APR 21—LEO-D
JUN 16—VIR-D
NOV 16-—LIB-D
1969
JAN 20—LIB-R
MAR 31—VIR-R
MAY 23—VIR-D
JUL 16—LIB-D
DEC 16—SCO-D
1970
FEB 19—SCO-R
MAY 01—LIB-R
JUN 23—LIB-D
AUG 16—CO-D
1971
JAN 16—SAG-D
MAR 23—SAG-R
JUN 06—SCO-R
JUL 24—SCO-D
SEP 12—SAG-D
1972
FEB 07—CAP-D
APR 24—CAP-R
JUL 25— SAG-R
AUG 25 —SAG-D
SEP 26 —CAP-D
1973
FEB 24 —AQU-D
MAY 30- AQU-R
SEP 28—AQU-D
1974
MAR 9—PiS-D
JUL 7—PIS-R
NOV 3—PIS-D
1975
MAR 19—ARI-D
AUG 14—ARI-R


DEC 10—ARI-D
1976
MAR 27—TAU-D
AUG 24—GEM-D
SEP 19—GEM-R
OC T 17—TAU-R
1977
JAN 15—TAU-D
APR 04—GEM-D
AUG 21—CAN-D
OCT 24—CAN-R
DEC 31—GEM-D
1978
FEB 20—GEM-D
APR 13—CAN-D
SEP 06-—LEO-D
1979
MAR 29—CAN-D
APR 21—LEO-D
SEP 30—VIR-D
DEC 29—VIR-R
1980
APR 26—VIR-D
OCT 28—LIB-D
1981
JAN 24—LIB-R
MAY 27—LIB-D
NOV 28—SCO-D
1982
FEB 25—SCO-R
JUN 27—SCO-D
DEB 27—SAG-D
1983
MAR 27—SAG-R
JUL 29—SAG-D
1984
JAN 20—CAP-D
APR 29—CAP-R
AUG 29—CAP-D
1985
FEB 06—AQU-D
JUN 04—AQU-D
OCT 03—AQU-D
1986
FEB 21—PIS-D
JUL 12—PIS-R
NOV 09—PIS-D
1987
MAR 03—ARI-D
AUG 19—ARI-R
DEC 14—ARI-D
1988
MAR 09—TAU-D
JUL 22—GEM-D
SEP 24—GEM R
DEC 01—TAU-R
1989
JAN 20—TAU-D
MAR 12—GEM-D
JUL 31—CAN-D
OCT 29—CAN-R
1990
FEB 24—CAN-D
AUG 19—LEO-D
NOV 30—LEO-R
1991
MAR 30—LEO-D
SEP 13—VIR-D
DEC 30—VIR-R
1992
APR 31—VIR-D
OCT 11—LiB-D
1993
JAN 28—LIB-R
JUN 02—LIB-D
NOV 11—SCO-D


1994
FEB 28—SCO-R
JUL 02—SCO-D
DEC 10—SAG-D
1995
APR 02—SAG-D
AUG 02—SAG-D
1996
JAN 04—CAP-D
MAY 04—CAP-R
SEP 03—CAP-D
1997
JAN 22—AQU-D
JUN 02—AQU-D
1998
OCT 08—AQU-D
FEB 05—PIS-D
JUL 18—PIS-R
NOV 13—PIS-D
1990
FEB 14—ARI-D
JUN 29—TAU-D
AUG 25—TAU-R
OCT 24—ARI-R
DEC 20—ARI-D
2000
FEB 15—TAU-D
JUL 01—GEM-D
SEP 29—GEM-R
2001
JAN 25—GEM-D
JUL 14—CAN-D
DEC 02—CAN-R
2002
MAR 02—CAN-D
AUG 02—LEO-D
DEC 04—LEO-D
2003
APR 04—LEO-D
AUG 28—VIR-D
2004
JAN 03—VIR-R
MAY 04—VIR-D
SEP 26—LIB-D
2005
FEB 02—LIB-D
JUN 05—LIB-D
OCT 26—SCO-D
2006
MAR 04—SCO-R
JUL 08—SCO-D
NOV 25—SAG-D
2007
APR 06—SAG-R
AUG 07—SAG-D
DEC 19—CAP-D
2008
MAY 09—CAP-R
SEP 08—CAP-D
2009
JAN 06—AQU-D
JUN 15—AQU-R
OCT 13—AQU-D
2010
JAN 19—PIS-D
JUN 07—ARI-D
JUL 23— ARI-R
SEP 10—PIS-R
NOV 18—PIS-D
2011
JAN 23—ARI-D
JUN 05—TAU-D
AUG 30—TAU-R
DEC 25—TAU-D
2012
JUN 12—GEM-D
OCT 04—GEM-D
2013
JAN 30—GEM-D


JUN 27—CAN-D
NOV 07—CAN-R
2014
MAR 06—CAN-D
JUL 17—LEO-D
DEC 08—LEO-D
2015
APR 08—LEO-D
AUG 12—VIR-D
2016
JAN 08—VIR-D
MAY 09—VIR-D
SEP 10—LIB-D
2017
FEB 06—LIB-R
JUN 09—LIB-D
OCT 11—SCO-D
2018
MAR 09—SCO-D
JUL 10—SCO-D
NOV 09—SAG-D
2019
APR 10—SAG-R
AUG 11—SAG-D
DEC 08—CAP-D
2020
MAY 14—CAP-D
SEP 13—CAP-D
DEC 20—AQU-D
2021
MAY 14—PIS-D
JUN 20—AQU-R
OCT 18-AQU-D
DEC 30—PIS-D
2022
MAY 11—ARI-D
JUL 28—ARI-R
OCT 29—PIS-R
NOV 23—PIS-D
DEC 21—ARI-D
2023
MAY 17—TAU-D
SEP 04—TAU-R
DEC 31—TAU-D
2024
MAY 26—GEM-D
OCT 09—GEM-R
2025
FEB 04—GEM-D
JUN 10—CAN-D
NOV 11—CAN-R

# Saturn Signs 1945-2025

**1945**
- JAN 01—CAN-D
- JAN 12—CAN-R
- MAR 05—CAN-D
- NOV 06—CAN-D

**1946**
- MAR 20—CAN-D
- AUG 03—LEO-D
- NOV 20—LEO-R

**1947**
- APR 03—LEO-D
- DEC 04—LEO-R

**1948**
- APR 17—LEO-D
- SEP 20—VIR-D
- DEC 17—VIR-R

**1949**
- APR 04—LEO-R
- MAY 02—LEO-D
- MAY 30—VIR-D
- DEC 30—VIR-R

**1950**
- MAY 15—VIR-D
- NOV 21—LIB-D

**1951**
- JAN 12—LIB-R
- MAR 08—VIR-R
- MAY 29—VIR-D
- AUG 14—LIB-D

**1952**
- JAN 24—LIB-R
- JUN 10—LIB-D

**1953**
- FEB 06—LIB-R
- JUN 23—LIB-D
- OCT 23—SCO-D

**1954**
- FEB 17—SCO-R
- JUL 06—SCO-D

**1955**
- MAR 02—SCO-R
- JUL 19—SCO-D

**1956**
- JAN 13—SAG-D
- MAR 12—SAG-R
- MAY 15—SCO-R
- JUL 30—SCO-D
- OCT 12—SAG-D

**1957**
- MAR 24—SAG-R
- AUG 11—SAG-D

**1958**
- APR 04—SAG-R
- AUG 24—SAG-D

**1959**
- JAN 06—CAP-R
- APR 16—CAP-R
- SEP 05—CAP-D

**1960**
- APR 26—CAP-R

- SEP 15—CAP-D

**1961**
- MAY 10—CAP-R
- SEP 27—CAP-D

**1962**
- JAN 04—AQU-D
- MAY 20—AQU-R
- OCT 09—AQU-D

**1963**
- JUN 03—AQU-R
- OCT 21—AQU-D

**1964**
- MAR 25—PIS-D
- JUN 15—PIS-R
- SEP 17—AQU-D
- NOV 02—AQU-D
- DEC 17—PIS-D

**1965**
- JUN 28—PIS-R
- NOV 14—PIS-D

**1966**
- JUL 11—PIS-R
- NOV 26—PIS-D

**1967**
- MAR 04-ARI-D
- JUL 25—ARI-R
- DEC 08—ARI-D

**1968**
- AUG 07—ARI-R
- DEC 21—ARI-D

**1969**
- APR 30—TAU-D
- AUG 21—TAU-R

**1970**
- JAN 03—TAU-D
- SEP 04—TAU-R

**1971**
- JAN 18—TAU-D
- JUN 19—GEM-D
- SEP 19—GEM-R

**1972**
- JAN 11—TAU-R
- JAN 31—TAU-D
- FEB 22—GEM-D
- OCT 02—GEM-R

**1973**
- FEB 13—GEM-D
- AUG 02—CAN-D
- OCT 17—CAN-R

**1974**
- JAN 08—GEM-R
- FEB 27—CAN-D
- APR 19—CAN-D
- OCT 31—CAN-R

**1975**
- MAR 14—CAN-D
- SEP 18—LEO-D
- NOV 14—LEO-R

**1976**
- JAN 15—CAN-R
- MAR 27—CAN-D
- JUN 06—LEO-D

- NOV 27—LEO-R

**1977**
- APR 11—LEO-D
- NOV 18—VIR-D
- DEC 11—VIR-R

**1978**
- JAN 06—LEO-D
- APR 25—LEO-D
- JUL 27—VIR-D
- DEC 24—VIR-R

**1979**
- MAY 09—VIR-D

**1980**
- JAN 06—VIR-R
- MAY 22—VIR-D
- SEP 22—LIB-D

**1981**
- JAN 18—LIB-R
- JUN 05—LIB-D

**1982**
- JAN 31—LIB-R
- JUN 18—LIB-D
- NOV 30—SCO-D

**1983**
- FEB 12—SCO-R
- MAY 7—LIB-R
- JUL 2—LIB-D
- AUG 25—SCO-D

**1984**
- FEB 24—SCO-R
- JUL 13—SCO-D

**1985**
- MAR 07—SCO-R
- JUL 25—SCO-D

**1986**
- MAR 28—SAG-R
- AUG 21—SAG-D

**1987**
- MAR 31—SAG-R
- AUG 25—SAG-D

**1988**
- FEB 24—CAP-D
- APR 21—CAP-R
- JUN 20—SAG-R
- AUG 30—SAG-D

**1989**
- APR 22—CAP-R
- SEP 11—CAP-D

**1990**
- MAY 04—CAP-R
- SEP 23—CAP-D

**1991**
- FEB 07—AQU-D
- MAY 17—AQU-R
- OCT 05—AQU-D

**1992**
- MAY 28—AQU-R
- OCT 16—AQU-D

**1993**
- MAY 22—PIS-D
- JUN 10—PIS-R

- OCT 28—AQU-D

**1994**
- JAN 29—PIS-D
- JUN 23—PIS-R
- NOV 09—PIS-D

**1995**
- JUL 06—PIS-R
- NOV 21-PIS-D

**1996**
- APR 08—ARI-D
- JUL 18—ARI-R

**1997**
- AUG 02—ARI-R
- DEC 16—ARI-D

**1998**
- JUN 10—TAU-D
- AUG 15—TAU-R
- OCT 26—ARI-R
- DEC 29—ARI-D

**1999**
- MAR 02—TAU-D
- AUG 30—TAU-R

**2000**
- JAN 12—TAU-D
- AUG 11—GEM-D
- SEP 12—GEM-R
- OCT 17—TAU-R

**2001**
- JAN 25—TAU-D
- APR 21—GEM-D
- SEP 27—GEM-R

**2002**
- FEB 08—GEM-D
- OCT 11—GEM-R

**2003**
- FEB 22—GEM-D
- JUN 05—CAN-D
- OCT 25—CAN-R

**2004**
- MAR 07—CAN-D
- NOV 08—CAN-R

**2005**
- MAR 22—CAN-D
- JUL 17—LEO-D
- NOV 22—LEO-R

**2006**
- APR 05—LEO-D
- DEC 06— LEO-R

**2007**
- APR 19—LEO-D
- SEP 03—VIR-S
- DEC 19—VIR-R

**2008**
- MAY 03—VIR-D
- DEC 31—VIR-R

**2009**
- MAY 17—VIR-D
- OCT 30—LIB-D

**2010**
- JAN 13—LIB-R
- APR 08—VIR-R
- MAY 30—VIR-D

- JUL 22—LIB-D

**2011**
- JAN 27—LIB-R
- JUN 13—LIB-D

**2012**
- FEB 07—LIB-R
- JUN 25—LIB-D
- OCT 06—SCO-D

**2013**
- FEB 18—SCO-R
- JUL 08—SCO-D

**2014**
- MAR 02—SCO-R
- JUL 20—SCO-D
- DEC 24—SAG-D

**2015**
- MAR 14—SAG-R
- JUN 16—SCO-R
- AUG 02—SCO-D
- SEP 19—SAG-D

**2016**
- MAR 25—SAG-R
- AUG 13—SAG-D

**2017**
- APR 06—SAG-R
- AUG 25—SAG-D
- DEC 21-CAP-R

**2018**
- APR 18—CAP-R
- SEP 06—CAP-D

**2019**
- APR 30—CAP-R
- SEP 18—CAP-D

**2020**
- MAR 23—AQU-D
- MAY 11—AQU-R
- JUL 02—CAP-R
- DEC 18—AQU-D

**2021**
- MAY 23—AQU-R
- OCT 11—AQU-D

**2022**
- JUN 04—AQU-R
- OCT 23—AQU-D

**2023**
- MAR 08—PIS-D
- JUN 17—PIS-R
- NOV 04—PIS-D

**2024**
- JUN 29—PIS-R
- NOV 15—PIS-D

**2025**
- MAY 26—ARI-D
- JUL 13—ARI-R
- SEP 02—PIS-R
- NOV 28—PIS-D

# Uranus Signs 1945-2025

**1945**
- JAN 1—GEM-R
- FEB 15—GEM-D
- SEP 23—GEM-R

**1946**
- SEP 27—GEM-R

**1947**
- FEB 25—GEM-D
- OCT 2—GEM-R

**1948**
- FEB 29—GEM-D
- AUG 31—CAN-D
- OCT 06—CAN-D
- NOV 13—GEM-R

**1949**
- MAR 05—GEM-D
- JUN 11—CAN-D
- OCT 11—CAN-R

**1950**
- MAR 09—CAN-D
- OCT 15—CAN-D

**1951**
- MAR 14—CAN-D
- OCT 20—CAN-R

**1952**
- MAR 18—CAN-D
- OCT 24—CAN-R

**1953**
- MAR 22—CAN-D
- OCT 29—CAN-R

**1954**
- MAR 27—CAN-D
- NOV 03—CAN-R

**1955**
- APR 02—CAN-D
- AUG 25—LEO-D
- NOV 08—LEO-R

**1956**
- JAN 29—CAN-R

- APR 05—CAN-D
- JUN 11—LEO-D
- NOV 12—LEO-R

**1957**
- APR 10—LEO-D
- NOV 17—LEO-R

**1958**
- APR 15—LEO-D
- NOV 22—LEO-R

**1959**
- APR 20—LEO-D
- NOV 27—LEO-R

**1960**
- APR 24—LEO-D
- DEC 02—LEO-R

**1961**
- APR 29—LEO-D
- NOV 02—VIR-D
- DEC 06—VIR-R

**1962**
- JAN 11—LEO-D
- MAY 04—LEO-D
- AUG 11—VIR-D
- DEC 11—VIR-R

**1963**
- MeY 09—VIR-D
- DEC 16—VIR-R

**1964**
- MAY 13—VIR-D
- DEC 20—VIR-R

**1965**
- MAY 18—VIR-D
- DEC 25—VIR-R

**1966**
- MAY 18—VIR-D
- DEC 30—VIR-R

**1967**
- MAY 28—VIR-D

**1968**
- JAN 04—VIR-R
- JUN 02—VIR-D
- SEP 29—LIB-D

**1969**
- JAN 08—LIB-R
- MAY 21—VIR-R
- JUN 07—VIR-D
- JUN 25—LIB-R
- JUL 01—LIB-D

**1970**
- JAN 13—LIB-R
- JUN 12—LIB-D

**1971**
- JAN 18—LIB-R
- JUN 12—LIB-D

**1972**
- JAN 23—LIB-R
- JUN 21—LIB-D

**1973**
- JAN 11—LIB-R
- JUN 26—LIB-D

**1974**
- FEB 01—LIB-R
- JUL 01—LIB-D
- NOV 22—SCO-D

**1975**
- FEB 02—SCO-R
- MAY 02—LIB-R
- JUL 07—LIB-D
- SEP 09—SCO-D

**1976**
- FEB 10—SCO-D
- JUL 11—SCO-D

**1977**
- FEB 14—SCO-R
- JUL 16—SCO-D

**1978**
- FEB 19—SCO-R
- JUL 21-SCO-D

**1979**
- FEB 25—SCO-R
- JUL 26—SCO-D

**1980**
- FEB 28—SCO-R
- JUL 30—SCO-D

**1981**
- FEB 19—SAG-D
- MAR 05—SAG-R
- MAR 21—SCO-R
- AUG 04—SCO-D

**1982**
- MAR 09—SAG-D
- AUG 09—SAG-D

**1983**
- MAR 14—SAG-R
- AUG 14—SAG-D

**1984**
- MAR 14—SAG-R
- AUG 22—SAG-D

**1985**
- MAR 22—SAG-R
- AUG 23—SAG-D

**1986**
- APR 01—SAG-R
- AUG 27—SAG-D

**1987**
- APR 01—SAG-R
- AUG 19—SAG-D

**1988**
- FEB 16—CAP-D
- APR 04—CAP-R
- MAY 28—SAG
- SEP 05—SAG-D
- DEC 03—CAP-D

**1989**
- APR 09—CAP-R
- SEP 10—CAP-D

**1990**
- APR 13—CAP-R
- SEP 14—CAP-D

**1991**
- APR 18—CAP-R
- SEP 22—CAP-D

**1992**
- APR 21—CAP-R
- SEP 22—CAP-D

**1993**
- APR 25—CAP-R
- SEP 27—CAP-D

**1994**
- APR 25—CAP-R
- OCT 02—CAP-D

**1995**
- APR 02—AQU-R
- MAY 05—AQU-R
- JUN 10—CAP-R
- OCT 06—CAP-D

**1996**
- JAN 13—AQU-D
- MAY 08—AQU-D
- OCT 10—AQU-D

**1997**
- MAY 12—AQU-R
- OCT 18—AQU-D

**1998**
- MAY 17—AQU-R
- OCT 18—AQU-D

**1999**
- MAY 11—AQU-R
- OCT 23—AQU-D

continued pg 224

| 2000 | MAY 25—AQU-R | 2005 | JUN 14—PIS-R | | AUG 15—PIS-R | 2016 | JUL 29—ARI-R | 2021 | JAN 14—TAU-R |
|---|---|---|---|---|---|---|---|---|---|
| | OCT 26—AQU-D | | NOV 16—PIS-D | | DEC 06—PIS-D | | DEC 29—ARI-D | | AUG 20—TAU-R |
| 2001 | MAY 29—AQU-R | 2006 | JUN 19—PIS-R | 2011 | MAR 13—ARI-D | 2017 | MAR 03—ARI-R | 2022 | JAN 18—TAU-D |
| | OCT 30—AQU-D | | NOV 16—PIS-D | | JUL 10—ARI-R | 2018 | JAN 02—ARI-D | | AUG 24—TAU-D |
| 2002 | JUN 03—AQU-R | 2007 | JUN 23—PIS-R | | DEC 10—ARI-D | | MAY 16—TAU-D | 2023 | JAN 22—TAU-D |
| | NOV 11—PIS-D | | NOV 27—PIS-D | 2012 | JUL 13—ARI-R | | AUG 07—ARI-R | 2024 | JAN 27—TAU-D |
| 2003 | MAR 11—PIS-D | 2008 | JUN 27—PIS-D | | DEC 13—ARI-D | | NOV 06—ARI-D | | SEP 01—TAU-R |
| | JUN 07—PIS-R | 2009 | JUL 01—PIS-R | 2013 | JUL 17—ARI-R | 2019 | JAN 02—ARI-D | 2025 | JAN 30—TAU-D |
| | SEP 16—AQU-R | | DEC 02—PIS-D | | DEC 21—ARI-D | | MAR 07—TAU-D | | JUL 08—GEM-D |
| | NOV 08—AQU-D | 2010 | MAY 29—ARI-D | 2014 | JUL 22—ARI-R | | AUG 12—TAU-D | | SEP 6—GEM-R |
| | DEC 31—PIS-D | | JUL 04—ARI--R | | DEC 21—ARI-D | 2020 | JAN 11-TAU-D | | NOV 9—TAU-R |
| 2004 | JUN 10—PIS-R | | | 2015 | JUL 26—ARI-R | | AUG 15—TAU-R | | |
| | NOV 11—PIS-D | | | | DEC 26—ARI-D | | | | |

# Neptune Signs 1945-2025

| 1945 | JAN 07—LIB-R | 1960 | FEB 10—SCO-R | 1977 | MAR 18—SAG--R | 1993 | APR 22—CAP-R | 2009 | MAY 29—AQU-R |
|---|---|---|---|---|---|---|---|---|---|
| | JUN 14—LIB-D | | JUL 18—SCO-D | | AUG 23—SAG-D | | SEP 30—CAP-D | | NOV 04—AQU-D |
| 1946 | JAN 10—LIB-R | 1961 | FEB 11—SCO-R | 1978 | MAR 20—SAG-R | 1994 | APR 25—CAP-R | 2010 | MAY 31—AQU-R |
| | JUN 17—LIB-D | | JUL 18—SCO-D | | AUG 29—SAG-D | | OCT 02—CAP-D | | NOV 07—AQU-D |
| 1947 | JAN 12—LIB-R | 1962 | FEB 13—SCO-R | 1979 | MAR 23—SAG-R | 1995 | APR 27—CAP-R | 2011 | JUN 03—AQU-R |
| | JUN 20—LIB-D | | JUL 23—SCO-D | | AUG 30—SAG-D | | OCT 05—CAP-D | | NOV 10—AQU-D |
| 1948 | JAN 13—LIB-R | 1963 | FEB 16—SCO-R | 1980 | MAR 24—SAG-R | 1996 | APR 29—CAP-R | 2012 | JUN 04—AQU-R |
| | JUN 21—LIB-D | | JUL 26—SCO-D | | AUG 31—SAG-D | | OCT 06—CAP-D | | NOV 10—AQU-D |
| 1949 | JAN 16—LIB-R | 1964 | FEB 18—SCO-R | 1981 | MAR 27—SAG-R | 1997 | MAR 02—CAP-R | 2013 | JUN 07—AQU-R |
| | JUN 23—LIB-D | | JUL 27—SCO-D | | SEP 03—SAG-D | | OCT 09—CAP-D | | NOV 13—AQU-D |
| 1950 | JAN 18—LIB-R | 1965 | FEB 20—SCO-R | 1982 | MAR 29—SAG-R | 1998 | JAN 30—AQU-R | 2014 | JUN 09—AQU-R |
| | JUN 26—LIB-D | | JUL 27—SCO-D | | SEP 05—SAG-D | | MAY 04—AQU-R | | NOV 16—AQU-D |
| 1951 | JAN 21—LIB-R | 1966 | FEB 22—SCO-R | 1983 | APR 02—SAG-R | | AUG 24—CAP-R | 2015 | JUN 12—AQU-R |
| | JUN 28—LIB-D | | AUG 02—SCO-D | | SEP 14—SAG-D | | OCT 11—CAP-D | | NOV 18—AQU-D |
| 1952 | JAN 23—LIB-R | 1967 | FEB 24—SCO-R | 1984 | JAN 20—CAP-R | 1999 | NOV 29—CAP-R | 2016 | JUN 13—AQU-R |
| | JUN 30—LIB-D | | AUG 03—SCO-D | | APR 02—CAP-R | | MAY 07—AQU-R | | NOV 20—AQU-D |
| 1953 | JAN 25—LIB-R | 1968 | FEB 27—SCO-R | | JUN 24—SAG-R | | OCT 14—AQU-D | 2017 | JUN 16—AQU-R |
| | JUL 02—LIB-D | | AUG 05—SCO-D | | AUG 29—SAG-D | 2000 | MAY 08—AQU-R | | NOV 22—AQU-D |
| 1954 | JAN 28—LIB-R | 1969 | FEB 28—SCO-R | | NOV 23—CAP-D | | OCT 15—AQU-D | 2018 | JUN 18—AQU-R |
| | JUL 05—LIB-D | | AUG 07—SCO-D | 1985 | APR 05—CAP-R | 2001 | MAY 11—AQU-R | | NOV 25—AQU-D |
| 1955 | JAN 29—LIB-R | 1970 | JAN 13—SCO-R | | SEP 12—CAP-D | | OCT 18—AQU-D | 2019 | JUN 21—AQU-R |
| | JUL 07—LIB-D | | MAY 04—SCO-D | 1986 | APR 07—CAP-R | 2002 | MAY 13—AQU-R | | NOV 27—AQU-D |
| | DEC 25—SCO-D | | AUG 10—SCO-D | | SEP 14—CAP-D | | OCT 20—AQU-D | 2020 | JUN 23—AQU-R |
| 1956 | FEB 02—SCO-R | | NOV 07—SAG-D | 1987 | APR 12—CAP-R | 2003 | MAY 16—AQU-R | | NOV 29—AQU-D |
| | MAR 13—LIB-R | 1971 | MAR 05—SAG-R | | SEP 17—CAP-D | | OCT 23—AQU-D | 2021 | JUN 25—AQU-R |
| | JUL 16—LIB-D | | AUG 12—SAG-D | 1988 | APR 11—CAP-R | 2004 | MAY 17—AQU-R | | DEC 02—AQU-D |
| | OCT 20—SCO-R | 1972 | MAR 07—SAG-R | | SEP 18—CAP-D | | OCT 24—AQU-D | 2022 | JUN 28—AQU-R |
| 1956 | FEB 02—SCO-R | | AUG 14—SAG-D | 1989 | APR 13—CAP-R | 2005 | MAY 19—AQU-R | | DEC 04—AQU-D |
| | JUN 18—LIB-R | 1973 | MAR 09—SAG-R | | SEP 21—CAP-D | | OCT 26—AQU-D | 2023 | JUN 30—AQU-R |
| | JUL 11—LIB-D | | AUG 16—SAG-D | 1990 | APR 16—CAP-R | 2006 | MAY 22—AQU-R | | DEC 06—AQU-D |
| | AUG 07—SCO-D | 1974 | MAR 13—SAG-R | | SEP 22—CAP-D | | OCT 29—AQU-D | 2024 | JUL 02—AQU-R |
| 1958 | FEB 05—SCO-R | | AUG 19—SAG-D | 1991 | APR 19—CAP-R | 2007 | MAY 22—AQU-R | | DEC 07—AQU-D |
| | JUL 14—SCO-D | 1975 | MAR 14—SAG-R | | SEP 26—CAP-D | | OCT 31—AQU-D | 2025 | JUL 04—AQU-R |
| 1959 | FEB 07—SCO-R | | AUG 21—SAG-D | 1992 | APR 20—CAP-R | 2008 | MAY 26—AQU-R | | DEC 10—AQU-D |
| | JUL 16—SCO-D | 1976 | MAR 15—SAG-R | | SEP 27—CAP-D | | NOV 02—AQU-D | | |
| | | | AUG 20—SAG-D | | | | | | |

# Pluto Signs 1945-2025

| 1945 | JAN 01—LEO-R | | AUG 20—VIR-D | 1970 | JUN 05—VIR-D | 1983 | MAR 02—LIB-R | 1995 | JAN 18—SAG-D |
|---|---|---|---|---|---|---|---|---|---|
| | APR 20—LEO-D | | DEC 04—VIR-R | 1971 | JAN 02—VIR-R | | JUL 07—LIB-D | | MAR 04—SAG-R |
| | NOV 13—LEO-R | 1958 | APR 12—LEO-R | | APR 12—VIR-D | | NOV 06—SCO-D | | APR-22—SCO-R |
| 1946 | FEB 07—LEO-R | | MAY 11—LEO-D | | OCT 16—LIB-D | 1984 | FEB 04—SCO-R | | AUG 08—SCO-D |
| | JUL 16—SCO-D | | JUN 11—VIR-D | 1972 | JAN 04—LIB-R | | MAY 19—LIB-R | | NOV 11—SAG-D |
| 1947 | APR 23—LEO-D | | DEC 06—VIR -R | | APR 18—VIR-D | | JUL 09—LIB-D | 1996 | MAR 05—SAG-R |
| | NOV 16—LEO-R | 1959 | MAY 13—VIR -D | | JUN 09—VIR-D | | AUG 29—SCO-D | | AUG 10—SAG-D |
| 1948 | APR 24—LEO-D | | DEC 08—VIR-R | | JUL 31—LIB-D | 1895 | FEB 05—SCO-R | 1997 | MAR 08—SAG-R |
| | NOV 17—LEO-R | 1960 | MAY 15—VIR-D | 1973 | JAN 06—LIB-R | | JUL 12—SCO-D | | AUG 13—SAG-D |
| 1949 | APR 05-—LEO-D | | DEC 10—VIR-R | | JUN 11—LIB-D | 1986 | FEB 08—SCO-R | 1998 | MAR 11—SAG-R |
| | NOV 19—LEO-R | 1961 | MAY 17—VIR-D | 1974 | JAN 09—LIB-R | | JUL 158—SCO-D | | AUG 16—SAG-D |
| 1950 | APR 28—LEO-R | | DEC 12—VIR-R | | JUN 14—LIB-D | 1987 | FEB 11—SCO-R | 1999 | MAR 13—SAG-R |
| | NOV 21—LEO-D | 1962 | MAY 19—VIR-D | 1975—JAN 11—LIB-R | | | JUL 18—SCO-D | | AUG 19—SAG-D |
| 1951 | JUN 28—LEO-D | 1963 | MAY 21—VIR-R | | JUN 17—LIB-D | 1988 | FEB 14—SCO-R | 2000 | MAR 15—SAG-R |
| | NOV 23—LEO-R | | DEC 17—VIR-R | 1976 | JAN 14—LIB-R | | JUL 20—SCO-D | | AUG 20—SAG-D |
| 1952 | JUN 30—LEO-D | 1964 | MAY 22—VIR-R | | JUN 21—LIB-D | 1989 | FEB 16—SCO-R | 2001 | MAR 18—SAG-R |
| | NOV 24—LEO-R | | DEC 18—VIR-R | 1977 | JAN 16—LIB-R | | JUL 23—SCO-D | | AUG 23—SAG-D |
| 1953 | MAY 02—LEO-D | 1965 | MAY 25—VIR-R | | JUN 21—LIB-D | 1990 | FEB 19—SCO-R | 2002 | MAR 20—SAG-R |
| | NOV 26—LEO-R | | DEC 21—VIR-R | 1978 | JAN 19—LIB-R | | JUL 26—SCO-D | | AUG 26—SAG-D |
| 1954 | MAY 02—LEO-D | 1966 | MAY 27—VIR-D | | JUN 24—LIB-D | 1991 | FEB 22—SCO-R | 2003 | MAR 23—SAG-R |
| | NOV 28—LEO-R | | DEC 28—VIR-R | 1979 | JAN 21—LIB-R | | JUL 28—SCO-D | | AUG 29—SAG-D |
| 1955 | MAY 06—LEO-D | 1967 | MAY 29—VIR-D | | JUN 27—LIB-D | 1992 | FEB 24—SCO_R | 2004 | MAR 24—SAG-R |
| | DEC 02—LEO-R | | DEC 26—VIR-R | 1980 | JAN 21—LIB-R | | JUL 30—SCO-D | | AUG 30—SAG-D |
| 1956 | OCT 21—VIR-D | 1968 | MAY 31—VIR-R | | JUN 28—LIB-D | 1993 | FEB 26—SCO-R | 2005 | MAR 29—SAG-R |
| | DEC 02—VIR-R | | DEC 27—VIR-R | 1981 | JAN 26—LIB-R | | AUG 02—SCO-D | | SEP 02—SAG-D |
| 1957 | JAN 16—LEO-R | 1969 | JUN 02—VIR-R | | JUL 02—LIB-D | 1994 | MAR 02—SCO-R | 2006 | MAR 29—SAG-R |
| | MAY 09—LEO-D | | DEC 30—VIR-R | 1982 | JAN 29—LIB-R | | AUG 05—SCO-D | | SEP 04—SAG-D |
| | | | | | JUL 04—LIB-D | | | | |

continued pg 225

| 2007 | MAR 31—SAG-R | 2010 | APR 07—CAP-R | 2015 | APR 17—CAP-R | 2020 | APR 25—CAP-R | 2024 | JAN 22—AQU-D |
|---|---|---|---|---|---|---|---|---|---|
| | SEP 07—SAG-D | | SEP 14-CAP-D | | SEP 25—CAP-D | | OCT 04—CAP-D | | MAY 02—AQU-R |
| 2008 | JAN 27—CAP-D | 2011 | APR 09—CAP-R | 2016 | APR 18—CAP-R | 2021 | APR 27—CAP-R | | SEP 03—CAP-R |
| | APR 07—CAP-R | | SEP 16—CAP-D | | SEP 26—CAP-D | | OCT 06—CAP-D | | OCT 12—CAP-D |
| | JUN 15—SAG-R | 2012 | APR 10—CAP-R | 2017 | APR 20—CAP-R | 2022 | APR 29—CAP-R | | NOV 20—AQU-D |
| | SEP 09—SAG-R | | SEP 18—CAP-D | | SEP 05—CAP-D | | OCT 08—CAP-D | 2025 | MAY 04-AQU-R |
| | NOV 28—CAP-D | 2013 | APR 12—CAP-R | 2018 | APR 22—CAP-R | 2023 | MAR 24—AQU-D | | OCT 14—AQU-D |
| 2009 | APR 04—CAP-R | | SEP 20—CAP-D | | OCT 12—CAP-D | | MAY 02—AQU-R | | |
| | SEP 11—CAP-D | 2014 | APR 14—CAP-R | 2019 | APR 24—CAP-R | | JUN 12—CAP-R | | |
| | | | SEP 23—CAP-D | | OCT 03—CAP-D | | OCT 11—CAP-D | | |

# GLOSSARY

## Ascendant

The constellation or sign that was on the horizon at the exact time and from the exact location where the individual was born.

## Aspects

Angular relationships between two or more planets by degrees.

## Conjunction

The conjunction aspect involves planets within 8-12 degrees of each other. They can be in the same sign or at the end of one and the beginning of the next, such as Moon 28 degrees Gemini and Venus 4 degrees Cancer. A conjunction can be harmonious or inharmonious, according to the nature of the planets involved. For example, Mars conjunct Moon may not work so well, because fiery Mars can be incompatible with watery Moon.

## Major "SOFT" Aspects are aspects of benefit

A **Trine** is an aspect of 120 degrees that is usually between planets in the same element., such as Sun in Taurus trine Mars in Virgo. Trines are considered very favorable.

A **Grand Trine** is an aspect among three signs of the same element... for example, the air signs Gemini, Libra, Aquarius. The planets in a grand trine form a triangle. This is considered tops!

A **Sextile** is an aspect between compatible elements 60 degrees apart, such as Venus in earth-Taurus sextile Moon in water-Cancer-or Sun in air-Gemini sextile Mars in fire-Leo. It is considered favorable, but you have to help it by taking some action to bring the benefits. It just won't fall in your lap like a happy trine.

## Major "HARD" Aspects are aspects of challenge!

A square, two planets 90 degrees apart, represents a challenge, a difficulty. Sometimes it seems as if you are held in a vise, or you swing from one thing to the other.

## Grand Square or Grand Cross —when all four of the mode of action signs square each other, or form a cross. A **cardinal cross** involves Aries, Cancer, Libra, Capricorn, a **fixed cross** involves Taurus, Leo, Scorpio and Aquarius, and a **mutable cross** involves Gemini, Virgo, Sagittarius and Pisces. A chart with a Grand Cross is said to be a karmic one, with many obstacles to work out (or lessons to learn) in this life. Children with such a configuration should be helped to understand this challenge so that they can learn to use it to accomplish, rather than allow it to have a non-beneficial effect. Help them to look at and accept each challenge as a very special opportunity. In general, one needs challenging "hard" aspects—to get tossed out of the hammock—to get going! The people who accomplish the most, whether in the world or within themselves, usually have many hard aspects in their charts.

## Transits—where the planets are NOW!

"Transits" is a term that means where in the zodiac each planet is they are NOW—at any given time—as can be seen in relationship of a transit to a birth chart. The transiting planets make temporary aspects to the birth chart, and this greatly assists an astrologer to understand what might be going on in the life of the person whose chart is being transited. To know and understand this important timing technique, you should consult a professional astrologer, and then undertake to learn more about astrology yourself so that you can watch the **transits** to guide your children, and your own life for the better! The more you know about your charts, and the timing of transits to them, the more you are able to work with them beneficially, the more forewarned you are, and the more you can take appropriate action.

Just as an example of how helpful understanding transits can be, one of my daughters who has always been very responsible, self-disciplined and a person you could count on to do the right thing, started acting very irresponsibly. A normal thought would be that somehow she had gotten involved with and was taking drugs and if I had not been aware of astrology I would have thought so too. However, when I looked at her chart I saw that she was having a Neptune transit which can mean that a person becomes very spacy. So instead of going down

the drug bunny trail, I simply had a conversation with her about Neptune and advised her that she needed to pay special attention to everything that she did to avoid the problems. Another advantage was that I could tell her how long the Neptune transit was going to last. She was relieved to know she wasn't "losing it" and that I understood. The situation was greatly improved. The importance of knowing is invaluable because it can bring such relief.

Another example: one of my grandsons was having terrible anxiety attacks, getting stomach aches and throwing up over going to school. When I looked at his chart I saw that he was having a Saturn transit. I told him what it was about, and that it would go away on a certain day. He called me right after that date and told me that he felt fine again. That saved his having to go to the doctor or a psychologist.

A final example is about friend of mine who had a girl about age four who would all of a sudden start crying and screaming for no reason and keep doing it until she collapsed. This had been going on for several weeks. Nothing would help or make her stop. I looked at her chart and saw that she had Uranus transiting her Mercury. I told her Mom how long it would be before it was over and sure enough the crying and screaming stopped at the time I told her. That too saved the need to seek professional help which probably would have been some kind of drug, if of any help at all.

It should be said here, that transits can have more than one meaning and there are always positive or negative potentials, so you must read them within the context of a particular situation. One meaning for Uranus can be sudden upset, but it could also mean a surprise or something exciting. Mercury is about one's thinking, mental capability, and nervous system. In this case of my friend's four year old daughter, it was obvious to me that Uranus was showing the tension in her nervous system, and this would likely calm down after the transit passed by her Mercury. At another time Uranus transiting Mercury could mean, for example. excitement, inventiveness and creative thinking or writing. I hope this helps you to see the value of seeking astrological counsel.

Also, it should be said that when your chart is contacted by a transiting benefic planet, good things are likely to be happening then! If you are aware of beneficial transits just ahead, welcome them, and use them!

# The Elements

The four **elements** are **fire, earth, air** and **water**. There are three signs in each element:

FIRE—Aries, Leo, Sagittarius
EARTH—Taurus, Virgo, Capricorn
AIR—Gemini, Libra, Aquarius
WATER—Cancer, Scorpio, Pisces.

The signs in the same element are compatible. Fire and air are compatible with each other, and earth and water are compatible. Less compatible combinations are fire and earth, or air and water. Imagery from nature offers examples of how this can work: fire burns earth, and earth can smother fire. Air can cause dust storms on earth; earth can suffocate air. Air can whip water into a hurricane, and water can put out fire.

Elements are concerned with tendencies of the temperament. Planets in earth will be practical doers. In air, this is mental and often intellectual. In water it is emotional and creative. In fire, it is action-oriented and inspirational.

## The Modes of Action

The three Modes of Action are **Cardinal, Fixed, Mutable**. There are four signs in each mode.

### CARDINAL—Aries, Cancer, Libra, Capricorn.

Usually considered the "movers and the shakers," the go-for-it signs. Too much cardinal in one person's chart compared to another person's cardinal can be extremely irritating -they both want to be first! To have their own way!

### FIXED—Taurus, Leo, Scorpio, Aquarius.

Each of these signs are in different elements. They are likened to Taurus/Earth/Rock, Leo/Fire/Torch, Scorpio/Water/Ice, Aquarius/Air/Tornado. They endure, they persevere and they get the job done. If two charts each have a lot of fixity, they tend to butt heads! If you are a cardinal person and want action, you will have to develop tremendous patience and tolerance, since these fixed individuals are difficult to bend, change, or move! If you are mostly mutable, you may have a challenge with their obstinacy. However, mutables are very clever, and will probably think of something!

### MUTABLE—Gemini, Virgo, Sagittarius, Pisces.

These four are the most adaptable of the signs, like reeds that move with the wind, not standing firm and fixed until they break. People with mutable signs dominant can be like chameleons. They can fit into many different environments. They are flexible, resourceful,

ingenious. Sometimes they also can be nervous, fluttery, or very changeable.

CARDINAL–initiates the concept, kicks it off.
FIXED—works persistently to produce a result.
MUTABLE—promotes and sells it.

# HOUSES

The horoscope or wheel of 360 degrees is divided into twelve parts which area called houses. Each house represents an area of life.

**House 1** Self-image, self-expression, personality, appearance, behavior, body.

**House 2** Money, income, financial source, spending, values, possessions, property, resources, monetary security.

**House 3** Communication, sense perception, learning, thinking, teaching, writing, commuting, errands.

**House 4** Home territory, roots, tradition, emotional security, parents, family, parenting.

**House 5** Creative expression, recreation, romance, entertainment, play, children, pets, speculation.

**House 6** Work, jobs, skills, productivity, analysis, criticism, correction, health.

**House 7** Relationships, partnerships, marriage, contracts, agreements, the law, politics, harmony.

**House 8** Sex, sexuality, crisis, catalytic experiences, death and rebirth, transformation, the occult.

**House 9** Knowledge, wisdom, philosophy, religion, higher education, publishing, journeys, exploration.

**House 10** Career, success, public recognition, ambition, prestige, status, authority, government.

**House 11** Friends, associates, groups, aspirations, expectations, plans, the future.

**House 12** Service, inspiration, spirituality, intuition, empathy, illusion, sacrifice, self-undoing, misfortune, tragedy.

# THE LUMINARIES and the PLANETS

## LUMINARIES

The Sun, the core of the being, the SELF

The Moon, one's emotional makeup, responsiveness.

## PLANETS

The planets symbolically represent different facets of human makeup.

## RULERSHIP

This indicates where a planet is at home, where it most easily expresses itself. When a planet is placed in the sign opposite its home, it is considered weaker or impaired, called "in detriment." It doesn't work at full power or utilize its true nature.

Mars rulers Aries, is in detriment in Libra

Venus rules Taurus, is in detriment in Scorpio

Mercury rules Gemini, is in detriment in Sagittarius

Moon rules Cancer, is in detriment in Capricorn

Sun rules Leo, is in detriment in Aquarius

Mercury rules Virgo, is in detriment in Pisces

Venus rules Libra, is in detriment in Aries

Pluto rules Scorpio, is in detriment in Taurus

Jupiter rules Sagittarius, is in detriment in Gemini

Saturn rules Capricorn, is in detriment in Cancer

Uranus rules Aquarius, is in detriment in Leo

Neptune rules Pisces, is in detriment in Virgo

# SIGNS and the HOUSES where they are naturally "at home"

## ARIES the Ram, First House

A cardinal fire sign ruled by Mars. Parts of the body ruled are head and face.

## TAURUS the Bull, Second House

A fixed earth sign ruled by Venus. Parts of the body ruled are the ears, neck, and throat.

## GEMINI the Twins, Third House

A mutable air sign ruled by Mercury. Parts of the body ruled are lungs (air in them), shoulders, arms, wrists, and fingers.

### CANCER the Crab, Fourth House
A cardinal water sign ruled by the Moon. Parts of the body ruled are breasts, stomach, and solar plexus.

### LEO the Lion, Fifth House
A fixed fire sign ruled by the Sun. Parts of the body ruled are heart, back, and spine.

### VIRGO the Virgin, Sixth House
A mutable earth sign ruled by Mercury. Rules the nervous system and the intestines.

### LIBRA the Scales, Seventh House
A cardinal air sign ruled by Venus. Parts of the body ruled are the kidneys.

### SCORPIO the Scorpion, Eighth House
A fixed water sign ruled by Pluto (ancient ruler Mars). Rules the reproductive system.

### SAGITTARIUS the Centaur, Ninth House
A mutable fire sign ruled by Jupiter. Parts of the body ruled are the hips and thighs.

### CAPRICORN the Goat, Tenth House
A cardinal earth sign ruled by Saturn. Rules the skin, teeth, skeleton in general and the knees in particular.

### AQUARIUS the Water Bearer, Eleventh House
A fixed air sign ruled by Uranus (ancient ruler Saturn). Body parts the calves and ankles.

### PISCES the Fish, Twelfth House
A mutable water sign ruled by Neptune (ancient ruler Jupiter). Parts of the body are the feet.

## SIGNS of the Zodiac
The **signs** were named for the **constellations** (star groups) that can be seen beyond the ecliptic (orbit of Earth around Sun) in the approximate area of the signs, although due to the precession of the equinox, the signs are no longer quite in the constellational areas for which they were named. Constellations are very different in size, while signs are equal 30 degree sections of the 360 degree circle. The constellations,

or stars in the sky, were arbitrarily considered by the Ancients to be a group because they suggested an outline of some animal or mythological being. If you look carefully at the glyph of each sign, you can see an outline that somewhat resembles the constellational being, such as a Ram's head (Aries ♈ ), a Bull's head (Taurus ♉ ), the Twins (Gemini ♊ ), the Cancer Crab ♋ ), the Lion (Leo ♌ ), the Virgin (Virgo ♍), the Scales of Balance (Libra ♎ ), the Scorpion (Scorpio ♏), the Centaur (Sagittarius ♐), shooting his arrow into the sky, the Seagoat (Capricorn ♑), the water flowing from the Waterbearer's pitcher (Aquarius ♒), and the two Fish swimming (Pisces ♓).

## Sign Polarities

The odd numbered signs, beginning with the first one Aries, are called "positive" or "masculine" the even numbered signs, beginning with the second one, Taurus, are called" negative" or "feminine." Think of these old-fashioned terms of positive and negative as two kinds of psychic current—one of them, called positive or masculine, is like a force flowing out and the other, called negative or feminine, is like a force pulling in. Positive is electric and outgoing; negative is magnetic and in-pulling.

In the elements, then, the "masculine" signs are fire and air, and the "feminine" signs are earth and water. Both natures are, of course, needed in a chart for proper balance of being.

## Zodiac

Also called the signs in astrology, zodiac refers to an imaginary belt in the Heavens made of twelve constellations that are along the apparent path ("apparent" meaning as viewed from Earth) of the Sun, the Moon, and the planets of the Solar System.

# About the Author

**Samantha Marshall,** an inspirational motivator in the human potential movement, as also been an entrepreneur in various businesses for over 40 years. She is considered an innovator, who has developed expertise in many areas including seminar leadership, writing, counseling/coaching, education, astrology, marketing, and the wholesale and retail business.

In 1972, Samantha was among the founders of Arizona Society of Astrologers, which boasts one of the largest memberships in the country today. Until 1979, she had alternately served on the board as Vice President, Director of Programs, and Director of Education. As a personal and business consultant in Arizona, she developed a large national clientele. Along with her teaching, speaking and writing articles for nationally recognized astrology magazines and a weekly newspaper column, she had her own radio program and has been a guest speaker on other people's show on both radio and TV.

In 1979, Samantha became a Certified Instructor of the Silva Method of Mind Development, with proficiency in teaching controlled relaxation, stress management, and self-empowerment. She managed her own Arizona territory, gaining experience in advertising and marketing. She then created and led relationship seminars called "Living with People," showcasing methods to enhance all forms of relationships, including the one you have with yourself. She has also taught many classes in astrology, interpersonal communication, relationship dynamics, personal responsibility, goal setting, financial success, emotional and physical health and healing, spirituality, and parenting.

At the heart of it all, Samantha is a mother who raised four children as a single parent and now has ten grandchildren. Her ability to understand human behavior and potential combine with a multitude of skills to make her a dynamic instrument for positive change and transformation in the lives of all who have the opportunity to experience her. Samantha says that, "This book is committed to helping parents, caregivers, teachers and therapists gain added insights into our children's personalities, and to assist them in learning new effective tools and methods for raising, guiding, and understanding the children of our world."

# The Other Side of Samantha

While astrology has been at the core of Samantha's life for 35 years, horses have played a huge part since she was a child. Now, they have once again come front and center—for two reasons. First, Samantha became a Certified Equine Gestalt Coach in 2011, after studying for two years with the Founder of the Equine Gestalt Coaching Method (EGCMtm ), Melisa Pearce in Colorado.

Gestalt is an experiential method with a focus on human dynamics, to identify interfering issues from the past, such as trauma, and bring them to the forefront for release, and this is added to normal coaching practice. In equine gestalt, horses are added as partners and co-facilitators. The Gestalt Coach is trained to be sensitively and intuitively tuned into the client to enhance the coaching session. The horses, since they are naturally intuitive, telepathic, sensitive and brilliant creatures, read the client as well. Samantha, by reading both, facilitates according to their evolving energy. It is quite a thorough and complete process, where for most people the issue or challenge is cleared permanently. For some people, there may be more than one layer to clear, as a result of experiences or influences gathered over a lifetime.

It is not necessary to have any previous horse experience to participate in this process, nor is riding involved. All you need is just a desire and a willingness to use a unique approach to get free from past or current burdens and to live a healthier, more fulfilling life. The process is effective across a range of human challenges, ranging from business coaching with team building and productivity enhancement, through personal performance encompassing empowerment and relationship skills, plus all the way to potential resolution of deep-seated trauma.

Find out more at:

## Samantha's Astrology websites:
*www.astro-dna.com*
*www.equiserene.com*

## And on the next page— find out about Horse-Scopes!

# Horse-Scopes!

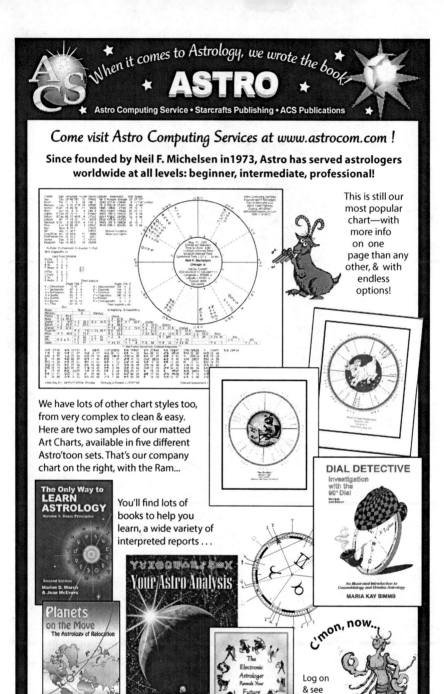

*Magical Child astrology options for the nurturing of your children... or your inner child Book, report and art by Maria Kay Simms*

Learn how each child is born with his or her own special magic in personality, style and talents. Discover how best you can assist his or her development of potential.

**Your Magical Child** book............**BYMC3 $19.95**

YOUR
MAGICAL CHILD
Astrology for Nurturing
Your Child or Inner Child
Expanded 3rd Edition

Maria Kay Simms

### *Your Magical Child* Interpreted Report

It's a personalized report for any child's (or your own!) birth date, time and place. (Each of us has an "inner child" that sometimes needs nurturing and undertanding. Recently we were told by a chart services customer that she orders the report for each of her adult clients. "It's a very good natal report," she told us, and added, "We don't change that much!")

(approx. 20 pages)............**AB5 $26.95**

## *Your Magical Child* Art Options

Personalized pictures and charts include a little poem about the zodiac character. Available as print only, or in art mat, as shown. Print only 8-1/2 x 11. Matted art is 11"x14". All twelve pictures and charts can be seen on *www.astrocom.com*. Charts include a 2nd page listing of the planets in signs, houses & aspects.

Notecards can be ordered as one sign individually or in boxed sets of 12, or boxes can be one of each sign.

**Your Magical Child Art Chart**
based on date, time & place... **$9.95**
**Chart or picture , matted .. $25.95**

**Your Magical Child notecards**
One card, ..... **MCC $3.50**

**YMC notecard set** (1 of each sign, or all 12 of one sign (state sign number).......**$25.00**

CPSIA information can be obtained at www.ICGtesting.com
Printed in the USA
BVOW05s1025250314

348697BV00007B/126/P